Transforming Anthony Trollope

**STUDIES IN
EUROPEAN COMICS
AND GRAPHIC NOVELS** ❹

Editorial board

Hugo Frey, Editor in Chief (University of Chichester)
Jan Baetens (KU Leuven)
Bart Beaty (University of Calgary)
Charles Hatfield (California State University, Northridge)
Ann Miller (University of Leicester)

Transforming Anthony Trollope

Dispossession, Victorianism and Nineteenth-Century Word and Image

Edited by
Simon Grennan & Laurence Grove

LEUVEN UNIVERSITY PRESS

© 2015 by Leuven University Press / Presses Universitaires de Louvain / Universitaire Pers Leuven
Minderbroedersstraat 4, B-3000 Leuven (Belgium)

All rights reserved. Except in those cases expressly determined by law, no part of this publication may be multiplied, saved in an automated data file or made public in any way whatsoever without the express prior written consent of the publishers.

ISBN 9789462700413
D / 2015/1869/26
NUR: 617

Layout: Frederik Danko
Cover design: Johan Van Looveren
Cover illustration: Simon Grennan

Contents

Simon Grennan and Laurence Grove   7
    Introduction

Part 1: *Dispossession*: Simon Grennan's graphic adaptation of Trollope's *John Caldigate*   13

Jan Baetens   15
    Adapting and displaying multiple temporalities: what became of Trollope's *John Caldigate* and Maupassant's *Boule de Suif* in Simon Grennan's *Dispossession* and Battaglia's *Contes et nouvelles de guerre*?

John Miers in conversation with Simon Grennan   33
    Dispossession: time, motion and depictive regimes

Hugo Frey   55
    The tactic for illusion in Simon Grennan's *Dispossession*

Part 2: Nineteenth-century visualisations   69

Frederik Van Dam   71
    Allegorical landscapes: the psychology of seeing in Anthony Trollope's later novels

David Skilton   89
    Complex meanings in illustrated literature, 1860-1880

Roger Sabin   107
    Comics versus books: the new criticism at the 'fin de siècle'

Barbara Postema   131
    The visual culture of comics in the last half of the nineteenth century: comics without words

Part 3: Using the Victorians: appropriation, adaptation and historiography   149

Marie-Luise Kohlke   151
    "Abominable pictures": neo-Victorianism and the tyranny of the sexual taboo

Ian Hague   175
    Drawing "the apprenticeship of a man of letters": adapting *Remembrance of Things Past* for 'bande dessinée'

Contents

Aarnoud Rommens 199
Allegories of graphiation: Alberto Breccia's counter-censorial versions of E. A. Poe's *Valdemar*

Peter Wilkins 217
An incomplete project: graphic adaptations of *Moby-Dick* and the ethics of response

Index 235
Gallery with colour figures 247

Simon Grennan and Laurence Grove

Introduction

At first sight – and sight is all important – Simon Grennan's *Dispossession* appears to be attempting the impossible: to create via a one-off, 94 sheets of twenty-first-century images a "novel of few words" that visualises the 600-plus pages of *John Caldigate*, originally serialised by Anthony Trollope between April 1878 and June 1879. The task of this introduction, and the volume it serves, might seem equally unlikely: to provide a bridge between the two.

But such worries are only pertinent if we take things too literally, which neither Trollope nor Grennan do. Trollope's work is laden with ambiguity, and the plot of *John Caldigate* turns on a postage stamp – the proof of a fraud – a humorous reference in a generally non-humorous book to Trollope's career as a Post Office civil servant and creator of the pillar box. Grennan's version underlines what should have been in Trollope's book – from a retrospective view of history – but was not, namely aboriginal Australians speaking Wiradjuri. In both versions of the Caldigate story we are reminded that any work is finally dependent on the audience's experience of the text's milieu and its historic moment, including subsequent interpretations of them. The chapters in this volume by Peter Wilkins, Ian Hague and Aarnoud Rommens reinforce this point, showing how other works from over a century ago, by Melville, Proust and Poe, have also taken on new significances in their late twentieth-century adaptations and readings.

A brief summary: *John Caldigate* tells the story of the eponymous hero's trip to New South Wales, and the relationship that develops on the crossing with Euphemia Smith. Upon his return to England, having made his fortune, Caldigate marries his sweetheart Hester Bolton, only to be accused and convicted of bigamy based upon his marriage – the veracity of which remains unknown to the reader – to Euphemia. The evidence, a letter written to Smith as 'Mrs Caldigate', is found to have a postage stamp made after the date of the postmark upon it, and thus a fabrication. *Dispossession* presents Caldigate's

Introduction

tale through consistent panels in three rows of two frames, and a stable viewpoint that eschews close ups or high or low angles. Yet this formal distancing of the reader contrasts with the enfolding, rich colours, and the streaking yellow identifying Caldicate via his hair, both of which ignore the sepia or monochrome conventionally used to represent an inaccessible past.

Although much is to be felt rather than explained, the first section of this companion volume gives some context to the techniques Grennan uses and their effects. Hugo Frey creates an illuminating analogy between the visual tricks in *Dispossession* and the mechanisms of illusion. Jan Baetens gives a critic's analysis of the process of adapting *John Caldigate* relative to the psychologising of Battaglia, whereas John Miers in conversation with Simon Grennan gives us the creator's view of that journey.

The bridge between creation and criticism, between the nineteenth century and the twenty-first, is highly fitting in our current context. The era of *John Caldigate* was one that saw key developments in the changing culture of representation: yes, it was the time of the serialised long novel from the likes of Dickens, Hugo, and of course Trollope, with implications for visual culture that Frederik Van Dam explores in detail in Trollope's later novels, but it also saw a parallel rise of the image itself, and moreover the image in par with the text.

It was the early nineteenth century that saw the birth of the modern comic, that is to say periodic publications whose satirical content mixed text and image, with widespread distribution. Widespread image distribution was possible thanks to the proliferation of wood engraving and lithography. It was in 1825 that the first comic was to use lithography: *The Glasgow Looking Glass*, published by William Heath in the industrial city of its name.

From its industrial birth therefore, and long before Grennan, the medium of comics has had much in common with Trollope's concerns: narrative, caricatures in relation to physiognomy, caricatures in and of society, the social classes, travel, the latest technology. Nonetheless the striking difference is of course the format, with the concision of images appearing diametrically opposed to textual length, and Trollope's originally pictureless tomes almost appearing as if in respectful homage to Gotthold Ephraim Lessing's *Laokoon* of 1766, whereby poetry and painting, text and image, were to be kept apart for fear of one bastardising the other. However as the century progressed it became increasingly common for Victorian novels to bear illustrations, often based on the visual regimes of contemporary stage productions, including notable versions of Trollope's works by John Everett Millais, as we shall see from David Skilton's chapter in this volume.

In terms of the history of the culture of comics – to be compared with book illustration – as the nineteenth century progressed, illustrated journals became increasingly popular and increasingly visual: Heath moved to London, set up an alternative *Looking Glass*, and spurred along the culture that saw *Judy*, *The London Illustrated News* and *Punch*; meanwhile in France *Le Charivari*, *Le Monde Illustré* and *Le Chat Noir* took off, as did *Daily Graphic*, *Puck*, *Life* and *Truth* in the USA, to name but a few. The common factor was a mainstay of visual elements in terms of sketches, and later photos, of the events and fashions of the day, but also portrayal and satire of associated mores through caricatures and sequential picture stories.

By 1878 and the appearance of *John Caldigate*, cartoon characters and their comic strips had become commonplace. *L'Illustration* had popularised M. Boniface by Cham (Amédée de Noé) – based on the characters of Swiss Schoolmaster and candidate for the accolade of inventor of the comic strip, Rodolphe Töpffer – and M. Verdreau by Stop (Louis Morel-Retz), whilst in England the readers of *Punch* were of course familiar with Mr Punch, and those of *Judy* were soon to know and love Ally Sloper. Ally Sloper is a linchpin of Roger Sabin's analysis, as he outlines the exchanges and tensions between the Victorian worlds of comics and 'proper books'.

Whereas Sabin presents reception and reaction to the 'pop culture' of comics and shows how attitudes in the Victorian era were to resurface and evolve in later times, Barbara Postema gives us an overview of the development of the comic strip and in particular the wordless narrative through image, as opposed to the texts of Trollope et al. The latter-day culmination of this trend is perhaps Grennan's "novel of few words", the picture-based telling of the story of John Caldigate.

However, as with *John Caldigate* and with *Dispossession*, things are not as simple as they might seem: Grennan looks forward, underlining key changes in the graphic novel, which in the twenty-first century is seeing transformation in terms of reception – becoming an accepted artistic form worthy of scholarly editions and study in academia – but also format, as technology allows for experimentation, for example via high-resolution reproduction in a variety of media. But Grennan also deliberately looks back, creating a work that might appear static and which draws upon the values of nineteenth-century popular entertainment in books, journals and the theatre, as he describes in this volume, in conversation with John Miers.

Above all, questions of adaptation bring us to those of overlap and spill-over, as the utilisation of the past, and the imagining of the past, allow us to understand the present, whereupon an adaptation becomes a self-standing creation, not a satellite. And here we can understand that the forms of neo-Victorianism are critical as much as, indeed maybe more than, neo-Victorian 'topics'. Marie-Luise Kohlke's chapter exemplifies this approach, demonstrating how supposed Victorian taboos are appropriated in current day popular culture – in particular television – so as to peddle, and enjoy, the taboos of our current era.

But the layering, as in Trollope and in Grennan, creates equivocation. In both cases we are left with unambiguous representations of ambiguity: such was a self-conscious method utilised in the nineteenth century, and in many ways Trollope's hallmark. And although Grennan's graphic adaptation plays it with finesse, ambiguity it is not simply a post-Modern symptom. Which leads us to end with the word 'Perhaps': the first word of both *John Caldigate* and *Dispossession*.

Introduction

***

More specifically, and less ambiguously, this companion volume to Simon Grennan's *Dispossession* is divided into three parts, each addressing different aspects of the adaptation process and surrounding context. *Part 1, 'Dispossession': Simon Grennan's graphic adaptation of Trollope's John Caldigate*, analyses directly the techniques used by Grennan, both in comparison with other literary adaptations and conventions, and on their own terms, via the interviewed words of Grennan himself. *Part 2, Nineteenth-century visualisations*, switches us from Grennan to Trollope, but keeps us within the graphic novel mode by emphasising the theme of visual, or text/image, culture. These analyses consider the visual nature of Trollope's work, the visualisation of Trollope's work (using illustrations), and the visual context of Trollope's work, including the culture of Victorian comics. *Part 3, Using the Victorians: appropriation, adaptation and historiography*, bridges *Part 1* and *Part 2*, the Victorian era and that of today, and the time of Trollope with the time of Grennan. This section contextualises the twenty-first-century adaptation of *John Caldigate* by comparison with other renditions of Victorian culture: from England, France and the USA, and into TV, novels, and graphic novels.

Part 1

Jan Baetens's *Adapting and displaying multiple temporalities: what became of Trollope's 'John Caldigate' and Maupassant's 'Boule de Suif' in Simon Grennan's 'Dispossession' and Dino Battaglia's 'Contes et nouvelles de guerre'?* introduces us to the key issues in adaptation theory, before applying them to the analysis of Grennan's adaptation of Trollope. By means of a comparison, Baetens considers similar or differing narrative strategies in Battaglia's graphic novel version of Maupassant, concluding with the importance of the methods used to depict the passing of time.

'Dispossession': time, motion and depictive regimes, the title given to the interview of Simon Grennan carried out by John Miers, alludes to the key themes of the basic rules that directed Grennan in his creation of *Dispossession*, and the move from Trollope's literary style to his own corresponding visual style. Grennan discusses his aims and some influences on his thought – Caillebotte, Holman Hunt, Stubbs, Daumier, but also the theorising of Italian Renaissance paintings – in the quest to transpose Trollope's ambiguity.

In *The tactic for illusion in Simon Grennan's 'Dispossession'*, Hugo Frey contextualises Grennan's work in terms of the modern graphic novel, comparing it with examples by Hergé, Moore and Gibbons, and Ware. Drawing on the theme of magic and its latter-day music hall associations, Frey concentrates on the effects achieved by Grennan in terms of what he shows and, equally importantly, does not show: in short 'an aesthetic of illusion', but one that shies away from the expected techniques of a graphic novel set in the Victorian era.

Introduction

Part 2

Frederik Van Dam's *Allegorical landscapes: the psychology of seeing in Anthony Trollope's later novels* examines Trollope's visuality, albeit an image-free one, created via descriptions of physiognomy, and enhanced by varying narrator viewpoints. Van Dam draws upon Benjamin's theories of physiognomy, originally applied to Second Empire Paris, to further our understanding of Trollope's particular visual psychology.

Moving from literary visualisation to images themselves, David Skilton's *Complex meanings in illustrated literature, 1860-1880* concentrates on Victorian illustrated fiction. Analysis of illustrations by Cruikshank for novels by Dickens and associated reading practices (appropriate narrative pauses at sections bearing pictures), as well as theatrical images relating to more than one narrative instance, suggests kinship with narrative sequences such as those by Hogarth or Rowlandson. Skilton introduces the idea of the 'active reader' in Millais's illustrations for Trollope's *Framley Parsonage* (1860) and *Orley Farm* (1862), comparing them with more equivocal approaches in the work of Tenniel and by Hopkins.

Roger Sabin brings us to the broader culture of the image at the time of Trollope, considering the tension between works considered to be literature – including *John Caldigate* – and the rising popular form of comics, the former seen as beneficial and, often, the latter as damaging. In *Comics versus books: the new criticism at the 'fin de siècle'* Sabin draws upon contemporary accounts of the culture of comics, including little known journalistic commentaries, to present and analyse nineteenth-century attitudes to visual culture and its social implications. He concludes with a general contextualisation of the ethical debate about comics, then and now.

Barbara Postema continues with a specific analysis of nineteenth-century comics, concentrating on the nature and influence of a precise sub-form. *The visual culture of comics in the last half of the nineteenth century: comics without words* gives an overview of the development, content and importance of silent strips within the broader field of image narratives, including proto-cinematography. Postema draws examples from England, France, Germany and the USA, focusing in particular on examples from Busch, Caran d'Ache, Schulz, Poitevin and Engl, and the journals, such as *Le Chat Noir*, in which they appeared.

Part 3

With this final section taking us into contemporary culture, Marie-Luise Kohlke presents the Victorians as seen in novels and on television. *'Abominable pictures': neo-Victorianism and the tyranny of the sexual taboo* draws upon a variety of TV productions (*The Siege of Krishnapur*, *Ripper Street*, *The French Lieutenant's Woman*, *Possession*, *Tipping the Velvet*...) so as to explore the appropriation of myths surrounding Victorian sexuality. Kohlke concludes by underlining the complex nature of neo-Victorianism that creates fetish cult

Introduction

objects and revels in forbidden images, thereby displaying 'repression-envy' but also potentially desired transgression of current taboos, in particular paedophilia.

Ian Hague's *Drawing "the apprenticeship of a man of letters": adapting* Remembrance of Things Past *for 'bande dessinée'* considers the visualisation of Victorian-age culture though the graphic novel and the specific example of Proust. Hague concentrates on the 1998 Heuet version of *À la recherche du temps perdu*, and its attempts, with varying degrees of success, to convey complexities of the flavour, narrative techniques and themes of Proust's original, thereby leading to more general musings on the challenges of literary adaptation.

Aarnould Rommens's analysis of Breccia's versions of Poe produced in the context of Argentina's National Reorganisation underlines how cultural updates inevitably carry and convey changing political context. *Allegories of graphiation: Alberto Breccia's counter-censorial versions of E. A. Poe's* Valdemar centres on the workings of the covert resistance to the Argentinian 'Proceso' at the heart of Breccia's renderings into comics of Poe's ambiguous tale of the mesmerising of death.

Finally in *An incomplete project: graphic adaptations of* Moby-Dick *and the ethics of response* Peter Wilkins underlines Melville's 1851 novel as being an 'open work' and explores the resulting implications for its numerous adaptive responses, including graphic novels. Rommens, in the previous chapter, demonstrates the nuanced power of comics via visual association, and Wilkins here emphasises the richness of ambiguity as compared to description of narrative, and the advantage of providing a visual equivalent, rather than an imitation, of prose. Together they form a fitting conclusion to the main themes of a volume on Grennan's *Dispossession* and Trollope's *John Caldigate*.

Part 1

Dispossession:
Simon Grennan's
graphic adaptation
of Trollope's
John Caldigate

Jan Baetens

Adapting and displaying multiple temporalities: what became of Trollope's *John Caldigate* and Maupassant's *Boule de Suif* in Simon Grennan's *Dispossession* and Battaglia's *Contes et nouvelles de guerre*?

The debate on visual adaptations of literary source texts has often taken the form of a dichotomy between two conflicting stances.[1] The traditional view claims that adaptation always involves the relationship between a source text and a target text (to use here the classic terminology of translation studies). Even if 'fidelity' is only a secondary issue here, although a very hotly debated one, what matters in all cases is the fact that an adaptation should always take into account the existence as well as the characteristics of the original work. In this regard, to adapt means chiefly to translate into another medium, whatever the translation policy or ethics one may follow. A more recent view, at least in the theoretical debate, tends to see the adaptation as an independent work, which has to be studied and evaluated according to the values and norms of its new context.

Part 1: *Dispossession*

To a certain extent, a similar shift can be observed in recent forms of so-called empirical translation studies, where the focus is no longer on the relationship between source text and target text, but on the multiple interactions between target text and target culture, which both shapes the translation and is being transformed by it. Taking as their point of departure the simultaneous presence or realisation of works in various media, the current spread of studies on convergence culture and transmediality exemplifies this larger move (which in turn it also reinforces).

Today it may seem as if the latter stance has become largely dominant, although it would be more correct to state that the conflict between both positions has become less doctrinaire. Fidelity, for instance, which entailed the *a priori* condemnation of the adaptation as 'never as good as the original', is no longer the F-word of adaptation studies. The idea, but also the practice of fidelity, can be studied once again in less anxious terms as part of the adaptation's target culture. In certain cases, fidelity is simply a commercial necessity (can one imagine a big budget Hollywood adaptation that would discard the expectations of a 'knowing' audience, for instance in the case of a *Harry Potter* movie?). In other cases, it can represent an artistic challenge, in the venerable and well-respected tradition of the 'paragone.'[2] However, the most general change in adaptation studies concerns the need to historicise and contextualise the works and processes under scrutiny. To put it in an oversimplified way: contemporary adaptations should not be studied the same way as nineteenth-century adaptations, while contemporary adaptations of past fiction – i.e. of fiction written in the past – do not raise the same problems as contemporary adaptations of contemporary historical fiction – i.e. of today's fictional (re)construction of the past. To simplify again: after more than a century, to adapt an 1878-1879 novel by Anthony Trollope (my main example here), or an 1880 short story by Guy de Maupassant (to which I will turn in the final part of this chapter, in order to sketch some convergences as well as well as dissimilarities with the Trollope comic), cannot be compared to the rapid adaptation of, for instance, Michael Cunningham's *The Hours* (I'm quoting this example from Collins who discusses several other adaptations of the same type).[3] This is not to say that the former type of adaptation is more difficult (or for that case, easier) than the latter one, but that both are different and ask for distinct approaches.

A practice-based art research project commissioned by Leuven University, Simon Grennan's *Dispossession* breaks with the two conventional types of literary adaptation.[4] These conventional approaches are didactic (keen to guide the reader to the original work) and hagiographic (aiming at highlighting the superiority of the original work), yet without reinventing the existing literary work in a completely new way, such as in the critically overlooked recreations of Edgar Allan Poe by Alberto Breccia from 1995, whose focus was definitely more on the present than on the creative relationship with the past, in his case the unspeakable present of the Argentinean military dictatorship.[5] Rather, Grennan begins from the historical awareness of the contemporary reader and creator, and their sensitivity to the differences between 'then' (Victorian culture) and 'now' (whatever that now may be).[6] Hence the ambition both to respect the past as much as possible as well as to show that it is seen from a modern point of view. Such an adaptation policy might be labeled 'fidelity 2.0', 'critical fidelity', or 'fidelity-through-infidelity', but it is important to stress that the in-depth study of Trollope's novel and its cultural and historical context was the very starting point of the creative enterprise.

The close reading of *John Caldigate* and other Trollopean books of that period provided the artist with two basic insights. First: any adaptation of the novel would take a (respectful) stance towards a basic feature of Trollope's style, namely 'realism'. Second: no adaptation can put between brackets the fact that Trollope's novelistic writing had many relationships with the visual culture of its time, most directly via the illustrations that used to accompany some of his most popular works. Given the fact that *Dispossession* is an adaptation in graphic novel form, the link between both characteristics is self-evident. However, it does not immediately reveal what will prove one of the key issues within both realism and illustration: time, or more precisely duration.

Realism in Trollope is not to be seen as the capacity of the author to describe a given world in full detail or even to add to his description those 'superfluous' details that determine, according to Roland Barthes in 1986, the 'reality effect'.[7] It is rather the consequence of a particular interaction with the reader, to whom the author presents a world in which everything appears as normal, in which nothing deserves any special mention since everything seems so perfectly self-evident, and in which the essential stylistic and narrative technique is that of 'evenness'.[8] The fact that the author does not find it necessary to highlight certain elements at the expense of others implies that for reader as well as author the fictional word is unproblematic, already known and therefore 'realistic'. However, if this is true for Trollope's first works, a novel such as *John Caldigate* exceeds this initial approach to realism. In most of his later works, Trollope introduces indeed a more complex form of realism, shifting towards a more psychologically oriented realism that not only offers a representation of a social environment (the Victorian middle class), but also a view of the interpretation of that world and that environment by those who inhabit and experience it. In this later Trollope, the world is no longer seen and described, but also frequently open to an ambivalent interpretation of the characters, who are not always capable of drawing definitive conclusions about their own world. *John Caldigate* is a typical example of this growing sophistication, for in this book the 'element of mystery' aspect is clearly nothing but a superficial layer. The question is not whether the protagonist committed bigamy or not, but a reflection on the very impossibility of ever knowing what really motivates people and their actions. This realism is less visual than more conventional definitions generally allow. Hence it is a challenge for an artist to have to find a visual equivalent for this kind of literary voice. Images, one may argue, do create a clear and present danger for this kind of psychological realism. On one hand, images inevitably show details the novelist can easily skip, the most simple example being that of the characters' faces, where even very stylised representations will have to fill in certain details that a writer is allowed to overlook. This fatal verisimilitude, so to speak, may of course jeopardise the psychological inclinations of the text. On the other hand, images are good at showing the look of things, and in certain cases also of events, but less good at suggesting their interpretation, certainly in those cases where many conflicting or competing interpretations are juxtaposed without ever producing a final explanation: this is what Grennan calls the difficulty of 'drawing the idea of "perhaps"'–for this is the first word of the novel–as well as of the graphic adaptation, and it exemplifies in his eyes the stylistic use of equivocation in *John Caldigate*.

This divide between word and image cannot but remind the contemporary reader of a similar change in the work of another famous writer of the late nineteenth (and early twentieth) century, Henry James. In his novels, it is also possible to discover a similar, although much more radical move. Katherine Biers, who analyses James's struggle with the problem that "Really, universally, relations stop nowhere, and the exquisite problem of the artist is eternally but to draw, by a geometry of his own, the circle within which they shall happily *appear* to do so." argues that:

> James's career can be understood as a series of shifting responses to this fundamental problem. In his realist phase, as exemplified by *Washington Square*, he limited the proliferating associations of words and their meanings by investigating the complex motives of well-delineated and discrete characters, understanding them (...) as 'types'. In later novels like *The Ambassadors* or *The Golden Bowl*, published in 1903 and 1904, the drama of limiting and circumscribing meaning, both by and between personas, becomes itself the subject.[9]

What makes James's work such a useful reference in this context is the fact that in his case, more clearly than in that of Trollope, the move beyond his initial type of realism had much to do with shifting attitudes toward the visual culture of the day, a point that cannot be separated from the larger discussion of realism. According to Biers, it was the multiplication of (mechanically produced) images and the sometimes-aggressive marketing of these images that explained a literary reaction against a kind of realism that refused to acknowledge the specific features of writing. In this regard, it is obvious that many existing illustrations of Trollope, with their strong emphasis on the material and objective properties of his fictional world, cannot do justice to the psychological subtleties of realism in the author's later works.

For this reason, the drawing model that Grennan felt attracted to was less the national, Victorian illustrators of Trollope, than the French Honoré Daumier. Nevertheless, visuality cannot be reduced to the issue of book illustrations alone, in spite of the commercial and cultural significance of this textual counterpart. Victorian literature was itself a good example of 'visual writing', given the influence of pictorialism throughout the whole nineteenth century.[10] As defined by Katherine Biers pictorialism, which has strong relationships with the 'melodramatic' imagination analysed by Peter Brooks, refers to an aesthetic that combines, among others, the following characteristics: 1) a preference for daily life scenes, but infused with timeless meaning (realism and idealisation go here hand in hand), 2) a predilection for scenes, tableaux, and situational conventions, 3) the possibility of realising these moments in various media.[11] In pictorial fiction, the story-world was organised around 'citable' scenes (rather than actions), which could freely 'migrate' from one medium to another, even in a period when the *ut pictura* ideology had been replaced, in the wake of Lessing's *Laocoon*, by a raised awareness of the specific features of each medium.[12] Trollope's fiction is a good example of such pictorialism, both in his own writing and in his dialogue with the illustrators. The example of James, however, whose relationships with the visual culture of his time were infinitely more difficult, may suggest the limits of this pictorialism and hence force the contemporary graphic novelist to rethink the whole issue of putting words into images. Indeed, the extreme facility with which certain late nineteenth-century novels have been transposed to other media, on the one hand, and the increasing number of these more and more mechanised media, on the other hand, tended to hollow out the very dynamics of pictorialism as well as the uniqueness of the written, literary text, coercing an author such as James to opt for different, more medium-specific ways of achieving the 'realisation of the ideal'. In James's case, an author traumatised by his (in)famous failure to transfer his prose from book to stage, it was of course convoluted syntax that was asked to play that role. In the case of a modern Trollope adaptation, the critical treatment of pictorialism will have to go beyond the mere aspect of visualisation – i.e. of translating a verbal scene into a drawn one – and to explore specifically visual ways of transposing complex elements of style and narration. It is here that the key problem of time comes into view.

The crucial feature of evenness is something that one can more or less easily transpose from the verbal to the visual as far as the representation of characters, objects, settings, and perhaps even events is concerned. It suffices to refuse any strong distinction between figure and background, for instance. Yet what to do with another aspect of evenness, which is not spatial (visual) but temporal (narrative)? What does the notion of temporal evenness mean in literature, and how can comics create a visual equivalent of it?

Technically speaking, such evenness can be defined in terms of isochrony or, in other words: similarity of time and rhythm. This term, and many others that belong to the same semantic field have been introduced in narrative analysis by and since the germinal work of Gérard Genette.[13] Narratologists tend to focus their reading of narrative speed at both story and discourse level. More specifically they measure speed by comparing time at story level (what is the time-span of the story that is being told?) and time at discourse level (how much time, expressed in words per page, does it take to tell these events?). This analysis cannot offer an 'objective' view of narrative speed (since no two readers will have exactly the same reading time), but it surely provides information on the 'relative' speed of narrative time, generally defined with the help of the following four basic ratios, equally introduced by Genette: ellipsis, descriptive pause, scene and summary.[14] However, the major limit of this approach is that it puts between brackets the very temporality of the narrative act itself, because in the broader field of narrative analysis many scholars are more interested in questioning the story as a whole (i.e. as a story having been told) than in scrutinising the story as it unfolds.[15] Yet storytelling time is a given of any story told, and its pace is absolutely key to a good understanding of realism-as-evenness.

In order to expand the field of narrative speed to the level of the act of storytelling, it is useful to make a distinction between time on one hand and duration and rhythm on the other hand. As summarised by Amit Yahav, whose work relies upon research in musicology and elocution theory, the opposition goes as follows:

> the difference between time and duration is a distinction between the abstract and the experiential, as well as between measures that assess the length of an expanse and measures that assess pace and its variations. Clock and calendar measure length and offer abstract notations of time; rhythm, by contrast, assesses pace, and though rhythm can be rendered through abstract notation and technical tools, it is never complete without a pulsating body to perform and experience their rendering. Finally [...] though rhythmic duration feels intimate, its intimacy is what makes if common.[16]

Are duration and rhythm, which materialise in 'isochronic tics', present in written texts as well? The answer given by various narratologists is unquestionably affirmative.[17] Certain stylistic devices, chiefly syntactic, can slow down or speed up the experience of storytelling while it unfolds, thus becoming a tool for the production of rhythm. The relevance of rhythm for realism can then be defined in two ways. First, evenness of rhythm should be seen as the (necessary) temporal complement of the spatial evenness created with the help of certain descriptive and visualising techniques. Second, the idea of rhythm as a shared experience of artist and audience, as suggested by the notion of 'intimacy' put forward by Yahav, is a supplementary argument to stress realism's approach in terms of common worldviews and experiences. The general notion of evenness already described is one of its cornerstones, since the ability to produce a story evenly is itself proof of the synchronicity between this type of storytelling and an audience's previous knowledge and expectations. But can one say that duration, which has recently become a hot issue in comics theory, is also a critical factor in the evaluation of realism in Grennan's Trollope adaptation? There are good reasons to believe that this is the case.[18]

First, one should not forget that *John Caldigate* is a very (although not unusually) long novel of more than 600 small print pages, which had to be shortened to the more or less conventional length of 94 six-panel pages (with very little text). Although *Dispossession* is anything but a Reader's Digest format, the fact remains that the dramatic shortening of the source text compels the artist to adopt an adaptive and stylistic policy that avoids a dangerous 'heating up' of the target text (to use a favourite term of Marshall McLuhan). Although *John Caldigate* is not, despite its length, a complex novel, it cannot be denied that its unabridged transposition would be close to unbearable to modern readers (in whatever format or medium). At the same time, however, Grennan's desire to be faithful to the even rhythm of Trollope's style is an important touchstone to assess his dealing with authenticity. As we will see, this 'cooling down' is definitely at the heart of various strategic decisions that Grennan made.

Second, Grennan's treatment of rhythmic devices also offers a good opportunity to highlight the uniqueness of both the source text and the target text, as well as to emphasise the necessity of adding new temporal dimensions to the analysis of visual culture. Given the dominant role of stand-alone visual productions such as paintings or illustrations, the shift from time to duration is something that can usefully enrich our current ways of reading the visual adaptation of literary material in static images.

How do comic authors and graphic novelists handle the problem of time and rhythm in visual terms? What are the basic techniques and devices that they use to link story time with the durational time of the narrative act? First, it is useful to keep in mind that the necessary interest in duration and rhythm cannot be separated from a similarly necessary focus on the relationship between story time and discourse time, as analysed in all classic forms of narratology. However, the assessment of the various (literary) ratios that can be distinguished (ranging from the tendency to 'speed up' by summarising to the opposite tendency to 'slow down' by indulging in descriptive pauses) will inevitably be influenced, if not modified by elements that are partly subjective, partly explainable by the active presence of durational elements. The play with boredom in comics is, for instance, a typical feature of many contemporary, post modern graphic novels, but does not imply that the reader will experience these works as boring, slow or uneventful. The work of Chris Ware comes to mind. Conversely, certain readers will consider high-action comics such as those in the classic superhero genre, as utterly dull and paradoxically lacking in speed or rhythm at all.

However, these observations, true as they may be, do not disclose the fundamental, but equally subjective intermingling of story-discourse time and durational time. Let us consider two elementary examples to suggest the kind of issues that may arise in this context.

In *Copper Calhoun*, one of the adventures in Milton Caniff's *Steve Canyon* (serialised between 1947 and 1955), a spectacular car crash is represented in a way that seems to stretch this very short event.[19] Two rows of four small panels detail how a speeding vehicle plunges into a ravine. The effect on the reader is difficult to pin down: the pace of the scene is both slowed down, by the multiplication of panels that are not easy to read, and dramatically quickened by the violent changes of black and white within the panels, but also by the dynamic shifts in point of view, distance and panel size.[20] A comparable yet opposite mechanism is materialised in Robert Crumb's famous one page (or poster format) comic, A Short History of America of 1979, which represents the gradual metamorphosis of a natural landscape from virgin wilderness to urban decay in twelve identical and similarly framed panels.[21] The fact that this poster image can be grasped at a single glance is obviously meant to increase both the fatality and the speed of nature's degradation through human action, yet at the same time this time-lapse effect is softened by a number of visual features that the reader may experience as a form of slowing down, as if we were experiencing less a crash-course in ecology than something almost taking place out of time. On a very intuitive level, it is not difficult to see what is going on in the highly nuanced drawings of Caniff and Crumb. In the former case, the accumulation of images representing very brief slices of time within an event that is itself extremely short, provokes a double feeling of chaos and stillness. In the latter, the reduction of something that hints at the notion of 'deep time' – for the story starts before human intervention and one is invited to read the opening panel in literally Eden-like terms – to just twelve near-identical images that one can mentally flip through in less than a second, so to speak, should leave the reader with a feeling of dizziness and bewilderment. However, the very symmetry of the composition and the highly isochronic pulse throughout the whole work tend to infuse a very different feeling, which, although not necessarily a positive or quieting one, is at least one that generates a paradoxical kind of standstill.

What narrative speed and rhythm actually mean cannot be studied alone by comparing the objective time of the story – a couple of seconds in Copper Calhoun, an incredible number of years in A Short History of America – and, at discourse level, the objective measure of panels per page in the respective comics. One has to complete this analysis with a closer reading of the visual techniques that visually organise the act of storytelling, for it is these elements that govern the durational, rhythmic, intersubjective dimension of time in comics.

If rhythm is linked with the notion of 'isochronic tics', it should not come as a surprise that the visual equivalent of this pulse has been initially located at the level of the panel structure of the strip, the (double) page, and the plot, in whatever publication format it is issued. In other words, layout principles are a good starting point for the analysis of rhythm. More particularly, Thierry Groensteen's proposal to distinguish between 'regular' and 'irregular' panel structure and page layout proves helpful here.[22] Although there certainly exists a 'regularity of irregularity' (and we will see that an author like Battaglia investigates the possibilities of this particular aesthetic mode), it is the regularity – i.e. repetition of panel structure and layout principles – that is most often used to turn out this basic beat. However, the brief discussion of the Caniff and Crumb examples has shown that panel structure is just one among several other aspects. No less decisive in this regard, and also considered by Thierry Groensteen, is the quantitative tension between information overload and information scarcity. Of course, overload or scarcity as such does not produce rhythmical effects. The reader may experience these features as criteria that either slow down or accelerate narrative pace, but the very changes – i.e. the shift from overload to scarcity and vice versa – are powerful tools in the visual manipulation of reading time and thus of rhythm and duration.

The shifting relationships between overload and scarcity, and their combination with the more or less strong presence of recognisable and reiterated panel structures, provides a primary general framework for the analysis of visual rhythm, which should always start from the interaction between the (ir)regularity of the panel on the one hand and the (ir)regularity of its content on the other hand. However, this general rule of thumb has to be completed by the study of other, properly visual features, such as the management of chromatic patterns. A famous and instructive example of this mechanism can be found in Moore and Gibbons' *Watchmen*, with its extremely regular nine-panel layout.[23] In many pages this grid is turned into a polarised checkerboard structure through the use of alternating colour schemes. In these cases, the beat is literally made visible. But alongside colour, theoretically any visual feature whatsoever can be used in order to create effects of isochronicity or non-isochronicity: distance, point of view, image resolution or stylistic unity or disarray. The list is almost endless and, for this reason, it is more practical to take a look at the specific examples of the work of Grennan and Battaglia, and their ways of linking the politics of realism with a visual methodology of drawing time.

As already stated, the drastic shortening of *John Caldigate* to a 94-page graphic novel format with an astonishingly conventional grid structure (three rows, two cells, only speech balloons and practically no captions inside the panels and none outside), constitutes a notorious challenge for an adaptation eager to respect the basic characteristics, aesthetic as well as ideological, of a Victorian novel. Of course, it is important to consider in detail what Grennan both left out and added to the original. Given the emphasis on evenness as a key element in the realistic narrative of Trollope, it is more important to start with an analysis of the central constraints Grennan followed in his attempt to shape or, more precisely, to reintroduce evenness in a fictional world whose abridged form provides numerous opportunities for an uneven treatment of form and content. At a general level, Grennan employs three major procedures, to which he sticks meticulously throughout the whole adaptation (Fig. 1.).

First, the systematic use of the grid, which reconciles a strong visual organisation of the page while also enabling its perfect sequential arrangement. It is vital to stress here the absence of any tendency towards 'tabularity' – i.e. the visual unification of the page as a global image – despite or beyond the apparent compartmentalisation in framed panels.[24] Nothing here prevents the reader from appreciating the transition from one panel to another; row after row, page after page, and everything helps the discovery and

Part 1: *Dispossession*

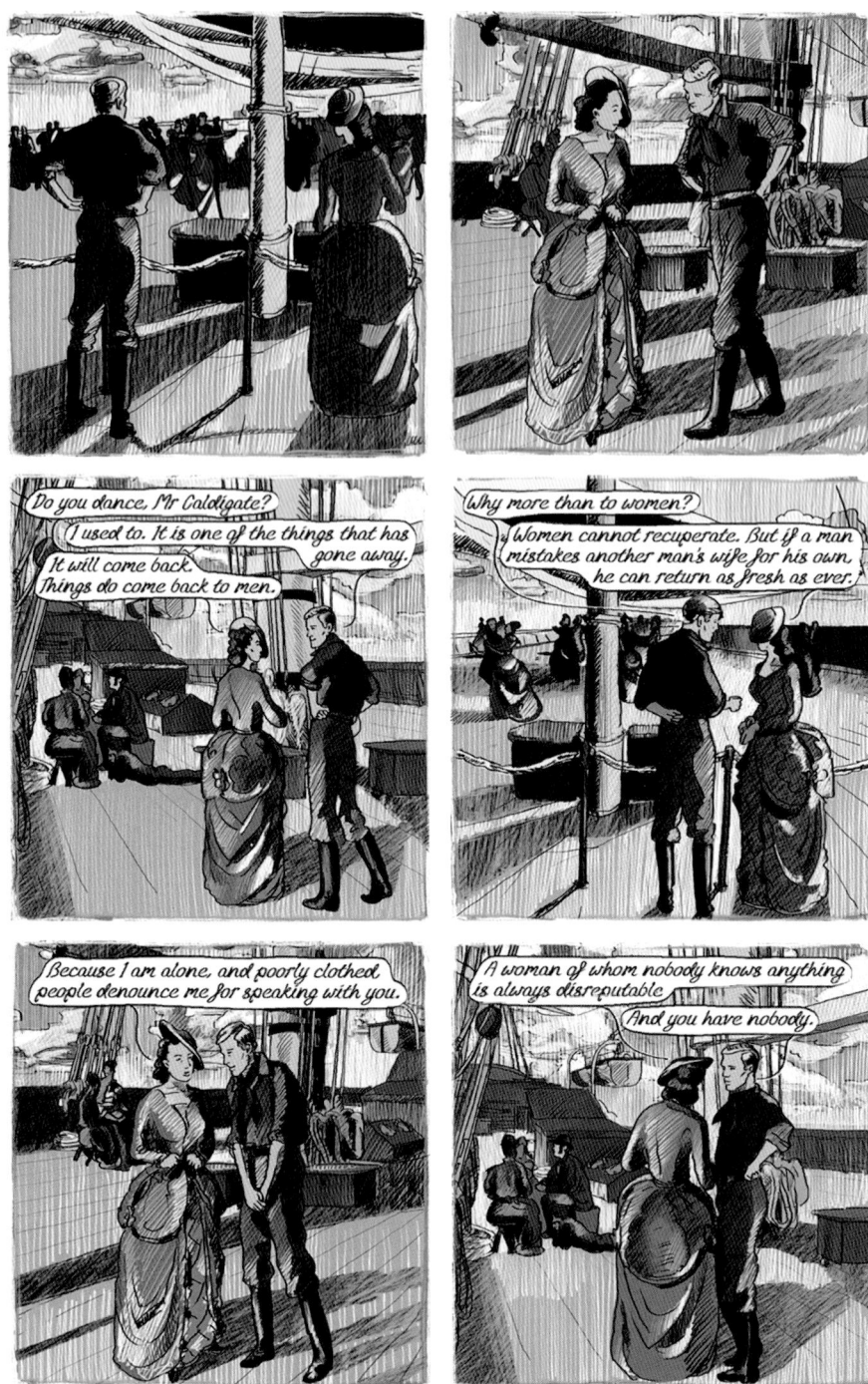

Fig. 1. Grennan, S. (2015) *Dispossession*. London: Jonathan Cape, page 23.

maintenance of the beat or pulse of the book. The regular dispatching of the text, always very smoothly integrated in the visual architecture of the panels, discreetly reinforces the linear trajectory of the images.

Second, the sharp division of the narrative into scenes or tableaux – on this level, the influence of pictorialist and melodramatic conventions is undeniable – which perfectly matches the division within pages, and here articulates the medium-specificity of the comics format. In *Dispossession*, it is not each image but each page that tells a story. On the one hand, all the images of a page are to be seen as variations on the same narrative action, not as successive fragments of an action unfolding in time. On the other hand, from one page to another, we shift from one action to another. The impact of this organisation on aspects of duration is profound, since it installs an authoritative rhythm based on the coincidence of story elements and material aspects of the host medium. This rhythm, moreover, is not a rapid one, for the reader knows that, to a certain extent, there is never something to follow: the whole action is displayed on the page, all its aspects are detailed, the page does not end on a cliff-hanger, and the next page will shift to another action rather than disclosing something left undisclosed on the previous page. This slowing down is an important counterweight to the dramatic shortening – and therefore accelerating – of the story, and thus contributes to the global aesthetics of evenness.

Third, the joining together of the grid's sequentialisation and the page's unification through a methodical application of a three-time, waltz-like rhythm, created by changes in reader point of view or movements of the characters in space, each row corresponding with one of these movements or changes. By doing this, the linear continuity of the panels of the grid is integrated in a larger structure, while the global action of the page is harmoniously fragmented into three even segments.

In fact, these general constraints must be completed by the reading of more fine-grained visual interventions, whose role in the global construction of evenness cannot be underestimated. Very striking in this regard, because apparently at odds with the aesthetics of evenness is the razor-sharp visual distinction between figures and background in *Dispossession*. Knowing Grennan's admiration for Daumier, one would have expected a less brutal opposition between the characters, which are often nearly monochrome blots always seen from the same distance, and the permanently shifting, habitually very variegated and almost motley background. This tension, which runs through the whole graphic novel, initially seems in blatant contradiction to the spirit of realistic evenness that both Trollope and Grennan claim to pursue. However, a closer reading reveals the presence of compensatory procedures, which ultimately tend to produce in the end a kind of 'second-degree evenness'. As far as the characters are concerned, it is their remarkable theatricality that catches the reader's eyes. The characters are always seen from the same distance, more or less the distance one conventionally relates with seeing characters on stage: the distance at which Grennan represents Trollope's characters is exactly the same as the distance that one finds in the cinema of the first years, where operators often tried to reproduce the view of the scene as if the scene was performed on stage in front of a live audience.

Monochromatic treatment of the figures, which makes them look as if they were silhouettes, adds further force to the theatrical representation. Nevertheless, this strong theatricality is also dissociated from any classic comics technique aimed at raising emotional involvement. First, the chosen viewpoint, although frequently shifting, is never a personalised point of view: it is only the omniscient narrator who looks at the characters, the perspective of the images is never subjective, and this feature prevents any easy identification. Second, the distance between the reader and the action always remains the same: the reader is never allowed to intrude on the intimate space of the characters, even at the most tragic and melodramatic moments of the story the reader is kept carefully at a distance, at the other side of the invisible but extremely present fourth wall.

In *Dispossession*, this absence of identification strategies has a twofold effect on the issue of evenness. On the one hand, it certainly hinders an exclusive focus on the characters themselves, who are never alone in the centre of the reader's attention: since we do not adhere completely to the character's thoughts and feelings (quite an achievement in so sentimental a story as this one), we can give our attention to all the aspects of the image, including the background. On the other hand, the paucity of information delivered by both the story – Trollope's elusive plot is rendered even more equivocal by Grennan's shortening and his refusal to show what Trollope does not say – as well as the reduced insights we can derive from physiognomy – the characters are shown at such a distance that it is difficult to interpret the movements of their faces or their eyes – force us to look more carefully at other parts of the drawing, more particularly the background, that inexhaustible source of permanent surprises and meaningful details. It is at this level of detail, of the endless oscillation between the tiny revolutions of what may first may go unnoticed and the strong, apparently overwhelmingly present general constraints structuring the whole work, that *Dispossession* carves out a balance between the general and the singular that offers a good example of a materialised evenness.

In Maupassant's short story *Boule de suif* (Ball-of-Fat or Dumpling), a totally different approach to realism is taken. At the same time, the similarities between Grennan's adaptation and the adaptive work of Battaglia are more profound than may be apparent on the surface. Leaving aside issues of shortening of plot and characterisation, which, as we have seen in *Dispossession*, is a relatively minor problem in adaptation, any comparison between Battaglia and Grennan should take as its starting point Maupassant's vision of realism, one that has almost no affinity with Trollope's. In Maupassant, realism is not the literary mode that relies on the complicity of author and reader, sharing the same worldview, the same experiences, in short, the same way of life, but rather the mode that instead enables their violent confrontation. For Maupassant, realism is not a way of writing that presents what the reader already knows, but something that lays bare what the reader does not yet know, particularly because he or she refuses to admit its very existence.

A masterpiece of French narrative art, Maupassant's short story is a biting satire of French bourgeois culture, set during the 1870 Franco-Prussian war.[25] The short story follows a group of French residents of Rouen, recently occupied by the Prussian army, who decide to flee to Le Havre in a stagecoach. The carriage constitutes a microcosm of French society: six bourgeois, two nuns, an anti-bourgeois republican, and 'Dumpling', a prostitute. At a stop in a local inn, they realise that, due to the terrible weather, they have blundered into Prussian-held territory. The German officer detains the stagecoach, not saying why. After a couple of days, 'Dumpling' tells the other travellers, who clearly despise her, that they will not be allowed to leave unless she sleeps with the officer. As a good patriot, she refuses to do so, to the increasing fury of her fellow travellers, but eventually gives in. The stagecoach leaves the morning after, but no one shows any form of thankfulness and all continue cruelly to ignore 'Dumpling'.

Contrary to Trollope's narrative, the narrator does not leave any doubt about the interpretation of the story. Although he refrains from direct authorial comments, he tells the story in a highly ironical but totally unambiguous way. There is no 'perhaps', nothing to interpret, no hidden or evanescent meaning. Here, realism is not a matter of evenness, but of breaking evenness, breaking the conspiracy of silence. From a temporal point of view, however, there is definitely a strong analogy with Trollope's realism, and this is how *Dispossession* helps us to reframe the spatial notion of evenness. In *Boule de suif* evenness is also dominant, but as a negative, not as a positive, marker of realism and reality. The key structural element is suspense, waiting, lack of action which, on the anecdotal plot level, reflects a broader view of a society frozen in hypocrisy. In the central part of the story, nothing happens until the final disruption of the forced immobility. After that, however, immobility takes over again: nothing changes after the protagonist's sacrifice, and everything goes back to normal, namely to the social status quo and the accompanying moral hypocrisy.

So what do we actually see in Battaglia's adaptation? How does his comic visualise the idea of immobility and lack of action, without simply freezing the plot or putting it between brackets, but by giving it a medium-specific comic treatment?[26] At first sight, what Battaglia's work presents is the exact opposite of Grennan's. The overall organisation of the pages bears no similarity to the conventional grid. Many images are partially deprived of a frame, in many cases the surface occupied by the verbal fragments is as large as the space taken by the images, and no two page layouts are similar. At the same time, however, the reader rapidly notices that this absence of regular patterns is only superficial, and very rapidly more complex forms of regularity appear. On one hand, it appears that while Battaglia avoids any direct mirror effect between left and right pages he pays also a lot of attention to their general (yet open) symmetry, which changes the visual perception of the work dramatically. The sequential arrangement of texts and panels is challenged and superseded, the reader's eye being progressively seduced by hidden relationships between left and right. On the other hand, the lack of framing, for

Part 1: *Dispossession*

Fig. 2. Battaglia D. (2002) *Contes et nouvelles de guerre*. St-Égrève: Mosquito, page 72.

instance, acts to enhance the balance between text and image. The boundaries between both spaces are blurred thanks to the partial un-framing of the panels, so that the reader moves almost imperceptibly from visual to textual zones and vice versa (Fig. 2).

The consequence of these delicate patterns is the gradual emergence of a way of visual storytelling that appears between comics and illustration.[27] This shift away from the classic comic mould means that less pressure is put on the sequential dimension of the work, and of course this characteristic is not totally dissociated with the fundamental theme of lack of action. One discovers in Battaglia's treatment of time and rhythm a kind of relative 'fading out' of comics narrativity, corresponding with the idea of waiting. The action is still there, the storyline remains perfectly readable, but one has the impression that a world sinks slowly down into a form of stasis that little by little seizes everything and everyone.

Various micro-stylistic features reinforce this reading. First, there is the typical 'vaporous' style of Battaglia that, contrary to that of Grennan, circumvents any clash between figure and background. Inside the panels, the merger of character and setting repeats the comparable fusion of text and image at page level. Second, there is the multiplication of non-narrative panels. Not only does Battaglia fold characters into backdrops and vice versa, he also privileges images that are either 'portraits' – characters deprived of backdrop – or 'landscapes' – views with no characters. In Grennan, figure and background violently meet. In Battaglia, their differences are softened, if not made irrelevant given the fact that they are represented separately. Third, Battaglia also favours horizontality, not only by including many very large panels but also by enriching these panels with elements that lengthen their reading time. His use of textual inscriptions in the fictional world is a good example of this tendency toward horizontality and the stretching of time within the image.

As in Maupassant's text, this general slowing down and dissolving of the story world is broken by stylistic surprises. In certain cases, the transfer of these elements is direct, so to speak: Battaglia quotes many ironical sentences and revealing dialogues directly from the short story. In other cases, the transposition is based on purely visual devices, such as the changing size of a panel or the changing distance of a character within such a panel. The technique used to depict 'Dumpling' is enlightening in this regard. When the narrator introduces the various travellers on the stagecoach the prostitute is shown at a greater distance than the others, as if suggesting the psychological remoteness to which she is condemned by the 'virtuous' fellow travellers. When the latter appear to be in need of her, first for food – she is the only one who had thought of bringing provisions for the trip – then for vicarious sex (with the German officer), she is drawn the same size on the page as the other characters. At the end, after her sacrifice and their ungrateful behaviour, her face is repeatedly shown in close-up, in strong contrast with the smaller-sized other characters, in a paradoxical and therefore all the more painful inversion of the initial difference between them.

Through these visual micro-events, Battaglia manages to reintroduce time and duration within a fictional universe whose linearity and sequentiality is always on the verge of collapsing into utter immobility and repetition. By so doing, he strongly reaffirms the importance of temporality in the representation of people, objects, and settings whose visual characteristics alone seem strong enough to represent a world in realistic ways. Just like *Dispossession*, Battaglia's adaptation of Maupassant foregrounds the impossibility of leaving out time and duration in the analysis of realistic images.

Notes

1. Cartmell, D. and Whelehan, I. Eds. (2000) *Adaptations*. London: Routledge.
2. The 'paragone' (Italian: 'comparison') is a Renaissance term for the qualitative comparison between media. It is based on the widely shared belief that all media are equal as far as their representation capacities are concerned (this is the reference of the Latin phrase 'ut pictura poesis', 'as is painting, so is poetry'), but unequal as far as their rhetorical power is concerned (according to the medium that one promotes, one will consider that images are stronger than words, or vice versa). The diversity of media was the starting point of a permanent competition between each medium to do the *same* as the others, only 'better'.
3. Collins, J. (2010) *Bring on the Books for Everybody*. Chapel Hill, NC: Duke University Press. The dates of Trollope's novel refer to first publication. The novel was first serialised in *Blackwoods Magazine*, April 1878 – June 1879, and published later that year as a typical 'three-decker'. Maupassant's story was first read in public in January 1880, and published later that year as part of the collective volume *Soirées de Médan*.
4. Grennan, S. (2015). *Dispossession*. London: Jonathan Cape. By 'practice-based' research, I am referring to a method of research that utilises practice as a method of research (alongside other methods such as historical analysis or theoretical reflection).
5. Breccia, A. (1995) *Le Cœur révélateur et autres histoires extraordinaires*. Paris: Les Humanoïdes Associés.
6. Sanders, J. (2006) *Adaptation and Appropriation*. London: Routledge. Sanders provides a general discussion of this historical awareness (it should be noted however that, although Sanders pays a lot of attention to Victorian literature, Trollope does not seem fashionable enough to be one of her examples). In the case of Simon Grennan, the influence of the impossibility of reading past fiction without taking into account contemporary perspectives can be seen in the treatment of what Trollope did not represent: aboriginal culture in the Australian episodes, for instance.
7. Barthes, R. (1986) "The Reality Effect", trans. by Richard Howard. In Barthes, R. *The Rustle of Language*. New York: Hill and Wang, pages 141 – 148.
8. I am quoting Simon Grennan, who frequently uses this word in the preparatory notes of *Dispossession*.
9. James, H. (1935) *The Art of the Novel*. London: Charles Scribner's Sons, page 5 and Biers, K. (2013) *Virtual Modernism: Writing and Technology in the Progressive Era*. Minneapolis: University of Minnesota Press, page 90.
10. In order to avoid any confusion: the term 'pictorialism' is used here in a much broader sense than the word that gives its name to the international style and aesthetic movement that dominated photography during the later nineteenth and early twentieth centuries.
11. Biers, K. (2013) *Virtual Modernism: Writing and Technology in the Progressive Era*. Minneapolis: University of Minnesota Press, page 76 and Brooks, P. (1995) *The Melodramatic Imagination: Balzac, Henry James, Melodrama, and the Mode of Excess*. New Haven: Yale University Press.

12. More generally speaking, the issue of 'citability' proves to be a dramatically crucial feature of a text's posterity, see De Guardia, J. (2013) "La Technique de la durée". *Poétique* Number 174, pages 173 – 188. The Latin phrase 'ut pictura poesis' was a quotation from Horace's *Ars poetica*, and it was often used in the 'paragone' discussion as a decisive argument in favour of poetry as the highest artistic medium. See endnote 2.
13. Genette, G. (1983) *Narrative Discourse. An Essay In Method*. Ithaca: Cornell University Press.
14. Although one may introduce experimental procedures to impose a metronomically paced reading time, similar to certain constraints used to generate texts or text fragments in clearly described temporal limits, but these are often experimental set-ups which do not cover the immense and immensely anarchic reality of concrete reading experiences. For a commentary, see Baetens, J. and Hume, K. (2006) "Speed, Rhythm, Movement: A Dialogue on K. Hume's Article 'Narrative Speed'". *Narrative* Volume 14, Number 3, pages 351 – 357.
15. That is, as a process rather than as an object; see Baroni, R. (2011) "Le Récit dans l'image". *Image (&) Narrative*, Voume 12, Number 1, pages 272 – 294, for an illuminating discussion of the antinomy. For similar remarks on comics narratology, see Miodrag, H. (2013). *Comics and Language: Re-imagining Critical Discourse on the Form*. Jackson: University Press of Mississippi.
16. Yahav, A. (2013) "Sonorous Duration: *Tristram Shandy* and the Temporality of Novels". *PMLA* Volume 128, Number 4, pages 872 – 887.
17. Yahav quotes Stewart, G. (2009) *Novel Violence: A Narratography of Victorian Fiction*. Chicago: University of Chicago Press, but one should add here all those who also emphasise the notion of 'narrative tension' as well as related notions as curiosity, surprise and suspense, see Baroni, Ibid.
18. Groensteen, T. (2012) *Comics and Narration*, trans. Ann Miller. Jackson: University Press of Mississippi, pages 133 – 157 and Baetens, J. and Pylyser, C. (2015) "Comics and Time". In Cooke, R., Meskin, A. and Bramlett, F. Eds, *The Routledge Companion to Comics*. New York and London: Routledge.
19. The *Copper Calhoun* episode, based on Caniff's interpretation of the film actress Carol Ohmart, appeared in 1947.
20. Remember that Caniff was called the Rembrandt of comics, for his mastery of chiaroscuro effects.
21. There exist several versions of this work, with the initial work in black and white eventually appeared also in colour. For example, the original 12 panels have been completed by a supplementary row presenting three possible futures; or the comic itself has been transformed into a cartoon or animated film version, which is easily found on YouTube. None of these differences changes however the analysis of time and duration under scrutiny in this chapter.
22. Groensteen, T. (2012) *Comics and Narration*, trans. Ann Miller. Jackson: University Press of Mississippi, pages 43 – 50.
23. Moore, A. and Gibbons, D. (1987) *Watchmen*. London: Titan Books.
24. On the tension between linearity and tabularity, see Peeters, B. (2007), "Four Conceptions of the Page". *ImageText* Volume 3, Number 3, available at: http://www.english.ufl.edu/imagetext/archives/v3—3/peeters/
25. An English version of the story can be found in Maupassant, G. (1999) *Short Stories of de Maupassant: Including The Necklace, Love, The Piece of String, Babette, and Ball-of-Fat*. New York: The Book League of America.
26. It may suffice to have a quick look at other, non-comic adaptations of the same short story to notice immediately the considerable differences between media, for instance at the level of visual characterisation. To give just one example: in the filmic adaptations, 'Dumpling' is always a... very pretty woman (sometimes even quite slender!).

References

Baetens, J. and Hume, K. (2006) "Speed, Rhythm, Movement: A Dialogue on K. Hume's Article 'Narrative Speed'". *Narrative* Volume 14, Number 3, pages 351 – 357.

Baetens, J. and Pylyser, C. (2015) "Comics and Time". In Cooke, R., Meskin, A. and Bramlett, F. Eds. *The Routledge Companion to Comics*. New York and London: Routledge.

Baroni, R. (2011) "Le Récit dans l'image". *Image (&) Narrative* Volume 12, Number 1, pages 272 – 294.

Barthes, R. (1986). "The Reality Effect", trans. by Richard Howard. In Barthes, R. *The Rustle of Language*. New York: Hill and Wang.

Battaglia D. (2002) *Maupassant : Contes et nouvelles de guerre*. St-Égrève: Mosquito.

Biers, K. (2013) *Virtual Modernism: Writing and Technology in the Progressive Era*. Minneapolis: University of Minnesota Press.

Breccia, A. (1995) *Le Cœur révélateur et autres histoires extraordinaires*. Paris: Les Humanoïdes Associés.

Brooks, P. (1995) *The Melodramatic Imagination: Balzac, Henry James, Melodrama, and the Mode of Excess*. New Haven: Yale University Press.

Cartmell, D. and Whelehan, I. Eds. (2000) *Adaptations*. London: Routledge.

Collins, J. (2010) *Bring on the Books for Everybody*. Chapel Hill, NC: Duke University Press.

De Guardia, J. (2013) "La Technique de la durée". *Poétique* Number 174, pages 173 – 188.

Genette, G. (1983) *Narrative Discourse. An Essay In Method*. Ithaca: Cornell University Press.

Grennan, S. (2015) *Dispossession*. London: Jonathan Cape.

Groensteen, T. (2012) *Comics and Narration*, trans. Ann Miller. Jackson: University Press of Mississippi.

James, H. (1935) *The Art of the Novel*. London: Charles Scribner's Sons.

Maupassant, G. (1999) *Short Stories of de Maupassant: Including The Necklace, Love, The Piece of String, Babette, and Ball-of-Fat*. New York: The Book League of America.

Miodrag, H. (2013) *Comics and Language: Reimagining Critical Discourse on the Form*. Jackson: University Press of Mississippi.

Moore, A. and Gibbons, D. (1987) *Watchmen*. London: Titan Books.

Peeters, B. (2007) "Four Conceptions of the Page". *ImageText* Volume 3, Number 3, available at: http://www.english.ufl.edu/imagetext/archives/v3—3/peeters

Sanders, J. S. (2013). "Chaperoning Words: Meaning-Making in Comics and Picture Books." *Children's Literature* Number 41(1), pages 57 – 90. Retrieved 14 November, 2014, from https://muse.jhu.edu/journals/childrens—literature/v041/41.sanders.html

Sanders, J. (2006) *Adaptation and Appropriation*. London: Routledge.

Stewart, G. (2009) *Novel Violence: A Narratography of Victorian Fiction*. Chicago: University of Chicago Press.

Yahav, A. (2013) "Sonorous Duration: *Tristram Shandy* and the Temporality of Novels". *PMLA* Volume 128, Number 4, pages 872 – 887.

John Miers in conversation with Simon Grennan, conducted by email, July and August 2014

Dispossession: time, motion and depictive regimes

John Miers: The research aims of *Dispossession* create unusual, highly specific constraints on both the selection and rendering of depicted scenes, so I thought we could start this discussion by considering, within the context of both general and comics-specific theories of drawing, the effect of these rules on its production.[1]

Patrick Maynard offers the term 'frameworks' to describe techniques for organising depictions "that can precede the drawing of any individual objects."[2] With regard specifically to drawing in the comics register, Groensteen identified 'quadrillage' ('gridding') as "an operation (or at least a stage of reflection that is not always incarnated) that intervenes very early in the process of elaboration in comics", which "operates as a primary repartition of the narrative material."[3]

Simon Grennan: Part of the process of creating *Dispossession* was the development of a number of rules to govern the graphic novel's storyboard, that is, the ways in which the reader relates to the action in each panel and the way in which panels relate to each other. As we begin our conversation, it might be useful to repeat these rules: a limited range of distances between viewer and scene; views of discrete actions, not divisions of actions; rhythmic changes of scene and episode on the page; consistent rhythmic changes of point of view in a visible 1-2-3 rhythm; no extradiegetic narrative; as small an amount of verbalisation in the plot as possible; generalisation: this treatment applied in all circumstances. I am sure that we will be discussing these rules further.

JM: The rule that individual cells should present "views of discrete actions, not divisions of actions" carries significant implications for the depiction of diegetic time before a single mark has been made. The simple phrasing of this rule belies what must have been a complex decision-making process at this level of primary repartitioning: how did you decide that the actions presented in a given cell constituted a discrete action rather than a division of one?

SG: The rules governing the storyboard were developed as part of the strategy for making the graphic adaptation of Anthony Trollope's 1879 novel *John Caldigate* that became *Dispossession*. I set myself the challenge of replacing Trollope's literary voice, his *John Caldigate* style of writing, with a visual style, along with the further task of being able to theorise this replacement. More than his plots, Trollope's writing style, his techniques of understatement, create the overwhelming sense of the world in which he lived, his novels being set in the very recent past of the mid and late nineteenth century. Virginia Woolf said of Trollope's style that the reader believes in it "as we believe in the reality of our own weekly bills."[4] However, although written at great speed, scrutiny of *John Caldigate* reveals that this effect is as much to do with the careful structuring of juxtapositions and omissions as with description. Trollope is both accurate and equivocal. 'Perhaps', he says, or 'it was said of'. Producing this sense of equivocation through the visual style of the graphic novel became one of the central challenges of showing, rather than telling, the plot: how does one draw 'perhaps'?

I made a distinction between storyboarding and mark making. It is useful to maintain this distinction at this point, because it allows us to talk about the partitioning of plot in terms of the structuring of reader points of view, relative to the panel, the page, the spread and the book. However, there are other ways in which the mark itself positions the reader relative to each scenario, to which I'm sure we will return. The rules governing the storyboard were intended to replace Trollope's equivocation with a set of consistent visual effects. As a result of the rules, the reader never views the main characters from a distance closer than 15 or 20 feet. There are single encompassing, locating panels, but there are no close-ups and no middling views. The major characters in each panel are always seen full figure and the reader invariably keeps his or her own feet on the diegetic ground. Rather, the reader moves around the action from panel to panel, even as the characters move in diegetic space, in a regular, repetitive round between three points of view: a sort of reader waltz with the diegesis.

The visual effect that is produced by the rules is part of the replacement of literary style with visual style. The visual world of *Dispossession* is not vague. It is vivid and distinct, but readers can only experience it from beyond the threshold of a small distance that they can never cross, that renders certain details unimportant. Keeping their feet on the ground, the reader is moved in a consistent rhythmic round of changes of point of view. Together, these effects both allow the visual world of *Dispossession* to appear materially robust and historically verisimilar and, at the same time, to deny the reader any single conclusive adjudication of views. This rationale prompted my approach to the partitioning of action in each scenario, in the sense that entire types of partitioning became unavailable, if the storyboard was to maintain its rhythm and distance. For example, the type of close scrutiny of the perfume bottle thrown by Laurie on page 195 of Moore and Gibbon's *Watchmen* was both impossible and undesirable within the regime of *Dispossession*.[5] The short trajectory of the bottle takes place over three panels according to the time it takes to read the overlying text, that is, 'in slow motion'. The way in which the action is fragmented and delayed by voiceover, and the close proximity to the reader that it creates, renders it privileged and unequivocal, exactly the kind of effect that the rules of *Dispossession* were established to avoid.

Rather, the divisions of action in *Dispossession* were pushed by the regime into tableaux, with historic theatrical roots. The distance and invariable mobility of the reader suggested gesture rather than facial expression as a meaningful expressive instance, for example. Similarly, I approached the actions comprising the plot as iconic rather than sensational. Hence, we can see on page two of *Dispossession* that distance and regular mobility tend to produce a series of divisions of action along the lines: 'John climbs a tree', 'John fights his father', rather than 'John feels the bark beneath his hand', 'Sweat beads John's brow'. In theatrical terms, this distinction might be described as the distinction between different performance practices: nineteenth-century melodrama, later represented by the work of Vsevolod Meyerhold for example, and twentieth-century psychological realism, represented by the work of, say, Constantin Stanislavski.[6] Although contemporary use of the word 'melodrama' has taken on the sense 'empty exaggeration', the practice of melodrama in the nineteenth century constituted a sophisticated system of gestures and groups of gestures recognised by contemporaneous audiences as communicating a comprehensive range of physical conditions and emotions. Both practices are codified regimes that utilise expressive resources and audience expectations in very different ways and, I suspect, the compelling strength of those expectations tends to universalise one regime at the expense of the other. I was aware that the storyboard rules in *Dispossession*, including this partitioning of action, would generate a book that twenty-first-century readers might find unusual to read. However, the adoption of an older theatrical tradition of action grouping and partitioning in the storyboarding of *Dispossession* also acts to place the plot in the nineteenth century. It is a cue for twenty-first-century readers. The visual style underwrites the relationships that *Dispossession* establishes with Trollope's text and with ideas of the nineteenth century that contemporary readers bring to the novel.

JM: *John Caldigate* was published in the year before Eadweard Muybridge used a series of cameras to record the successive moments in a horse's gallop, thereby creating the first set of depictions of precise divisions of actions, and indicating the shift in the visual apprehension of motion that the camera would enable. This ability to see motion through

Part 1: *Dispossession*

Fig. 3. Grennan, S. (2015) *Dispossession*. London: Jonathan Cape, page 2.

time as fragmentary, causally connected time-slices frequently informs accounts given by cartoonists of what constitutes effective communication of narrative. McCloud, in a page that opens with the text "When clarity is your *sole purpose…*" describes the depiction of successive moments as a "dot-to-dot puzzle".[7] While he asserts that "each panel shows a complete *action*", the interpolation of extra cells at the bottom of that page to extend the depicted action demonstrates that the division of time described here is precisely that excluded by the frameworks that structure *Dispossession*. Jeff Smith, discussing his response to Frank Miller's *Dark Knight Returns*, highlights the link between the camera and the division of motion: "It was the first time I had seen you could do visual, cinematic storytelling in comics. You can *really* manipulate timing."[8]

A significant effect of this divided-action approach to narrative drawing, and one well exemplified in Smith's own work, is the cartoonist's focus on the reader's ability to infer specific trajectories of bodies in space during sequences that depict physical action. I would suggest that the reader is largely denied this ability in *Dispossession*. For example, the last three panels of page fourteen, or page two (Fig 3).

In page two, there is no definite succession of movements that would fill the gaps between panels three and four, or four and five. Panel five in particular strongly suggests an action whose depiction has not been distributed across the preceding or following panels. The young John's leap towards his father in the fifth panel must, given his trajectory, have taken place after John has been placed on the ground, and the complex movements that must have taken place between panels four and five cannot be inferred from their contents. The depictions of John in the fifth and sixth panels, if considered in isolation, easily yield a reading in which he hits the ground running and continues in the direction he was already facing, but this reading – suggested by the visual redundancy of the two appearances of John on the page's surface - is denied by the rotation of viewpoint between the two panels.

SG: I mentioned that I think that audience expectations tend to universalise one visual story-telling regime at the expense of others. Jeff Smith's term 'manipulation' suggests to me both that his insight into the temporal structure of *Dark Knight Returns* delights in finding movie conventions in the storyboarding of the comic, and that these conventions are an apotheosis of the craft of visual story-telling, for him. But the import of conventional movie divisions of time into a graphic storyboard is only one type of possible 'manipulation'. All images and sequences of images produce a temporal order of some sort. The association of 'divided motion' with movie storyboarding conventions is only one type of many possible temporal orders. I am really talking about the storyboarding and editing conventions of movie, but these conventions rely, to a great extent, both upon the type of images produced by a lens as an ordering principle and upon the idea of visual illusion and the possibility of the occasional deployment of visual illusions.

Because, in general, each panel In *Dispossession* presents an icon of action rather than the sensation of action, the anaphoras of the plot are categorically different from the

Part 1: *Dispossession*

Fig. 4. Grennan, S. (2015) *Dispossession*. London: Jonathan Cape, page 21.

anaphoras in a graphic novel structured by a movie-type regime. Anaphoras constitute what the reader can know about the diegesis that is not shown in the plot. I am using the term 'anaphora' in its linguistic sense, to refer to types of knowledge that are indexed by a text, but which do not appear in a text. Anaphoristic knowledge has causal relationships to the events of the plot. For example, if a plot shows a mature oak tree, then we also understand that there has been an acorn, in the past, and that, at some future time, the tree will disappear. Neither of these anaphoristic facts are shown explicitly in the depiction of the mature tree. With a movie-type comics storyboard, knowledge of the trajectory of a body moving in space might form a crucial aspect of the anaphora, as a present-time sensation for the reader. The storyboard rules in *Dispossession* make this type of knowledge largely unimportant.

So what types of dramatic effect are produced by what I might call the non-*Dark Knight Returns* storyboard regime developed for *Dispossession*? I have touched on the visual production of narrator equivocation relative to the writing style of Trollope through *Dispossession*'s storyboard regime, or the unambiguous presentation of ambiguity. I also thought of this as a part of my technique for representing the nineteenth century for twenty-first-century readers. The 1870s are represented through the carefully researched use of verisimilar visual appearances, such as historically accurate styles of dress, locations and technologies. Further, a small number of visual cues as to character and the meaning of specific situations are overdrawn, to give twenty-first-century readers a hint of the significance that they would have had in the past. Mrs Smith's straw hat alone is a cue to a world of social associations that underwrite her character. For a modern reader, it is an icon for significance, even if the reader doesn't necessarily understand the nature of this significance (Fig. 4).

However, the storyboard regime was by far the most important way in which I represented what I consider to be the fundamental strangeness of the nineteenth-century world: its near/far proximity to our own world. As well as replacing Trollope's literary voice, my rules also replaced many of the rules of western comics storyboarding expected by contemporary comics readers. I intended the strangeness of the experience of reading *Dispossession*, compared with habitual expectations of reading a new graphic novel in English or French, to inculcate the strangeness of the diegetic world of the 1870s. In a sense, this 'displacement', as you call it, aims to place the reader in an affecting relationship with a vision of the period that is both coherent and comprehensively dis-habituating. *Dispossession* is meant to be dis-habituating to read, in the way that reading some comics of the mid- and late nineteenth century is dis-habituating. I'm thinking particularly of Marie Duval's pages from the 1870s, the period in which the plot of *Dispossession* takes place. *Dispossession* purposefully shares some of its storyboard regime with these comics in order to create a specific sense of proximity to the past for the reader.

JM: To develop the comparisons between *Dispossession* and comics contemporary to Trollope's novel a little further, I wanted to ask whether you see the iconic rather than sensational status of the depicted actions in *Dispossession* as something also present in nineteenth-century narrative drawing? George Cruikshank's *The Progress of Mr. Lambkin*, produced in 1844 but republished in 1865 and 1883, differs from *Dispossession* and Duval's work by presenting a single image per page, but shares their dense use of line work and presentation of discrete rather than fragmented actions.[9] The selection of depicted moments in *Lambkin* might even be closer to *Dispossession*'s rules than those made in Duval's pages, which often present to the reader purely informative drawings of objects that play a role in the diegesis. Page nine of *Lambkin* captions its single image of Mr. Lambkin being introduced to a lady at what appears to be a society ball with text beginning, "Mr Lambkin of course visits *all* the theatres and *all* the saloons", attaching to the image a weight of narrative information similar to your suggestion that what is communicated by the tableau in *Dispossession* page 2 panel 5 could be stated as 'John fights his father'. Without wishing to take our attention away from depictive regimes, an obvious contrast between these two nineteenth-century drawn narratives and *Dispossession* is the prevalence of verbal text: both *Lambkin*'s and *Sloper*'s illustrations are accompanied by substantial anchoring verbal text, whereas *Dispossession*'s rules include "no extradiegetic narrative" and "as little verbalisation in the text as possible". Would you say that deliberate avoidance of verbal text with an anchoring function and the frequent appearance of 'silent' panels and sequences of panels are features of *Dispossession* that rely on the reader's familiarity with contemporary comics-reading protocols, or are these features more closely linked to the theatrical roots of its depictive regime?[10]

SG: Rather than extradiegetic verbal text anchoring the image, I suggest that the image anchors the verbal text in the examples from Cruikshank and Duval. There is a long history of theorising images as accumulating meanings, an aspect of which is the idea that images, unlike verbal text, are beyond the bounds of law or literally 'unruly'. Joe Sutliffe Sanders has recently interrogated this idea, arguing that reading practices generate media forms, with radical consequences for the idea that verbal text 'rules' image.[11] I think that the image makes the verbal text epistemologically immanent, rather than the other way around. Habitually, we see images unequivocally, in that what we recognise is what they show, whereas verbal text founders on its processes of agreed semiosis, and meaning only emerges in the diexical relationship between sign and signifier. In this sense, I think one could argue that an image shows precisely what is meant by a verbal text.

JM: Modern cartoonists do not, of course, universally share the movie-influenced conception of narrative drawing. Chris Ware has frequently lamented what he sees as movie's overbearing influence on comics production and reception.[12] The high level of visual redundancy that emerges from the focus on networked co-presence of serial depictions of characters and locations in his work is also denied the reader of *Dispossession* by the constant rotation around diegetic space. While the consistent framing and the circling around the diegetic space solidify our sense of the world in which these actions are taking place, the latter combines with the treatment of motion to reduce our certainty about the precise events taking place within that space. Gridding as well as facture participates in the adaptation of Trollope's equivocation: could we say that this uncertainty operates as a microcosm of the central uncertainty in the plot, regarding Caldigate's marriage to Mrs Smith?

SG: Trollope never tells us if Caldigate and Mrs Smith were married or not. The relevant parts of his plot, describing a period of three years in which he consolidates a gold strike by going into partnership with Mrs Smith in a mine and returning home a wealthy man, are told very briefly, in retrospect, by Caldigate, his father and members of the Bolton, Shand and Babbington families in Cambridgeshire. This presented a challenge in a medium that shows events. However, the storyboarding regime in *Dispossession* suggested that a scene could clearly show a course of events that distance renders ambiguous for the reader. On page 42 of *Dispossession*, Caldigate and Mrs Smith seem to be getting married in a scenario that takes place across four panels, but they could, just as plausibly, be playing at getting married. What ARE they doing, laughing uproariously, drinking and reciting vows with (is that...) a priest outside that tent at the gold fields? If it were a marriage, would Anna Young laugh out loud at one of the most solemn moments in the ceremony? Is it a joke or an actual marriage? The reader is not allowed to get close enough to be able to decide.

In similar vein, the continual waltz that the reader makes with the diegesis offered opportunities to depict and indicate the significance of the complete separation of the Wiradjuri and European characters in New South Wales. The two groups of people pass within feet of each other, both in the New South Wales countryside, the mining town of Nobblc (Grenfell) and in Sydney. Their activities parallel and cross each other, but they never meet and don't exchange a word. This separation was facilitated to a great degree by the imperative to rotate continually around the action: sometimes, it is the Europeans in the foreground, sometimes the Wiradjuri, as the reader moves round and round.

JM: The movie-influenced conception of the visual presentation of time expressed by Jeff Smith is also embedded in some of the best-known attempts by cartoonists to describe the operation of narrative drawing, as in McCloud's suggestion that "*before* it's projected, film is just a very very very very *slow* comic" and Eisner's conception of individual depictions within a comic as 'postures' from which the preceding and succeeding movements are readily extrapolated by the reader.[13] Although the approach to breakdown in *Dispossession* contradicts such accounts by obscuring the precise nature of preceding and succeeding moments, expectations regarding the ability of a single image to imply temporal continuity remain an important point of comparison between the behaviour towards narrative pictures exhibited by nineteenth-century and twenty-first-century audiences.

SG: Although I can't think of any theorist who has said this explicitly, there might be a narratological argument to be made for the plotlessness of single images, in which the image is only meaningful as an anchor for its anaphoras. I think that a change in the relative importance accorded to different categories of anaphoras by viewers took place with the advent of movie and photography. If we compare two paintings form the period in which modern photography and then movie appeared, La Place de l'Europe, temps de pluie of 1877, a painting by Gustave Caillebotte with The Children's Holiday of 1864, a painting by William Holman Hunt, we can see the differences between these categories of 'unshown' knowledge, in which the images become meaningful. In Caillebotte's painting, it is the sense that we know that the image depicts a moment almost identical to the preceding and successive ones that is significant. In Holman Hunt's painting, the identification of the moment of depiction, relative to surrounding moments, is unimportant. Rather, it is knowledge of the histories of each element in the image, and the juxtaposition of these histories, that is significant. To twenty-first-century viewers immersed in lens-based media, Holman Hunt's image highlights the loss of the habit of significantly relating the histories of elements to each other, whereas Caillebotte's extraction of a moment from a continuity of moments exploits the now-expected significance of a type of knowledge of before and after similar to that which makes the 'snapshot', the phone movie or the 'selfie' comprehensible.

JM: According to Donald H. Ericksen's discussion of Victorian and art and illustration, viewers of images in the late nineteenth century would have been familiar with the types of viewing habits assumed by both Caillebotte's and Holman Hunt's paintings.[14] He emphasises the status of Victorian narrative paintings as tableaux of carefully arranged details, as in Hunt's *The Children's Holiday*, but also claims that their primary distinguishing feature is their emphasis on 'story telling', in the specific sense of allowing the reader to infer moments that directly precede and follow the depicted scene, as in Caillebotte's *La Place de L'Europe*. The low critical status of narrative painting in the first half of the twentieth century is often ascribed to a rejection of the sentimentality expressed in much Victorian painting.[15] However, analysing different depictive regimes by means of the types of anaphoras they create opens another reading: the tableau-style, with its sense of distilled rather than passing time, is unsuited to the expectations of audiences whose visual culture is being transformed by lens-based media. Caillebotte's work, and that of the Impressionists more generally, expresses a conception of image-as-moment that is at odds with the image-as-tableau that characterised British painting of the same period. The shift between these two regimes that took hold with the advent of photography can be clearly seen by comparing two commentaries, each about a century distant from the publication of *John Caldigate*. Gotthold Lessing famously argued that the representation of time was the domain of the literary rather than visual arts, as a picture can only ever express a single moment. That single moment, in his work, should not aim to allow the viewer to infer specific moments occurring immediately before and after the depicted scene. Rather, what he called the 'pregnant moment' was the one "which allowed the freest scope to the imagination of the spectator, who the more he looked at what was represented, the more he ought to exercise thought."[16] Lessing's principle that "plastic art ought not to exhibit the last and extremest thing" is directly at odds with Stan Lee's instruction to the aspiring illustrator of superhero comics to "notice how the first drawing and the last one in that particular sequence seem to have the most impact … in a Marvel story, the artist would use either of those shots rather than the tamer ones in between."[17]

SG: Of course, Lessing never describes how the decisive moment of depiction is suggestive, or what it might be suggestive of. For him, it seems that the most successful depictions offer a summary of some type or types of anaphoristic knowledge, but he remains vague as to what types of knowledge these might be. Because he was theorising in the eighteenth century, I think it is safe to conjecture that Lessing accords significance to the type of accumulated histories of elements piled up in Holman Hunt's painting, rather than to the 'moment of time' approach made commonplace by photography. This approach to the relative significance of the histories of depicted elements need not diminish with single depictions of dramatic actions. George Stubbs' painting *Horse Frightened by a Lion*, painted within Lessing's lifetime (in 1763) depicts such a moment of action, and the significance of the moment of arrest derives from knowledge of the longer histories of the rocks, lion, horse and clouds rather than from understanding that these elements are significant as knowledge of an entire concatenation of anaphoristic before and after moments.

JM: The position of the viewer relative to the depicted action, the movement of which emphasises both the grid and the regular compartmentalising of time, strongly emphasises what Philip Rawson calls the 'floor' of a drawing, "the ground surface which, the drawing suggests, rises into the format from under the spectator's own feet", and which he argues begins to disappear from Modernist art, starting with Cezanne's late paintings.[18] The floor is certainly prominent in much popular narrative art of the mid-Victorian period, such as William Powell Frith's *Derby Day* of 1858, whose dense agglomeration of figures provides an example of both the depictive regime discussed in relation to Holman Hunt above, and realism's focus on the details of the social milieu of its middle-class audience.

SG: In *Dispossession,* I thought of this 'floor' as a theatre stage and, on reflection, the floor of the stage is quite unlike Rawson's 'floor' of a drawing. Rawson's 'floor' is fixed by a geometric projection that locates points precisely in a closed, systematic representation of space, of which the position of a single eye is the absolute arbiter. The floor of the stage, on the other hand, is a generalised ground that continually shifts in relation to both viewers and actors. A close visual analogy exists in the regimes for representing space in the Chinese painting tradition.[19] In these regimes, either the top or right of a handheld of hanging scroll forms a nominal 'most distant' area and the bottom or left forms a nominal 'least distant' area or, elements that are darkest are 'least distant' and elements that are lightest are 'most distant'. In proscenium theatre, stage scenery, flats and drops, stage left/stage right and front can all occupy 'most distant' or 'least distant' positions. Even 'up' and 'down' are mobile concepts, relative to both spectator and action.

JM: Despite the emphasis above on the ways in which *Dispossession*'s frameworks act to create a depicted inference of time and motion that is distinct from that enabled by photography and later, movie, the creation of photo-collages as the basis for the drawings in *Dispossession* is a notable aspect of the process of its creation. This is not an unusual technique – apart from the reliance on photo-reference by artists such as Neal Adams and Bryan Hitch, Rutu Modan's *The Property* (of 2013) makes very similar use of actors to stage scenes, the documentation of which is then drawn over.

SG: In *Dispossession*, the diegetic 'floor' is certainly depicted as something on which the reader might stand, because the reader's eye level most often lies at a similar level to those of the characters. However, this 'floor' is geometrically incoherent, due to the accumulation of a depicted elements from a variety of sources, that bring vestiges of their own, diverse spacial regimes with them into each panel. In particular, rather than utilising geometric projection to unify the view in each panel, I often made characters, props and locations spacially distinct, in order to refer the reader to the idea of 'the stage'. Paradoxically, this process was much aided by the use of collaged photographic elements in constructing each diegetic location and the action taking place within it. These elements finally succumbed to the specific motivation of the drawings, and were erased. But they contributed some of the local details and internal proximities that produce the historic verisimilitude in the drawings and left a residue of contrasting spacial regimes deriving from the process of collage itself. This is most obvious in panels where I have used the extreme changes of scale in close proximity, such as pages 35 and 37, or a type of 'discordia concors' (union of opposites) associated with both Mannerism and, in theatrical terms, the early performance traditions of the Commedia dell'Arte.[20]

JM: By placing the viewer consistently within what Cutting and Vishton call 'action space', an imagined physical relationship with the characters is emphasised throughout *Dispossession*, one in which, as the characters never enter 'personal space', leads to the reading of expression and intention through gesture and pose rather than the scrutiny of facial expressions.[21] This, combined with the constancy of layout, provides an experience of the story-world that has more in common with theatre than movie.

SG: This seems like a good place to turn to the facture of the drawings themselves, because I suspect that there is a link between aspects of drawing technology in particular and the way in which I've tried to produce the sense of relative historic position and diegetic time that contributes to this sense of a theatre tradition rather than a movie tradition. I am currently in the process of imagining a drawing equivalent to Jean Louis Baudry's and Christian Metz's 'apparatus' theory, in which the social, formal and technological terms of depictive drawing are ideological in themselves.[22] Unlike movie, the traces that constitute depictive drawings are attenuated directly to the body and the physical resources of the body embed them. In a sense, depictive drawing belongs to a category of intersubjective processes that directly transform the body and directly utilise the body to transform the world. Such direct transformations arise out of crises of representation (for instance, the perennial 'problem' of depiction) of a type unknown to movie, but which are commonplace in theatre.

In direct co-present communication with others, the body reforms itself according to what are known as 'image schemas', which stand for a physically felt but abstract sense.[23] These schemas can represent our experience of others, of physical activities, of the apprehension of movement and time, of our use of objects and our understanding of space.[24] Although they arise afresh according to the needs of each situation, across both theatrical and depictive traditions, body schemas form the basis for the lexica, although not necessarily the syntaxes, of an actor's or artist's craft, unmediated by the structuring principal of the lens. They also underpin the culturally habituated processes by which we recognise depictive drawings as the situations that they depict, as we struggle to achieve depictive recognition of the mark. In the case of the 'problem' of depiction, or how we come to recognise other visual situations in groups of marks that are entirely unlike them, image schemas spontaneously generate solutions that constitute successful depictions, through a process of catachresis. I'm conjecturing that the totality of this schematic catachresis in drawing is equivalent to movie's apparatus. Rhetorically, catachresis is the use of an existing word in a new way to describe something for which no other word exists. Catachresis uses words to break lexical rules so as to communicate something beyond the lexicon.[25] Visually, this is exactly how a depictive drawing functions to elicit recognition successfully. Every drawing transforms the situation of both drawing and viewing by 'solving' the problem of depiction afresh in each new situation, using the tools at hand to substitute others, as the body makes its marks.

JM: The movie-like approach to narrative drawing can be very frequently observed in contemporary comics, and cinematic vocabulary operates as something of a default lexicon for (non-scholarly) discussions of the comics register's affordances. However, the well-known practitioner treatises I've mentioned earlier do bear traces of something like a theatrical gestural lexicon even as they operate from a standpoint that sees 'divided time' as inherent to depiction in comics. For example, Eisner precedes his discussion of 'postures' as "movement[s] selected out of a sequence of related moments in a single action" with the notion of 'gestures', which are much closer to the habits you describe in nineteenth-century melodrama, being "generally almost idiomatic to a region or culture."[26] To take a more recent example of comics scholarship, Forceville et al acknowledge that, in comics, "Physical activities (walking, throwing, fighting, giving, kissing etc.) are often depicted in highly stereotypical ways," a statement that seems more compatible with a theatrical than a cinematic regime.[27] Invoking a much more cinematic conception of time, they also insist that "it is crucial that viewers correctly judge the nature of any physical activity" and "the key moment of a movement needs to be chosen to convey the entire action."[28] Your characterisation of the nature of narrative drawing as an intersubjective process that uses the body to transform the world implies that the viewer's experience of reading a comic will always include an awareness of drawn marks as the trace of a body moving in space, and the differing conceptions of depicted action expressed in both of these texts would seem to support this idea. However strong the influence of lens-based media may be on these accounts of storytelling in comics, the foregrounding of the importance of gestures and stereotypes also emphasises the potential of the body as a carrier of meaning.

SG: It seems to me that Forceville makes the 'key moment' a characteristic of comics' 'stereotypical' depiction of action, so that, unlike movie, recognisable and expected still postures underwrite the communication of action itself in comics. Other than this, his commentary could as easily be describing a movie regime. However, In terms of melodrama as practice, for example, the still moment is not 'inactive', but rather indicates a moment of crisis in the plot, in which the action is at its most intense and at which points the audience becomes fully sensate. Simon Shepherd calls these still moments 'pauses of mutual agitation', which present "a foregrounding of the moments of coming to knowledge, of 'apprehension'."[29] This is one of the reasons that I think that consideration of different categories of anaphoras relative to lens, performance and visual depictive regimes is important. Readers and viewers understand if they are meant to pay attention to a still image as immanent (or coming to knowledge), as isolating a moment (as Caillebotte's painting) or as an a-temporal accumulation of icons. Hence, different types of still image anchor different types of anaphoras and are schematically inscribed by the body in different ways.

JM: The concept of image schemas is one that only a few writers have applied to the analysis of comics. One example that may be particularly relevant to the distinctions we've been proposing between nineteenth and twenty-first-century depictive schemas is Potsch and Williams' discussion of superhero comics.[30] Their opening statement that "comics is cinema without motion or sound" is controversial within the context of most contemporary theoretical discussions of comics, but might appear slightly less problematic when applied exclusively to superhero comics.[31] It supports the observation derived from Jeff Smith's response to *The Dark Knight Returns,* that a reader of a contemporary superhero comic is likely to expect from the comic an experience that is, in ways outlined earlier, comparable to movie. With the connection Baudry draws between movie apparatus and the tradition of linear perspective in post-Renaissance Western art in mind, the idea that the expectation of a movie-like experience is created and to some degree fulfilled by many superhero comics is supported by the fact that while *How to Draw Comics the Marvel Way* devotes two chapters to drawing in perspective, the technique is discussed over just four pages in McCloud's *Understanding Comics* and receives a single paragraph in Abel and Madden's *Drawing Words & Writing Pictures.*[32]

According to Potsch and Williams, comics' lack of movement means "the comics reader must add motion and dynamics to the story conceptually, mentally animating the narrated events."[33] 'Must' here needs to be qualified: according to the present discussion it might be more appropriate to say that the reader of superhero comics expects that they will provide access to anaphoras that include relatively specific information about the positions of bodies in space at successive moments. This information, at least in this genre, is provided in large part by depictive devices that utilise the 'source-path-goal' schema identified by Talmy.[34] In keeping with the fundamental tenet of cognitive linguistics, he states that we understand abstract concepts by structuring our conception of them around our knowledge of physical experiences, arguing that we understand the abstract notions of cause and effect by applying force-dynamic image schemas.[35]

The use of a complex pattern of ribbon paths and impact flashes to depict a large and complex battle between two groups of super-powered characters at the opening of Kurt Busiek and George Perez's *JLA/Avengers …2* invokes, through image schemas, the reader's experience of gestures and sensations similar to those depicted in the panel.[36] Although broad equivalents to these specific depictive devices can be found in lens-based images, the total network presented across the panels is not something that lens-based media could depict. Such devices would appear at least in part to emerge, as you say, unmediated by the lens, in comparison to more recent developments in the depiction of motion in comics that have been influenced by the development of digital drawing technologies. For example, the explicit invocation of lens-based motion blur in Bryan Hitch's work on Marvel Comics' *Ultimates* series.[37] The influence of movie on comics may be more to do with the expectations of knowledge about spatial, temporal and causal relations within the narrative that readers bring to comics texts than any specific, identifiable drawing conventions. Comparing the *JLA/Avengers* sequence – what we might call a typical action scene – with a highly kinetic sequence by Jeff Smith such as *The Great Cow Race* from his long-running series *Bone*, reveals that Smith makes relatively infrequent use of the sort of conventionalised devices discussed by Potsch and Williams.[38] His interest in the cartoonist's ability to 'manipulate time' seems to be more focused on presenting depictions that will create anaphoras that include specific physical trajectories than showing those trajectories in the plot, as ribbon paths do.

If Talmy is correct in saying that our understanding of cause and effect is grounded in force-dynamic schemas, then depictive regimes that make use of ribbon paths, motion lines, or that display Smith's concern with creating specifically physical anaphoras may also be interpreted as providing an unambiguous representation of the causes, nature and results of events taking place within the diegesis. This seems particularly appropriate for superhero comics in which, to make a sweeping generalisation, characters' motivations tend to be simply stated and the influences on, and outcomes of, a given event are generally made explicit in the plot. The absence of such devices in *Dispossession*, as well as being commensurate with nineteenth-century comics, supports the adaptation's aims of visually presenting the equivocation that we've been discussing as central to the plot of *John Caldigate* and Trollope's style more generally. In an image-schematic interpretation, the adoption of a depictive regime that placed emphasis on the communication of force-dynamic events, whether through Smith's 'manipulated time' or the sort of non-pictorial drawing conventions described above, would metaphorically be interpreted by the reader as also providing an unambiguous account of more abstract causes and effects. Conversely, are there any image schemas already identified (for example, those listed in Johnson) that you see as strongly invoked by *Dispossession*'s depictive regime?[39]

SG: The question is made complex by the fact that facture itself, the act of drawing, can be discussed as belonging to the resources of the enunciator's body or bodies and hence as appearing under the expressive aegis of the body's image schemas. In this sense, depictions always produce an image-schematic 'observer viewpoint'. McNeill describes body transformations that place us at the centre of the gestural images we create as showing 'character viewpoint'. He describes transformations that place us at the periphery of the image as showing 'observer viewpoint'. The actions of our transforming bodies are located in different places depending on the image made with the body.[40] A character viewpoint image includes our bodies in the substance of the image, whereas in an observer viewpoint image, our body is excluded. When our gestures display 'observer viewpoint' we are joining the social sphere to perceive our own communication from the positions of other people. This is an emic position. On the other hand, when we display 'character viewpoint' in our gestures, we establish social distance from other people, creating a single position that we inhabit and from which we view others. This is an etic position.[41]

However, I think that you are referring to the particular appearance of diegetic image schemas in *Dispossession*, ranging from the depicted gestures of characters through to changes in reader point of view. Because I depict action in the book as both iconic and immanent, in the sense of Shepherd's melodrama practice of performing 'coming to knowledge' pauses, I think that Johnson's 'Centre-Periphery' and 'Cyclical Climax' schemas effect the reader whilst being specifically rooted in the gestures, movements and postures of the protagonists, particularly in ensemble, whilst the movement of the reader around the action is continually confirmed by these diegetic schemas. Together, the effects of these visual schemas conspire to create a fundamental rhythm of the book.

JM: Lakoff makes some brief comments on the image-schematic structure of Caillebotte's *Le Pont de l'Europe*, 1876, that support your description of the importance his painting places on successive moments. Describing the largest three figures in the painting, he observes that "the man and the woman are in the middle phase of walking, with one foot outstretched" and that the man leaning on the railing is in a posture that communicates specific detail about his shifting of his weight from moment to moment.[42] Lakoff describes the painting as a whole as being structured by the 'parallel lines' schema. None of the lines he identifies are parallel on the picture plane, but instead are read as depicting parallel objects in pictorial space due to the painting's emphatic use of linear perspective, which, as Baudry claims, serves as the original model for cinematic apparatus.[43] In these pictures, the precise location of points (and therefore of the observer) in continuous space and the precise occurrence of instances in continuous time are irrevocably bound together.

SG: When I was drawing *Dispossession*, I had in mind depictive lexica visible in the drawings of a small number of artists in whose drawings I recognised shared solutions to the problem of depiction and hence whose works generate, for me, related visions of the world, such as Cham, Honoré Daumier, John Piper and Edward Ardizzone. It was in part my sense of the meteorology of the worlds depicted that caused me to link them, by which I mean the ways in which their visual worlds share similar light and air. It was also my sense that recognition of this particular weather system would contribute to produce the effect of the strangeness of the historic period upon the reader. On one level, I made associations between idea, period and depictive lexica that were not strictly historical but, rather, derived from shared aspects of the lexica themselves, which I sought to emulate.

JM: I briefly mentioned Rutu Modan's *The Property* earlier as a recent example of a graphic novel that shares *Dispossession*'s use of photo-collage as a preliminary stage of the drawing process. While Modan distils her source imagery with 'ligne claire' rendering, *Dispossession* instead blankets the story-world with a web of lines both dense and insubstantial. Although the opposing styles of facture in these two comics denies the idea that this use of photography implies any specific use of line, could we say that the presence of the photo-collaged 'underdrawing' contributed to enabling an approach to facture that communicates equivocation? With forms already placed, the role of mark-making in creating enclosures and dividing space is diminished in favour of a use of drawing that fills surfaces, creating a flickering pattern of tone across the pages. Just as Trollope avoids privileging any of the opinions on the events of *John Caldigate* presented in the novel, neither does this visual fug highlight specific areas of *Dispossession*'s pages, an effect bolstered by the consistent use of a single digital brush of fixed width with fixed characteristics.

SG: I wouldn't agree that the type of mark making in *Dispossession* is itself equivocal, as this establishes a false distinction between its 'flickering patterns of tone' and 'the forms' that it depicts. Drawing does not dress form. It is form. It seems to me that depictions are always absolutely unequivocal, even if diegetic ambiguity pushes us to fail to recognise what is depicted, or the atmosphere is so thick that we recognise that little can be seen, or when a depiction unambiguously presents ambiguity. So we return to the central problem of attempting to replace an equivocal text with unequivocal drawing, as we first discussed. However, making a distinction between 'flickering patterns' and 'forms' has relevant historic precedents, particularly in Italian Renaissance 'paragone' or 'comparisons' between the depictive styles of paintings.[44] In these comparisons, on one hand, 'colore' described the depiction of the diegetic light by means of which an image exists, with 'colorito' describing the technical methods for producing a depiction of this type.[45] On the other hand, 'disegno' described the identification of divisions and contours as a method for depicting encompassed volumes and the boundaries between one object and another.[46] The distinction can still prove useful and I had it in mind when drawing *Dispossession*. The book adopts a 'colore' depictive regime inspired by the work of the artists I have mentioned, in which light and air are themselves being depicted. In cuing the reader to an idea of a strange nineteenth-century past, this approach also acts to equalise the status of people, objects and locations, unifying them across the whole book. Everything in the diegesis is seen as having the same light and air, from the most significant gesture by a major character to the least significant book tucked away on an office shelf. According to this approach, the light encompasses changes of season, time of day and continent. Everything can be either illuminated to centre-stage brightness or made invisible by a cloaking gloom. No hierarchy exists in the palette used to achieve this pervasive light that would render a cloud less important than an eyebrow. This equality of treatment extends to every drawn line in *Dispossession*. It is often the matter of the slightest inflection or shift in context that makes a white line into the tail of a speech balloon rather than a depiction of the light reflected on an old oak floor. Hence, according to 'colorito' it is in the 'flickering' of *Dispossessions* drawings that we recognise both what is depicted and the ultimate subservience of every visual element of the plot to a profound fiction of the past.

Notes

1. Grennan, S. (2015) *Dispossession*. London: Jonathan Cape.
2. Maynard, P. (2005) *Drawing Distinctions: the Varieties of Graphic Expression*. Ithaca: Cornell University Press, page 173.
3. Groensteen, T. (2009) *The System of Comics*. Jackson: University Press of Mississippi, page 144.
4. Woolf, V. (2012) *Granite and Rainbow,* New York: Girvin Press, page 100.
5. Moore, A. and Gibbons, D. (1987) *Watchmen*. New York: DC Comics, page 195.
6. Piches, J. (2003) *Vsevolod Meyerhold*. London: Routledge and Stanislavski, C. (1988). *An Actor Prepares*. New York: Methuen.
7. McCloud, S. (2006) *Making Comics: Storytelling Secrets of Comics, Manga and Graphic Novels*. New York: HarperCollins, page 14.
8. Smith, J. (2012) "The Jeff Smith Interview" Groth, G. (ed.) November 21. www.tcj.com/the-jeff-smith-interview/3/ accessed March 5, 2014.
9. Patten, R. (1974) *George Cruikshank: A Revaluation*. Princeton: Princeton University Press, page 185.
10. I am adopting the term 'anchoring functions' from Barthes, R. (1977) *Image-Music-Text*. London: Fontana, pages 32 – 51.
11. Sanders, J. S. (2013). "Chaperoning Words: Meaning-Making in Comics and Picture Books" *Children's Literature* 41(1), pages 57 – 90. Retrieved May 20, 2014 from https://muse.jhu.edu/journals/childrens—literature/v041/41.sanders.html.
12. Hignite, T. (2006) *In the Studio: Visits With Contemporary Cartoonists*. New Haven: Yale University Press, page 241.
13. McCloud, S. (1994) *Understanding Comics: The Invisible Art*. New York: Harper Perennial. 8 and

Eisner, W. (1985) *Comics & Sequential Art*. Tamarac: Poorhouse Press, page 106.

14 Ericksen, D. H. (1983) "*Bleak House* and Victorian Art and Illustration: Charles Dickens's Visual Narrative Style." *The Journal of Narrative Technique*. Volume 13, Number 1, pages 31 – 46.

15 Thomas, J. (2000) *Victorian Narrative Painting*. London: Tate Publishing.

16 Lessing, G. E. and Phillimore, R. J. (1874) *Laocoon: Translated from the Text of Lessing with Preface and Notes*. London: Macmillan, page 18.

17 Ibid. and Lee, S. and Buscema, J. (1984) *How to Draw Comics the Marvel Way*. New York: Simon & Schuster, page 53.

18 Rawson, P. S. (1987) *Drawing*. Philadelphia: University of Pennsylvania Press, pages 204 – 207.

19 Hearn, M. (2007) *How to Read Chinese Paintings*. Yale University Press, New York.

20 Castagno, P. (1992) *The Early Commedia dell'Arte (1550–1621): The Mannerist Context*. New York: Peter Lang.

21 Cutting, J. E. and Vishton, P. M. (1995) "Perceiving Layout and Knowing Distances: The Integration, Relative Potency, and Contextual Use of Different Information about Depth." in Epstein, W. and Rogers, S. Eds. *Perception of Space and Motion*. London: Academic Press, pages 69 - 117.

22 Baudry, J-L. (2004) "Ideological Effects of the Cinematographic Apparatus." in Braudy L. and Cohen, M. Eds. *Film Theory and Criticism*, Oxford: Oxford University Press and Metz, C. (1977) *The imaginary Signifier: Psychoanalysis and the Cinema*. Bloomington: Indiana University Press.

23 Gibbs Jr, R. W. (2005) *Embodiment and Cognitive Science*. Cambridge: Cambridge University Press, page 90.

24 Johnson, M. (1987) *The body in the mind*. Chicago: University of Chicago Press, Lakoff, G. (1987) *Women, fire and dangerous things: What our categories reveal about the mind*. Chicago: University of Chicago Press and Talmy, L. (1988) "Force dynamics in language and cognition" in *Cognitive Science* Number 12, pages 49 – 100.

25 Smyth, H. W (1920). *Greek Grammar*. Cambridge: Harvard University Press, page 677.

26 Eisner, W. (1985) *Comics & Sequential Art*. Tamarac: Poorhouse Press, pages 104 – 105.

27 Forceville, C., El Refaie, E. and Meesters, G. (2014) "Stylistics and Comics" in Burke, M. Ed. *The Routledge Handbook of Stylistics*. New York: Routledge, page 489.

28 Ibid.

29 Shepherd, S. (1994) "Pauses of Mutual Agitation" in Bratton, J., Cook, J. and Gledhill. G. Eds. *Melodrama: stage, picture, screen*. London: BFI, page 27.

30 Potsch, E. and Williams, R. F. (2012) "Image Schemas and Conceptual Metaphor in Action Comics" in Bramlett, F. Ed. *Linguistics and the Study of Comics*. London: Palgrave Macmillian, pages 13 – 36.

31 Ibid. Page 13.

32 McCloud, S. (1994) *Understanding Comics: The Invisible Art*. New York: Harper Perennial, pages 172 – 175 and Abel, J. and Madden, M. (2008) *Drawing Words and Writing Pictures*. New York: First Second, page 178.

33 Potsch, E. and Williams, R. F. (2012) "Image Schemas and Conceptual Metaphor in Action Comics" in Bramlett, F. Ed. *Linguistics and the Study of Comics*. London: Palgrave Macmillian, page 13.

34 Talmy, L. (2000) *Towards a cognitive semantics*. Cambridge, MA: MIT Press.

35 Langacker, R. (1999) *Grammar and Conceptualisation*. Berlin and New York: Mouton de Gruyter, pages 23 – 27.

36 Busiek, K. and Perez, G. (2004) *Avengers/JLA …2*. New York: DC Comics. n. p.

37 For example: Millar, M. and Hitch, B. (2002) *The Ultimates*. Vol. 1 no. 8. New York: Marvel Comics.
38 Smith, J. (2004) *Bone: The Complete Cartoon Epic in One Volume*. Columbus: Cartoon Books, pages 217–238.
39 Johnson, M. (1987) *The body in the mind*. Chicago: University of Chicago Press, page 106.
40 McNeill, D. (1992) *Hand and mind: What gestures reveal about thought*. Chicago: University of Chicago Press.
41 Pike, K. L. (1996) *The Mystery of Culture Contacts: Historical Reconstruction and Text Analysis - An Emic Approach*. Washington: Georgetown University Press.
42 Lakoff, G. (2006) "The Neuroscience of Form in Art" In Turner, M. Ed. *The Artful Mind: Cognitive Science and the Riddle of Human Creativity*. New York: Oxford University Press, page 166.
43 Baudry, J-L. (2004) "Ideological Effects of the Cinematographic Apparatus." In Braudy L. and Cohen, M. Eds. *Film Theory and Criticism*. Oxford: Oxford University Press, page 347.
44 Plett, H. (2004) *Rhetoric and Renaissance Culture*. Boston: De Gruyter.
45 Land, N. E. (1994) *The Viewer as Poet: The Renaissance Response to Art*. Pennsylvania: Pennsylvania State University Press.
46 Vasari, G. (2008) *The Lives of the Artists*. London: Oxford Paperbacks.

References

Abel, J. and Madden, M. (2008) *Drawing Words and Writing Pictures*. New York: First Second.
Barthes, R. (1977) *Image-Music-Text*. London: Fontana.
Baudry, J-L. (2004) "Ideological Effects of the Cinematographic Apparatus." in *Film Theory and Criticism*, Braudy L. and Cohen, M. Eds. Oxford: Oxford University Press.
Busiek, K. and Perez, G. (2004) *Avengers/JLA* …2. New York: DC Comics.
Castagno, P. (1992) *The Early Commedia dell'Arte (1550–1621): The Mannerist Context*. New York: Peter Lang.
Cutting, J. E. and Vishton, P. M. (1995) "Perceiving Layout and Knowing Distances: The Integration, Relative Potency, and Contextual Use of Different Information about Depth." in Epstein, W. and Rogers, S. Eds. *Perception of Space and Motion*. London: Academic Press.
Eisner, W. (1985) *Comics & Sequential Art*. Tamarac: Poorhouse Press.
Ericksen, D. H. (1983) "*Bleak House* and Victorian Art and Illustration: Charles Dickens's Visual Narrative Style." *The Journal of Narrative Technique*. Volume 13, Number 1, pages 31 – 46.
Forceville, C., El-Refaie, E. and Meesters, G. (2014) "Stylistics and Comics" in Burke, M. Ed. *The Routledge Handbook of Stylistics*. New York: Routledge.
Gibbs Jr, R. W. (2005) *Embodiment and Cognitive Science*. Cambridge: Cambridge University Press.
Grennan, S. (2015) *Dispossession*. London: Jonathan Cape.
Groensteen, T. (2009) *The System of Comics*. Jackson: University Press of Mississippi.
Hearn, M. (2007) *How to Read Chinese Paintings*. Yale University Press, New York.
Hignite, T. (2006) *In the Studio: Visits With Contemporary Cartoonists*. New Haven: Yale University Press.
Johnson, M. (1987) *The body in the mind*. Chicago: University of Chicago Press.
Killeen, J. (2013) "Emptying Time in Anthony Trollope's *The Warden*", in Ferguson, T. Ed. *Victorian Time*. Basingstoke: Palgrave Macmillan.
Lakoff, G. (1987) *Women, fire and dangerous things: What our categories reveal about the mind*. Chicago: University of Chicago Press.
Lakoff, G. (2006) "The Neuroscience of Form in Art" in Turner, M. Ed. *The Artful Mind: Cognitive Science*

and the Riddle of Human Creativity. New York: Oxford University Press.

Land, N. E. (1994) *The Viewer as Poet: The Renaissance Response to Art*. Pennsylvania: Pennsylvania State University Press.

Langacker, R. (1999) *Grammar and Conceptualisation*. Berlin and New York: Mouton de Gruyter.

Lee, S. and Buscema, J. (1984) *How to Draw Comics the Marvel Way*. New York: Simon & Schuster.

Lessing, G. E. and Phillimore, R. J. (1874) *Laocoon: Translated from the Text of Lessing with Preface and Notes*. London: Macmillan.

Metz, C. (1977) *The imaginary Signifier: Psychoanalysis and the Cinema*. Bloomington: Indiana University Press.

Maynard, P. (2005) *Drawing Distinctions: the Varieties of Graphic Expression*. Ithaca: Cornell University Press.

McCloud, S. (1994) *Understanding Comics: The Invisible Art*. New York: Harper Perennial.

McCloud, S. (2006) *Making Comics: Storytelling Secrets of Comics, Manga and Graphic Novels*. New York: Harper Collins.

McNeill, D. (1992) *Hand and mind: What gestures reveal about thought*. Chicago: University of Chicago Press.

Millar, M. and Hitch, B. (2002) *The Ultimates*. Volume 1, Number 8. New York: Marvel Comics.

Modan, R. (2013) *The Property*. London: Jonathan Cape.

Moore, A. and Gibbons, D. (1987) *Watchmen*. New York: DC Comics.

Patten, R. (1974) *George Cruikshank: A Revaluation*. Princeton: Princeton University Press.

Piches, J. (2003) *Vsevolod Meyerhold*. London: Routledge.

Pike, K. L. (1996) *The Mystery of Culture Contacts: Historical Reconstruction and Text Analysis - An Emic Approach*. Washington: Georgetown University Press.

Plett, H. (2004) *Rhetoric and Renaissance Culture*. Boston: De Gruyter.

Potsch, E. and Williams, R. F. (2012) "Image Schemas and Conceptual Metaphor in Action Comics" in Bramlett, F. Ed. *Linguistics and the Study of Comics*. London: Palgrave Macmillian.

Rawson, P. S. (1987. *Drawing*. Philadelphia: University of Pennsylvania Press.

Sanders, J. S. (2013). "Chaperoning Words: Meaning-Making in Comics and Picture Books" *Children's Literature* Number 41(1), pages 57 – 90. Retrieved May 20, 2014 from https://muse.jhu.edu/journals/childrens—literature/v041/41.sanders.html

Sfar, J. and Blain, C. (2011) *Ulysse (Socrate le demi-chien)*. Paris: Dargaud.

Shepherd, S. (1994) "Pauses of Mutual Agitation" in Bratton, J., Cook, J. and Gledhill. G. Eds. *Melodrama: stage, picture, screen*. London: BFI.

Smith, J. (2004) *Bone: The Complete Cartoon Epic in One Volume*. Columbus: Cartoon Books.

Smith, J. (2012) "The Jeff Smith Interview" Groth, G. Ed. 21 November, accessed March 5 2014. http://www.tcj.com/the-jeff-smith-interview/3

Syth, H. W. (1920) Greek Grammar. Cambridge: Harvard University Press.

Stanislavski, C. (1988) *An Actor Prepares*. New York: Methuen.

Talmy, L. (1988) "Force dynamics in language and cognition" in *Cognitive Science* Number 12, pages 49 – 100.

Talmy, L. (2000) *Towards a cognitive semantics*. Cambridge, MA: MIT Press.

Thomas, J. (2000) *Victorian Narrative Painting*. London: Tate Publishing.

Vasari, G. (2008) T*he Lives of the Artists*. London: Oxford Paperbacks.

Woolf, V. (2012) *Granite and Rainbow*. New York: Girvin Press.

Hugo Frey

The tactic for illusion in Simon Grennan's *Dispossession*

Simon Grennan's new interpretation of Anthony Trollope's *John Caldigate* is a remarkable artistic and literary achievement. This is true in terms of its ambition, as well as for an unerring ability to convey period and place. It is also the case because Grennan is quite as much a thoroughly contemporary graphic novelist, enriched by the narrative and visual strategies offered by the form, as he is a skilled practitioner of literary adaptation.

Dispossession is a very nineteenth-century tale of money, romance, corruption and redemption, but it is also a vibrant, intelligent and nuanced twenty-first-century work in its own right. The history and medium-specific possibilities of the graphic novel suffuse Grennan's work. For example, there are several little snippets of the Hergéan 'ligne-claire' school. One thinks here for instance of Grennan's use of the bold cover image – the mysterious, full-page image of Caldigate at Hester Bolton's doorway – that is evocative of the classic covers from the Tintin series that so often also included protagonists passing through or approaching gateways and thresholds. Similarly, in his constant use of the six-panel page layout Grennan nods to Alan Moore's and Dave Gibbon's famous nine-panel *Fearful Symmetries* section of *Watchmen*, as well as to cult titles that also make use of a regular grid design, such as Gary Spencer Millidge's *Strangehaven* series.[1] Furthermore, Grennan's controlled use of colour and his manipulation of a sense of the space of the page directly echo Chris Ware's comparable exactness of tone.

In *Dispossession*, during John Caldigate's voyage to Australia, an unnamed character from the second class of passengers remarks of the depleted food supplies on board the ship, on pages 28, 29 and 30. In what Grennan subtitles *A novel of few words*, a ship's steward nearby is heard to reply: "There's nothing to be done, we can't magic meat". However, just such a magic trick is then quickly proffered when a baby is placed under a silver cloche and sent to the upper deck diners for their presumed amusement if not their actual nourishment. As readers of *Dispossession* we are only ever shown the silver-serving cloche; and hence do not get literally to view or read the encounter with the first class passengers – Grennan insures that what occurs there is left open to our imaginations. In this short but telling sequence Grennan underlines the extreme class stratification that is magnified in the confined world of the ship 'Danaë'.

The same intriguing passage also prepares the reader for the next, more radical break in plotting that occurs shortly thereafter, in the section dedicated to the unhappy Aboriginal Wiradjuri marriage. Furthermore, the scene also provides something of a meta-commentary on the 'trickiness' of graphic novels per se and especially of this work in particular. Meat is 'magicked up', or maybe it is not, for while Grennan shows the baby being placed on the tray, he then withholds images of the serving to the elite passengers. Similarly text contradicts image, for at the end of the sequence some kind of meat is found (after all) – even if it is as a rather sadistic joke. Maybe inspired by the phrase 'magicked up' Grennan further underlines the theatrical – music-hall illusionist – quality of the episode by drawing the ship's steward gliding and then wobbling across the deck. Here the depiction of his body evokes a silent film (a Chaplin; Laurel and Hardy or Harold Lloyd work), while neatly also channelling something of Henry Raeburn's painting *Robert Walter Skating on Duddingston Loch* (circa 1790s). As I will explore in much of the rest of this essay, graphic novelists are able to play with a wide range of visual tricks, just as Grennan does here. What the reader sees or misses, the ordering and explanation of visual material through symmetry, or dissonance, with the words on the page, is at the very heart of the medium of the graphic novel. Certainly, the skilled control of what is shown and what is known (that is illusion) marks *Dispossession* apart from any kind of standard pattern bowdlerisation of the *Classics Illustrated* era of comics that in the 1940s and 1950s adapted many different literary novels.

Before going further, let me define the key term for this article and the thesis that I will discuss within it. I am using the term 'illusion' to mean the rhetorical use of the form (in our case the form of the graphic novel) to manipulate a reader's attention and focus, that is to use the medium to push for a particular vision of a thing, while simultaneously offering knowledge that contradicts it. The comic as a mass form (the precursors to graphic novels) emerged precisely when Western society was slowly exchanging religious and ritualistic interpretations (magic) for precisely this world of illusion. Card tricks, rhetorical uses of the stage in the theatre, photography, film and comics, used printed and material devices to make suggestive interpretations to their audiences and readers. As Walter Benjamin underlined in *The Work of Art in the Age of Mechanical Reproduction*, the world of a single art object, evoking a ritual function for a religious belief system, was slowly giving way to mechanical and multiply reproducible art forms providing a sense of awe through the cultural industries of repeatable illusions. The important point about illusion is that, as readers or audiences, we always know that there is a complex manipulation of our attention occurring and that, unlike in the world of supernature or theology, we have a choice either to enjoy the pleasure of the trick or to try to understand and decode its creator's processes. In other words, there is an 'openness' in illusion that allows for this kind of multiplicity of reading. This is especially pertinent for engaging with graphic novels that, as a form, offer complex layers and tracks of communication through features such as page design and word and image relations, as well as narrative sequence.

As I will now explain, Simon Grennan's *Dispossession* maximises an aesthetic of illusion. Shortly, I will argue for and analyse how Grennan reinvents Anthony Trollope through rehearsing a number of techniques that push and pull a reader as if they were watching a music hall magician. This reading through the notion of illusion will, in particular, underline the ways in which Grennan, as an artist, uses the devices of graphic novels to achieve a powerful range of rhetorical effects. It will underline how a skilled artist can suggest meaning, allow for multiple interpretations, and weave seemingly contradictory emphasises together in a single space. By way of a conclusion, I will underline what may be particularly interesting for critics is the fact that, while Grennan knows and deploys the 'tricks of the trade', he also adamantly rejects some of the more typical genre expectations for a neo-Victorian graphic novel. There is an interesting and critically significant 'dérapage' (slippage) between formal rhetoric and the framing story-world. That is to say, Grennan very subtly deploys the tactics of illusion and does not draw special attention to them through any correspondence in plotting. Relatively commonly, graphic novels that use the nineteenth century as a setting provide stories of gothic horror, fantasy or the quasi science fiction of steam punk. Therein the technical, formal, devices of illusion found in graphic narrative are mirrored in plots relating to suspense, mystery, or the esoteric. What is clever about *Dispossession* is that it retrieves and smuggles in the devices of illusion while boldly telling its own and Trollope's narration: a plot about economics, empire, law, moral and social attitudes, relationships, in other words nothing much that is suggestive of mystery or suspense.

As it is often remarked in the field of narratology, some forms of storytelling seem more comfortable recounting certain types of story than others. Part of the critical commentary on the rise of the graphic novel often makes precisely this point regarding the medium's facility for autobiography, reportage or historical representation. Since the publication of Art Spiegelman's *Maus* it is accepted that these are the things the medium is especially good at communicating. Notably, the comics page and the standard grid layout that organises material through panels, is recognised as being especially powerful at historical narration.[2] To repeat, Spiegleman's famous *Maus* remains the 'locus classicus': it exemplified how the comic book page allowed for information from different time

Part 1: *Dispossession*

periods to be presented simultaneously. It gave readers a present day (the father and son interviews and interactions; Art Spiegelman's thoughts while working on the strip) and a history (the detailed reconstructions of the 1930s and 1940s). This richness of potential for historical reconstruction is further demonstrated where Spiegelman directly redraws historically authenticated photographic images, or when he includes authentic photographs of his father and lost brother. With the publication of *Meta-Maus* (with its many digital-archival aspects providing an electronic museum of the Spiegelman family history, as well as the more general horrors of twentieth-century European history), this potential has been further added to.[3]

Nonetheless, sensitively managed historical reconstruction is not all the graphic novel has to offer or can achieve. In the thirty years since *Maus*, contemporary graphic novelists have regularly played with the themes of esoterica and magic and use visual illusion as a theme or an aspect of their stories. The medium is commonly used literally to play tricks with its readers, to stimulate ambiguity, doubt, interest, or just re-reading. Just as graphic novels are able to convey sophisticated historical-autobiographical narratives, several of the medium's formal properties also allow for a powerful rhetoric of and for illusion. The range of techniques is extensive, including relatively simple ways of playing with a reader's response to visual material on one hand, to sophisticated plotting and a nuanced manipulation of the verbal and visual tracks that make up the medium, on the other hand. For example, surveying works from writers and artists today considered masters of the form, such as Alan Moore, Hugo Pratt, Hergé, Charles Burns, Daniel Clowes and others, five recurrent techniques are commonly repeated to make illusion.[4] Such tactics are helpful to summarise in general terms, as they allow one to return to *Dispossession* and to identify Grennan's similar but also unique skill for the making of illusion.

(1) Disturbance or variation of the scale of the images. Notably, this is the sudden use of 'close up' drawing of unexplained visual details (a piece fabric on an item of clothing; the detail of a physical form) with no narrative explanation of what is occurring. Such close up panels disorientate the reader and lend an air of mystery to a work. This is particularly strong when a verbal text seems to have no direct correspondence with what is shown in the extreme close up. It is also more effective when the reader is given no preliminary narrative explanation and therefore the strategy makes for a powerful introduction to a sequence of plot or a work as a whole. In other words, what we see as readers is 'real' but we are made to be so close to it, we believe we may be in a dream or experiencing an encounter with the surreal. Hugo Pratt uses this technique in the Corto Maltese stories to powerful rhetorical effect. For example, in *The Ethiopians* three panels on a page are composed of detailed images of zebra skins that, on first reading, could be lines on a map, or traces in the sand, or maybe stripes on a flag. Similar abstraction through magnification is found in many other works that aim to offer a sense of the unexplained: Gary Spencer Millidge, for example, offers a page of abstract details of Masonic-like robes in *Strangehaven*, athough

on a first reading they could be simply abstract lines on a page.[5] These are 'extreme close ups' where contextual information is withheld because the image is so enlarged, relative to point of view, that it becomes abstracted. The above examples use this form of illusion to generate a sense of the uncanny or strangeness. The same device works well to achieve other things, such as a slowing of the reading speed, which in turn can force a greater sense of concentration on the part of the reader. This can achieve an enhanced sense of psychological realism for a work that somewhat paradoxically also allows for greater narrative clarity.

(2) Unexplained shifts in time inside the story-world of the strip. Here, creators introduce panels that are flashbacks but, on first reading, are not fully explained as such by the plot or other visual material that sits around them on the page, as helpful explanatory context. Often it is only when completing a first reading that one can return to re-explore these time-lapse panels. This is a technique exploited with great effect by Charles Burns in his new trilogy of titles, *X'ed Out*, *The Hive* and *Sugar Skull*. It is very disorienting because it throws into question the temporal consistency of the plot and makes the reader ask of each panel: when is this occurring and indeed, where? Such a device forces a truncated and slow reading of any graphic novel because it requires the reader to move forward and backward between sections of plot to try to find any signs of a clear temporal anchoring for a given passage. The effect is more powerful in a graphic novel compared with experiences of viewing a movie, precisely because, when such loops occur in a movie (e.g. *Pulp Fiction*), they resolve themselves more quickly and are consumed in a single sitting in an auditorium. Of course such viewing habits have been changing for some 40 years and if video recorders offered 'pause', 'fast forward', 'slow motion' and 'rewind' options, it is true that DVDs, the internet and streaming are further attacks on filmic linearity.

(3) The retrospective signification of a coded image. A more controlled and similar technique is to reveal narrative information about the images in the work only at its final conclusion, or through coded and hinted references that are very difficult to spot on a first reading. Hergé (maybe following Alfred Hitchcock) was the master of this technique: see for example his famous uses of it with the umbrella in *The Calculus Affair* and the magpie in *The Castafiore Emerald*. This device for illusion, that is the manipulation of how we see/read a text-image narrative, relies on the information delivered through the plot to encourage a re-reading to address the work 'in the knowledge of' initially hidden codes.[6]

(4) Experiments with narrative structure. When an easy linear reading experience is stopped in its tracks, the creator implies that the story is a never-ending Moebius Strip wherein the beginning and end of the narration are permanently conjoined as an ever-looping narrative world. An excellent example of this features in Floc'h and Rivière's *Rendez-vous de Sevenoaks*. In such works time seems to stand still; the detective or investigator is trapped in a permanent exploration where panels from the beginning of the work suddenly return as a part of its conclusion.[7] Incidentally, a similar effect can be achieved in

Part 1: *Dispossession*

a single panel. Inside the panel a creator will set up a series of dialogues from protagonists that have no clear reading order and hence are open to be read as an endless circle of possibilities, with no guidance given. This is a device Alan Moore claims to have invented for his incomplete graphic novel of the early 1990s, *Big Numbers*. Therein a panel showing a family talking around a kitchen table seems endlessly readable because there is no sequence in the discussion and therefore no movement beyond it.[8] Here each of the speech balloons function simultaneously without a clear order of how to interpret their relation to each other. More simply, in some fantasy titles, Moore has simply instructed his artist to draw Moebius Strips for characters to walk around: see the well-known example from *Promethea*.[9]

(5) Sudden and unexplained interruptions and changes in drawing style, including a tendency towards 'magic realism'. Thus, for long passages a work will follow one aesthetic and then there will be a break, a rupture in drawing style, perhaps playing with expectations around what classic cartoon images look like when suddenly they are used in a more realist work. The pact of verisimilitude between creator and reader is temporarily suspended, through either visual changes in style or through impossible/fantastical interventions of word-image association: the waves on the sea start to think, a pet animal adds their point of view, for example. Again, the rhetorical effect draws attention to the formal potential of the graphic novel to combine any image with any word and to use it to introduce a dream-like or illusory quality to the work.

What do these strategies for illusion have in common? They rely on always deferring the meaning of the plot; placing explanation of inferred symbolism towards the end of a work, if at all. They also often rely on a play of interference between the words on the pages and the images nearby. As René Magritte famously noted in his writings on this subject, when linked with pictures, words can re-enforce a meaning but they can also confuse, distract, defer or even conjure surreal effects.[10] Form does not always dictate content, but the graphic novel allows for a form of nuanced illusion with the same ease as it facilitates telling moving life narratives, oral history or reportage. These tactics for illusion work well together and are commonly found in narratives on uncanny or esoteric subjects. They reverse the discourse adopted by Spiegelman for *Maus*. Therein his purpose was to offer as clear and readable a communication as possible. Everything had to make sense, words and images function to support each other, narrative material moves forward without confusion. For graphic novels of illusion, the artist may invert these processes to stop linear reading; to confuse our vision of what we think we are seeing; and to dissociate word from image and image from word.

Dispossession achieves a complex balancing act between the two types of communication associated with the graphic novel that, for heuristic reasons, I have rapidly sketched in place. On one hand, there is a very strong and clear narration that recounts the trials and tribulations of Caldigate. For example, the plot entirely follows his life (with the exceptional digression in Australia that focuses on the Wiradjuri people and to which I will return shortly). Rarely is there a page in which Caldigate's short golden hair is not glimpsed. In that way Grennan is quite as 'transparent' and smooth a communicator through words and images as Spiegelman is in *Maus*. Tactics for illusion are also employed and pursued through formal mechanisms that are comparable to those identified above. Certainly one cannot reduce the possibilities for illusion to a simplistic schema. Furthermore, Grennan is a subtle innovator of new modes for illusion, while no doubt being cognisant of the tricks of the profession I have, for now, finished enumerating.

Notably, the dominant visual structure in *Dispossession* of the six panel grid and each panel with its shifting point of perspective, is not only suggestive of a dance, or of an extremely controlled literary hand (such as Trollope's), it is also a quite frightening, almost uncanny, regularity that offers the reader no variation or escape. The almost invariable shifting angles of the positions of the bodies of the characters inside the constant six panels, further draws one in to a mesmeric encounter with the page. What I think Grennan is also attempting, and succeeding at here, is to use this formal regularity of panel and panel content to intimate the constricted and constraining values of Victorian society. Just as Caldigate must comply to merit his fortune, so we as readers must accommodate and accept Grennan's system of representation. This is visual illusion in the sense of achieving a metaphor or implied storytelling process through a formal structure. It is the systematic image creation, page after page, that tells us we are in a world of order and hierarchy where gambling, romance, flirtation, sex, are to be always contained within the same formulaic page designs. Characters may visually move around a page through the changing angles that Grennan sets up, but they never break free from the orientation of the grid. Similarly the reader is held in this same highly controlled space: their visual perspective locked into the frame Grennan has encoded into the work as a whole.

The above rhetorical mode of page layout makes the single scenes of landscape or seascape a huge visual relief, for it is here that there is something of a variation or pause in the style, making the shifting angles of perspective less evident. So too, as a reader, we encounter those few pages where the regularity is slightly nuanced. Thus, just very occasionally, Grennan deploys two panels to capture an extended image or at least a conjoined picture that works as a whole. For instance, the horse race panels on page 7, wherein Caldigate loses his bets, work as one picture, quite as well as the two panels. For readers less familiar with modern graphic novels we should add here that this formalism of the never changing grid is itself a radical move away from convention. Some other graphic novelists use comparable devices but, far more commonly, there are changing sizes of panels, variations on the grid that turn part of the page into a larger, freer, single image or sets of varying panel shapes and sizes.[11] To repeat, *Dispossession* makes its first tactical visual illusion through breaking with the more 'free' panel structures of most graphic novels.

The dominance of this basic framing also tends to conceal, control and accommodate examples of instances when Grennan has directly redrawn images from Victorian fine art

Part 1: *Dispossession*

or used them quite clearly to achieve his own depictions. The dominant grid imposes a complete universe on the work as a whole, wherein those images inspired by, or borrowed from, Martineau (*Last Day in the Old Home*, first referenced on page 14 of *Dispossession*); Daumier, (*Bathers*, on page 24), Ford Maddox Brown (*Take Your Son Sir!*, on page 26), sit quite naturally disguised alongside Grennan's original creations. It is for this reason that, as readers, we do not ever really clearly spy an obvious pastiche of Victorian images but instead sense their presence almost everywhere. Similarly, the regular and regularising control of the grid, and the shifts of the angle of view, conceal several other inter-textual reference points: a set from the 1970s BBC television adaptation *The Pallisers*; one or two famous contemporary and historical actors, who were used as models for the protagonists.

There are no cases of the 'extreme close up' device that I described above. However, a comparable effect of claiming the reader's attention and disturbing their progress through the work is achieved through the repetition of key panels at important points of the narration: notably, the image of Hester Bolton that occurs twice on two pages of the depiction of Caldigate's journey to Australia. In fact, she is present in Trollope's original description of Caldigate's flirtation with Mrs Smith, when for example he underscored Caldigate's ambiguity of sentiment, writing: "How did it come to pass that she was so completely alone, so poor, so unfriended, and yet possessed of such gifts? [...] The puzzle was much too intricate for Dick Shand's rough hands. Then giving his last waking thoughts for a moment to Hester Bolton, he went to sleep in spite of the snoring".[12] However, Grennan, and the form of the graphic novel, can magnify this short passage of 'memory' of Hester Bolton into a consistent and dominant image: Hester figuring twice and making up one of six images on both pages 24 and subsequently 32.

Indeed, these are the first single dominant images of Hester in the graphic novel. At this point in the narrative we are encouraged by Grennan to take a more sympathetic view of Mrs Smith, the woman who later claims to be Caldigate's wife, who has had a far greater narrative and visual role by this point of the work than in Trollope's text. The repeated and magnified deployment of Hester in this early part of the work compared to her appearance in Trollope's work is therefore most powerful. On page 24 of *Dispossession* she first appears in one of the few sections of the work where the European characters are depicted without clothes. They are seemingly sleeping and washing on board deck under an implied tropical heat. She returns, in an identical panel, when Caldigate and Mrs Smith have exchanged their romantic promises. Such placements can be read in many different ways, none of which are fully grounded in any textual or other explanation, and this is what I mean by a 'tactic' for illusion, the illusion being the graphic novelist's invitation to the reader to decide for themselves what is occurring and then believe it to be so. The recurrence of Hester on pages 24 and 32 leaves us to ponder (i) that Hester is thinking of Caldigate – hence her appearance here (ii) that Caldigate is thinking of Hester (as described by Trollope and cited above) or (iii) if one so chooses, if Hester recurs as a figure holding judgement or at least emotional concern over John's actions. This could already relate to his encounter with Mrs Smith, which has just begun, or it could similarly concern his enjoyment of the physicality of the sunbathing and washing pictured in the panel next to her image. These are images that also implicitly look forward to the second and final occasion we are presented with Caldigate's naked body, when he makes love with Hester, as well as to the relative nakedness of the indigenous Wiradjuri. However, the point I am making is not narratological but formal. This re-distribution of the same image of Hester allows for such explanation and consideration. It absolutely does not push one reading or another in any prescriptive direction. It raises narrative questions (because we all want to find a story in a picture or picture sequence) but also remains a relatively abstract intervention, as on a first reading, we do not fully see the meaning, or exactly the right single meaning.

The somewhat cryptic depictions of Hester on the journey to Australia anticipate a more extended sequence where Grennan disturbs the reader's assumptions and orientation: the several panels and pages that recount the troubled Wiradjuri marriage. Precisely because of the sense of ambiguity that has developed around John, Hester and Mrs Smith (and because we know no backstory of the Wiradjuri), one is invited, but not forced, to explore these sections as somehow a commentary on the British protagonists; a 'comic within a comic' that functions just as a 'play within a play', to comment upon or evoke the main themes. As readers we have no idea who these Wiradjuri people are and, if we follow the textual narrative track of the work, we would read the 'second wife' potentially to be Mrs Smith (as she would become a wife for a second time on her marriage to Caldigate; and also because the sequence follows immediately after Mrs Smith and Caldigate's arrival in Australia, suggestive almost that they are transformed into the Wiradjuri couple). This is an interesting and productive line of enquiry set running in the work, for it is in fact this 'second wife' who is discontent with her status and marriage. To repeat, for a reader with no foreknowledge we are likely to see this as metaphorically evoking Mrs Smith's life with Caldigate in Australia. However, on a second reading, or for a Trollope specialist with foreknowledge of the preceding novel, the episode anticipates Hester's reactions to Mrs Smith's return in England. As such, the episode is predictive of Caldigate's impossible status when marrying Hester, but also awaiting the resolution of Mrs Smith contractual claim.

As a tactic for illusion the above 'comic within a comic' is intriguing. Grennan refuses to break with his six panel page and movement of viewpoint. He does not raise this section as being specifically different from any other. And yet, through the dominant colours of green and brown that are used here, it is defiantly marked out as a separate and different element. Also there are more words here: the double presentation of speech in two languages, the Wiradjuri language and either an English or French language translation, adding to the otherness of this section. For these visual reasons a reader is likely to want to return, to explore what is occurring here. Just as with the repetition of images of Hester discussed above, there are no simple answers provided. Instead, we have

Part 1: *Dispossession*

to re-read in order to evaluate and re-evaluate our own interpretations. When there is no full or single dominant message being communicated, the work becomes nearer to a mirror; reflecting back what the reader brings to the page.

Finally, while Grennan never allows the reader close proximity to the action, he does use the opposite strategy of reduction and relative concealment. This is particularly evident in the depiction of the death of a child on the ship to Australia. On first reading it is not so clear why this material is here or what is even occurring. Perhaps a reader might thinks that the dead infant is served as food for the first class passengers, as the different scenes are close to each other. These episodes are not found in Trollope's novel but gleaned by Grennan from research into emigrants' own letters and accounts of the time. And yet if one reads Grennan's images carefully and in detail everything is clear. A child has died and has been thrown overboard. Just such a tiny image of the dead child sinking amidst the ice flows can only just be spied out on page 27 in one of the entirely wordless pages that one could read very quickly if only following the work (quite wrongly) as a bowdlerised version of Trollope's novel. Moreover, Grennan encourages the Trollope enthusiast to be utterly distracted here by also using the page to emphasise his emblematic change of name of the ship – from Trollope's 'The Goldfinder' to his classically-derived 'Danaë'.[13] Such a distraction would push some readers through the page to the next, wondering simply as to the reason for the change of the ship's name and not reading the brutal but tiny image of the abandoned dead baby surrounded by icy floes.[14]

To the more alerted reader, aware of the possibilities for ambiguous and coded presentation in graphic novels, then this sequence is where the graphic novel takes control of the source novel. Grennan is telling us precisely that here: in *Dispossession* the ship will be called 'Danaë'; and in Grennan's storyworld the intolerable hardships of the colonial ship's journey will be more clearly evidenced. Thus, Grennan uses the 'mise en abime' effect of a reduction of image size to conceal and force readers to engage in greater detail than otherwise would be normal for reading a page of illustration without words.[15] In its inclusion he requires the reader to study his drawing and not cling to any knowledge of Trollope's work. Indeed, the social critique buried in the above 'reduced' image of the child about to sink in the icy water is to some extent replicated in the comparable treatment of the threat posed by western culture to the Wiradjuri community. Almost in passing (on page 45) some of the tribe have reached George Street in central Sydney and one is asking how they will obtain liquor if they no longer visit towns. As Caldigate and Mrs Smith walk along in the next panel, the reader may also note the drawing of the indigenous Wiradjuri seated together in the gutter. In these episodes it is clear that Grennan's work follows Georges Didi-Huberman's arguments on the politics of aesthetics: *Dispossession* restores to view the victims of history who are not seen in Anthony Trollope's work (the 'sous-exposé'), while also being sensitive to the dangers of over-representation ('sur-exposé') and hence the danger of neglect through trivialisation.[16]

To summarise, as a medium the graphic novel is able to communicate clear and very compelling information, with an emotional and historical plausibility. It is similarly capable of generating complexity, illusion and, maybe most importantly, ambiguity. None of the above sequences in *Dispossession* repeat famous tropes used by many other graphic novelists to achieve one kind of illusion or another. However they do share the common purpose of using form to communicate implied content, to raise open-ended questions of the plot, and carefully weave together multiple stories wherein information can be foregrounded for a first reading or withheld and offered up for a second closer investigation. As Jan Baetens and I have argued, it is this ability of pictures and page design to produce the story, to add to the narrative, that is one key defining feature of the modern graphic novel.[17] Grennan's *Dispossession* achieves precisely this dynamic. The work is a modern graphic novel precisely because of Grennan's use of the formal devices of the medium to generate the work's underlying energy and spirit.

Coda. Yet, for all of Grennan's loyalty to the potential for illusion in graphic novels and his use of the tactic, maybe his most assertive piece of 'magic' in *Dispossession* is to bury these technical devices away inside a storyworld that does not much evoke them. They really are often concealed from a reader unfamiliar with how graphic novels can use illusion, because Grennan offers so few narrative hints as to their presence. Let us recall that time and again other graphic novelists frame the Victorian period through stories of the horror, fantasy or science fiction genres – the so-called steam punk tradition.[18] This material captures the period's original pulp fiction 'penny dreadfuls' and to some extent the post First World War fashion for esotericism. In these works there is a coherence between the plot/story-world and the deep tactic for illusion I have implied to be central for graphic novels, in much of this chapter. This makes for an accessible and cohesive kind of cultural form where stories of the surreal use illusion and estranging visual rhetorical devices to communicate. Grennan's approach is far more radical, for he embeds the techniques of illusion, analysed in this chapter, into a story-world that is far more normal, more Trollope-like, and also seemingly neo-realist, than is the case in comparable works by Grennan's contemporaries.[19]

In *Dispossession* the reader is placed in a world of legal agreements, inheritance and dis-inheritance, fortune hunting, class, individual endeavour, labour, attack and the defence of privilege. No clues here to the illusions inside the pages and throughout the book as a whole. Clearly, Trollope's novel of course pre-dates the classic literary examples in fantasy or science fiction writings (Wells's, *The Time Machine*, of 1895; Stevenson's, *Dr Jekyll and Mr Hyde*, of 1886), by some years, and Grennan avoids any temptation to insert anything of that genre into *Dispossession*. The passage cited in the introduction to this chapter, the stage magic episode with the baby under the cloche, is the only notional reference to the world of magic in the work. It is in this context, of a semi-realist adaptation of Trollope, that Grennan develops the organisation of his material to achieve visual illusions.

Arguably, then, the work is closer to Stendhal's idea of the realist novel as "a mirror carried on a high road" than maybe anything else one can suggest for comparison. In *Dispossession* Grennan gives us the road (the faithful Victorianism of Trollope), and he also offers the watchful observer glimpses of the socially painful conditions it captures but, just as importantly, we see the mirror itself, or the sense that the visual is to be controlled and shaped for readers as much as any written text. In conclusion, what I propose is that there is a meta-illusion that surrounds the more localised examples discussed in the body of this essay, that *Dispossession* is not only a bright and cheerful piece of enthusiastic literary adaptation, 'tout court', but that it is also a work of intricate visual games and deft spatial and visual ploys, employing the mechanics of illusion offered by the form of the graphic novel.

Yes, there is a very brightly coloured, neatly Victorian Trollope plot on offer to us here. But maybe that is only the serving cloche that conceals a more feisty, flesh and blood, living work existing beneath. For inside Grennan's tactics of illusion, we find page after page of carefully developed graphic narrative that use old and new visual-rhetorical modes through which to gain a reader's attention, stimulate our minds and ask us to rethink our perceptions of both Trollope's novel and the wider cultural-political environment that produced it.

Notes

1. See Moore, A. and Gibbons, D. (1987) *Watchmen*. New York: DC Comics and Millidge, G. S (2000) *Strangehaven*. Leigh on Sea: Abiogenesis Press, Vol 2.
2. For example, see this argument in Chute, H. (2010) *Graphic Women: Life Narrative and Contemporary Comics*. New York: Columbia University Press and Gardner, J. (2012) *Projections: Comics and the History of Twenty-First-Century Storytelling*. Stanford: Stanford University Press and Baetens, J. and Frey, H. (2015) *The Graphic Novel: An Introduction*. Cambridge and New York: Cambridge University Press.
3. See Spiegleman, A. (1987) *Maus*. New York, Pantheon and Spiegelman, A. (2012) *Meta-Maus*. New York: Panthon.
4. In addition to works directly cited above or below, see Burns, C. (2010) *Xed' Out*. London: Jonathan Cape and Burns, C. (2012) *The Hive*. London: Jonathan Cape and Burns, C. (2014) *Sugar Skull*. London: Jonathan Cape and Clowes, D. (2000) *David Boring*. New York Pantheon.
5. See Pratt, H. (2008) *Les éthiopiques*. Paris: Casterman-Gallimard and Millidge, G. S (2000) *Strangehaven*. Leigh on Sea: Abiogenesis Press, Vol 2.
6. For the famous deconstruction of this aspect, and much more as well, see Peeters, P. (2007) *Lire Tintin*. Brussels: Les Impressions Nouvelles.
7. See also Frey, H. (2008) "Trafic d'Outre-Manche: réflexion sur *Une trilogie anglaise* de Floc'h et Rivière", *Lendemains: Études comparées sur la France*, Vol 33. No 129, pages 43 – 60.
8. See Moore, A. and Sinkiewicz, W. (1990) *Big Numbers,* discussed at length by Moore biographer and graphic novelist Spencer Millidge on his blog: http://createsilence.com/Blog/transcending/ (accessed November 30, 2014).
9. See Moore, A., Williams III, J. A. and Gray, M. (2003) *Promethea, Vol 3*. La Jolla: Wildstorm.

10 See Magritte, R. (2012) *Les Mots et les Images*. Brussels: Espace Nord, pages 34–35.
11 Many contemporary graphic novels use panels to split single landscape images (so called 'false framing') or to offer readers variety of layout, including mixtures of 'close ups' and 'wide angles'. The artist behind a lot of the *Walking Dead* horror series offers many good examples. A good primer is therefore Kirkham, R. and Adlard, C. (2010) *The Walking Dead, Compendium 1*. New York: Image Comics.
12 Trollope, A. (1955) *John Caldigate*. Oxford: Oxford Univerity Press, page 55.
13 Grennan re-titles the ship 'Danaë' in light of the resonance of Greek mythology to Trollope's own plot of a search for gold. Therein, Zeus 'showers' Danaë with golden rain, precipitating the birth of Perseus; a legend that is depicted in famous works by Rembrandt (1636) and Klimt (1907).
14 Specialists of historical treatments in graphic novels cannot help but compare this panel with the work of Kyle Baker (Baker, K. [2010] *Nat Turner*. New York: Abrams). Therein Baker depicts a slave ship, including a magnified full-page image of a child being thrown off the ship to be attacked by sharks. It is a brutal historical representation that stays in the mind and is coincidentally echoed here in *Dispossession*. My focus on this aspect of Grennan's work may have been primed because of the searing nature of Baker's imagery. The two graphic novels merit an extended comparison not possible in this more general analysis.
15 It is also the case that the reduction or concealment of images does literally reduce their significance/interference with the central plot development. Placing the 'dead child in the icy water' in the bottom left panel of the page places this image in one of the rhetorically least powerful panels. Top left panel and bottom right panel are the key visual zones of interest for any fast reader moving their eyes down a page, in a conventional horizontal eye movement. There is an impossible ambiguity: the reduced/concealed image forces a closer reading; it also allows for a graphic novelist to push forward the main plot development, which is obviously important in a creative response to a pre-existing literary work.
16 See Didi-Huberman, G. (2012) *Peuples exposés, peuples figurants: L'Oeil de l'histoire, no. 4*. Paris: Editions de Minuit.
17 Baetens, J. and Frey, H. (2015) *The Graphic Novel: An Introduction*. Cambridge and New York: Cambridge University Press.
18 These works are usually described as beginning with Bryan Talbot's *The Adventures of Luther Arkwright*. This was first published in serialied form in 1978.
19 This chapter has not discussed in detail the role of colour in the creation of *Dispossession*, which merits an essay of its own. For now, let me note that in some ways this aspect captures exactly my arguments here. Colour functions to create a visual illusion: each main character is evoked by the colour of their dress and this facilitates recognition and quick reading. However, colour also normalises the text compared to the conventions of other neo-Victorian graphic novels. Very often these works use black and white (notably *From Hell*) and hence Grennan's decision to use a bright palette distances *Dispossession* from those titles. It assists in making *Dispossession* a neo-realist, literary piece, rather than a gothic-horror title.

References

Baetens, J. and Frey, H. (2015) *The Graphic Novel: An Introduction*. New York and Cambridge: Cambridge University Press.
Baker, K. (2008) *Nat Turner*. New York: Abrams.

Part 1: *Dispossession*

Burns, C. (2010) *Xed' Out*. London: Jonathan Cape.
Burns, C. (2012) *The Hive*. London: Jonathan Cape.
Burns, C. (2014) *Sugar Skull*. London: Jonathan Cape.
Chute, H. (2010) *Graphic Women: Life Narrative and Contemporary Comics*. New York: Columbia University Press.
Clowes, D. (2000) *David Boring* (New York Pantheon.
Didi-Huberman, G. (2012) *Peuples exposés, peuples figurants: L'Oeil de l'histoire, no. 4*. Paris: Editions de Minuit.
Gardner, J. (2012) *Projections: Comics and the History of Twenty-First-Century Storytelling*. Stanford: Stanford University Press.
Grennan, S. (2015) *Dispossession*. London: Jonathan Cape.
Frey, H. (2008) "Trafic d'Outre-Manche: réflexion sur *Une trilogie anglaise* de Floc'h et Rivière", *Lendemains: Études comparées sur la France*, Vol 33. No 129, pages 43 – 60.
Kirkham, R. and Adlard, C. (2010) *The Walking Dead, Compendium 1*. New York: Image Comics.
Magritte, R. (2012) *Les Mots et les Images*. Brussels: Espace Nord.
Millidge, G. S. (2000) *Strangehaven*. Leigh on Sea: Abiogenesis Press, Vol 3.
Millidge, G. S. 'Homepage/Blog' http://createsilence.com/Blog/transcending (accessed November 20, 2014).
Moore, A. and Gibbons, D. (2987) *Watchmen*. New York: DC.
Moore, A. and Campbell, E. (1999) *From Hell*. London: Knockabout.
Moore, A. Williams III, J. H. and Gray, M. (2003) *Promethea, Vol 3*. La Jolla: Wildstorm.
Peeters, B (2007) *Lire Tintin*. Brussels: Les Impressions Nouvelles.
Pratt, H. (2008) *Les éthiopiques*. Paris: Casterman-Gallimard.
Spiegeleman, A. (1987) *Maus*. New York: Pantheon.
Spiegelman, A. (2012) *Meta-Maus*. New York: Pantheon.
Talbot, B. (2007) *The Adventures of Luther Arkwright*. Milwaukie: Dark Horse Books.
Trollope, A. (1955) *John Caldigate*. London: Oxford University Press.

Part 2

Nineteenth-century visualisations

Frederik Van Dam

Allegorical landscapes: the psychology of seeing in Anthony Trollope's later novels

The novels which Anthony Trollope wrote in the last decade of his career differ from his earlier works in their apparent disregard for the necessity of a visual dimension. At times, Trollope's narrator even points out that the task of illustrating his story-worlds with visual details is one he performs only grudgingly. "Of Marion Fay's appearance," he sighs, "something has already been said; enough, perhaps – not to impress any clear idea of her figure on the mind's eye of a reader, for that I regard as a feat beyond the power of any writer, – to enable the reader to form a conception of his own."[1] All the novelist must do, the narrator here seems to propose, is sketch a silhouette: readers will use their own knowledge and experience to fill in the blanks. Showing how Trollope's later novels put this theory into practice, the present chapter explores how Trollope uses stylistic and narratological means in order to leave certain elements out of the picture. As such, the following pages analyse two intertwined features: the role of description (the physiognomy of characters and settings, the function of mysteries, and the use of imagery) and the mediation of descriptions through the use of certain forms of perspective (neutral omniscience, external focalisation, the unreliable narrator, and internal focalisation). Walter Benjamin's early writings about allegory, I suggest, shed light on the visuality of the story-worlds, which Trollope created in the last decade of his life. It is helpful to begin this inquiry, however, with a consideration of Benjamin's unfinished *Arcades Project*, one of the most influential works for the study of nineteenth-century visual culture.[2] While it is true that Walter

Part 2: Nineteenth-century visualisations

Benjamin's reading of Charles Baudelaire's poetry against the construction of Georges-Eugène Haussmann's Paris cannot be easily mapped onto the study of the Victorian novel, Benjamin's discussion of physiognomy in one of the preliminary articles based on the *Arcades Project*, *The Paris of the Second Empire in Baudelaire* of 1938, can nevertheless, through contrast, illuminate the psychology of seeing in Trollope's later novels.[3]

The art of physiognomy, which operates on the assumption that "the 'signs' of the body can be 'read' to reveal character and psychological attributes", experienced a revival in the nineteenth century.[4] According to Benjamin, this revival was part of a wider attempt to obscure the more threatening aspects of modern urban life.[5] The genre of the 'physiologie', the sketch of city life as perceived by the 'flâneur', the stroller, made scientific physiognomy available to a broader audience, "assur[ing] people that everyone could – unencumbered by any factual knowledge – make out the profession, character, background, and lifestyle of passers-by. The physiologies present this ability as a gift which a good fairy lays in the cradle of the big-city dweller."[6] Physiognomy was thus subsumed within the phantasmagoria of the marketplace, "the stage on which the commodity makes its breathtaking appearance".[7] When the popularity of the physiologies began to decline, their purpose and techniques were recuperated by popular literature, in which the *physiologue*, the flâneur, was refashioned as a detective: "The flâneur required a social legitimation of his habitus. It suited [the flâneur] very well to see his indolence presented as a plausible front, behind which, in reality, hides the riveted attention of an observer who will not let the unsuspecting malefactor out of his sight."[8]

Although Benjamin is primarily concerned with nineteenth-century Paris, he also illustrates his claims with references to American and English writers, such as Edgar Allan Poe and Charles Dickens. Dickens's fiction, indeed, is certainly understood as part of the discourse that Benjamin delineates.[9] Even though Dickens did have reservations about the merits of scientific physiognomy, his early sketches are close to the 'physiologie'.[10] True to the petty-bourgeois spirit of the genre, *Sketches by Boz* offer harmless and superficial caricatures of London and its inhabitants, especially the lower middle class. Begun in 1833, they also fall within the same timeframe. Dickens's novels build on these sketches. His characters' faces are generally inscribed with a particular trait, which is a concentrate sublimated by exaggeration. Take, for instance, Quilp in *The Old Curiosity Shop* of 1840: "what added most to the grotesque expression of his face was a ghastly smile, which [...] constantly revealed the few discoloured fangs that were yet scattered in his mouth, and gave him the aspect of a panting dog."[11] Clothing and gait, too, are reliable indices of a character's social station and personality: "it is true that Dickens can appear to skimp on his characters' personalities, and even what they look like from the neck up, when compared to the loving attention he lavishes on their outfits".[12] Henry James not inaccurately pays him the compliment of being "the greatest of superficial novelists."[13] Dickens's later novels extend this concern with appearances, in their fantastical depiction of city life. In addition to his penchant for stories that revolve around mysteries, Dickens was one of the first writers to portray the professional detective, Inspector Bucket, in *Bleak House*, published in 1853.[14] It is clear, then, that for Dickens character resides in appearance.

Given Anthony Trollope's mixed feelings about the melodramatic realism of Dickens, whom he memorably satirised as Mr Popular Sentiment in *The Warden,* of 1855, one would expect Trollope's stance vis-à-vis physiognomy to be different.[15] The grotesque and caricatured descriptions of gait and build that one finds in Dickens's novels are, indeed, by and large absent in Trollope's fiction. Although most of Trollope's characters are introduced with a description of their face and demeanour, these descriptions are all too conventional and repetitive. The very fact that there is a clear method in Trollope's use of physiognomy, with 'good' girls being brown and imperfect, and 'bad' girls white and beautiful, makes the interpretative value of his comments limited.[16] The exceptions to this rule reveal an important assumption underlying Trollope's understanding of human nature. Take, for instance, George Vavasor's features in *Can You Forgive Her?* of 1865:

> He would not generally have been called ugly by women, had not one side of his face been dreadfully scarred by a cicatrice, which in healing, had left a dark indented line down from his left eye to his lower jaw. That black ravine running through his cheek was certainly ugly. On some occasions, when he was angry or disappointed, it was very hideous; for he would so contort his face that the scar would, as it were, stretch itself out, revealing all its horrors, and his countenance would become all scar.[17]

It is no coincidence that the legibility of George Vavasor's face, marked as it is by a trace, reflects his villainous nature. In Trollope's fiction, the two are closely intertwined: wicked characters' faces tend to be a palimpsest. In general, however, such emphatically readable faces are rare in Trollope's universe, which is peopled by characters in whom there is a balance between good and bad, and whose faces, as a result, tend to resist interpretation. Although the description of faces is a standard ingredient, it is one that adds little to the flavour of Trollope's novels.

If in his earlier novels Trollope still pays lip-service to the model of correspondence between inner mind and outward appearance on which physiognomy relies, in his later novels he becomes more interested in the discrepancy between visual impressions and the reality they are supposed to represent. Towards the 1870s, Trollope seems to have become intrigued by protagonists whose appearance does not correspond with their minds – characters, that is, whose appearances are deceptive: Lizzie Eustace in *The Eustace Diamonds* of 1872, dated 1873, who seems clever but is a charlatan, Ferdinand Lopez in *The Prime Minister* of 1876, who poses as a gentleman but is a speculator, John Caldigate in the eponymous novel of 1879, who is silent about his colonial past, Mr Scarborough

Part 2: Nineteenth-century visualisations

in *Mr Scarborough's Family* of 1883, who revels in deceiving all other characters, or Mr Whittlestaff in *An Old Man's Love* of 1884, who seems strong-willed but is shamefaced. As a result, the conventions of physiognomy become a point of concern.

Trollope's scepticism about the possibility of interpreting surface appearances correctly is also apparent in his fascination with situations in which characters find that their behaviour is interpreted in ways that run counter to their intentions. In *Is He Popenjoy?* of 1878 and *Marion Fay* of 1882, for instance, Trollope reflects on the nature of 'oligoptic' spaces such as the suburb and the boulevard, which were both designed to ensure that citizens could observe and supervise one another, and in which citizens could thus consciously mould the signs coded in their appearance.[18] *Is He Popenjoy?* shows, however, that oligoptic spaces can be a social minefield. Knowing that Captain Jack de Baron's name has been mixed up with too many women, Lady George can still enjoy his flirtations without compunction, as long as these take place in public. Their rides in Hyde Park are supervised. Even so, she creates impressions she had rather avoid:

> 'Now, Captain de Baron, would you like to be a dog?' This she said turning round and looking him full in the face.
> 'Your dog I would.' At that moment, just over his horse's withers, she saw the face of Guss Mildmay who was leaning on her father's arm. Guss bowed to her, and she was obliged to return the salute. Jack de Baron turned his face to the path and seeing the lady raised his hat. 'Are you two friends?' he asked.
> 'Not particularly.'
> 'I wish you were. But, of course, I have no right to wish in such a matter as that.'
> Lady George felt that she wished that Guss Mildmay had not seen her riding in the park on that day with Jack de Baron.[19]

Lady George feels uncomfortable chiefly because she knows that Augusta Mildmay has set her heart on marrying the Captain, but also because she knows that her husband, Lord George Germain, thinks that by associating with Captain de Baron she exposes herself (and him) to calumny. Matters take a turn for the worse at Mrs Montacute Jones's ball. Dancing the Kappa-Kappa, Lady George trips and "could hardly have been saved without something approaching to the violence of an embrace."[20] Jack de Baron has the decency to catch her; Lord George, in his jealousy, reprimands her in front of all assembled. Lord George realises only belatedly that it is his intervention that really disgraces her, however, not the dance. *Marion Fay* embroiders on this theme. Lord Hampstead unwittingly creates a sensation when he visits a suburban street: "He did not see why a man on horseback should attract more attention at Holloway than at Hyde Park Corner. Had he guessed the effect which he and his horse would have had in Paradise Row he would have come by some other means."[21] Whereas Hampstead does not seem to have studied physiognomy, the women observing him are skilled readers of the street. Nothing is known about George Roden's mother, for example, but they successfully guess the identity and background of one of her friends, Mrs Vincent.[22] Yet, they are unwilling to be observed themselves: Lord Hampstead does not "know from what window exactly the eyes of curious inhabitants were fixed upon him. But he was conscious that an interest was taken in his comings and goings."[23] These women's anonymity tallies with their lack of empathy. They are oblivious of a tragedy that is taking place in front of their eyes: their neighbour Marion Fay, with whom Hampstead has fallen in love, is dying. Trollope's representation of oligopacity thus suggests that physiognomy can easily descend into parochialism.[24]

Trollope's portrayal of the detective and of mysteries reinforces this impression. Trollope's detectives are guided by intuition more than logic: they are either raffish and underhand (Inspector Bunfit in *The Eustace Diamonds*, Mr Prodgers in *Mr Scarborough's Family*), obstinate and lucky (Madame Marie Max Goesler in *Phineas Redux*, Mr Apjohn in *Cousin Henry*), overly specialised and subservient (Samuel Bagwax in *John Caldigate*), or reckless and resentful (Captain Yorke Clayton in *The Landleaguers*). None of them, in any case, comprehends the crowd in the way that Dickens's Inspector Bucket does; the only one to immerse himself in the mass, Yorke Clayton, loses his target and is shot. The detective story, too, is subject to parody. Trollope's scepticism about the interpretation of surface appearances resurfaces in his treatment of mysteries. In his novels of the 1870s, secrets do not create suspense; their existence is in itself often of no importance to the way in which the plot unravels. The Eustace diamonds are stolen, twice, but they are never recovered; what matters is how Lizzie Eustace is haunted by the knowledge that the first theft was unsuccessful, which causes "a morbid desire of increasing the mystery [to take] possession of her."[25] The narrator of *Phineas Redux*, of 1873, reveals almost immediately that Mr Bonteen was murdered by Mr Emilius, not by Phineas Finn, a pre-emptive strike that allows the reader to appreciate the injustice Phineas Finn endures when put on trial. *The American Senator*, of 1877, presents a case of displacement similar to *The Eustace Diamonds*. When a poisoned fox is found, the local hunters are quick to blame a disgruntled farmer, Goarly, who, however, turns out to have been an accomplice of a character who is introduced at the end of the novel. In *Cousin Henry*, published in 1879, Henry Jones knows that his uncle Indefer had made a second will, according to which his cousin Isabel Brodrick should inherit his property. This more recent will is apparently lost, but Henry Jones discovers it by accident. *Dr Wortle's School*, of 1881, and *Kept in the Dark*, of 1882, extend this theme: both feature protagonists with a chequered past – Mr Peacocke's American wife is actually married to another man, whom they believe to be dead; and Cecelia Holt hides the fact that she is a jilt – whose disclosure of their secrets prompts other characters to re-examine their own standards and values. Mountjoy Scarborough's mysterious disappearance after his fight with Harry Annesley in *Mr Scarborough's Family*, of 1883, is never fully detailed, even though he reemerges at the right moment. In *The*

Landleaguers, published in 1883, Florian Jones's murderer's identity is finally known, but he is never caught. Unlike Dickens or Wilkie Collins, then, Trollope does not write detective stories. It is the effect of a secret on the individual and the collective conscience that Trollope is concerned with, not the secret itself.

One might interpret Trollope's parodic treatment of detective fiction as a sign of his lifelong attempt to distance his realism from the 'popular' form and ethos of the sensation novel.[26] However, more is at stake. For all Trollope's irony and scepticism about appearances and about our human inability fully to understand what lies beneath them, it is significant that many mysteries are tied to certain trivial objects whose significance only becomes apparent in due course: the strongbox in *The Eustace Diamonds*, the coat and the mould in *Phineas Redux*, the envelope in *John Caldigate*, or the volume of Jeremy Taylor's sermons in *Cousin Henry*. Described in detail, these containers substitute for the more important objects they once held (the diamonds, the life-preserver and the latch-key, the letter, the second will), whose particulars are taken for granted. In fact, these containers, these outer garments, take on the role of the mystery: whereas at first they seem just a suggestive piece of background information, they turn out to be the actual lynchpins in the story.

One might invoke Roland Barthes's terminology here, according to which would show that the 'containers' hiding secrets in Trollope's fiction are 'indices' that begin as 'informative' and gradually become 'pure.'[27] It might be more worthwhile, however, to interpret these containers as embodying the concept of allegory. Like figures such as the emblem, the fragment, the mosaic, the ruin, or the torso, Trollope's 'containers' posit a relation between a particular instance and its context that is not organic, but artificial. They do not represent a larger whole or a complement; instead, they show that the relationship between them and the reality they should capture has been broken and become arbitrary. Like allegories, they are hollow: from an allegorical point of view, according to Benjamin, any "person, any object, any relationship can mean absolutely anything else. With this possibility a destructive, but just verdict is passed on the profane world: it is characterised as a world in which the detail is of no great importance."[28]

A lack of attention to detail, however, does not mean "that details themselves have lost all meaning; indeed, precisely the opposite is the case."[29] *John Caldigate* provides an exemplary instance. Caldigate's trial revolves around an envelope that he addressed to Euphemia Smith as 'Mrs Caldigate' but which he, so Caldigate maintains, never sent. Since this is the only material fact that supports Smith's case, Caldigate's barrister declares that it is on "this envelope [...] that the case hangs."[30] The jury does not pay attention to this detail, however. It is only through the efforts of a Post Office official, Samuel Bagwax, that its meaning (or the absence thereof) becomes clear. Bagwax is convinced that the postmark is suspicious and spends his time pouring over photographs to discover the truth. Trollope devotes a disproportionate amount of space to this mystery. Suddenly, however, all this becomes inconsequential when Bagwax notices another detail, the stamp, hidden underneath the postmark, which was fabricated at a later date than the letter was purportedly posted. All the while, both readers and characters lose sight of the fact that Caldigate did write a letter, posted or not, to Euphemia Smith as 'Mrs Caldigate'. The envelope, then, is like an allegory: it illustrates how the truth has become irrelevant and irretrievable. These images thus provide a helpful clue with which to interpret Trollope's distrust of surface appearances.

Allegory is more than just a literary form; it also implies a certain view of the world. This view came into its own, according to Benjamin, with the advent of the Protestant Reformation, when "[s]omething new arose: an empty world."[31] In contrast to a symbolic perspective, through which "the transfigured face of nature is fleetingly revealed in light of redemption," allegory reveals "the *facies hippocratica* of history as a petrified, primordial landscape," thus providing "the dark background against which the bright world of the symbol might stand out."[32] When a form of representation is allegorical, this has certain implications: it entails a secular explanation of a world "whose importance resides solely in the stations of its decline."[33] Such primordial landscapes abound in Trollope's later novels, which tend to open with semi-naturalistic descriptions of landscapes in decline. In *The Landleaguers*, discontented tenants have flooded the Ballintubber marshes; in *The American Senator*, the town of Dillsborough suffers from "decreasing business," the Bush Inn is "fallen from its past greatness," and there is a general atmosphere of "decadence"; and in *John Caldigate*, "the property is bisected by an immense straight dike, [...] which is so sluggish, so straight, so ugly, and so deep, as to impress the mind of a stranger with the ideas of suicide."[34] Even more telling than these allegorical landscapes is Trollope's allegorical imagery. In his earlier work, Trollope favours the symbol: consider the gates to the Gresham estate in *Doctor Thorne*, of 1858, which are "not merely elements of an external decor, but [...] the junction of the collective and the person, [...] molding [the] subjectivity [of individuals] in ways bound to seem unfathomably mysterious".[35] Similarly, the spire of Barchester cathedral, is "the product of an organic national history, a cherished legacy, 'the beautiful and decorous' parts of which, like the 'theatrical show' Walter Bagehot more cynically described in *The English Constitution*, of 1867, proved a crucial symbolic function."[36] In Trollope's later fiction, symbolic images are less frequent. When they appear, they are often destroyed, as the poisoned fox in *The American Senator*, which is, "on a clean sward of grass, laid out as carefully as though he were a royal child prepared for burial."[37]

One of the most interesting examples in this regard is the trope of the flower in *John Caldigate*. When John Caldigate meets his future wife, Hester, after his return from Australia, she is surrounded by symbolic images:

> When [Caldigate] had been [at Puritan Grange] before, the winter had commenced, and everything around had been dull and ugly; but now it was July, and the patch before the house was bright with flowers. The roses were in full bloom, and every

morsel of available soil was bedded out with geraniums. As he stood holding his horse by the rein while he rang the bell, a side-door [...] was suddenly opened, and a lady came through with a garden hat on, and garden gloves, and a basket full of rose leaves in her hand.[38]

The lady in question, Hester, is the only ray of light in the darkness that pervades *John Caldigate*. Even when all evidence points to the contrary, she continues to believe in her husband's innocence, a belief that instigates Bagwax's researches and thus eventually redeems Caldigate. By introducing Hester in a symbolic scene, Trollope emphasises her redemptive qualities. As Benjamin suggests, however, the symbolic and the allegorical are often intertwined, and Trollope follows suit. When Caldigate meets Euphemia Smith, she uses the image of the dying flower: "You," Smith tells him, "have a resurrection – I mean here upon earth. We never have. We burst out into full flowering early in our spring, but long before the summer is over, we are no more than huddled leaves and thick stalks."[39] This image of decay is paradigmatic: "allegories fill out and deny the void in which they are represented, just as, ultimately, the intention does not faithfully rest in the contemplation of bones, but faithlessly leaps forward to the idea of resurrection."[40] The example that Benjamin himself adduces is remarkably similar: a plate "which shows a rose simultaneously half in bloom and half faded, and the sun rising and setting in the same landscape."[41]

The image of the dying flower returns frequently in Trollope's fiction of the 1870s. In *An Old Man's Love*, too, the return of a colonial adventurer is bound up with huddled leaves and thick stalks. Mr Whittlestaff's house is called Croker's Hall. A cultivator or seller of saffron, the 'croker' essentially sells dead flowers, since saffron is derived from the crocus, a flower that is traditionally associated with love and youth. The reader is thus told, in code, that youth and love are in decline. Indeed, Mr Whittlestaff's love for his young ward is thwarted. His misfortune is a product of colonial imperialism. Just as John Caldigate touches Hester Bolton before he bolts, John Gordon extracts a promise of love from Mary Lawrie before he sets out for the diamonds fields of South Africa. Even though for many years he does not even write a letter, Gordon eventually returns to claim what he believes to be his, only to find that he is a few hours late. The allegorical motif of the dying flower also appears in *The Way We Live Now*. Roger Carbury tries to woe his nice by bringing "a white rose from the hot-house, and placed it in a glass on the dressing table. Surely she would know who put it there" – an attempt that, as Carbury's touching self-doubt suggests, will fail.[42] There is a pattern in these novels: Caldigate, Gordon and Montague return from the frontier (Australia, South Africa, and California) and bring with them an atmosphere in which flowers do not bloom, but whither.

Up until this point, this chapter has suggested that visual descriptions in Trollope's later novels resist totalisation and often point to what cannot be seen or what has been hidden. As such, they are part of an allegorical aesthetic. The mediation of descriptions through the use of perspective reinforces this hypothesis. Trollope's distrust of surface appearances is compensated by his increasing focus on the mind – a focus is admittedly germinal in his earlier work. Where Dickens's skill lies in delineating and exaggerating what is addmittedly visible to the naked eye, Trollope's craft lies in limning mental states – exultation, vacillation, happiness, guilt, which are by definition invisible. Most significantly, Trollope's art revolves around doubt, around characters self-consciously caught up between the two sides of every question. For Trollope, character resides in the mind. In Trollope's later novels, this theory is intensified. Take, for instance, Trollope's introduction of Mr Whittlestaff in *An Old Man's Love*, of 1884:

> We seldom think how much is told to us of the owner's character by the first or second glance of a man or woman's face. Is he a fool, or is he clever; is he reticent or outspoken; is he passionate or long-suffering – nay, is he honest or the reverse; is he malicious or of a kindly nature? Of all these things we form a sudden judgment without any thought; and in most of our sudden judgments we are roughly correct. It is so, or seems to us to be so, as a matter of course, – that the man is a fool, or reticent, or malicious; and, without giving a thought to our own phrenological capacity, we pass on with the conviction. No one ever considered that Mr Whittlestaff was a fool or malicious; but people did think that he was reticent and honest. The inner traits of his character were very difficult to be read. Even Mrs Baggett had hardly read them all correctly. He was shamefaced to such a degree that Mrs Baggett could not bring herself to understand it.[43]

Trollope alludes to phrenology, physiognomy's little brother, only to highlight its limits. Dissecting the brain, Trollope jokes, will not shed light on men's inner thoughts. The novelist, however, has the instruments to make such an attempt: through long passages in free indirect speech, in which the voices of the narrator and character mingle, *An Old Man's Love* presents a meticulous psychological analysis of one man's inner struggle with shame and desire. Trollope's approach, in short novellas such as *An Old Man's Love* and *Cousin Henry*, is the opposite of Dickens's presentation of a character's personality through his or her appearance, and echoes Gustave Flaubert's disdain for the banality of phrenological observations.

The way in which Trollope's characters turn their minds inward also has repercussions for the way in which they perceive the world. Meditation and perception are intertwined. If his descriptions become fragmentary, so does his use of perspective. More precisely, if Trollope's later novels can be understood as a series of experiments in representing characters' minds through the intensified use of free indirect speech, they can also be understood as a series of experiments in representing the world through the

Part 2: Nineteenth-century visualisations

manipulation of point of view, a narrative element that is closely tied to the position of the narrator. In his novels of the 1850s and 1860s, Trollope's narrators share many affinities with what Norman Friedman calls the editorial omniscient narrator.[44] This type of narrator surveys the plot in its totality and frequently intervenes to criticise characters' thoughts or to reveal secrets, thus taking the reader into their confidence. The narrator's pose, his or her omniscience, tallies with the fact that he or she is not part of the world of the story; not a character within the tale, but a narrative construction encapsulating the whole. At the same time, the narrator does represent every character's individual view on what takes place. To use the more technical terms introduced by Gérard Genette, whose project famously seeks to make a clear-cut distinction between narrator and perspective, the narrator is heterodiegetic, while there is zero focalisation.[45] For a textbook example, one could do worse than turn to the narrator's comments about Eleanor Harding's marital prospects in *Barchester Towers*, of 1857:

> Our doctrine is that the author and the reader should move along together in full confidence with each other. Let the personages of the drama undergo ever so complete a comedy of errors among themselves, but let the spectator never mistake the Syracusan for the Ephesian; otherwise he is one of the dupes, and the part of a dupe is never dignified. I would not for the value of this chapter have it believed by a single reader that my Eleanor could bring herself to marry Mr. Slope, or that she should be sacrificed to a Bertie Stanhope. But among the good folk of Barchester many believed both the one and the other.[45]

In his later novels, however, Trollope begins to experiment and toy with these conventions. The narrator's intrusions, first of all, become limited. As David Skilton notes, even in a work of characteristically Trollopian realism such as *The Prime Minister*, the narrator helps readers make up their minds about the significance of the action far less than in his earlier novels, and leaves more play for an unmediated reading of the characters' states of mind.[46] In Friedman's terms, the narrator's editorial omniscience is replaced by a neutral omniscience.[47] But Trollope goes even further. In some novels, the narrator's knowledge of the story's events and characters' minds has become partial or selective. It is possible, for instance, that the narrator will use a particular form of focalisation for specific characters, such as Mr Melmotte in *The Way We Live Now* (1875). On the morning after the disastrous dinner-party for the Emperor of China, Melmotte realises that he should begin to cover his tracks. Normally, Trollope would seize this opportunity and give us Melmotte's thoughts and secrets in great detail. Instead, Trollope presents an enigmatic tableau:

> Mr Melmotte on entering the room bolted the door, and then, sitting at his own table, took certain papers out of the drawers – a bundle of letters and another of

small documents. From these, with very little examination, he took three or four – two or three perhaps from each. These he tore into very small fragments and burned the bits – holding them over a gas burner and letting the ashes fall into a large china plate. Then he blew the ashes into the yard through the open window. This he did to all these documents but one. This one he put bit by bit into his mouth, chewing the paper into a pulp till he swallowed it.[48]

In this scene, Trollope uses what Friedman calls 'camera-eye mode' or 'dramatic mode' or what Genette calls 'external focalisation', in which the reader is not given insight into the inner workings of a particular character's mind, but in which the narrator simply shows what is happening.[49] There is a maximum of mimesis, or showing, and an absence of diegesis, or telling. The most famous nineteenth-century example of this technique is arguably Henry James's *The Awkward Age*, published in 1899, a tour de force in which a story is told without any comment about characters' consciousness.[50] Trollope, too, experiments with this technique – it is rife, for instance, in the dry, icy, almost naturalistic descriptions of rural Irish life in *The Landleaguers* – but he does not push it to its limits.

In one experiment, *The Fixed Period*, of 1882, Trollope did venture beyond the limits of realism. This novella is unique in two respects: it is set in the future, around the year 1980, and it figures a first-person narrator, John Neverbend, who presents his story as a memoir of his disposition as President of the independent colony of Britannula. Trollope never uses an I-protagonist or a homodiegetic narrator in his novels, apart from *The Fixed Period*, (although in his short stories he does experiment with this form); he considered it to be "too egoistic" and even "dangerous".[51] In *The Fixed Period*, however, he uses it to good effect. Like E. T. A. Hoffmann's Kater Murr, Mr Neverbend is a bit too full of himself, but he cannot always maintain his pose. While he presents his case as if the population unconditionally supports him, there are certain inconsistencies in his account. He may initially present his subjects as "the very cream [...] that had been skimmed from the milk-pail of [...] a wider colony", but also mentions that there "had always been a scum of the population, the dirty, frothy, meaningless foam at the top".[52] The narrator, then, is fallible, even unreliable; his presentation of reality is skewed. As a result, readers are forced to interpret and reconstruct the story.

Finally, Trollope's later novels manipulate perspective through the use of internal focalisation. Compare the confidence implied in the excerpt from *Barchester Towers* with the opening of *John Caldigate*: "Perhaps it was more the fault of Daniel Caldigate the father than of his son John Caldigate, that they two could not live together in comfort in the days of the young man's early youth".[53] This sentence is fraught with ambiguity. Introducing an element of uncertainty that pervades the novel as a whole, the word 'perhaps' indicates that the argument between father and son is a matter of perspective. Trollope often creates internal focalisation through his phrasing; 'of course' and 'certainly' are familiar signs that what follows must be considered as in some way subjective. Here, however, it is unclear through whose eyes the world is presented, because 'perhaps' announces a point of view even before the story has begun – a point of view, furthermore, that is challenged as the story develops: Daniel Caldigate gradually emerges as his son's staunchest ally. Importantly, Daniel Caldigate's development is a matter of showing rather than telling: the narrator does not explicitly point out that he is supporting his son when John Caldigate is accused of bigamy, but, rather, shows how he makes sure that daughter-in-law and his grandson are sheltered and taken care of while his son is in prison. The novel's opening sentence, then, is misleading: it nudges the reader towards a point of view on the basis of information that is epistemologically unclear. One might say that John Caldigate and the narrator seem to have struck a deal. The narrator, indeed, withholds compromising facts, such as John Caldigate's relationship with Euphemia Smith in Australia. This may require a short summary. Having run into debts which his father won't pay, Caldigate decides to go hunting for gold and sets off for the mining fields near an Australian settlement called Ahalala. During his journey and his enterprising activities afterwards, Caldigate forms a romantic attachment to Euphemia Smith. Then there is a sudden gap. In the space of one chapter, all details of his gold-digging operations in Australia vanish: we are just told that Caldigate strikes gold and that over the course of five years he reconciles with his father. The following fifty-one chapters slow down dramatically: they take up only two years and centre on a trial that deals with the repercussions of what has never been narrated. To be sure, the reader knows that Caldigate fell in love with Euphemia Smith during the voyage south, but to what extent they continued their relationship afterwards remains a matter of doubt. This formal ingenuity did not escape the notice of a contemporary reviewer such as the budding biographer Edmund Sheridan Purcell (1823-1899), writing in *The Academy* that "in the sudden transition by which he avoids the dubious part of the young man's story, his construction is both masterly and judicious."[54] The missing part of the narrative provides the fuel for its development. It continues to remain a matter of perspective whether Caldigate has been acting in good faith. When he returns to England, for example, he reflects that in his wife Hester he has found "where the gold lay at this second Ahalala", even though he resolves that "at the very first mention of a British wife he must declare himself to be wedded to Polyeuka", his Australian mine.[55] Trollope thus uses internal focalisation to remind the reader that Caldigate's Australian secrets are still very much present in his thoughts. Trollope further emphasises the narrator's selective omniscience by, all of a sudden and at the very end, suggesting that the narrator is actually a character: "When last I heard from Folking, Mrs John Caldigate's second boy had just been born."[56] This beautiful example of metalepsis, in which the narrator shifts his position from an extradiegetic to an intradiegetic level, occurs in other later novels as well, such as *Marion Fay*.[57]

In his later novels, then, Trollope explores forms of perspective that differ from the editorial omniscient narrator's use of zero focalisation: neutral omniscience, external focalisation, the unreliable narrator, and internal focalisation. These fragmentary forms of perspective tie in with the verbal texture of his descriptions: both, this chapter has argued, are essentially allegorical. Trollope's forms of vision and perspective in his novels of the 1870s may not reflect the phantasmagoria of the marketplace as analysed by Benjamin in his work on the visual culture of nineteenth-century Paris and as represented (to some extent) in the work of Charles Dickens, but Benjamin's earlier conceptualisation of allegory in his work on the German baroque drama does dovetail with some aspects of Trollope's thinking about visuality in the last decade of his life. Trollope's late novels are allegorical insofar as they present an image of the world that is incomplete and marked by ellipsis, resisting the semblance of unity and totality that the omniscient narrator in his earlier novels pretended to uphold. The loose ends in Trollope's plots and the selective or partial forms of focalisation utilised by his narrators highlight that something is missing, that these novels' meaning is constructed around a void.

Notes

1. Trollope, A. (1985) *Marion Fay: A Novel*. Ann Arbor: University of Michigan Press, page 111.
2. Benjamin, W. (1999) *The Arcades Project*. Cambridge, MA: Belknap.
3. Critics have fruitfully elaborated Benjamin's ideas in the context of the postcolonial frontier: see, for instance, Brand, D. (1991) *The Spectator and the City in Nineteenth-Century American Literature*. Cambridge: Cambridge University Press and McCann, A. L. (2004) *Marcus Clarke's Bohemia. Literature and Modernity in Colonial Melbourne*, Melbourne: Melbourne University Press. Chris Otter has recently argued that it is wrong to assume that the 'flâneurie' was the dominant form of visual practice in nineteenth-century London. Benjamin's narrow focus on the arcades "occludes understanding of more prevalent modalities of vision that were at once visible, embodied, and voluntary. It also ignores the ways in which vision was an active subjective technique: the knowledge gained from judicious observation was useful largely for the subject alone." Otter, C. (2008) *The Victorian Eye: A Political History of Light and Vision in Britain. 1800-1910*. Chicago and London: University of Chicago Press, page 49.
4. Anger, S. (2005) *Victorian Interpretation*. Ithaca and London: Cornell University Press, pages 19 – 20.
5. 'Scientific' physiognomy began with Johann Kaspar Lavater's *Physiognomische Fragmente* (1775-1778; translated into English as *Essays on Physiognomy*, 1789-1793). This discourse had a precursor in the philosophy of art, such as Charles Le Brun's (1619-1690) *Méthode pour apprendre à dessiner les passions: proposée dans une conference sur l'expression générale et particuliere* (1698). For more extended analyses of the development of this discourse in nineteenth-century thinking, see Gray, R. T. (2004) *About Face: German Physiognomic Thought from Lavater to Auschwitz*, Detroit: Wayne State University Press and Pearl S. (2010) *About Faces: Physiognomy in Nineteenth-Century Britain*. Cambridge, MA: Harvard University Press. Physiognomy also played a significant part in the theorisation of the early graphic novel, such as Rodolphe Töpffer's (1799-1846) *Essai de physiognomonie* (1845); see Groensteen, T. (2014) *M. Töpffer invente la bande dessinée*. Brussels: Les Impressions Nouvelles.
6. Benjamin, W. (2003), "The Paris of the Second Empire in Baudelaire." In Eiland, H. and Jennings, M. *Selected Writings: Volume 4, 1938-1940*. Cambridge, MA: Harvard University Press, page 20.

Part 2: Nineteenth-century visualisations

7. Otter, C. (2008) *The Victorian Eye: A Political History of Light and Vision in Britain, 1800-1910*. Chicago and London: University of Chicago Press, page 2.
8. Benjamin, W. (1999) *The Arcades Project*. Cambridge, MA: Belknap, page 442. The story-world of these sketches could be understood a counterpart to the nostalgia of the bourgeois interior; see Brown, J. P. (2008) *The Bourgeois Interior: How the Middle Class Imagines Itself in Literature and Film*. Charlottesville and London: University of Virginia Press.
9. For a Benjaminian reading of Dickens's fiction, see Piggott, G. (2012) *Dickens and Benjamin: Moments of Revelation, Fragments of Modernity*. Farnham: Ashgate.
10. Zirker, A. (2011) "Physiognomy and the Reading of Character in *Our Mutual Friend*," *Partial Answers* Vol. 9, No. 2: 379-390. Carey, J. (1973) *The Violent Effigy*. London: Faber and Faber, pages 89 – 91.
11. Dickens, C. (1997) *The Old Curiosity Shop*, Oxford: Clarendon, page 27.
12. Douglas-Fairhurst, R. (2011) *Becoming Dickens: The Invention of a Novelist*. London and Cambridge, MA: Belknap Press, page 59.
13. James, H. (1971) "Our Mutual Friend." In Collins, P. Ed. *Dickens: The Critical Heritage*. London: Routledge, page 481.
14. For a narrative account of Bucket's original, Jack Whicher, see Summerscale, K. (2008) *The Suspicions of Mr. Whicher; or, the Murder at Road Hill House*. London: Bloomsbury.
15. For Trollope's views on Dickens, see Trollope, A. (1999) *An Autobiography*. Sadlier (Ed.), Oxford University Press, pages 247 – 49.
16. Ammar, J. (2010) "Saints and Sinners: The Physiognomy of Trollope's 'Good' and 'Bad' Girls," *Trollopiana* No. 87, pages 10 – 17.
17. Otter, C. (2008) *The Victorian Eye: A Political History of Light and Vision in Britain, 1800-1910*. Chicago and London: University of Chicago Press, pages 60 and 74.
18. Trollope, A. (1998) *Is He Popenjoy?* London: The Trollope Society, page 127.
19. Ibid., page 303.
20. Ibid., page 40.
21. Ibid., page 33.
22. Ibid., page 121.
23. For more on Trollope's ideas about urban sociability, see Van Dam, F. (2014) "'Wholesome Lessons': Love as Tact between Matthew Arnold and Anthony Trollope," *Partial Answers* Vol. 12, No. 2, pages 291 – 92.
24. Trollope, A. (1990) *The Eustace Diamonds*. London: The Trollope Society, page 363.
25. Taylor, J. B. (2011) "Trollope and the Sensation Novel." In Dever, C. and Niles, L. Eds. *The Cambridge Companion to Anthony Trollope*. Cambridge: Cambridge University Press, pages 85 – 98.
26. Barthes, R. (1977) *Introduction to the Structuralist Analysis of Narratives*. New York: Hill and Wang, pages 95 – 96.
27. Benjamin, W. (2009) *The Origin of German Tragic Drama*. London and New York: Verso, page 175.
28. Weber, S. (2008) *Benjamin's –Abilities*. Cambridge, MA: Harvard University Press, page 241.
29. Trollope, A. (1995) *John Caldigate*. London: The Trollope Society, page 325.
30. Benjamin, W. (2009) *The Origin of German Tragic Drama*. London and New York: Verso, page 139.
31. Ibid., pages 166 and 161.
32. Ibid. page 166.
33. Trollope, A. (1999) *The American Senator*. Oxford: Oxford University Press, pages 3 and 4. Trollope, A. (1995) *John Caldigate*. London: The Trollope Society, page 3.

34 Herbert, C. (1991) *Culture and Anomie: Ethnographic Imagination in the Nineteenth Century*. Chicago: University of Chicago Press, page 272.
35 Goodlad, L. M. E. (2009) "Trollopian 'Foreign Policy': Rootedness and Cosmopolitanism in the Mid-Victorian Global Imaginary," *PMLA* Vol. 124, No. 2, pages 867 – 875. Bagehot, W. (2001) *The English Constitution*. Cambridge: Cambridge University Press, page 30.
36 Trollope, A. (1999) *The American Senator*. Oxford: Oxford University Press, page 62.
37 Trollope, A. (1995) *John Caldigate*. London: The Trollope Society, page 105.
38 Ibid., page 36.
39 Benjamin, W. (2009) *The Origin of German Tragic Drama*. London and New York: Verso, page 233.
40 Ibid., page 194.
41 Trollope, A. (1992) *The Way We Live Now*. London: The Trollope Society, page 120.
42 Trollope, A. (1998) *An Old Man's Love*. London: The Trollope Society, page 13.
43 Friedman, N. (1955) "Point of View in Fiction: The Development of a Critical Concept," *PMLA* Vol. 70, No. 5, pages 1160 – 1184.
44 Genette, G. (1980) *Narrative Discourse: An Essay in Method*. Ithaca NY: Cornell University Press, page 208.
45 Trollope, A. (1995) *Barchester Towers*. London: The Trollope Society, page 122.
46 Skilton, D. (1998) "Introduction." In Trollope, A. *An Old Man's Love*. London: The Trollope Society, page ix.
47 Friedman, N. (1955) "Point of View in Fiction: The Development of a Critical Concept," *PMLA* Vol. 70, No. 5, page 1172.
48 Trollope, A. (1992) *The Way We Live Now*. London: The Trollope Society, page 527.
49 Friedman, N. (1955) "Point of View in Fiction: The Development of a Critical Concept," *PMLA* Vol. 70, No. 5, page 1178. Genette, G. (1980) *Narrative Discourse: An Essay in Method*. NY: Cornell University Press, page 191.
50 See Miller, J. H. (2005) "Henry James and 'Focalisation,' or Why James Loves Gyp." In Phelan, J. and Rabinowitz, P. J. Eds. *A Companion to Narrative Theory*. Oxford: Blackwell, 124 – 135.
51 Friedman, N. (1955) "Point of View in Fiction: The Development of a Critical Concept," *PMLA* Vol. 70, No. 5, page 1175. Genette, G. (1980) *Narrative Discourse: An Essay in Method*. NY: Cornell University Press, page 245. Trollope, A. (1983) *The Letters of Anthony Trollope*. CA: Stanford University Press, page 429.
52 Trollope, A. (1997) *The Fixed Period*. London: The Trollope Society, pages 11 and 97.
53 Trollope, A. (1995) *John Caldigate*. The Trollope Society, page 1.
54 Smalley, D. (1969) *Trollope: The Critical Heritage*. London: Routledge, page 451.
55 Trollope, A. (1995) *John Caldigate*. The Trollope Society, pages 16 and 107.
56 Ibid., page 498.
57 Genette, G. (1980) *Narrative Discourse: An Essay in Method*. Ithaca NY: Cornell University Press, page 234. Trollope, A. (1985) *Marion Fay: A Novel*. Ann Arbor: University of Michigan Press, page 422.

References

Anger, S. (2005) *Victorian Interpretation*. Ithaca and London: Cornell University Press.
Ammar, J. (2010) "Saints and Sinners: The Physiognomy of Trollope's 'Good' and 'Bad' Girls," *Trollopiana* Number 87, pages 10 – 17.
Bagehot, W. (2001) *The English Constitution*. Cambridge: Cambridge University Press.
Barthes, R. (1977) *Introduction to the Structuralist Analysis of Narratives*. New York: Hill and Wang.

Part 2: Nineteenth-century visualisations

Benjamin, W. (1999) *The Arcades Project*. Cambridge, MA: Belknap.
Benjamin, W. (2003), "The Paris of the Second Empire in Baudelaire." In Eiland, H. and Jennings, M. Eds. *Selected Writings: Volume 4, 1938-1940*. Cambridge, MA: Harvard University Press, pages 3 – 92.
Benjamin, W. (2009) *The Origin of German Tragic Drama*. London and New York: Verso.
Brand, D. (1991) *The Spectator and the City in Nineteenth-Century American Literature*. Cambridge: Cambridge University Press.
Brown, J. P. (2008) *The Bourgeois Interior: How the Middle Class Imagines Itself in Literature and Film*. Charlottesville and London: University of Virginia Press.
Carey, J. (1973) *The Violent Effigy*. London: Faber and Faber.
Dickens, C. (1997) *The Old Curiosity Shop*. Oxford: Clarendon, 1997.
Douglas-Fairhurst, R. (2011) *Becoming Dickens: The Invention of a Novelist*. London and Cambridge, MA: Belknap Press.
Friedman, N. (1955) "Point of View in Fiction: The Development of a Critical Concept," *PMLA* Volume 70, Number 5, pages 1160-1184.
Genette, G. (1980) *Narrative Discourse: An Essay in Method*. NY: Cornell University Press.
Goodlad, L. M. E. (2009) "Trollopian 'Foreign Policy': Rootedness and Cosmopolitanism in the Mid-Victorian Global Imaginary," *PMLA* Volume 124, Number 2, pages 867 – 875.
Gray, R. T. (2004) *About Face: German Physiognomic Thought from Lavater to Auschwitz*. Detroit: Wayne State University Press.
Groensteen, T. (2014) *M. Töpffer invente la bande dessinée*. Brussels: Les Impressions Nouvelles.
Herbert, C. (1991) *Culture and Anomie: Ethnographic Imagination in the nineteenth century*. Chicago: University of Chicago Press.
James, H. (1971) "Our Mutual Friend." In Collins, P. Ed. *Dickens: The Critical Heritage*. London: Routledge, pages 479 – 482.
McCann, A. L. (2004) *Marcus Clarke's Bohemia. Literature and Modernity in Colonial Melbourne*. Melbourne: Melbourne University Press.
Miller, J. H. (2005) "Henry James and 'Focalisation,' or Why James Loves Gyp." In Phelan, J. and Rabinowitz P. J. Eds. *A Companion to Narrative Theory*. Oxford: Blackwell, pages 124-135.
Otter, C. (2008) *The Victorian Eye: A Political History of Light and Vision in Britain, 1800-1910*. Chicago and London: University of Chicago Press.
Pearl, S. (2010) *About Faces: Physiognomy in Nineteenth-Century Britain*. Cambridge, MA: Harvard University Press.
Piggott, G. (2012) *Dickens and Benjamin: Moments of Revelation, Fragments of Modernity*. Farnham: Ashgate.
Skilton, D. (1998) "Introduction." In Trollope, A. *An Old Man's Love*. London: The Trollope Society.
Smalley, D. (1969) *Trollope: The Critical Heritage*. London: Routledge.
Summerscale, K. (2008) *The Suspicions of Mr. Whicher; or, the Murder at Road Hill House*. London: Bloomsbury.
Taylor, J. B. (2011) "Trollope and the Sensation Novel". In Dever, C. and Niles, L. Eds. *The Cambridge Companion to Anthony Trollope*. Cambridge: Cambridge University Press, pages 85 – 98.
Trollope, A. (1983) *The Letters of Anthony Trollope*. Stanford, CA: Stanford University Press.
Trollope, A. (1985) *Marion Fay: A Novel*. Ann Arbor: University of Michigan Press.
Trollope, A. (1989) *Can You Forgive Her?*. London: The Trollope Society.
Trollope, A. (1990) *The Eustace Diamonds*. London: The Trollope Society.
Trollope, A. (1992) *The Way We Live Now*. London: The Trollope Society.
Trollope, A. (1995) *Barchester Towers*. London: The Trollope Society.
Trollope, A. (1995) *John Caldigate*. London: The Trollope Society.

Trollope, A. (1997) *The Fixed Period*. London: The Trollope Society.
Trollope, A. (1998) *Is He Popenjoy?*. London: The Trollope Society.
Trollope, A. (1998) *An Old Man's Love*. London: The Trollope Society.
Trollope, A. (1999) *The American Senator*. Oxford: Oxford University Press.
Trollope, A. (1999) *An Autobiography*. Oxford: Oxford University Press.
Van Dam, F. (2014) "'Wholesome Lessons': Love as Tact between Matthew Arnold and Anthony Trollope," *Partial Answers* Volume 12, Number 2, pages 287 – 310.
Weber, S. (2008) *Benjamin's – Abilities*. Cambridge, MA: Harvard University Press.
Zirker, A. (2011) "Physiognomy and the Reading of Character in *Our Mutual Friend*," *Partial Answers* Volume 9, Number 2, pages 379 – 390.

David Skilton

Complex meanings in illustrated literature, 1860-1880

There is often assumed to be a direct evolutionary link between nineteenth-century literary illustration and the later art forms of the comic book and the cinema, and yet it is difficult to make a rigorous, art-historical case for a causative link.[1] This chapter will identify features of mid-Victorian illustrated fiction that appear to have been adopted from a longer-established narrative form, the drama, or bequeathed to these later art forms. It will focus in particular on a few of the characteristics of illustrations to novels in the period 1830 – 1885, which have proved to be of particular interest during the creation of Simon Grennan's 2015 adaptation of Trollope's *John Caldigate* of 1879, in English as *Dispossession* and in French as *Courir deux lièvres*.[2]

One strategy which illustrators of novels in the nineteenth century inherited from those of the eighteenth century was the representation of fictional action as though it was being played out on a stage, though in examining this phenomenon we must bear in mind that there was probably an existing convergence between visual art and drama derived from pre-existing conventions of ocular interpretation of the 'real' world, and that in many works, such as those of Thomas Rowlandson and Pierce Egan, for example, the illustrations and the written episodes to which they are attached are referred to in the pages of those books as 'scenes'. What is certain is that writers and graphic artists were content to recognise the connection. The representation of a room can easily be seen as a pictured stage set, and in the hands of an illustrator as able as George Cruikshank, street scenes too are arranged in a comparable way. Examples from Cruikshank's work for Dickens are *Oliver Surprised* in *Oliver Twist*, of 1838, and *Seven Dials* in *Sketches by Boz*, of 1836. The figures are disposed as though viewed from the auditorium, and the townscape is represented by a number of two-dimensional pictures, as though on the flats of the stage flies. The readers of early Dickens, Cruikshank was suggesting, were the equivalent of an audience at a popular theatre – a view from which Dickens, with his well-documented enthusiasm for the theatre, would certainly not have dissented.[3] This link between prose fiction and the stage was confirmed by the use of one of Cruikshank's images for Harrison Ainsworth's immensely popular novel, *Jack Shepperd*, of 1839 – 1840, to advertise one of the numerous stage adaptations which followed. The chosen illustration, *The Name on the Beam*, already bears a striking resemblance to a stage set, and to make the link more obvious, the image from the novel is decked out with the trappings of a theatre, including lighting and a curtain.[4] This example depends on the uni-directional viewing associated with indoor theatres with proscenium arches, and not the multi-directional viewing, partly in the round, of the Greeks and of Shakespeare's day.

A quasi-dramatic illustration often presents a complex action or a sequence of actions extended over time. For example, the unexpected announcement of a visitor may surprise a person in an act of concealment, and the defensive action that succeeds the recognition of the intrusion must occur a fraction later. The interval, however brief, might seem to be eliminated in an illustration that, perforce, has to present everything simultaneously. Nathalie Ferrand, in her ground-breaking book on the illustrated novel in eighteenth-century France, *Livres vus, livres lus*, records an illustration of one such moment in Mme Riccoboni's *Lettres d'Adelaide de Dammartin*. Quoting an extract from the letter in the text in which the comtesse relates the event to a correspondent, Ferrand concludes:

> Nous sommes comme au théâtre: une 'action' a lieu dont la protagoniste a saisi tous les mouvements et qu'elle sait restituer à son correspondant…. Ainsi l'illustration que nous voyons est-elle une réponse à un appel du texte à être mis en image. (We are as though in the theatre: an incident is taking place, every action of which the protagonist has captured and recreated for her correspondent…. Thus the illustration we see is a response to a call from the text to be converted into an image.)[5]

This call by the text for an illustration is not only found in the presence of an actual illustration, but is also recognisable in a pause in the narrative to allow for the description of a scene as though it were a picture. This is commonplace from the eighteenth century and into the early decades of the nineteenth century, particularly in comic and sentimental writing, and an example of the practice teaches us something of the accepted and 'usual' way of reading an illustration in the period. The following description is from Thackeray's *The Adventures of Philip*, which appeared in the *Cornhill Magazine* from 1861 to 1862, a period when a new style of illustration had become dominant, one which promised to give middle-class readers the feeling that the story was set in a world they recognised and to which they belonged. It demonstrates strikingly the resultant diegetic arrest that often accompanies description or illustration, and the use the reader is intended to make of it. The scene is written to be enjoyed visually, the narrator proposing that comic pleasure is to be derived from an examination of its composition:

> Here is a picture I protest. We have – first, the boarders on the first landing, whither, too, the Baynes children have crept in their nightgowns. Secondly, we have Auguste, Françoise, the cook, and the assistant coming up from the basement. And, third, we have Colonel Bunch, Doctor Martin, Major MacWhirter, with Charlotte in his arms; Madame, General B., Mrs. Mac, Mrs. General B., all in the passage, when our friend the bombshell bursts in amongst them.[6]

The reading of this comic moment is formalised – almost ritualised – as the action is arrested for the narrator to show where the comic quality lies. Thackeray did not, in fact, choose this particular incident for illustration, and it would have been an old-fashioned choice for that year and that magazine should he have done so. Rather Thackeray is using a self-aware device inherited from the eighteenth century, but this degree of self-awareness was out of fashion in the politer sixties, the 'Golden Age' of the kind of illustrations Millais drew for the works of Tennyson and Trollope. Texts now called for images in altogether subtler ways. What the reader is invited to construct in the above passage from *Philip* is a plate in the style of Cruikshank. In the absence of an actual illustration, the reader is taken through the narrator's composition and reading of an imaginary one. An actual plate should perhaps be looked at in the same way, and the action, however rapid in the verbal text, should be thus interrupted for an interval of non-verbal laughter. Images requiring the process of reading which Thackeray's description presupposes continued to circulate throughout the Victorian period, but were not often found in the realistic novel of modern life.

The fact that theatrical images commonly relate to more than one instant in the action is also carried over into novel illustration, as in Cruikshank's illustration to *Oliver Twist, of* 1837 – 1838, *Oliver escapes being bound apprentice to the sweep*, which is not composed of moments and gestures which occur simultaneously in the narrative, but presents a sequence of events of some duration. 'Correct' viewing or reading of this kind of image entails following the sequential events around the plate in a particular order, which would be easily identified by those brought up on the work of Hogarth and his successors, especially Rowlandson, Combe and Gillray. In this case there are eight chronologically successive actions specified in Dickens's text, and Cruikshank has presented them all, assuming in his readers the knowledge of how to allow the text to direct the reading of the image. The eight actions are narrated as follows:

> 1) The old gentleman stopped, laid down his pen, and looked from Oliver to Mr. Limbkins:

2) who attempted to take snuff ...
3) 'My boy!' said the old gentleman, '... What is the matter?'
4) 'Stand a little away from him, Beadle,' said the other magistrate: laying aside the paper, and leaning forward with an expression of interest.
5) 'Now, boy, tell us what's the matter ...'
6) Oliver fell on his knees,
7) and ... prayed that they would [not] ... send him away with that dreadful man.
8) 'Well!' said Mr. Bumble, raising his hands and eyes with most impressive solemnity, 'Well! of all the artful and designing orphans ...'

The introduction of duration into a single image is an ancient device which today is commonplace in static advertisements for motion pictures, in which compound images frequently show both an action and its consequences in the way that this form permits, but which realism would not allow. The particular type of 'realism' which found favour with the mid-Victorian middle-classes under the name of 'Truth to Life', demands that the entire 'content' of a picture be given equal standing, the existence of one element not being dependent upon or subservient to another. Part of this equality of course is simultaneity. At very least the illusion of simultaneity must be maintained. Some fundamental features of the processes by which people learn to perceive an event as a 'scene' may account for the fact that quasi-theatrical art has been successfully exploited to please publics as dissimilar as Boz's and the polite, French novel-readers of the mid-eighteenth century.

In early Dickens the aligning of prose narrative and drama is perfectly appropriate because of the nature of that narrative. Many scenes are comic and the narrative is frequently openly didactic, rather as we find in the popular theatre of the day.[7] Another of Dickens's great illustrators, Hablôt K. Browne ('Phiz'), specialises in reinforcing didactic and comic narrative by other means. *Coming Home from Church,* an illustration to Chapter 31 of Dickens's *Dombey and Son*, of 1846 – 1848, shows Mr Dombey returning from his ill-fated wedding. Much can be deduced about the characters' states of mind from this and other plates by examination of the visual environment, which is loaded with indirect, externalised representations of mental and moral states and awarenesses. The gulf between wealth and poverty is expressed in this image in the ragged figures clustering near the wealthy couple, and this is more than a device for visual variety and more than simplistic social criticism, because it tells us a great deal of about Dombey's ethos. We cannot miss the ill-omened funeral in the background. In other plates in *Dombey*, Browne, like Hogarth before him, includes pictures on the walls and statues in the hall that allude to well-known myths or dramatic works.[8] Such illustrations convey meaning by a combination of verbal and visual referencing, or bimodal intertextuality, as it is now increasingly called. Later in the Victorian period the dominant mode of middle-class fiction shifts from exemplary narrative heavy with moral didacticism, towards a psychological and moral analysis of the individual and collective situations of multiple characters in a complex and problematic world.

In Millais's rendering of the Crawley Family in *Framley Parsonage*, of 1860, we have a typical mid-Victorian focus on an individual case of poverty – that of a scandalously low-paid perpetual curate in the Church of England, forced to appear a gentleman and remain a scholar on the income of a semi-skilled labourer. A modestly prosperous middle-class neighbour is visiting. This is not a case of the contrast of extreme wealth and extreme poverty – not a case of Lady Bountiful and the pauper – and it sets up complex conflicts in all the fictional adults concerned. The delicacy and ambiguities are emphasised by the enigmatic figure seen behind the door, which is ajar. Mr Crawley is teaching his young daughters a boys' curriculum. The elder is already competent in Greek, but it is the younger who has the better ear for the scansion of Greek poetry. Crawley is in many ways a very difficult man, and this is a complicated case of poverty and pride, and a useful case against which to test our assumptions when we make judgments about fictional characters. Most people today will applaud the father's intention of equipping his daughters with the learning a son should receive, even if some now consider that Greek may not of itself deliver the greatest possible benefits. The author's 'advanced' acquaintance (such as George Eliot) almost certainly approved. On the other hand it could be taken to confirm the view of many in the Diocese, and expressed frequently throughout the *Chronicles of Barset,* that Crawley was mentally unstable. We enjoy it today as an example of mid-Victorian social transgression, and may read the scene as Crawley standing up to Victorian prejudice, proud of his integrity and his poverty. The distress of the family of a brilliant university graduate like Crawley was a perfect subject to excite the interest of the middle-class readership of the *Cornhill*.

In the spirit of a good Victorian novel, this chapter will now turn from poverty to conspicuous consumption, and an impressive steel engraving by John Tenniel, another leading artist of the day, who is now most widely remembered for his *Punch* cartoons and his illustrations to *Alice in Wonderland*. The engraving, which appeared in 1862 as the frontipsiece.to the second edition of F.W. Robinson's novel, *Grandmother's Money*, depicts a fashionable white, ball-gown descending a staircase (Fig. 5.).

Two other young women, less flamboyantly dressed in white, are behind, as is the eponymous, hatchet-faced grandmother. The young belle in the dress, is eclipsed by it. This is a less finely-tuned image of economic standing and psychology than Millais's 'Crawley Family'. There is no subtlety to the fashionable display, and the emotions of the participants are not complex. The grandmother is what Stanley Holloway famously called 'an awkward old party', and the others look merely disapproving.[9] The young belle herself is pretty, but having no strongly markedf eatures,is a blank canvas upon which the conventional Victorian reader is invited to inscribe sweetness and virginity.

Part 2: Nineteenth-century visualisations

Fig. 5. Tenniel, J. (1862) Untitled illustration in Robinson, F. W. (1862) *Grandmother's Money*. London: Hurst and Blackett, frontispiece.

Further consideration reminds us that this is a frontispiece, which was introduced for the first time into the second edition of this novel, not the first. It represents a significant financial investment, and it must have been a commercial motive that drove the publishers, Hurst and Blackett, to commission it. Almost certainly they wished to compete with the highly successful new monthly magazines, including the *Cornhill* and *Macmillan's Magazine*. The *Cornhill* in particular had immediately achieved great success with illustrated fiction and poetry when launched in 1860, because the publisher, George Smith, called on well-known names to enhance its visual appeal. Frederick Leighton, for example, had illustrated Elizabeth Barrett Browning's poem *Pan*, of 1860 and George Eliot's novel, *Romola*, of 1862 – 1863. John Everett Millais, celebrated as a founder-member of the Pre-Raphaelite Brotherhood and latterly as one of the most commercially successful mainstream artists, illustrated Trollope's *Framley Parsonage*, of 1860 – 1866 and the *Small House at Allington*, of 1862 – 1864, in the *Cornhill*, as well as providing forty-eight plates for the novelist's *Orley Farm*, of 1861 – 1862, for a rival publisher, Chapman and Hall.

Millais was particularly adept at highlighting the glamour (as we now might call it) of Trollope's texts. One of his illustrations to *Framley Parsonage*, *Was it not a lie?*, is particularly striking, showing a young woman face down on her bed in despair, but more importantly devoting most of the block to her extraordinarily elaborate crinoline. This may well be what Hurst and Blackett tried to emulate by commissioning the frontispiece we have discussed from Tenniel. *Framley Parsonage* was consumed with great enthusiasm, and the references to ladies' fashions in it, and their role in social climbing, were commented on by critics as the talk of the moment.[10] In fact this is Millais's least appropriate illustration to a Trollope novel, since in his haste (presumably) he misattributes the 'fashionista' Griselda Grantly's wealth and extravagance to the modest sister of the parish clergyman, Lucy Robarts. That aside, the image was successful. Millais had invented a new style, not seen before in any of the fashion publications, but established in the real world a few months later when Princess Mary of Cambridge, the woman with one of the largest dress bills in London, was seen wearing a copy of it.[11]

The publisher of *Grandmother's Money* seems to have decided to compete, and commissions a sensational picture of a dress from the celebrated artist John Tenniel, to boost, it appears, the sales of that novel in a second edition. His weapon is the portrayal of female consumption for the female reader. The precursor of the 'sex and shopping' novel is born. For the moment, Trollope and Millais were calling the tune.

We continue the shopping theme, but in this case it is fictive shopping, the more significant for being neither seen nor believed in. In *Your son, Lucius, did say – shopping* of 1862, an attractive young widow is visiting her lawyer, giving shopping as the excuse for her journey into London from Harrow (Fig. 6.).[12]

The lawyer's wife, suspecting that her husband is being manipulated by Lady Mason's undoubted charms, has detected Lady Mason in what might be a white lie or might be

Part 2: Nineteenth-century visualisations

"Your son Lucius did say—shopping."

Fig. 6. Millais, J. E. (1862) "Your son, Lucius, did say – shopping." in Trollope, A. (1862) *Orley Farm*. London, Chapman and Hall, page 97.

something far more serious, and so, without breach of social decorum, announces that she has uncovered a deceit. A dramatist could not have better presented and punctuated that line, and Millais gives it a suitable but very low-key dramatic presentation, which is the more quietly powerful for being so subdued. The setting, the location by the door, indicating transition and the imminent resumption of movement, the arrangement of the figures and their interaction bring out the reading I have summarised, and their stances – poised for an instant but almost in motion – impel narrative exploration or speculation. The caption is a skilful case of innuendo. Novelist and artist – Anthony Trollope and John Everett Millais – seem to understand this scene in the same way. It is a very effective illustration, and points forward to future developments in Trollope's narrative. One has the impression of characters that have sufficiently complex internal and external characteristics to be seen from more than one point of view, both morally and physically. The grouping here is excellent and suggestive of there being other views which might be taken. The interpretation of the scene, though seen identically by the verbal and the visual artist, is importantly left to the reader to elaborate on, with author and artist guiding not insisting. This is the very stuff of later Trollope, in which readers are often left uncertain about important facts, so that they must become active in their collaboration in the processes of meaning-production – becoming for the moment inhabitants of the fictional world, knowing no more and no less than can be told by garnering the awarenesses of a variety of characters. Millais does something very similar in his graphic works and his paintings, and it is this perspective that links Trollope and Millais so closely.

We do not know whether or not Millais, in highlighting these moments, encouraged the novelist's further development of the active reader and the equivocal narrative, but the question is relevant in the present volume, since *John Caldigate* is a particularly interesting example of this new narrative approach, which suggests an irresistible but undefined onward movement in the narrative. This sort of illustration was one of Millais's specialities. Two or more characters are caught at a moment of what is obviously significant interaction, the text providing more or less the remainder of the information needed to read the illustration in its entirety. Here I use the word 'illustration' in its fullest form, not to designate an image that is an addition to a verbal text, but, rather, a complex art form containing both verbal text and visual image, with the addition, very often, of a caption which may or may not consist of words taken from the verbal text. In one of these richly suggestive illustrations, the relevant text may be distributed widely through many chapters of the text, and, equally, the image may cross-refer to other illustrations. It is the role of the image of such a significant moment to create this instability. The situation is one that cannot last. The very poses of the characters make that apparent. The reader may know the cause of this instability, but cannot predict for sure what will happen as a consequence of it. Such moments are almost overloaded with implication: loaded with meaning about the present, and pregnant with alternative, future, narrative possibilities.

This type of illustration which, if it was not invented by Millais, was perfected by him during the period when he was illustrating *Orley Farm*, gave rise to the so-called 'problem picture' for which he and other artists became celebrated, in which an enigmatic or ambiguous social situation is portrayed, and made more complex by a cryptic title. The viewer is thus presented with what is in effect an illustration involving a narrative which is hidden – an illustration, that is, from which the verbal narrative has been removed so that viewers have to construct and debate their own interpretations.

The responsibility given to the reader is paralleled in what is often regarded as the first 'problem picture', *Trust Me*, a large oil painting dating from the period during which Millais was staying in Perthshire while executing drawings for wood engravings to *Orley Farm*.[13] It shows a moment's interaction between a well-dressed woman and an older man, who is in hunting pink and holding a riding-crop. She is holding what appears to be a letter behind her back, while he is holding out his hand as though to receive it. One character is saying to the other 'Trust me', yet it is not apparent who is speaking. Is the man saying that he can be trusted to read the letter, or is the woman saying that he can be confident that she has nothing to hide from him? We have no idea what their relationship might be, older husband and younger wife, or father and daughter, legal guardian and ward – the possibilities are numerous. Aspects of the personages have long reminded some viewers of Sir Peregrine Orme and Lady Mason in *Orley Farm*,[14] despite counter-indications: Sir Peregrine is known not to hunt in the traditional pink coat, and that no such situation arises between the two characters in the novel. It may be that Millais provides the precedent for some of Walter Sickert's problematically titled, pictures such as the four that constitute the so-called *Camden Town Murder* group, of 1906.[15]

In *An Autobiography* Trollope writes, "I am fond of *Orley Farm*, – and am especially fond of its illustrations, by Millais, which are the best I have seen in any novel in any language."[16] This and other passages are often quoted as though they show how completely Millais met Trollope's expectations as to the appearance of his characters. These illustrations, we are asked to believe, can provide us with the means of visualising the fictional personages, and particularly their physiognomies. To make such a simplistic connection is, in my view, a mistake. Descriptions of fictional characters rarely provide enough to facilitate a complete visualisation of their faces, and Trollope's certainly do not. He describes a relatively small number of facial features, and for those he uses interpretative terms that are intended to control the reader's reaction to non-visual as much as to visual characteristics.

Let us take the most celebrated example, the moment when, at an advanced stage in the story of *Orley Farm*, in Chapter 63, the narrator asks for the reader's cooperation:

> In an early part of this story I have endeavoured to describe how this woman sat alone, with deep sorrow in her heart and deep thought on her mind, when she first

learned what terrible things were coming on her. The idea, however, which the reader will have conceived of her as she sat there will have come to him from the skill of the artist, and not from the words of the writer. If that drawing is now near him, let him go back to it. Lady Mason was again sitting in the same room – that pleasant room, looking out through the verandah on to the sloping lawn, and in the same chair; one hand again rested open on the arm of the chair, while the other supported her face as she leaned upon her elbow …[17]

Trollope imagines someone reading part fifteen of *Orley Farm*, and sends this reader back to the second part, published thirteen months earlier and shelved elsewhere, perhaps, or, if reading the two-volume edition from the second volume published 25th September 1862 to the first, published nine months earlier. As N. J. Hall points out, '[i]n the earlier description we read simply that Lady Mason "seated herself in her accustomed chair"; the details mentioned in the latter passage are in fact a description of Millais' drawing'.[18]

The novelist describes himself as 'very proud' when he was first told that Millais was to illustrate *Framley Parsonage*. "He afterwards illustrated *Orley Farm*, *The Small House of Allington*, *Rachel Ray*, and *Phineas Finn*", he tells us.

Altogether he drew from my tales eighty-seven drawings, and I do not think that more conscientious work was ever done by man (…) An artist will frequently dislike to subordinate his ideas to those of an author, and will sometimes be too idle to find out what those ideas are. But this artist was neither proud nor idle. In every figure that he drew it was his object to promote the views of the writer whose work he had undertaken to illustrate, and he never spared himself any pains in studying that work so as to enable himself to do so.[19]

I think we must take the promotion of 'the views of the writer' to relate to socio-economic standing and physical type, not details of appearance. Rather than facial detail, Millais conveys the stance of a person in a particular situation, such as the dynamic of the plate described above, and also the significant arrangement of figures within groups to indicate interpersonal perceptions.

Comparison with the work of another well-regarded illustrator, Arthur Hopkins, will highlight Millais's strengths. *Look at her, Matt*, the frontispiece to volume one of Payn's *A Confidential Agent*, of 1880 (Fig. 07.), is a scene set in a lower-middle-class suburban garden, and is a good example of a plate and its caption which should arouse the interest of the reader without indicating what, in narrative terms, it is 'about'.[20]

The image demonstrates the dangerously thin line between a 'realistic' grouping of characters, which would be 'True to Life' as the Victorians would say, and a posed group portrait, which is what this tends towards. This wood engraving is characteristic of 1880 in

Part 2: Nineteenth-century visualisations

Fig. 7. Millais, J. E. (1880) "Look at her, Matt." in Payn, J. (1880) *A Confidential Agent*. London: Chatton & Windus, frontispiece.

prioritising attractive design above narrative impulse. All this is perfectly appropriate in the first novel in the language to centre on the 'framing' of an innocent man for a meticulously planned crime. The tension this image sets up stems from the three characters' focused gaze on the fourth, whose eyes are downcast. It also prepares for the then unusual fictional situation in which the eponym, the 'agent', is of interest thanks to what he *doesn't* do, while his wife is going to be visibly the more active. Wilkie Collins is perhaps fairer in his *The Law and the Lady*, of 1875, in which the 'lady' who is the active character is credited in the title. As far as individual psychology, conveyed by facial expressions, is concerned, we marvel, as so often we must, at how life was conducted by men sporting the fashionable 'seventies beard. The four people are grouped as though posing for a portraitist or photographer. There is no reason incorporated into the narrative as to why they should be so conveniently arranged. That is, their positions are not motivated by the narrative. There is, of course, no reason why an illustration to a novel with a commonplace suburban setting should avoid stylisation. A later novelist, though, might bring such an image as this into the fiction by presenting it as a domestic snapshot, and indicating how and why it was taken. As it is, the artifice of the illustrated, realistic novel is unintentionally laid bare.

A very successful full-page plate by Millais for *The Small House at Allington*, *It's All the Fault of the Naughty Birds*, shows the better artist solving the problem of how to present numerous characters with faces towards the viewer, without any impression of conscious posing for a group portrait.[21] The occasion is the return, empty-handed, of a group of men who have been shooting. This time the arrangement of the figures is saved from awkwardness by the boot-scraper, which is centre-stage, and, humble object though it is, guarantees that the men and dogs have just arrived at the squire's door, and are therefore seen as a motivated array facing the squire rather than as a randomised group. Gender is important here once more, and the point of view, visual and narrative, is particularly interesting. The caption, "It's all the fault of the naughty birds.", is a quotation from the text of the novel at this moment in the action. The sarcastic remark is made by Lily Dale, the vivacious younger daughter of the 'Small House', and calculatedly presented so as to be the reader's favourite character. The satirical tongue of the attractive heroine is an accepted part of English literary tradition since Shakespeare's *As You Like It*, and is sanctioned in the domestic novel by the example of Elizabeth Bennet in Jane Austen's *Pride and Prejudice*, of 1813. There is, therefore, little problem for Trollope, but he has set Millais a problem: how the intelligent and much-loved Lily is to be shown in this present situation. After all she is openly mocking the men (marginally permissible in this case in Victorian terms because one of them is her avowed lover), but this mockery and the lack of sporting success makes the men look extremely sheepish. How is Lily's status as an ideal young candidate for marriage to be maintained if she sounds for the moment like Kate, the 'Shrew' who has to be 'tamed' in Shakespeare's play?

Millais's solution is to place her at the back of the group, alongside her sister, the two of them identically dressed and demurely veiled. The reader/viewer sees the diminution of the sportsmen as though through that rather rare perspective of 'the Victorian female gaze'. That is to say, conventions are overturned. Yet this visual rendering of the men is not in fact Lily's, though it is her words that have called for it. Both Millais and Trollope are 'having their cake and eating it', as the proverbial expression puts it. The caption constructs the Victorian middle-class male as potentially ridiculous and thus motivates the image in an unusual way for the period. We seem to be submitting the male characters to a female gaze, and it is we, the readers, whether male or female, who are manoeuvred into actually delivering what it seems should be her 'gaze', to correspond to her satirical words. Such an illustration raises the interesting possibility that a scrutiny of visual and narrative points of view could help develop a new illustrative typology. In the present instance, the opposing directions of the two 'views' might help define a new category of irony which, because it involves an assumed mid-Victorian reader and a distinctly different, twenty-first-century reader, is far more complex than the simple irony of Lily's sarcasm acting safely within the fiction as artefact. The multiple viewpoint is utterly appropriate to Trollope's narrative method, and is perhaps the single most important historical precedent on which Simon Grennan draws in *Dispossession*.

My last example, *Monkton Grange*, from *Orley Farm*, is interesting in many ways (Fig. 8.).[22] First, it is strikingly original. Inevitably England once had a National Museum of Fox-Hunting – a museum, that is, devoted entirely to fox-hunting – and the staff of this

Part 2: Nineteenth-century visualisations

"Monkton Grange."

Fig. 8. Millais, J. E. (1862) "Monkton Grange." in Trollope, A. *Orley Farm*. London, Chapman and Hall, page 215.

museum believed that this plate of Millais's could well be the first artistic representation of a meet before the hunt has moved off.[23] Hunting prints, which in the Victorian period sold very well, usually depicted action, and generally showed plenty of cantering and jumping. Horses were all too often shown in impossible positions, flying over hedges with all four legs stretched out, in defiance of anatomy, or galloping with a gait that no horse could ever adopt. There were also easel paintings a-plenty of hunting scenes, often of stag hunts, which were as much group portraits of the riders and their mounts, carefully arranged into a tableau, as records of hunting as a sport. Oils of static scenes of hunts were usually celebrations of a landowner, his house, his estate, the riders and their valuable horses, and these were (and still are) extensively reworked as engravings or etchings.[24] These paintings doubled as celebrations of wealth and landed estates, and as images of expensive mounts, not unconnected with the immortalising of famous horses by George Stubbs some decades earlier. Staghounds were all the more fashionable because Sir Walter Scott included hunting scenes in his novels, and he himself was painted with his beloved staghound, Bran, beside him.[25] Indirectly, Millais follows this path to a certain extent, but of course, with no landed patron to flatter, he is free to take a view that does not overtly glorify the owner of the house. On the other hand, he had two very experienced foxhunters that the picture had to satisfy – himself and Anthony Trollope, who rode together for many years. Everything in this plate is fictitious. Not one of the people or horses or places is recognisable, nor is the house, but what is not fiction is that the architectural style of the country house in the background was very fashionable. Landowners were building pseudo-Elizabethan mansions or transforming their genuine old houses back to this earlier style, obliterating a century and a half of neo-Grecian masquerade.[26] The artist has radically adapted a subject that was traditionally calculated to please a landowner into an image to appeal to the middle-class readers of the *Cornhill Magazine*.

The most striking thing about this illustration, therefore, is the re-positioning of the spectator. As you view it, you are standing near the dogs and horses (and the people as well), close to but not necessarily of them, positioned as befits a *Cornhill* reader, socially of or near the gentry, and part of or a sympathetic observer of that sort of country life. The active social grouping shows no awareness of being pictured – seems to feel no pressure to form a tableau. This image is a perfect example of the best that the 'realistic' illustrators of the day could achieve. We can see everything in it with almost equal clarity, and any messages we decode from it are our contribution to the act of perception. If we decide to become involved, that is our doing. The interpretative scope this gives the reader maps accurately not only on to the social standing of the viewer/reader but on to the way Trollope is increasingly giving his readers responsibility for creating the fiction as it is actually to be consumed.

In this account of some of the ways in which historical habits of the illustration of literary texts in English locate the reader and generate meaning, I have indicated some generalities and read a number of particular images to show them in action. The first inherited habit is the exploitation of a long-standing link between illustration and the theatre, but a link which manifests itself in ways which subtlety but importantly change over time. As the mid-Victorian illustrated novel adapts itself to a newly prosperous middle-class market, the very nature of the fiction which is illustrated changes, from the strong effects and the rather simple characterisation which is typical of the popular theatre and the mass-produced, illustrated fiction of the early nineteenth century, to a product aimed at a middle-class readership, who expect a to be introduced into a world rather like the one they hope they live in, where people are motivated by complex moral and religious beliefs, and are conscious of a multiplicity of interpersonal relations set within a larger, more intimidating world. Moral judgments, and with them character portrayal, are expounded more thoroughly. Despite the stratification of British society at the time, characters from a wider social spectrum can be taken seriously. Meanwhile, because the fictional world of written narrative and illustration now seems an extension of the world in which readers live, they are given narrative and visual viewpoints that reinforce the illusion of reality. Thus, also, the picture of the world admits new features into the narrative art: fashion in clothing, behaviour and architecture is suddenly more immediately important to a larger body of consumers than was the case in the eighteenth century. The illusion of closeness of the characters to the readers brings many of the stresses of middle-class life into prominence, in particular gender rules for nearly everybody, and genteel poverty for the unfortunate. Debt, investment, risk and fraud join inheritance as the economic drivers of the fictional world. The fictional world is now to be understood rather as the world of everyday life – as complex, not entirely explicable, and to be lived in so that individuals achieve the most morally acceptable life they can (by Victorian standards), by the exercise of will and strength of character. Both verbal narrative and image combine to project the complexities of individual life in a dangerous but practical, and usually negotiable world.

Despite the suasiveness of Trollope's narrative voice, his fiction often leaves us free to do our own mental work, to engage ourselves actively in his fictional world. Millais has appreciated that quality entirely. It is a quality that is eminently visible in *John Caldigate* and opens up this fiction to new remaking in a later century. An examination of Victorian literary illustration with such wisdom as hindsight and acquaintance with the modern graphic novel may provide, reveals that narrative poses problems which are common to different media, but which each artistic form has to tackle with its own tools.

Notes

1. See Lopes, P (2009) *Demanding Respect: the Evolution of the American Comic Book*. Philadelphia: Temple University Press, pages 4 – 6, for the view that developments in publishing connect illustration in pulp magazines to the comic book.
2. Grennan, S. (2015) *Dispossession*. London: Jonathan Cape and Grennan, S. (2015) *Courir deux lièvres*. Brussels: Les Impressions Nouvelles.

3. Dickens at first wished the cover of *Martin Chuzzlewit* to bear the motto "Your homes, the scene. Yourselves, the actors, here!", but was dissuaded from this by John Forster, who thought he would thereby offend his readers. See Forster, J. (1874) *The Life of Charles Dickens Volume 2*. New York: Bibliobazaar, page 59.
4. An uncredited illustration in an unpaginated, undated publication, probably a pirate edition from the third quarter of the nineteenth century, of W. H. Ainsworth's novel *Jack Sheppard*.
5. Ferrand, N. (2009) *Livres vus, livres lus: une traversée du roman illustré des Lumières*. Oxford: Voltaire Foundation SVEC, 2009.03, pages 12 and 200.
6. Thackeray, W. M. (1862) *The Adventures of Philip on His Way through the World* first appeared serially in the *Cornhill Magazine* between January 1861 and August 1862. This passage occurs on *Cornhill Magazine* 5 (January 1862), page 9.
7. See note 3 for evidence for this assertion.
8. "Florence and Edith on the Staircase" in Chapter 47 of *Dombey and Son* is a perfect example, analysed in Steig, M. (1978) *Dickens and Phiz*. Bloomington and London: Indiana University Press, pages 101 – 103.
9. Marriot. E. (1935) "The Jubilee Sov'rin" in Edgar, M. (1935) *Albert, 'Arold and Others … performed by Stanley Holloway and Marriott Edgar*. London, Francis, Day and Hunter, pages 25 – 26.
10. See Skilton, D. (1972) *Anthony Trollope and His Contemporaries: a Study in the theory and Conventions of mid-Victorian Fiction*. London: Longman and New York: St Martin's Press, pages 19 – 20.
11. Skilton, D. (2007) "The Centrality of Literary Illustration in Victorian Visual Culture: the example of Millais and Trollope from 1860 to 1864." *Journal of Illustration Studies*. (December 2007). http://jois.uia.no/articles.php?article=30 accessed 27 September 2014.
12. Millais, J. M. (1862) "Your son, Lucius did say – shopping." in Trollope, A. (1861-2) *Orley Farm Volume 1*. London: Chapman & Hall, recto opposite page 98.
13. For a reproduction and full details of this painting see the sale catalogue of the Forbes Collection, lot 17: (2003) *The Forbes Collection of Victorian Pictures and Works of Art* Volume 1. London: Christie's, pages 124 – 127. There is a repeated misprint on page 124, where the date of first purchase is twice given as 1891 instead of 1861.
14. Ibid., pages 126 – 127.
15. *The Camden Town Murder* is a title given to a group of four paintings by Walter Sickert painted between 1908 and 1914.
16. Trollope, A. (1996) *An Autobiography*. London: Penguin, 1996, page 110.
17. Trollope, A. (1862) *Orley Farm*. London: Chapman and Hall, pages 178 – 179.
18. Hall, N. J. (1980). *Trollope and His Illustrators*. London: Macmillan, page 44.
19. Trollope, A. (1996) *An Autobiography*. London: Penguin, pages 98 – 99.
20. XXX
21. John Everett Millais, "It's all the fault of the naughty birds." in Trollope, A. *The Small House at Allington* in *Cornhill Magazine* 6 (November 1862), verso facing page 663.
22. John Everett Millais, "Monkton Grange." in Trollope, A. (1861) *Orley Farm, Volume 1*. London: Chapman and Hall, recto facing page 216 (first issued as the part of September 1861).
23. Personal communication from the curator, 2001. The Melton-Carnegie Museum, which contained the Hunting Museum, has been taken under the care of the Leicestershire County Museums service. I am grateful for the help of the staff of the museum service.
24. For example, see the painting by Dean Wolstenholme, Senior (1757-1837) *Lord Glamis and his Staghounds* of 1823, or, later, the painting by Joseph Francis Walker (1831-1906) *A Meet of Sir*

Clifford Constable's Stag Hounds at Burton Constable of 1858. I am grateful for the assistance of the curator of the Burton Constable Foundation.

25 See Lockhart, J. G. (1838), *Memoirs of the life of Sir Walter Scott, Bart.* London: John Murray and Whittaker and Company, Volume 7, page 428. John Gibson Lockhart lists as number XV "An excellent half-length portrait, by John Watson Gordon, of Edinburgh, done in March 1830, for Mr Cadell. See this volume, page 276. Scott is represented sitting, with both hands resting on his staff. The stag hound Bran on his left. The engraving in Volume 33 of the Waverley Novels does no justice to this picture."

26 Mark Girouard comments on the gloriously vague 'Old English' designation, which was "widely used [...] to describe both Tudor-Gothic and Elizabethan houses." Mark Girouard (1979) *The Victorian Country House.* Newhaven CT: Yale University Press, page 71.

References

Ferrand, N. (2009) *Livres vus, livres lus: une traversée du roman illustré des Lumières.* Oxford: Voltaire Foundation SVEC, 2009.03.

Forster, J. (1874) *The Life of Charles Dickens Volume 2.* New York: Bibliobazaar.

Girouard M. (1979) *The Victorian Country House.* New Haven CT: Yale University Press.

Hall, N. J. (1980) *Trollope and His Illustrators.* London: Macmillan.

Lockhart, J. G. (1838) *Memoirs of the Life of Sir Walter Scott, Bart.* Edinburgh: Robert Cadell and London: John Murray and Whittaker and Co.

Payn, J. (1880) *A Confidential Agent.* London: Chatto & Windus.

Skilton, D. (1972) *Anthony Trollope and His Contemporaries: a Study in the theory and Conventions of mid-Victorian Fiction.* London: Longman and New York: St Martin's Press.

Skilton, D. (2014) "The Centrality of Literary Illustration in Victorian Visual Culture: the example of Millais and Trollope from 1860 to 1864." In *Journal of Illustration Studies.* December, accessed 27 September 2014. http://jois.uia.no/articles.php?article=30

Steig, M. (1978) *Dickens and Phiz.* Bloomington: Indiana University Press.

Thackeray, W. M. (1862) *The Adventures of Philip on His Way through the World.* London: Smith, Elder & Company.

Trollope, A. (1996) *An Autobiography.* London: Penguin.

Trollope, A. (1861) *Framley Parsonage.* London: Smith, Elder & Company.

Trollope, A. (1862) *Orley Farm.* London: Chapman and Hall.

Trollope, A. (1864) *The Small House at Allington.* London: Smith, Elder & Company.

Roger Sabin

Comics versus books: the new criticism at the 'fin de siècle'

This chapter concerns some of the debates around comics in Britain in the late nineteenth century, and in particular their relationship to 'literature'. Simon Grennan's *Dispossession* is a remarkable book, and represents the bringing together of 'classic' literature (in this case, a story by Anthony Trollope) with comics. Although we are very familiar with this kind of crossover today (indeed, it's been popular since the 1930s, reaching its apogee with the *Classics Illustrated* line), in the nineteenth century itself, when Trollope was active as a writer, it would have been inconceivable. 'Literature' and 'comics' – albeit in their fledgling form – were often perceived to be on different trajectories: one 'improving', and the other damaging.

The aim here, then, is not to trace the way in which adaptations became acceptable (a worthwhile project though that would be), but instead to survey the discourses that emerged around early comics. Why, exactly, were they seen as lesser literature? Who judged them thus? What codes and class barriers were being erected, and why such fear about their transgression? What were the imagined prohibitions that kept the two forms apart? Why, in total, were they positioned at opposite ends of the spectrum of respectability? Using new evidence in the form of selected quotes from the contemporary press, this chapter will build an argument about the first great age of comics criticism – and the first great age of prejudice against comics.[1]

'Comics', for our purposes, means the wave of publications that came after *Punch* and its main rivals, *Fun* and *Judy* (founded 1841, 1861, and 1867 respectively).[2] In particular, the more visually orientated, more slapstick, and more 'working class' publications that flourished at the end of the century. The pioneering title was *Ally Sloper's Half-Holiday*, appearing from 1884, which claimed to be the market leader through the late 1880s and 1890s, followed by *Comic Cuts* and *Illustrated Chips*, appearing from 1890, *Funny Wonder*, appearing from 1892, *Larks!* appearing from 1893, *Big Budget*, appearing from 1897 and a slew of others.[3] These titles were primarily aimed at an adult readership, and mainly men, though women and younger readers became significant demographics towards the end of the century. They consisted of a mix of humorous cartoons, strips, illustrated stories, news stories (related in satirical fashion), competitions, letters pages, and adverts (often illustrated).

It is important to note at the outset, therefore, that physically these comics contained a lot more than cartoons and strips – and that some had an appearance and aura that was closer to what we would think of as a newspaper or magazine. They were emphatically not straightforward collections of stories told in sequential images, and sometimes as much as 50 per cent of their space was given over to text. The question of whether they were 'comics' at all depends on definitions. If a comic is something that's mass-produced on a regular basis, contains as a significant proportion of its content cartoons and strips, and stars recurring characters, then they count; the fact that they were increasingly referring to themselves as 'comics' is not insignificant.[4]

Who were the critics? Unsurprisingly, they were mostly men (though, as we shall see, arguably the most important of their number was a woman) and overwhelmingly middle class – engaged in talking about a working class art-form, and talking about it primarily to a middle class readership. The nature of their critique typically turned on the question of 'what was best for "them" to read' (the 'othering' of the working class was therefore very much part of their process), though it should be noted that middle class readers of comics were not small in number.[5] Such arbiters of taste can be seen as self-credentialising – essentially carving a niche for themselves by talking about pop culture.[6] There were more of them than ever before in the late nineteenth century, because there were more outlets for their work (for reasons that will become clear), and their opinions appeared in newspapers, magazines, and occasionally in the comics themselves.

Their criticism, therefore, was a discourse – with its own parameters and rules, and emanating from a variety of sources that had distinct editorial points-of-view.[7] To an extent, this period saw a new kind of more aggressive opinionating, often seen as an aspect of the 'New Journalism': the more outraged the opinion, the better, because this is what sold units.[8] So we need to bear in mind that these critics were habitually 'being outraged' for money, week after week, and were constantly on the lookout for new stories – the place of comics in culture being one of them. Inevitably, similar views were advanced about other aspects of pop culture – notably music hall, the fashion for advertising, and, later, cinema. Nevertheless, the discourse is revealing, and the very words that are used indicate deep-seated values.

The quality of the criticism was not monolithic, taking different forms in different venues. In the more 'intellectual' journals, it consisted of longer pieces, often many pages, which dwelt upon looking for patterns and asking big questions about meaning – examples to be offered in a moment. These were often penned by star journalists, who got a by-line, and who worked freelance (though that term requires to be contextualised). The other main kind of criticism took the form of passing commentary and consumer reviews in the weekly and daily press, which was aimed at a mixed-class readership. This kind of writing was not interested in cultural patterns, and instead concerned itself with snap judgements (e.g. 'funny or not') and advice to readers on whether a particular title was worth their money. 'Cuttings from the Comics'-style columns, collecting choice jokes from the latest crop, also became popular in the 1880s.

The reviewing system was open to bias. For example, it was common for critics to favour comics that happened to be published by the same media empire as the papers for which they were writing (some critics actually worked for the comics simultaneously). Also, views expressed in the elite publications tended to 'trickle down' to the less upmarket press, and thus 'agenda setting' tended to be the preserve of a select few critics. We are familiar today with these caveats about cultural journalism in the context of the modern media, and analyses like those by Noam Chomsky and Robert McChesney have been important in promoting political economy approaches that can be relevant when applied historically.[9]

Finally, it is important to note that critics did not always differentiate between the new-style comics, and the old *Punch*-style journals. Although today it is customary for many historians to see *Ally Sloper's Half-Holiday* as a break point between the two forms, this was not so evident at the time. Thus, the 'Cuttings from the Comics' mentioned above might include excerpts from *Punch*, *Judy*, and *Fun* as well as *Ally Sloper's Half-Holiday*, *Comic Cuts*, *Illustrated Chips* and the rest. Definitions are always fluid, always under construction, and thus ahistoricism is a risk: as philosopher and comics theorist Aaron Meskin cautions: "Nothing could have counted as jazz in the seventeenth century."[10]

In terms of the general intellectual background to this discourse, why did criticism become so intense in the late nineteenth century? The period c.1880-1914 is now acknowledged to have been the 'first great age of leisure', meaning in particular that working class people had more leisure time (less work) and more disposable income.[11] The expansion of the cities made the 'economics of entertainment' viable, undergirded by the expansion of the railways and other transport systems. This was the era of organised sport (football especially), hobbies like smoking, trips to the seaside, and of variety entertainment. It was also the era of a new kind of popular press, as cheap publications flourished. The 1870 Education Act had been significant in raising literacy levels, and it was only a matter of time before reading would become an ideological battleground, with positions staked around 'good, improving reading' versus 'negative, frivolous, and harmful reading'.[12]

Part 2: Nineteenth-century visualisations

What gave the debate an added depth was, by the end of the century, that 'big ideas' were in play, notably socialism. Marx and Engels' investigations into capital had been inspired by observing the British working class, and the rise of organised labour parties offered a fresh arena for the discussion of culture. Old questions were given urgent spins: what place should the new leisure occupy in a democracy – ideally a socialist democracy? Who is leisure 'for': all workers – skilled and unskilled? Women? If a measure of capitalism was allowable, then was it necessary to control working class taste, in order for the market to function successfully? Was the new leisure harmful? This essentially ethical framework for the debate thickened it, and politicised it in explicitly class-based terms.[13]

This meant a challenge to the very notion of what 'culture' could be. Such a concept had been dominated by the enduring view of a leading intellectual from earlier in the century, Matthew Arnold, who famously believed that culture was "the best that has been thought and said in the world."[14] For him, this meant high culture, the kind of culture enjoyed by the upper and middle classes – with the concomitant notion that the working class simply had no culture. Arnold's elitism was attractive to conservatives for obvious reasons, but it was also a factor in the thinking of some leisure reformers, who believed that instead of legitimating what the working class actually did for amusement, it would be preferable to guide them in the direction of 'the best that has been thought and said'.

Finally, the context for the debate included one further element that was ever-present in the background – the legacy of the 'penny dreadfuls' panic of the 1860s. The so-called 'dreadfuls' were fictional illustrated story books, often about violent crime and sometimes glamorising criminals, which were read primarily by young men. They quickly became the subject of a panic, based on the idea that they were contributing to delinquency, and a campaign was organised to get them banned. There was an accompanying effort by publishers to combat the threat with more 'wholesome' literature. Historians have argued that some of the dreadfuls' politically subversive storylines could be as panic-inducing as anything to do with violence, and were a factor in the backlash.[15] The comics that came in the late nineteenth century were certainly different to the dreadfuls – they were humorous to begin with, and read by a broader constituency – but their 'low culture' aura meant they were often tarred with the same brush, and accused similarly of inciting bad behaviour.[16]

To look at the anti-comics case first of all, we can generalise that the tone of the criticism was sanctimonious, melancholic, despairing, angry, nostalgic and full of fear. It never cohered into a 'campaign' as such – as had happened with the dreadfuls and would happen again with the horror comics in the 1950s – but it was a persistent, if sporadic, feature of the press. At its most hyperbolic, it was as if the end of civilization was nigh: comics, along with the rest of the vulgar new pop culture, were bringing an end to a 'golden age' when everybody knew where they stood, and when hierarchies (both social and cultural) were secure. In the face of the working class finding its voice, the middle class was on the defensive. New ways had to be found to mark out distinctions and to re-inscribe Arnoldian values. Thus, cultural capital became a focus: as sociologist Pierre Bourdieu has famously theorised, taste can be a weapon, and the majority of negative commentary about comics circulated around 'good versus bad' binaries.[17]

Why the idea of 'the working class finding a voice' should have been so disturbing has to do with a heightened awareness, post the 1860s, of its political ramifications. Fears about delinquency, rioting and revolution had not gone away, and in the context of the aforementioned rise of socialist (and anarchist) ideas, and the anxiety-stoking effect of a newly vocal sensationalist media, the event that jolted the middle class more than any other was a particularly violent riot in Whitehall in 1887 (so-called 'Bloody Sunday'), during which the police had nearly lost control. After this 'wake up call', the comics did not actually have to say anything bad to be a focus for fear and disdain.

A flavour of this general feeling can be gleaned from this anonymous quote from a daily newspaper in 1890:

Critics of the modern newspaper [including comic newspapers] – and how multitudinous they are! – are apt to overlook the fact that journalism is but a reflection of public opinion. It is just what public opinion makes it, and if *Ally Sloper* and that fungus growth of the press flourishes, it is because there is a class of people whose intellectual cravings must have it.[18]

Note here the language. The word 'fungus' was the same as had been used against the dreadfuls, and would be the same again as used in the 1950s against the horror comics (it was the analogy favoured by key campaigner Dr Fredric Wertham).[19] A powerfully expressive noun, it connoted a blight: something that spreads uncontrollably, is aesthetically unpleasant, and is likely to be poisonous when consumed. A fungus also gets its sustenance from other living or decaying things. Here, the market is allowing growth to happen, and we can detect an additional fear concerning the unpredictable nature of supply and demand.

Consider, also, the word "cravings". Who has cravings, exactly? Clearly, an addict, and the suggestion here is that comics are addictive; undoubtedly a reference to the fact that they are serial in nature, and that repetition breeds a kind of intensification and dependence.[20] Possibly, too, there's an acknowledgement that comics weren't just cheap, they were very cheap, meaning that working class addicts could afford to buy more than one – again suggesting amplification. And finally, perhaps there is a nod to the idea that because comics were portable and throwaway, they tended to get passed around (in pubs, coffee houses, in railway carriages, etc.), sometimes to as many as an estimated four other people – another magnification of the 'craving'.[21]

Seriality, therefore, was something of which to be suspicious. Not only were the comics 'addictive' and profligate, they were also associated with advertising – a necessity for their economic viability as serial publications, and another marker of the new commercial vulgarity. This set them apart from books, though the irony was that the Victorian period saw books increasingly published in bit-parts: everybody from Trollope to Dickens was publishing in this way, and their serialised pamphlets would similarly carry advertising. Snobbery from critics was still in evidence, however, and even Queen Victoria was chastised for reading *Oliver Twist* in its serialised form.

Finally, note how in the quotation the critic bundles-in comics (symbolised by the mention of *Ally Sloper's Half-Holiday*) along with other "modern newspapers", thus suggesting a blanket judgement about the lowbrow popular press of the day. It's taking over and it's a plague – "how multitudinous they are!" According to this (presumably middle class) journalist, the 'class of people' with no taste, and who are prone to being addicts of trash, are encouraging a very unhealthy kind of publication to flourish. Other critics would use the term 'railway literature' in a pejorative fashion to make a similar point: suggesting publications designed to be bought at railway stations at places like W. H. Smith's, and then discarded after a journey.[22]

Elsewhere, this kind of prejudice could just as easily be invoked by referring to the dreadfuls: as we've seen, they were always 'there' haunting the public imagination. For example, many of the new comics were priced at one penny, thus making a psychological connection: *Ally Sloper's Half-Holiday* was priced as such, undercutting *Punch* by a penny, and led the way. When the comics got cheaper, as competition heated-up and technology became more efficient, so the complaints against them increased. Another quotation, usually attributed to A. A. Milne (later author of *Winnie-the-Pooh*), despairs that, "Harmsworth [the biggest publisher of comics in the 1890s] has killed the penny dreadful by the simple process of producing the ha'penny dreadfuller".[23] This encapsulates the idea that the new halfpenny titles (typified here by *Comic Cuts*, *Illustrated Chips* and the other Harmsworth staples) might be *worse* than the dreadfuls – with all that association entailed in terms of perceived deleterious effects on working class behaviour.[24]

The fact that Milne's quote refers to comics starring characters who were tramps and other 'low-lifes', more interested in loafing and scheming than working, was an obvious factor in the level of disgust. Ally Sloper was the archetype: a ne'er-do-well who was shabby and tramp-like: in early iterations he dossed by the Thames, though by the time of *Ally Sloper's Half-Holiday* he lives in a slum. His success spawned a host of imitators. The most famous of these were *Weary Willie and Tired Tim* (in *Illustrated Chips*) who were a pair of vagrants, while later examples included *Nobbler and Jerry* (in *Funny Cuts*), *The Three Lodgers* (in *Larks!*) and *Airy Alf and Bouncing Billy* (in *Big Budget*). These were not the role models for the working class that middle class critics wanted to see – how could capitalism function successfully if this was the message being broadcast? How could an Empire, built as it was on the myth of superiority, be sustained?

Similarly, some characters were partial to drink, and this was not good according to many moral guardians. The prime example, once again, was Ally Sloper, red-nosed through over-indulgence and with a gin-bottle sticking out of his back pocket. His comic also featured supporting characters such as The McNab, a whiskey-sodden Scotsman, and

McGoosely, who was typically too paralytic to have adventures of any kind; and the public was devoted to the new workers' 'half-holiday', perceived in sections of the middle class media as license for drunken debauchery. The links between alcohol and criminality were not lost on critics, and the Temperance movement in particular took up the challenge, settling on three targets: the pubs, the music halls and the penny press.[25]

Such comics characters seemed to embody a subversion of the 'moral duty' to work hard and improve oneself – a Victorian obsession that had grown with industrialisation.[26] If Samuel Smiles' book *Self-Help* of 1859, about how the working classes could better themselves in this fashion, was a kind of Victorian blueprint for this way of thinking – a quarter of a million copies sold by 1904 – then the new wave of shabby comics anti-heroes was its obverse.[27] Sloper, Weary Willie and the rest were 'helping themselves' alright; just not in the way that Smiles had hoped.

In short, these characters were setting an example that was somehow un-Christian and un-British, which was a problem for both conservatives and liberals: some socialists had the added concern that their antics implied for readers an ideological distraction from the 'real politics' of the day (comics as an opium of the masses). When the critic in the newspaper *Brighton Society* made the point, in 1896, about Sloper that "They [working class people] pay more attention to him than any eminent socialist", it was meant as a witty aside; but another interpretation is possible.[28]

Indeed, could the new comics actually be subversive, in a directly state-threatening way? This was an underlying theme in the backlash against the dreadfuls, as we have seen. Similarly, historians today, who engage in close readings of nineteenth-century comics, ask about the power of their representations of society, and whether they offered a glimpse of a more equitable world in which the status of the bourgeoisie was challenged: for example, historian Scott Banville argues that certain scenes in *Ally Sloper's Half-Holiday*, in which Sloper is clothed in the garb of his 'betters', might represent a vision of the kind of lives he could have had if he'd been higher-born.[29]

To put the question another way, if the 'establishment' was mocked week after week, surely this would undermine 'the social contract', and lead to unrest. There were fears about how far the comics would go (especially in the light of events like the Whitehall riot), and reports of striking railway workers in 1890 wearing 'Ally Sloper masks' can't have steadied nerves.[30] Indeed, such fears were part of a general feeling about the penny press, as noted by famed critic Augustus Sala:

> There existed, not only among the Conservatives, who thought that the cheap daily press could only be the prelude of sedition and revolution, but also among a large number of journalists, and Liberal journalists, too, of high standing, the most violent of prejudices against the new order of journals, which were usually contemptuously called the 'penny papers'.[31]

Part 2: Nineteenth-century visualisations

If the representation of men *per se* raised questions about the work ethic and sedition, then that of women raised other issues. For example, it's unsurprising that the titillating nature of much of that representation – scenes of female bathers at the seaside in 'summer specials'; 'pin-up' cartoons of music hall performers; and so on, was not to the taste of the more conservative critics. Once again the Temperance leagues were in the forefront of the fight against indecency, whether that be in the music halls, or in the (very much connected) comics, and the fear was that such imagery would inflame the passions of young men, and lead to 'base urges'. Such cartooning was perceived to be becoming more pornographic, due to the advances in photography and more realistic photo-referencing. Plus, the fact that some comics contained 'classifieds', a form of advertising sometimes linked with prostitution, magnified unease.[32]

Finally, other content in the comics caused alarm. For example, the fact that nearly all of them ran competitions and puzzles with a reward of prizes (ranging from pocket watches to cash), raised anxieties about a 'something for nothing' society in which working class people became beguiled by the prospect of winning, to the detriment of a concentration on the work ethic. Critics saw this as being akin to gambling, and one more layer to the comics' baleful influence. Once again the self-improvement ideal popularised by Samuel Smiles and others, and rooted in a conservative religious outlook, was being undermined, and the Temperance-minded were to the fore; while in the socialist camp some objected on the grounds that a disdain for material things (and unselfishness) should be key to a socialist future.

A bigger complaint was the 'danger to reading' posed by comics. Thus, according to another anonymous critic, this time employed by a magazine devoted to literature:

> To devour *Ally Sloper* and *Tit-Bits* is not to read. Nothing can be more enervating to the mind than this class of literature, if literature it may be called. Such sheets as these destroy the appetite for real reading, and the healthful hunger for books.[33]

Again, the wording is interesting. Reading proper books is positioned as 'healthful', while the opposite, reading comics, is unhealthy (again, like consuming a poison fungus). In fact, according to this critic, the latter doesn't even count as 'reading' – it is only looking – and thus, the visual is conceived as somehow extra-suspect. This binary opposition had a long history: for example, William Wordsworth had written a poem entitled *Illustrated Books and Newspapers*, published 1850, in which he contrasted respectable "prose and verse" with the rise of a "dumb Art/ that best can suit/ the taste of this once-intellectual land", ending with "Avaunt this vile abuse of pictured page!" Fifteen years later, the inclusion of illustrations had been perceived as a key factor in making the dreadfuls so potent.

Thus, the quote sees comics as beyond the pale of literature: the real authors – Trollope, Smiles, Shakespeare or anybody else – were 'over there', somewhere separate. It's as if comics are by their very nature crass, 'noisy' and communal – as opposed to reading books, which is private, quiet and soulful. They therefore undermine any conceptions associated with book reading, such as self-improvement and the diffusion of 'useful' knowledge. Again, comics – typified by *Ally Sloper's Half-Holiday* – are put in the same bracket as other 'lowbrow' publications (in this case, *Tit-Bits*, a compendium magazine consisting of competitions, jokes, and sensationalist and human interest stories). They are all part of the same drive towards vulgar commercialism. Finally, the phrase "enervating to the mind" suggests a kind of stupefaction of the reader, which links back to the idea that comics are like an opium hit – unhealthy and addictive.

This argument chimed with others that were in the air. For example, an enduring opinion about cheap publications, proffered earlier in the century (i.e. pre-comics), argued that the working classes did not have any time to think, because their lives were dominated by labouring. Therefore their reading matter had to be fast and immediate and not in any way philosophical. Their social conditions limit what they read, and they become like 'children or savages' fit only to gaze upon mindless pap.[34] Later, many critics (including Sala) echoed this view, albeit in less florid terms, and registered disappointment that the working classes, instead of using the opportunity to read improving literature, chose entertainment instead.

A good instance of this kind of thinking appeared in a polemical fiction story ("Patty – a Sketch.") from *All the Year Round*, of 1893, a weekly literary magazine, in which the middle class narrator attempts to 'improve' Patty, a semi-literate maidservant, by giving her some Shakespeare to read.[35] He despairs, however, when Patty prefers a copy of *Ally Sloper's Half-Holiday*, which, she says, is "'better than anythink [sic].'" The narrator relates how "she sat and grinned over it for two hours", and goes on to sigh that Patty's father also enjoys the comic. He concludes the story by saying "[I find it] impossible to cultivate the taste of the masses [...] when 'Slopers' [stand] in the way." If we pick apart the language here, the assumptions seem obvious. The narrator sees his role as being to "cultivate the taste of the masses", but Patty's idiotic "grinning at" the comic for two hours suggests child-like or 'savage' behaviour, and thus the new comics are positioned as a barrier to serious reading. Shakespeare versus comics: the divide couldn't be more clear.

Finally, critics made a taste distinction regarding the kind of comedy to be found in comics. Specifically, slapstick was contrasted with satire: coded as 'unsophistication' versus 'sophistication'. Comics, with their gormless, often tipsy, characters (who go around getting water splashed in their faces, tripping over, and falling down a lot), were deemed to be inferior to the satirical print tradition (Hogarth, Gillray, Cruikshank, etc.) and to its natural heir, in the form of *Punch*, which instead dealt in the more serious business of skewering the pretensions of the powerful and mocking 'affairs of the state'. One kind of humour was 'mindful' and had a political aim, while the other was 'mindless' with no meaning beyond frivolity. As one anonymous critic put it, making an explicit case about cultural capital: "The 'classes' [i.e. middle classes] – we will define for present purposes as those who buy *Punch* rather than *Ally Sloper* upon a railway journey."[36]

This criticism was commonly reinforced with reference to the poor production quality of the new comics, and the perceived crudeness of the artwork. Harmsworth's titles, in particular, were known for using low-grade ink and paper stock (how else was he going to keep them priced at a halfpenny?), and a critic of *Judy* pointed to the 'general poorness of its drawings' – many of which were republished in *Ally Sloper's Half-Holiday*.[37] As historian Brian Maidment has shown, this kind of complaint had precedents from within the print tradition itself, a few decades before, concerning the move to mass production, when, "genteel hand-coloured aquatints and etchings were turned into tonally crude wood engravings."[38] Thus, the objection to comics was an iteration of an ongoing argument about declining standards.

To sum-up, the perceived 'influences' of the new comics were deemed to have their most devastating effect on young men – the same demographic who had been so corrupted (allegedly) by the penny dreadfuls. These were the potential delinquents, the potential anti-patriots, the potential revolutionaries, the potential illiterates, the potentially over-sexualised, the potential giggling sinners, and the potential addicts of low culture who would have to be policed and otherwise 'carried' by more responsible members of society.[39]

By contrast, it is interesting that the female readership is absent from the discussion – apart from our fictional story about 'Patty' from *All the Year Round* quoted above. Noted critic and novelist Walter Besant's rather charming admission that, "as regards the women… I have never been able to find out anything at all concerning their amusements." belies the fact that they were fast becoming a significant market for comics.[40] Female literacy levels were rising exponentially, and they were consuming cheap publications of all kinds in an unprecedented fashion.[41] Moreover, women were a much more visible feature of music hall audiences (the halls having always been locked in a symbiotic relationship with the comics), and the 'New Woman' was making her way out of the home in all sorts of other ways.[42] Unsurprisingly, this phenomenon would raise new fears, and historian Lynda Nead has written of the perceived 'dangers' to women of reading visual literature, and the emotions this might stir i.e. how "the codes of respectable behaviour advocated for women" might be compromised.[43]

As for younger readers, these became more of a focus for concern as the intended age-range for the comics was reduced over time. They had been a part of the readership since the beginning, however, and were sometimes incorporated into complaints about comics in order to make a point about the corrupted 'innocence of childhood'. For example, one critic for a Christian youth organisation publication speculated despairingly on what an average boy would spend his money on: "Give him 3d. to expend on current literature and he will probably select *Scraps, Ally Sloper, Comic Cuts, the Joker*."[44] The battle for young minds was thus engaged, and would become more intense as the culture of pocket money began to take hold early in the next century, thus creating a whole new market of juvenile consumers of comics.

In conclusion, did these anti-comics critiques have any effect outside of a sporadic media outcry? It's difficult to say. Certainly, there was nothing as spectacular as the clampdown against the dreadfuls, but occasionally there were efforts to censor the comics, usually for misdemeanours such as libel against famous people, mismanagement of competitions, and, on occasion, stories that were politically contentious.[45] Such attacks might seem minor, but their implications could be severe, as the following report indicates:

> Sir John Bridge, the principal London Police magistrate, has given a decision that the prize competition in *Ally Sloper's Half-Holiday* is a breach of the Lotteries Act, and has inflicted a nominal penalty. This decision governs many other cases, and unless it is reversed by the judgment of a Superior Court, it is likely to be the ruin of a class of periodicals which well might not exist.[46]

If one test case could ruin an entire stratum of publishing, then it seems pertinent to ask whether these backlashes were undergirded by the general prejudice that existed against comics, and penny literature. Or even, as argued in the case of the penny dreadfuls and the horror comics whether there were bigger political motivations.[47]

In fact, most of the real-world impact was less dramatic, and consisted of initiatives to 'fight bad literature with good' by, for example, ensuring that 'proper books' were made available in working class districts.[48] Meanwhile, feeling under pressure, the comics industry itself reacted. Characters were increasingly portrayed in pro-establishment situations: Sloper was often to be pictured oozing up to the Queen, or dressed as a cop, and his comic revelled in insults about socialists, anarchists, strikers, and the unemployed. Characters in other comics were similarly patriotic and outwardly conservative (the first issue of *The Big Budget*, in 1897, saw Airy Alf and Bouncing Billy take part in a Jubilee Procession). The intention was to say that these were lovable characters – rough round the edges, but not likely to revolt. Comics also attempted to prove their moral worth by instigating charity drives and 'poor relief' appeals. Finally, when Harmsworth launched his line of comics, he explicitly stated that they would be a wholesome alternative to the penny publications that were out there. (Ironically, as we've seen, they were slapped down for being "halfpenny dreadfuls".) It all added up to a sense of comics being forced onto the back foot.

To turn now to the 'pro' case for comics, we can say immediately that, contrary to what might be imagined, and for all the bluster in the 'anti' camp, most of the passing commentary about them (in newspapers and magazines) was, in fact, approving. Characters like Sloper and Weary Willie and Tired Tim were referenced as 'friends', and their adventures applauded by the week. Some journals even went so far as to run long features about the new comics, their history and star cartoonists (for example, *Studies in*

Part 2: Nineteenth-century visualisations

Illustrated Journalism: The Rise of the Comic Paper in *The Magazine of Art*, 1891, and *Hi Hi Hi* in *St James' Budget* in 1894). Such is the volume of warm notices that the impression formed is that the panic about baleful effects was confined to a few conservative critics ranting to a small audience of the already-anxious.

In terms of locking horns with the specific points these critics raised – and it was true that most 'pro' criticism was reactive – counter-arguments tended to be advanced by elite critics who aligned themselves with liberal-leaning magazines such as *The Contemporary Review*. Such magazines made a point of expressing opinions about 'the new leisure', setting a template for future media to incorporate a space for cultural criticism, and were often inflected with a kind of paternalistic socialism. It was not lost on these commentators that significant numbers of their class were readers, even fans, of the comics (famous examples would include Sloper aficionados William Morris, artist and founder of the Socialist League, and William Gladstone, the Prime Minister), and that the majority of publishers, writers and artists producing the comics were similarly middle class.[49] If 'people like us' could enjoy the comics, they seemed to argue, then surely there was nothing wrong with others doing similar.

By the same token, for all the middle class fear of a 'rising' (more assertive) working class, there was a vocal minority who viewed it with equanimity, and even idealised it. The increasing popularity of socialism among middle class campaigners (like Morris), and sympathy for the struggle for a working class vote, was mirrored by cultural representations: for example, in paintings of muscular male factory hands and farm labourers, and of stoic female service workers, and in novels involving working class characters who were 'progressive', nuanced and more than a bundle of 'noble savage' characteristics. The idea of the working class as a potential 'friend and ally' would be developed further as the century progressed as other ideas, such as the German concept of the 'volk' (literally 'people'), were co-opted.

Which is not to say there was a coherent political line taken in the pro- camp. For example, there were disagreements about categorisation. Should comics, along with music hall and other aspects of the new commercial culture, be seen as part of the same tradition as coal miners' songs and Morris dancing? If so, how was this to be theorised? Was one 'pop culture' and the other 'folk culture'? Or was it all the same thing? It is perhaps no surprise that well-meaning middle class critics, speaking on behalf of the working classes but rarely taking into account their actual opinions, could sometimes come to contradictory conclusions.

Some accusations against the comics were more difficult to quell than others. On the question of whether they led to bad behaviour (delinquency, even sedition), Victorian commentators did not have the benefit of twentieth and twenty-first-century research into 'effects theory' (how the media impacts upon, and is used by, consumers), and so deflected the argument onto discussions of the comics' intrinsic worth – for example, the value of their humour and their 'Britishness'. Today, 'effects' are understood within the framework of the social construction of crime.[50] Having said that, occasionally, comics were seen as a safety valve, a diversion from violent or base urges (in the same way as other manifestations of pop culture were held to perform the same function). Walter Besant had this to say in the *Contemporary Review*: "The cheap excursions…the concerts given for the people…the Bank holidays, the Saturday half-holiday, all point to the gradual recognition of the great natural law that men and women, as well as boys and girls, must have play."[51] The key word here is 'must', as in 'they must have play': Besant doesn't say 'or else…', but he could have.

Similarly, the complaint that reading comics was detrimental to reading 'proper books' was engaged with indirectly. It was not as if the working class was as illiterate, or as averse to reading, as some of the critics implied. The story about Patty being incapable of sustained attention was obviously propaganda. Historian Jonathan Rose, for example, has shown that large sections of the working class were avid consumers of (some kinds of) high culture, especially when it came to reading.[52] The 'classics' were known via the public libraries and the thriving trade in twopenny second hand editions – and thus the cultural capital afforded by knowing what such classics were about could be easily attained. More than this, the comics themselves were often text-heavy, involving stories with a complex vocabulary and syntax (sometimes unnecessarily complex – the penny-a-liner writers were not known for their economy of style because it wasn't in their financial interests). Thus, we can imagine another version of the Patty story in which the reason she takes two hours over the comic is because there is so much to read.[53]

Therefore, it's not surprising that all the comics made reference to 'high literature' because it was part of the cultural diet of their readership. Famous books were parodied, and often quite obscure references to the Arnoldian canon were made (especially to Shakespeare). Meanwhile, comics characters gleefully mimicked celebrity literary figures, posing as novelists, playwrights and Poets Laureate. Perhaps the most eloquent riposte to the general grievance about books versus comics came in *Ally Sloper's Half-Holiday* on October 30, 1886, in the form of a cartoon of two boys, one looking malnourished and ill and holding thick books (labelled "heavy literature"), and the other sprightly and happy and holding a copy of – yes – *Ally Sloper's Half-Holiday* (Fig. 9.).

Other complaints were more directly addressed. For example, were the new comics heroes really setting such a bad example? We have seen how the comics bent over backwards to appear politically 'acceptable', and how (no doubt partly for this reason) they had their defenders in the wider media. For example, this was even true in the world of religious tracts – not a place where allies were normally found. In a pamphlet boldly and rather incongruously titled *Christ and Ally Sloper*, it is cheerfully acknowledged that many people enjoy "the quaint old man's preposterous doings" and further that "those who like drinking humour think of him as 'a jolly good fellow'". The pamphlet goes on to make a

Part 2: Nineteenth-century visualisations

·WHAT·EVERY·BOY·SHOULD·READ·

Fig. 9. Anonymous (1886) illustration in *Ally Sloper's Half-Holiday*. London: Gilbert Dalziel, October 30, no page.

rather tortured analogy between the spread of Sloper's fame, and that of Christ's.[54] Thus, the comics were just a bit of fun, and the antics of their stars shouldn't be taken too seriously.

Similarly, the idea that the new comics humour was inferior to that of the tradition of broadsheet prints, which had peaked earlier in the century, was vehemently denied by a number of key critics. Hume Nisbet, artist, author and sometime historian of graphic satire, writing in 1892, specifically identified *Ally Sloper's Half-Holiday* as the modern equivalent of the satirical canon of previous centuries:

Ally Sloper is the only paper of the present day to which the peculiar genius of the old caricaturists has descended; the Hogarthian satire and Rabelaisian humour is, in this much-illustrated weekly paper, reproduced in modernised costume and surroundings ...[...]. blend[ed] with the broad buffoonery with which Cruikshank delighted his audience of the past.[55]

Other critics reminded the complainers that rose-tinted nostalgia had a habit of editing-out the 90 per cent of poor material that existed in the print tradition alongside the 10 per cent of good; and that, therefore, a more sensible account of the modern day would have to acknowledge that a similar percentage of excellent cartooning existed.

As if to underline the point, in 1889, a major exhibition was held at the Royal Institute of Painters of the 'great cartoonists', which included the work of William Baxter (contributor of drawings to *Ally Sloper's Half-Holiday*, *Judy*, *Momus/Comus*) alongside that of Hogarth and Cruikshank – thus describing a direct lineage. (It was widely reviewed.) Baxter was not the only modern cartoonist to be feted in the media: other names included Tom Browne (contributor of drawings to *Comic Cuts*, *Illustrated Chips*, *The Big Budget,* etc.), Archibald Chasemore (contributor of drawings to *Judy*, *Ally Sloper's Half-Holiday*, etc.), and Jack Yeats (contributor of drawings to *Comic Cuts*, *Funny Wonder*, etc.).

The same sentiment went for comparing the new comics unfavourably with *Punch*. In the quote above, Hume Nisbet claims *Ally Sloper's Half-Holiday* as "the only paper" to inherit the mantle of the great cartoonist of the past – *Punch* is not mentioned. Elsewhere, too, *Punch* is not necessarily treated as automatically superior. For one thing, it was common knowledge that *Punch* and the new comics shared cartoonists and writers. Not only this, but satire was a staple of all the comics, however much they lent towards slapstick, and *Punch* itself evolved with the times and included a lot more 'falling over' humour by the end of the century. Thus, there was no easy divide between 'sophisticated' and 'unsophisticated' humour, as some of the 'anti' critics had suggested. Only after circa 1905 and the shift to comics being more orientated towards children did the distance from *Punch* become more marked.

Moreover, even if it was acceded that the new comics weren't quite up to the standards of the old print tradition or *Punch*, then did it really matter? Surely undemanding humour had something going for it even beyond the idea of a safety-valve? Indeed, could it be seen as rather civilised in comparison? In an article in *The Magazine of Art*, in 1891, critic David Anderson applauded *Ally Sloper's Half-Holiday* for its "gentle humour" and lack of venom – a plus, in the critic's eyes, when compared to the vicious satire of Gillray and so on.[56] The same feeling was echoed in a sympathetic piece in *The Glasgow Herald*, "It is not art, it is not caricature even, that Ally Sloper oftenest invites us to look at, but mere buffoonery... Baxter never becomes gross".[57] These critics saw nothing inherently dubious in the publications the working classes were enjoying, and were phlegmatic about the benefits of 'buffoonery'. As the *Newcastle Weekly Courant* concluded, "*Ally Sloper* and kindred illustrated periodicals are more likely [than books] to brighten the monotony of their lives."[58]

But the most ambitious argument advanced by the 'pro' camp had to do with idealising the new comics as a 'new vernacular'. This was most eloquently expressed in an eight page essay *The Modern Comic Newspaper* by Elizabeth Pennell in *The Contemporary Review*, number 50, of October 1886.[59] In it, she argues for a "folk culture" reborn, with comics at its centre (thus echoing the debates that were happening within liberal and socialist circles about where 'pop culture' might begin and end). She relates comics to the 'authenticity' of medieval peasant culture, and praises in particular their 'now-ness' and ability to pick up on the zeitgeist. In a passage that takes on golden age nostalgists and Arnoldian purists alike, she berates elitist critics for living in the past and forever looking back to the better days of high culture (thus revealing what she calls a "contemptuous indifference to the modern world").[60] Instead she argues provocatively that the working classes have better taste because they live in the present.

This slightly self-flagellating stance was not original to Pennell. It was a strain in the thinking of several middle class romanticisers of the working class, and implied that the former social group could never be as 'free' as the latter because they were shackled by their self-imposed sense of decorum and manners. Therefore, the prospect of 'letting themselves go' was never a possibility, with the concomitant suggestion that the only 'true', spontaneous and natural culture was to be found lower down the social order.[61] It was an idealistic idea in one way, but conversely there were hints of old prejudices about 'childlike' or 'savage' behaviour.[62]

Getting into her stride in the essay, Pennell takes *Ally Sloper's Half-Holiday* as a focus. Her emphasis on folk culture was clearly influenced by the fact that the character of Sloper had already become something of a folk-myth, being merchandised extensively and becoming a feature of popular performances – whether they be on the music hall stage, where comedians would imitate him, or in localised events where amateurs would dress up as Sloper in pageants and at country fetes. She writes: "At almost all amateur entertainments… there is sure to be an Ally Sloper as there must always be a Pulchinello to lead the Carnival revels." She then makes an all-important leap into a nationalistic mode: "after all, [Columbine, Harlequin] and Pantaloon were originally foreign importations; their real character forgotten in [Britain], and they can be allowed to go now that there is a genuine English creation [Ally Sloper] to succeed them".[63]

By pointing to how home-grown (comics-originated) characters were taking over from 'importations' – in this case from the Commedia dell'arte tradition – and emphasising their "genuine English" qualities, Pennell was doing something quite profound. Contra the critics of comics, she was saying that this supposedly un-British artform was, in fact, the quintessence of Britishness.[64] In terms of her vision of a new vernacular, here we can see her borrowing from Germany the idea of the 'volk', a romanticisation of 'the common people' as an organic entity, with a culture linked to ancient folklore, that is the foundation of the state, but – importantly – somehow anterior and superior to it. This almost supernatural nationalistic idea had been finessed by a succession of German philosophers since the early nineteenth century, and had become of increasing interest to intellectuals in the UK, of whom Pennell was one. The concept had been implicit in the work of Henry Mayhew (the great social researcher and co-founder of *Punch*), and explicit in the writings of later socialists like Thomas Wright. The difference was that instead of locating 'the soul of the volk' in books and music, as most other thinkers had, Pennell was making the case for comics and their associated manifestations.

This argument had implications beyond simple advocacy. It entailed a construction of the working class that de-fanged it, and made it manageable psychologically for the middle class, and in this way, pop culture now had the potential for being mobilised in the service of various political ends that were not necessarily as 'liberal' or 'progressive' as Pennell might have hoped. The comics may represent 'mere buffoonery', in the words of another critic quoted above, but Pennell had underlined that it was 'British buffoonery' (spontaneous, ironic, self-deprecating, pro-establishment) which set up an exclusionary zone based on a geographical (volk) identity. This perspective became more evident as time progressed: for example, American critic Walt McDougall, looking in from the outside, confirmed that the comics were dealing in content that was "a fundamental of the national humour."[65]

Thus, Pennell's vision of a volk, with comics as a key expression, could be used against enemies both abroad and at home. Comics characters were perfect embodiments of a new kind of self-effacing British resolve in the face of international challenges – a kind of 'soft power' at a time when countries like Russia and Germany were in the ascendant.[66] At the same time, Pennell was clear about who 'the enemy at home' might be, and in a throwaway sentence mentions that Sloper is "led astray" by "the swindling Jew" (a reference to his best pal in the comic).[67]

Perhaps we should not be too surprised, therefore, that the stars of the new comics were increasingly marshalled in support of the aims of the nation-state. Instead of ruining the Empire, as critics on the other side of the debate had argued, they were now seen as key elements in propping it up. It was a short step from cartoonists portraying such characters as being 'politically safe' (deferring to the Queen, supporting the police, and so on) to placing them in more overtly nationalistic situations. Victoria's late colonial wars saw them dressed in fatigues and 'doing their bit': Sloper against the 'fuzzy-wuzzies' (tribal warriors) in Sudan and then the Boers in South Africa; Weary Willie and Tired Tim organising a 'tramp army' to fight in the Transvaal; and so on (always accompanied by a Union flag). Come the First World War, things came to a logical head, with Sloper's daughter Tootsie leading recruitment drives, Sloper himself being adopted as a mascot for one regiment (the Army Service Corps becoming known as 'Ally Sloper's Cavalry'), and Weary Willie and Tired Tim bringing down a Zeppelin. Here was the new British volk in full throttle – an idea borrowed from Germany being used against Germany.

To sum-up, the pro-comics critique was many things. It was about middle class critics coming to terms with a new kind of working class entertainment ("their leisure", as Walter Besant would have it). It meant making a pact with it, and theorising it in such a way that it was understandable and manageable. Inevitably, there was a certain level of romanticisation, both of the working class and of comics, but also a recognition – a legitimation – of an already-existing middle class interest in the form. Above all, it meant fighting the nay-sayers – and the backlash against comics would have been far worse without the intervention of the 'pro' camp.

Yet, in 'othering' the working classes and their leisure, there was undoubtedly a sense of 'class tourism' for middle class readers. Some socialists at the time complained of how the vitality of the lower orders was being leeched-upon, in vampire-like fashion, and begged for middle class critics of all hues to stay away.[68] As for the motivations of journalists in the first place, the media was expanding and heated opinionating was a way to fill column inches. Comics can be seen as one more topic of interest for a self-credentialising elite of tastemakers, busy writing their own job descriptions. Which does not necessarily invalidate anything they said, or detract from the importance of this era in intellectual history.

In conclusion, it is possible to see in retrospect that this debate about comics was a cyclical phenomenon. The anti-comics backlash came soon after that against the penny dreadfuls, and then recurred several times in the twentieth century; most notably against the horror comics in the 1950s, and then, to a lesser extent, against the underground comix in the 1960s and 70s, *Action* in 1976, and manga in the 1990s. Other countries experienced a similar history. Each time, many of the concerns were the same, centring on the effect on readers and the potential for cultural debasement. The intrinsic controversy about 'comics versus books' was never far from the surface, and arguments about literacy, and taste in reading matter, continued to be markers of cultural capital.

Similarly, in defining the contours of the larger discourse involving the place of pop culture in the nineteenth century, the critics were anticipating much of the thinking we are familiar with today, via the Frankfurt School and the discipline of Cultural Studies (for the record: at present, Matthew Arnold is forgotten, commercialism is very much at the centre of definitions of 'pop', and the idea of 'culture' *per se* has stretched so far as to include 'anything that isn't nature').[69] The fact that comics were at the centre of this discussion is significant but rarely acknowledged. Meanwhile, the style of journalism pioneered at that time has become a staple of newspaper Sunday supplements, TV and radio 'culture review' shows, and arts websites and blogs. Thus, the 'fin de siècle' was a time not just of defining culture, but of defining the cultural critic.

Notes

1. Which is not to say there were not commentators upon comics before this date – Rodolph Töpffer in the 1840s being an often-cited example. However, it was only now that the form came under sustained scrutiny from a number of quarters.
2. The word 'comic' here being an abbreviation of 'comic book' or 'comic paper' – not of 'comic strip', as would be more common in the United States in the twentieth and twenty-first centuries. For further explanation, please see below.
3. For a quick sense of them, please see the Kevin Carpenter-curated online exhibition *Wonderfully Vulgar*: http://www.wonderfullyvulgar.de. For a more thorough listing, see Kirkpatrick, R. J. (2013) *From the Penny Dreadful to the Ha'Penny Dreadfuller*, London: The British Library and Oak Knoll Press, pages 368 – 369. *Ally Sloper's Half-Holiday* would frequently boast of being "The Largest Selling Penny Paper in the World", and its publisher cited sales of over 350,00 per issue in the 1880s and early 1890s; but statistics are never trustworthy, and detailed records for this and other comics do not exist.
4. The latest scholarly contribution to the debate about 'first' comics is Thierry Smolderen's excellent *The Origins of Comics*, which takes an essentially postmodern view.
5. This essay has refrained from defining 'working class'/'working classes' and 'middle class'/'middle classes'. Clearly these categories are contentious and constructed differently at different times – see, for example, Munt, S. Ed. (2000) *Cultural Studies and the Working Class*. London: Cassell. When talking about the nineteenth century, a substantial majority of the population was still rural and agricultural, so 'equivalence' with modern definitions is doubly difficult.
6. On the rise of the 'critical class', see Faulk, B. J. (2004) *Music Hall and Modernity*. Athens, Ohio: Ohio University Press.
7. Space forbids a description of each of the publications quoted in this essay: please refer to Brake, L. and Demoor, M. Ed. (2009) *Dictionary of Nineteenth-Century Journalism*, London: British Library Publishing.
8. For more on New Journalism, see Cox, H. and Mowatt, S. (2014) *Revolutions From Grub Street*. Oxford: Oxford University Press, especially Chapter 2.
9. For example, Chomsky's *Manufacturing Consent* and McChesney's *Rich Media, Poor Democracy*.
10. Meskin, A. "Defining Comics?" *The Journal of Aesthetics and Art Criticism* 65:4 Fall 2007, page 374.
11. See Bailey, P. (2003) *Popular Culture and Performance in the Victorian City*. Cambridge: Cambridge University Press.
12. Debates around 'the dangers of reading' stretch back a lot further, of course – to ancient Greece and also interpretations of the Bible. For more on the nineteenth-century context, see McAleer, J. (1992) *Popular Reading and Publishing in Britain 1914-1950*. Oxford: Clarendon Press, Chapter 1.
13. On socialism, see Waters, C. (1990) *British Socialists and the Politics of Popular Culture, 1884-1914*. Manchester: Manchester University Press. To quote page 1: "the Social Democratic Federation (SDF), the Socialist League (SL), the Independent Labour Party (ILP), the Fabian Society, and Robert Blatchford's 'Clarionettes' shared many assumptions which ultimately informed their critique of popular culture."
14. Arnold, M. (1969) *Culture and Anarchy*. London: Smith, Elder and Company. Incidentally, it was Arnold who is accredited with coining the phrase 'New Journalism'.
15. See in particular, Barker, M. (1989) *Comics: Ideology, Power and the Critics*. Manchester: Manchester University Press.

Part 2: Nineteenth-century visualisations

16 For more on the dreadfuls panic *per se* see Springhall, J. (1998) *Youth, Popular Culture and Moral Panics: Penny Gaffs to Gangsta Rap 1830-1996.* London: St Martin's. On juvenile delinquency, see: Pearson, G. (1983) *Hooligan: A History of Respectable Fears.* London: Palgrave Macmillan.

17 Bourdieu's *Distinction* is his most relevant work, but readers are advised to consider it in conjunction with Shusterman, R. Ed (1999) *Bourdieu: A Critical Reader.* London: Wiley-Blackwell. To quote *Distinction*, page 468: "The network of oppositions between high (sublime, elevated, pure) and low (vulgar, low, modest), spiritual and material, fine (refined, elegant) and coarse... is the matrix of all the commonplaces which find such ready acceptance because behind them lies the whole social order."

18 Anonymous. (1890) *Freeman's Journal and Daily Commercial Advertiser*, Nov 13.

19 In various articles in the 1940s and 50s, Wertham uses phrases like 'mushroom growth' (e.g. Wertham, F. (1957) *High Points in the Work of the High Schools of New York City Volume 39.* New York: New York Board of Education), but in his most famous book, *Seduction of the Innocent*, of 1954, he prefers analogies involving disease. Other historical uses of the word 'fungus' from earlier in the nineteenth century, referring to pre-comics publications, include: "that flood of Cheap Literature which [...] continues to spring up, with the mysterious fecundity of certain fungi" from Anonymous. (1859) "Cheap Literature." *British Quarterly Review*, April 1859, page 316. Also: "the mushroom growth of a sudden impulse, rapid and multitudinous to meet the occasion, came springing up a host of penny magazines – spontaneous and natural publications." from Oliphant, M. (1858) "The Byways of Literature: Reading for the Million." *Blackwood's* 84, August, page 203.

20 Repetition is a recurring theme in criticism. In the words of one American journalist, using quote marks in pointed fashion, "[comics deal in] the same 'funny' situation." from Burgess,G. (1901) "London's Ha'penny Comics." in *The (American) Bookman* Volume 14, Issue 4. Also: "*Ally Sloper* is amusing enough once, but it requires hereditary British stolidity to take him perennially in large weekly doses." From Ananymous, *Glasgow Herald*, June 8, 1889.

21 The idea of addiction in popular culture has been explored in various conferences and publications by the Repetition Repetition research group at the University of Kent and the Popular Seriality: Aesthetics and Practice research unit at the University of Gottingen.

22 See Brake and Demoor, *op cit*.

23 This quote is difficult to source: It appears in Turner, E. S. (1976) *Boys Will Be Boys.* London: Penguin, page 126, and is referenced in both Springhall and Kirkpatrick (*op cit*).

24 The quote is ironic because Harmsworth's comics were intended to be 'wholesome alternatives' to the dreadfuls and the rest of the penny press (see below). In fact, they often repeated formulas. Also, please note, prices did fluctuate over time: for example, by 1891, *Comic Cuts* was being priced at one penny.

25 See, for example, Walker, P. (2005) *Pulling the Devil's Kingdom Down: The Salvation Army in Victorian Britai.* Berkeley: University of California Press.

26 See Tosh, J. (2005) "Masculinities in an Industrialising Society: Britain 1800 – 1914" in *Journal of British Studies*, Volume 44, Number 2, April.

27 On Smiles, see Strachan, J. (2010) "Satirical Print Culture" in O'Gorman, F. *The Cambridge Companion to Victorian Culture.* Cambridge: Cambridge University Press.

28 Judex Junior "Letters to Local Somebodies" Nov 21.

29 Banville, S. (2008) "Ally Sloper's Half-Holiday: The Geography of Class in Late-Victorian Britain." in *Victorian Periodicals Review* Volume 41, Number 2, Summer, pages 150 – 173.

30 Anonymous (1890) "The Railway Crisis." in *Aberdeen Weekly Journal*, December 31. The parallels with the wearing of 'V' masks (derived from the graphic novel *V for Vendetta*) at the 2011/2012 Occupy protests are obvious.

31 Sala, G. A. (1895) *The Life and Adventures of George Augustus Sala*. New York: Charles Scribner's Sons, page 332.
32 See Cocks, H. G. (2004) "Peril in the Personals: the Dangers and Pleasures of Classified Advertising in Early Twentieth-Century Britain." in *Media History*, Volume 10, Issue 1, pages 3 – 16.
33 (1897) *Central Literary Magazine*, Volume 13, page 243.
34 Oliphant. *Op cit*, page 215. These attitudes are usefully contextualised in Fyfe, P. (2009) "The Random Selection of Victorian New Media." in *Victorian Periodicals Review*, Volume 42, Issue 1, pages 1 – 23.
35 Quoted in Banville, *op cit*.
36 (1890) "The Poetry of Bank Holiday." in *Pall Mall Gazette*, 26 May.
37 White, G. (2009) *English Illustration 'The Sixties': 1855-70 (1895)*. New York: Bibliobazaar, index entry.
38 Maidment, B. (2013) "The Persistent Regency - The Presence of the Past in Victorian Illustrated Comic Literature." in Korte, B. and Lechner, D. Ed. (2013) *History and Humour - British and American Perspectives*. Bielefeld, Germany, page 41.
39 For a twenty-first-century take on the problem, see Jones, O. (2012) *Chavs: the Demonisation of the Working Class*. London: Verso.
40 Besant, W. (1884) "The Amusements of the People." in *Contemporary Review* Number 45, March, page 346.
41 See McAleer, J. (1992) *Popular Reading and Publishing in Britain 1914-1950*. Oxford: Clarendon Press.
42 See Clark, L. L. (2008) *Women and Achievement in Nineteenth-Century Europe*. Cambridge: Cambridge University Press.
43 Nead, L. (2011) *Victorian Babylon*. New York: Yale University Press, page 149. For information on rising literacy levels, see Price, L. (2012) *How to do Things With Books in Victorian Britain*. Princeton, Princeton University Press.
44 (1893) *The Boys Brigade Gazette*.
45 For example, all three applied to *Ally Sloper's Half-Holiday*: there were several libel cases: the most famous being in 1889 (reported on 2 February in the comic) and 1897 (reported in *Reynolds Newspaper*, 28 February): the competition lawsuit was in 1913 (reported on in *The Times*), and the 'political censorship' incident happened in 1904 when the comic appeared with its front cover 'blanked out' due to a story about the Tsar: details are unclear.
46 Anonyous (1890) *The Leeds Mercury*, June 17.
47 The work of Martin Barker has been key in teasing out the often hidden political motives behind backlashes against comics. See, in particular: *A Haunt of Fears* and *Comics: Ideology, Power and the Critics*, which also briefly talks about penny dreadfuls.
48 See McAleer, *op cit*.
49 See Chapman, J. (2011) *British Comics: A Cultural History*. London: Reaktion.
50 See, for example, Barker, M. and Petley, J. Ed. (1997) *Ill Effects*. London: Routledge.
51 Besant, "The Amusements of the People." *op cit*, page 342.
52 Rose, J. (1995) *The Intellectual Life of the British Working Classes*. New York: Yale University Press.
53 How far the comics might have been a spur to reading e.g. with people of all ages learning to read using a comic, is unknown. Certainly there were critics who felt that any reading was 'good', though they often saw fiction as a step to non-fiction.
54 Standring, S. (1890) "Christ and Ally Sloper." In *Truth Seeker Pamphlet Number 2*. Bradford: Truth Seeker Company.

55 *The Gentleman's Magazine*, March.
56 This 'gentleness' had the added advantage of not upsetting advertisers.
57 Anonymous. (1889) June 8.
58 Anonymous. (1893) "Au Courant." September 9. The context for this quote was that a set of books had been delivered "to supply inmates of poor-houses with high-class literature" in Newcastle by well-meaning benefactors, but had included science books, and volumes in German that were "not likely to enjoy a wide circulation among the poor inmates."
59 For more on Pennell, see Faulk, *op cit*.
60 Elizabeth Pennell in the *The Contemporary Review*, Number 50, October 1886, page 520.
61 See also, for example, Emile Zola's *Germinal*.
62 In the twentieth and twenty-first centuries we have become familiar with similar ideas involving, say, the supposed 'street credibility' of punk, or the 'real-ness' of hip-hop. Regarding the former, one of the most famous lyrics by Clash frontman Joe Strummer, himself the son of a diplomat, had it that "the truth is only known by guttersnipes." (1977) *Garageland*. London: CBS Records.
63 Pennell, *op cit*, page 521.
64 'Englishness' and 'Britishness' have been conflated for the purposes of this essay (lack of space forbids problematisation, though clearly there is much to be said).
65 McDougall (1896) *Weekly News and Courier*, 4 March.
66 There were historical precedents e.g. Hogarth's depictions of the French.
67 Pennell, *op cit*, page 521.
68 The socialist and composer Rutland Boughton was known for this kind of opinion (see Waters, *op cit*, page103) and it has recently become fashionable among 'neo-Marxists' such as Slavoj Zizek.
69 See, for example, Strinati, D. (2004) *Introduction to Theories of Popular Culture*. London: Routledge.

References

Bailey, P. (2003) *Popular Culture and Performance in the Victorian City*. Cambridge: Cambridge University Press.
Banville, S. (2008) "Ally Sloper's Half-Holiday: The Geography of Class in Late-Victorian Britain" in *Victorian Periodicals Review* Volume 41, Number 2, Summer, pages 150 – 173.
Barker, M. (1984) *A Haunt of Fears*. London: Pluto.
Barker, M. (1989) *Comics: Ideology, Power and the Critics*. Manchester: Manchester University Press.
Barker, M. and Petley, J. Ed. (1997) *Ill Effects*. London: Routledge.
Bourdieu, P. (1984) *Distinction*. Cambridge MA: Harvard University Press.
Brake, L. and Demoor, M. Ed. (2009) *Dictionary of Nineteenth-Century Journalism*. London: British Library Publishing.
Carpenter, K. Ed. *Wonderfully Vulgar* at: http://www.wonderfullyvulgar.de.
Chapman, J. (2011) *British Comics: A Cultural History*. London: Reaktion.
Cocks, H. G. "Peril in the Personals: the Dangers and Pleasures of Classified Advertising in Early Twentieth-Century Britain." in *Media History*, Volume 10, Issue 1, pages 3 – 16.
Cox, H. and Mowatt, S. (2014) *Revolutions From Grub Street*. Oxford; Oxford University Press.
Chomsky, N. (1995) *Manufacturing Consent*. London: Vintage.

Clark, L. L. (2008) *Women and Achievement in Nineteenth-Century Europe*. Cambridge: Cambridge University Press.

Faulk, B. J. (2004) *Music Hall and Modernity*. Athens, Ohio: Ohio University Press.

Fyfe, P. (2009) "The Random Selection of Victorian New Media." In *Victorian Periodicals Review* Volume 42, Issue 1, pages 1 – 23.

Jones, O. (2012) *Chavs: the Demonisation of the Working Class*. London: Verso.

Kirkpatrick, R. J. (2013) *From the Penny Dreadful to the Ha'Penny Dreadfuller*. London: The British Library and Oak Knoll Press.

McAleer, J. (1992) *Popular Reading and Publishing in Britain 1914-1950*. Oxford: Clarendon Press.

Maidment, B. (2013) "The Persistent Regency – The Presence of the Past in Victorian Illustrated Comic Literature." in Korte B. and Lechner D. Ed. *History and Humour - British and American Perspectives*. Bielefeld, Germany: transcript.

McChesney, R. (2001) *Rich Media, Poor Democracy*. New York: New Press.

Meskin, A. (2007) "Defining Comics?" in *The Journal of Aesthetics and Art Criticism* 65:4, Autumn.

Munt, S. Ed. (2000) *Cultural Studies and the Working Class*. London: Cassell.

Nead, L. (2011) *Victorian Babylon*. New Haven CT: Yale University Press.

Pearson, G. (1983) *Hooligan: A History of Respectable Fears*. London: Palgrave Macmillan.

Price, L. (2012) *How to do Things With Books in Victorian Britain*. Princeton: Princeton University Press.

Rose, J. (2003) *The Intellectual Life of the British Working Classes*. New Haven CT: Yale University Press.

Shusterman, R. Ed. (1999) *Bourdieu: A Critical Reader*. Oxford: Wiley-Blackwell.

Smolderen, T. (2014) *The Origins of Comics*. Jackson: University Press of Mississippi.

Springhall, J. (1989) *Youth, Popular Culture and Moral Panics: Penny Gaffs to Gangsta Rap 1830-1996*. London: St Martin's.

Strachan, J. (2010) "Satirical Print Culture." in O'Gorman, F. Ed. *The Cambridge Companion to Victorian Culture*. Cambridge: Cambridge University Press.

Strinati, D. (2004) *Introduction to Theories of Popular Culture*. London: Routledge.

Tosh, J. (2005) "Masculinities in an Industrialising Society: Britain, 1800-1914." in *Journal of British Studies* Volume 44, Number 2.

Turner, E. S. (1976) *Boys Will Be Boys*. London, Penguin.

Walker, P. (2005) *Pulling the Devil's Kingdom Down: The Salvation Army in Victorian Britain*. Oakland: University of California Press.

Waters, C. (1990) *British Socialists and the Politics of Popular Culture, 1884-1914*. Manchester: Manchester University Press.

Wertham, F. (1954) *High Points in the Work of the High Schools of New York City Volume 39*. New York: New York Board of Education.

Wertham, F. (1954) *Seduction of the Innocent*. New York: Rinehart and Company.

Barbara Postema

The visual culture of comics in the last half of the nineteenth century: comics without words

While the narrative in pictures that we now call 'comics' was in vogue in the second half of the nineteenth century, with most magazines and newspapers including them on a regular basis, the mass circulation of picture stories was still new at the time, having developed rapidly over the course of only sixty years or so. By the second half of the century there were already a number of distinct national traditions in comics, with comics in English publications being significantly different from those in France and Germany, for example, and in fledgling form these comics already displayed the great range of work in comics form that we encounter today, with comical as well as tragic stories being told, in serialised as well as one-shot occurrences, in long-form and short, and in a huge range of visual styles, with captions, word balloons, or silent. By the end of the nineteenth century, art historian David Kunzle contends, wordless comics were recognised as the most advanced form of graphic storytelling, the pinnacle to which every cartoonist should aspire, with the *Chat Noir* magazine being the exemplary place to publish them, because despite it being only a four-page weekly periodical, it had the reputation of being bohemian and artistic.[1] Since the silent strips did not include explanatory text or narrative captions, wordless comics drew on the full artistic range of their creators, and if in some cases the pictorial stories being told remained somewhat mysterious, this ambivalence was seen as part of their appeal.[2]

Part 2: Nineteenth-century visualisations

In the early nineteenth century, comics were an elite publishing endeavour, with Rodolphe Töpffer (1799-1846) distributing his labours of love in handsome bound volumes to be circulated amongst friends, not via the bookstore or the news-stand, though some of them were later reprinted in albums and illustrated journals such as *L'Illustration*.[3] The best known of Töpffer's stories include *Histoire de M. Vieux Bois*, of 1837, and *Histoire de Monsieur Cryptogame*, of 1845. These works consisted of several illustrated panels per page, drawn in a scratchy, caricature style, with hand-written narrative captions underneath. Another early master of the long-form graphic narrative was Cham, pseudonym for French caricaturist Amédée-Charles-Henri de Noé (1818-1879). His books, which ranged in style from Töpfferian caricature to a more naturalistic style, include *Monsieur Lajaunisse*, of 1839, and *Les Folies de la Commune*, of 1871, which was in colour. *Les Folies de la Commune* was more serious and political than much of Cham's earlier work, and was made up of single full-page images with short printed captions below that offered context for the pictures by setting the scene or providing some dialogue. Comics may have begun by courting respectability and artistic recognition in the way they were circulated, but as Thierry Groensteen suggests in his history of silent comics, they were quickly discovered and exploited by the popular press, as magazine and newspaper printing expanded rapidly over the course of the century.[4]

Both the number of titles and circulation numbers of popular publications increased exponentially, and as printing technologies advanced, newspapers and magazines began to include more images. They did this to break up swaths of text, to draw attention to products in advertisements, to illustrate reports, stories and poems, but just as often the images were themselves the point of the entertainment, in the form of a satirical cartoon, large illustrations that could be taken out and hung on the wall as a poster, or of course as the short graphic narrative. Comics tended to be included in the popular press to tell humoristic stories like anecdotes or visual jokes. While serialisation had become extremely popular for textual narratives and had also been used for graphic narratives in the first half of the eighteen hundreds, as Jennifer Hayward traces in *Consuming Pleasures: Active Audiences and Serial Fictions from Dickens to Soap Opera*, newspaper and magazine comics, even if they used recurring characters, might be series but not "true serials": the strips sometimes featured recurring characters, but the narratives were episodic and repetitive.[5] Hayward argues that comic strips did not start telling continuing narratives until the 1920s and the 'Golden Age' of the adventure strip in the 1930s and 40s.[6]

In his *History of the Comic Strip: The Nineteenth Century*, Kunzle's main subject is the European comic, and he admits that due to the increasingly large volume of material being published over the course of the century, he had to leave the United States outside of his purview.[7] Kunzle's focus is very much on the formal developments of the comics in the nineteenth century, and in fact he ends his study just before the moment the newspaper strip as a comics form really establishes itself with significant economic success, widespread popular recognition, and syndication, though these elements were prefigured in the success of Charles Ross' and Marie Duval's newspaper hero and series *Ally Sloper*, which started in the late 1860s. Various elements relevant to newspaper comics publishing, that had been developing in a number of ways in Europe, including artistic styles, character building, and publication practices, came together fortuitously in the last decade of the nineteenth century in the United States, with technological advances in printing and public tastes all aligning to make the newspaper strip a popular form.[8] In *Comic Strips and Consumer Culture, 1890-1945*, Ian Gordon picks up where Kunzle's history leaves off, both by giving an overview of comics in mass publications in the U.S. that led up to newspaper strips becoming a fully established and commercially very successful form, as well as by shifting focus in foregrounding consumerism, thus exploring a different link between comics and the publication practices of the popular press.[9]

In the United States, many key developments during the last decade of the nineteenth century built on important groundwork that had been laid in previous years, with the development of the popular magazine press, printing techniques, and the use of techniques such as caricature, influences coming from both the U.S. and Europe. Weekly magazines like *Puck*, *Judge*, and *Life* included many illustrations, including numerous political cartoons. Narrative comics were less common, but a major contributor of short comics to American periodicals was Franklin Morris Howarth in the 1890s. His strips tended to be captioned, but occasionally he would also create wordless narratives.[10] In his discussion of the evolution of newspaper comic strips, it is also interesting to note that Gordon mentions in passing that several of the early ongoing comic strips were wordless, or 'pantomime', in their first appearances, for example Rudolph Dirks' *The Katzenjammer Kids* in 1897 and Frederick Burr Opper's *Happy Hooligan* in 1900. This silence was short-lived, however, and soon the strips took on the increasingly standardised newspaper strip format, with "[recurring] characters, panels, and word balloons."[11] Gordon spends some time discussing developments in the use of word balloons, in a way that implies that strips that use word balloons are more advanced than strips with textual captions underneath, or outside the panel, or strips without text. This is obviously very different from Kunzle's evaluation of the development of pictorial narrative in the European context, where pantomime comics were the height of achievement at this time.

The topics addressed in comics on both sides of the Atlantic were similar. Many late nineteenth-century comics deal with city life: busy streets, immigrants and vagrants, and apartment living, as Jared Gardner notes in *Projections: Comics and the History of Twenty-First-Century Storytelling*. The magazines and newspapers that comics appeared in were published in cities, and most of their readerships lived there, making city life a natural topic. Kunzle and Gordon also point to similar themes, and draw parallels between the 'modern' world and the comics form: Kunzle shows how the increasing movement of the outside world, on trains and in automobiles, was captured in the frequently frenetic activity on the comics page, often inspired by photographic effects, while Gordon draws attention to the reliance of comics on the processes of (mechanical) modernisation and notes the ways in which comics create an artistic outlet for commenting on the resulting societal change. Gordon writes: "As an outcome of modernisation comic strips appear as a social phenomenon, in this case one of the first widely consumed commodities produced by the mass entertainment industry." He goes so far as to say "comic strips helped create Modernism in both its formal art meaning and its broader cultural denotation", a claim that is also implied in Kunzle's work.[12] Gardner points out that the growing readership for the new entertainment media of comics as well as film were not completely unfamiliar with these forms that captured movement on the page, in contrast to the common assumption that audiences had a hard time adapting to new media forms.[13] Optical toys like the zoetrope and the phenakistiscope had already familiarised people with images that were fragmented into brief moments, breakdowns of action over space or the area of strips of paper and discs of cardboard.[14]

Zoetropes and phenakistiscopes showed movement taking on life from its fragments, and users could see those individual, fragmented moments when the instrument was at rest. It is not a big stretch from there to narratives broken down into fragments on paper. Töpffer's first comics were more or less contemporary with the popularisation of these optical toys. Earlier picture narratives, such as those by William Hogarth and Thomas Rowlandson in the eighteenth century, and George Cruikshank in the nineteenth, had used images as scenes, what comics historian Thierry Smolderen calls "readable images."[15] These plates were crammed with meaningful details that needed to be interpreted and took time to take in, besides being considered in their sequence.[16] The difference with Töpffer's picture stories was that his single images were simple and direct and relied on their sequence to be animated. Beyond representing movement on the page, Töpffer's work also showed the freedom that comics enjoyed in comparison with optical toys. Where the zoetrope and the phenakistiscope were limited to forever repeating the same action, Töpffer's visual stories were wide-ranging, rambling even, showing all kinds of increasingly absurd actions and situations in which his heroes ended up. In addition, the optical toys had very little space to allot for each instant, while comics were able to give more room on the page to individual moments. Where such moments in earlier picture stories had been carefully staged and often implied several actions, in stories by Töpffer individual panels generally represented only an instant, like the fragments on a zoetrope.[17] Töpffer's comics already use increased and decreased panel sizes for pacing and visual effect, variations that are impossible with proto-filmic moving pictures (as it is, of course, with film itself). A few decades later, the silent comics in the German weekly *Simplicissimus* often use wide horizontal panels that take up an entire tier, taking the space and thus time to set up an atmosphere for their settings and giving the eye, which was regimented in looking at and through a zoetrope, time to wander and take things in.

While comics are often called fragmented and the products of a frenetic world, they also gave readers the freedom to set their own pace and dwell on details in a way that many of the other popular entertainment forms of the time, such as vaudeville and eventually film, did not.[18] Audiences had witnessed the development of photography and numerous optical devices such as the zoetrope and, by the end of the century, the kinetoscope and the cinematograph, and were familiar with all kinds of fragmented pictures, artificially moving images, whether drawn or photographic, as well as caricature images, which was a form that had been evolving for over a century. While comics developed very rapidly through the middle of the nineteenth century, readers were well prepared to follow along with its progress, based on the many forms of visual culture that surrounded them.

Comics from earlier in the nineteenth century, such as those by Töpffer and Wilhelm Busch, told longer stories, as the adventures of M. Vieux Bois, and the seven tricks of Max and Moritz demonstrate. Later in the century, reading audiences were also familiar with narratives in instalments through the serial works of Charles Dickens, Anthony Trollope, and others. But as comics began to appear with more regularity in popular weekly magazines, they did not yet apply the same kind of narrative or the serial form.[19] Comic strips in the popular press in the later nineteenth century tended to be one-off vignettes as opposed to series, setting up characters, situation and punch line all in one page. And though comics would often deal with recurring types, they tended not to have recurring characters. An important exception is England's Ally Sloper, who was the hero of continuing episodes in various publications, including *Judy* and subsequently his own title, *Ally Sloper's Half Holiday*. He was one of only a few ongoing comics characters published in the 1870s, and though Sloper's adventures continued to be episodic and did not form a continuous, serialised narrative, the figure does constitute what Roger Sabin has called the "first comics superstar."[20] *Ally Sloper* also illustrates the difference between comics traditions in England and the continent. The strip had a format that was uncommon in France and Germany. Recurring characters were uncommon in Continental comics before the 1890s, including in the popular silent comic format, and they tended to be humorous. The great exceptions to this were Steinlen's black cat and Willette's Pierrot in the *Chat Noir* magazine in the 1880s. However, their stories were so dreamlike and surreal, that there is barely a sense of narrative, certainly not an ongoing one. One could go so far as to question whether it is in fact the same cat, or even the same Pierrot, who appears in these comics.[21]

Töpffer had put considerable effort into the narrative captions of his graphic narratives, making them as quirky and distinctive in their prose style as his drawings were visually. The comics that post-dated his also incorporated text in various forms, but usually with less attention to their composition. One exception was the German Wilhelm Busch (1832-1908) who is almost as famous for his sardonic rhyming couplets as for his much-imitated drawing style.[22] He is now best remembered for his story *Max und Moritz*, of 1865, which consists of seven sections or *Tricks* that the two naughty boys play. The

Part 2: Nineteenth-century visualisations

L'Humidité. Dessin de Caran d'Ache.

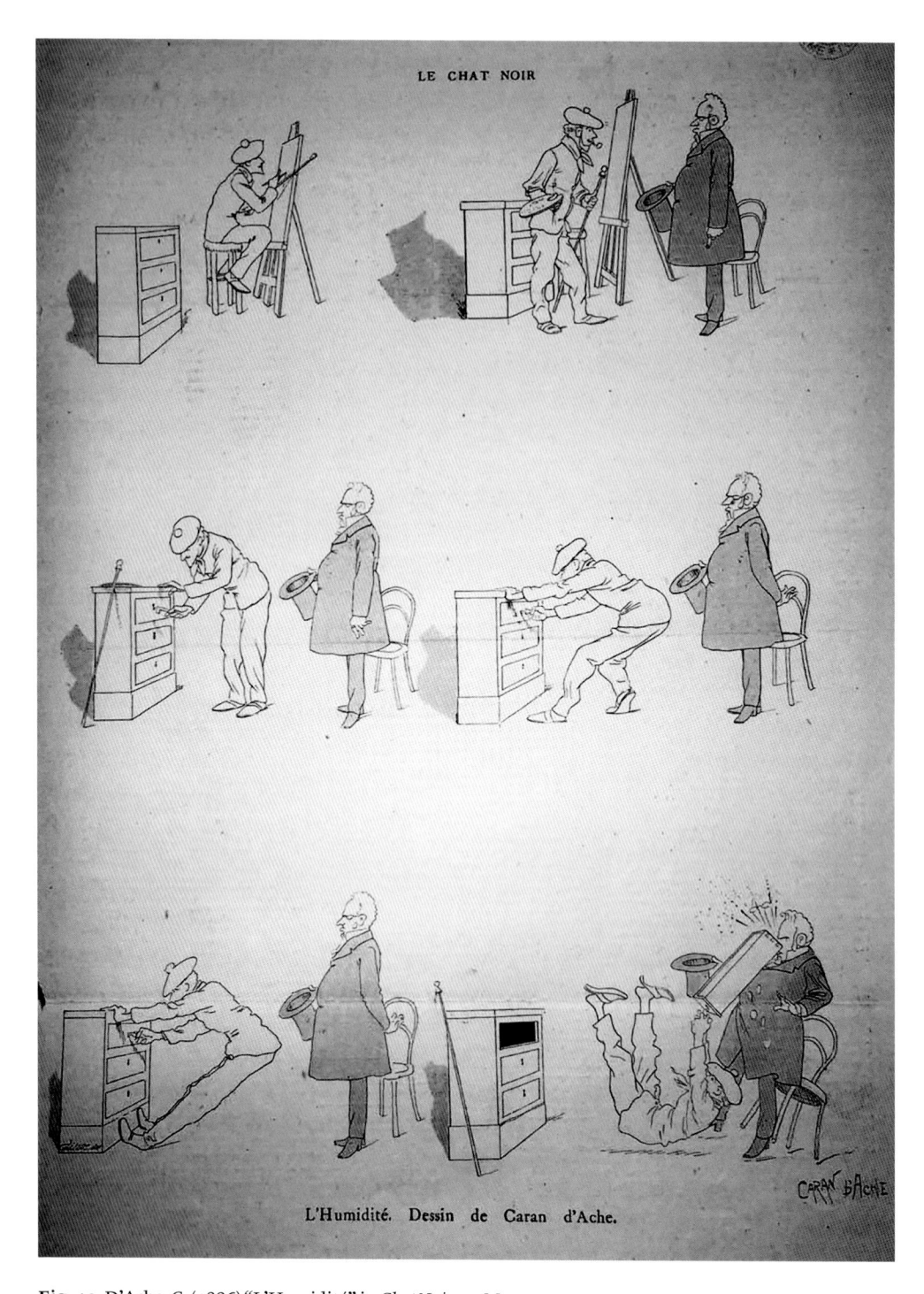

Fig. 10. D'Ache, C. (1886) "L'Humidité" in *Chat Noir*, 29 May, page 711.

drawings of *Max und Moritz* are accompanied by rhyming couplets that underscore the cruelly funny morality tale in the pictures. Ironically, Busch seems to have been the first cartoonist to start telling picture stories without the support of captions in the industrial age and for mass circulation. When he started his career as a cartoonist in 1859, making illustrations for the German weekly magazine *Fliegende Blätter*, many of his picture stories were wordless, allowing his dynamic and expressionistic art to shine. Groensteen calls Busch the pioneer of the wordless form, and indeed many other cartoonists quickly started following his example, first in Germany and then in France.[23] Adolf Oberländer (1845-1923) was another German wordless cartoonist of note, but it was in France that the genre really came into its own. Both David Kunzle and Thierry Groensteen point to Caran d'Ache as the most likely person to have introduced the wordless comic into the popular press in France, and he was certainly prolific in the form, contributing strips to numerous publications.[24]

Caran d'Ache is the pseudonym of Emmanuel Poiré (1858-1909), a Russian-born French son of a military man, who travelled throughout the continent before settling in France. He took his 'nom de plume' from the Russian word for pencil, 'karandash', which may explain why a Swiss colouring pencil manufacturer later took his name as its brand name. Caran d'Ache is also credited with having created, or at least planned, the first wordless long-form comic, with *Maëstro*. He discussed plans for the work in an 1894 letter to an editor of *Le Figaro*, where he summarised the story and projected it would run about 360 pages in length. The project was considered only a plan, until sections of the manuscript were discovered in the late twentieth century, and since then it has been published for the very first time by the Musée de la bande dessinée, reconstructed as far as possible by Thierry Groensteen, who also supplied the history of the work.[25]

Despite Caran d'Ache's ambitions for a long narrative, most of his work has the familiar short comic episode format that was common at the time. *L'Humidité* is such an anecdote, published in issue 229 of the *Chat Noir* weekly magazine on May 29, 1886 (see Fig. 10.). The strip is made up of six panels, two per tier, and though the page has a regularly structured layout, there are no borders separating the panels. The drawing is in very clear, simple pencil lines, with some stippling to provide shading. The strip demonstrates both the elegance of Caran d'Ache's line work, as well as the economy of his style, for example in the little variations in body language of the artist's visitor which betray his impatience. The title of the strip offers no clarification as to the plot, except to give the meteorological cause for the sticking drawer. The story is extremely simple, and though it may not strike one as a particularly funny punch line to see a rent collector violently struck in the face with a wooden object, Caran d'Ache's rendering is energetic, and fits into an ongoing dialogic series of comics about financially and otherwise challenged artists at the time.[26] This was a recurring theme in *Chat Noir* comics, with one strip even showing an artist feigning his own death to avoid paying what he owed – perhaps a veiled criticism against

Part 2: Nineteenth-century visualisations

Fig. 11. Schulz, W. (1896) "Umsonst" in *Simplicissimus*, 7 November, page 8.

the working conditions at the magazine, since Kunzle notes that Rodolphe Salis, editor of the magazine and owner of the famous cabaret of the same name, often did not pay his illustrators.[27] Alternatively, the continuous ribbing of fine artists in the *Chat Noir* and other publications may be an early indicator of the longstanding rivalry and jealousy between cartoonists or commercial artists and creators of the beaux arts.[28]

The *Chat Noir* made its silent one-page comic a regular weekly feature, one of its signature elements. This was by no means the case for all publications of the time. The satirical weekly magazine *Simplicissimus*, published in Munich starting in 1896, was heavily illustrated but contained only occasional one-page comic strips. These tended to be silent, although very rarely they included some text for dialogue. What sets the comics in *Simplicissimus* apart from *Chat Noir* and other contemporary publications is that they were frequently not humorous, nor meant to be. The most striking example of this tendency is the strip *Umsonst* by Wilhelm Schulz (1865-1952). Schulz was one of the original contributors to the magazine, and stayed with it throughout its almost fifty-year-long existence.[29] Schulz drew covers, illustrations for stories and poems (some of them his own), and the occasional comic. Schulz's visual style here is not one usually found in nineteenth-century comics. The pictures of this strip (which ran in issue 32, on November 7, 1896) appear to be drawn in a mix of ink pen, crayon and watercolour, with the grain of the paper showing through in some of the shading (See Fig. 11.). The page also uses red as an accent colour, notably in the child's bedding. Rather than the caricature outline drawings that we encountered in the previous example, Schulz's style is painterly, full of dark areas and shading. On the other hand, *Umsonst* does display what may strike us now as a very traditional use of panels.

The page has seven panels, all clearly framed, with neat gutters separating them. This is in contrast to most of the *Chat Noir* strips, which tended to have separate panels only implied by distribution across the page, as with the Caran d'Ache strip. The page is carefully balanced, with a diagonal symmetry in the panel layout, and inverting the scenes and settings of the two panels in the top and bottom tiers: the mother is going downstairs in the small panel at the top right, and going back upstairs upon returning home in the small panel in the bottom left. This symmetry draws attention to the sameness of the very first and last panels, the image of the child in bed, but also foregrounds the terrible difference between the two, the figure of the worried mother in the first panel replaced by the figure of Death at the bedside in the final image. The title *Umsonst*, which means 'in vain', adds the last tragic twist: the mother had gone out to earn money to take care of her ill boy, only to find him already taken away from her when she returns. The red of the blankets on the bed, which gave the room some cheer in the first panel, now accentuate the dead child's ashen face. Both in visual style and narrative content this silent comic from *Simplicissimus* is very different from the fare one encounters in *Chat Noir* or *Le Figaro*. However, the subject of prostitution, which here is treated simultaneously realistically and tragically, is a common one.[30]

Part 2: Nineteenth-century visualisations

The one-page strip *Cruelle Énigme* by F. Poitevin also deals with prostitution, but in a much lighter manner. This wordless comic appeared in issue 206 of *Chat Noir*, on December 19, 1885. The page is made up of nine borderless panels, three per tier, with the delineation of the panels often implied by the edges of furniture elements – a door, a pillow, and the recurring room screen, all in a scratchy pen and ink style. The first two panels show a well-dressed man arriving home and relaxing while reading his newspaper and smoking. In the third panel a woman arrives, who, from the way they shake hands, appears not to be his wife or another kind of acquaintance. In the second tier they get intimate over the newspaper: the woman reads to him from the paper and they embrace. When he gets too passionate she goes behind a room screen to get undressed, in the third panel. As she is disrobing, and one wonders to what extent her state of undress was regarded scandalous at the time, the woman notices that the man is reading the newspaper again. With a wagging finger (and a tapping foot?) she reprimands him from behind the screen, and in the final panel the newspaper has joined the woman's clothes behind the room screen, which now hides from view whatever the couple is doing on the other side.

In this case the story is amusing and quite daring, with the woman having to compete with the newspaper for the man's attentions, a light use of metafiction for the reader of the magazine. The mystery is provided here rather by the inclusion of a title, *Cruelle Énigme*, or 'cruel enigma,' which makes one wonder who or what is being cruel, and who or what the enigma is. Is the woman the enigma, since as a prostitute she is previously unknown to the client who has her over, and is she cruel for making him give up his newspaper? Or is there another play on words at work? The titles of silent comics pages carry a lot of weight, even if they are often only short. The title in Caran D'Ache's *L'Humidité* gave the cause for the landlord's misfortune, since it was the humidity that caused the drawer to get stuck due to the expanded wood of the cabinet. The word 'umsonst' adds a layer of tragedy to the comic of that title, while, to this reader at least, the title *Cruelle Énigme* could just as easily have been omitted. For a final example, the title *Der Triumph des Realismus* is essential to the meaning of the comic, adding a biting critique of contemporary art.

Der Triumph des Realismus was published in *Jugend* No. 25, on June 20, 1896. Like *Simplicissimus*, the weekly magazine *Jugend* started publication in 1896.[31] Whereas the former periodical was satirical and political in tone and focus, the latter foregrounded culture and aesthetics, and notably gave its name to the German term for Art Nouveau – 'Jugendstil' – based on the style of the illustrations that appeared on almost every single page. The three-tier wordless comic *Der Triumph des Realismus* is by Joseph Benedict Engl (1867-1907) and shows a painter at work in a farm yard. This painter had appeared before in Engl's work, in a wordless strip published in *Simplicissimus* in May of the same year. This earlier comic was called *Inspiration* and showed the artist trying to come up with ideas. When a bird lets its droppings fall on the painter's head he gets a sudden rush of inspiration, and in the final two panels we see the prize-winning magnum opus that he has created drawing crowds, and the painter resting happily on his laurels.

The comic published in June apparently shows the actual creation of the artist's famous work, since he is here in the process of painting that very same rural scene – a dung heap in a farm yard. When the artist has stepped away from his easel in the second panel, the farmer mistakes the painting for reality and tries to push his wheelbarrow up the painted plank instead of the real plank behind it. In the third panel the artist is shocked to find that the pigs have embraced his work and are wallowing on top of his painting. This little narrative is amusing enough on its own, but the title amplifies the ironic jab at the expense of the by then rather old-fashioned style of Realism in painting. Even the pigs love it, as do the so-called art lovers in *Inspiration*, but real connoisseurs, such as the discerning readers of *Jugend*, know that there are more interesting and important movements going on in the arts at this time. And while the realistic style may take in pigs and farmers, connoisseurs understand that painting cannot actually attempt to reproduce reality, and that the artist's own unique vision, as in Impressionism and Post-Impressionism, and of course Jugendstil itself, is more relevant.

The examples discussed above have illustrated some of the common subjects in wordless comics of the late nineteenth century. Besides the adventures of prostitutes and artists of various sorts, these subjects also included wives cuckolding their husbands, illicit romantic dalliances between servants of various sorts, and the pain of love in general, in addition to military life, petty crime, and, not unconnected, poverty, topics that had been common in popular culture since the Middle Ages. The German periodicals *Jugend* and *Simplicissimus* are striking for the originality of the subject matter in many of their comics, especially in comparison with the *Chat Noir*. While Caran d'Ache had introduced the form in France, Willette and Steinlen were the first artists to contribute the 'histoires sans parole', wordless stories, for *Chat Noir*, and they created a signature style for the periodical with their numerous comics in its first few years of publication. Their work stands out for its symbolist treatment of the common themes, wherein cupids, clowns, and cats stand in for mere mortals to populate morality tales, and though *Chat Noir* readers, literate and sophisticated as they were, often found the stories ambiguous, opaque, mysterious, the director of the magazine apparently never demanded the artists change their format and the weekly comic in *Chat Noir* remained silent throughout the existence of the magazine, even when other artists started contributing.[32] In many of these early strips a coherent story is hard to identify, or if events are recognisable, then the moral or ultimate meaning are still left distressingly open. Reading these episodes in the twenty-first century, one may wonder if it is due to a lack of historical and cultural knowledge that it is not clear what one is supposed to make of the story, or what the joke is. It may be of some comfort that Kunzle contends that even at the time readers had unanswered questions about the strips, and perhaps their open-endedness was part of the appeal. Kunzle discusses the one instance when Willette relented to the requests of the audience for more narration to his strips, and he provided, on a separate page, a text summary of the comic *Deux Pages d'Amour*. Kunzle demonstrates that this text version not only obliterates much of the charm and mystery of the wordless comic, it in fact raises more questions than it settles.[33]

Kunzle differentiates between various national traditions in comics by the late nineteenth century. The silent form was flourishing on the continent, and he discusses the French and German schools of wordless comics in detail, while in England, where the ground had seemed so fertile for comics earlier in the century, the comics format was languishing. England had been a leading force for illustrated journalism due to its relative freedom of the press and technological capacity, but publications were reluctant to take on narratives in comic strip form, and generally stuck with humorous spot illustrations, 'comic cuts,' instead.[34] After England's initial promise earlier in the century, by the second half of the nineteenth century, French and German periodicals took over in terms of the development of the comics form. Many well-known English humorous artists (Leech, Keene, Tenniel) never even tried the comics form, and Cruikshank did so only briefly.[35] Kunzle blames this on a dearth of sketch-like thinking. He writes "England lacked a figure in that peculiar balance of literary and pictorial, comic and narrative gifts that we find in Töpffer, Busch, and to a lesser degree in several French artists." Kunzle notes that the comics form in England "lacked prestige," as is demonstrated by the fact that the popular magazine *Punch* refused to print comic strips until well into the 1850s.[36] With this lack of institutional support, the form thus failed to attract the caliber of artists that it did on the continent, despite the important groundwork that had been laid by the likes of Hogarth, Rowlandson, and Gillray.

Whatever the overall quality of comics production in these areas, it is clear that the comics traditions in England did not incorporate a significant number of wordless comics or picture stories at the time. However, Kunzle perhaps somewhat overstates the importance of the wordless strip. He notes, "For Willette, Steinlen, and Caran d'Ache it became an index of graphic mastery to dispense with conventional verbal clarification", and render a narrative in images only.[37] He calls the trio "masters of the genre working at their best", but thereby also acknowledges his prejudice towards this particular form, apparently preferring it over more traditional comics.[38] Kunzle's inclinations lie in particular with the French practitioners of the form, and most notably Steinlen and Willette. He points to a development during the 1880s where "like painting, like poetry, the comic strip attains self-sufficiency and a certain purity by a process of abstraction and elimination: of shading, of background, of rational connections between scenes, of gridlike frames and layouts, and finally of text."[39] Of all wordless artists, that characterisation fits the comics of Willette and Steinlen best, as does the description that these comics are "like symbolist poetry, like impressionist painting, [where] the action flows in an open, atmospheric, rather than closed, perspectival space."[40] While his admiration is evident, it is perhaps also somewhat problematic that Kunzle singles out those works for his particular praise, which fit best into fine art traditions of image making. Even more problematic is equating these two singular artists with a French comics tradition, or even a *Chat Noir* signature style. In his article *The Voices of Silence*, Kunzle draws differences between the French and German styles of wordless comics, for the most part favouring the pages that Willette and Steinlen created for *Chat Noir*, which are atmospheric and ethereal. Kunzle contrasts this imagistic style with the spot-on, clearly rendered, "abbreviated" caricature of the "German school" spearheaded by Busch.[41] However, most of the later *Chat Noir* artists, and notably Caran d'Ache, had an abstracted, caricature style, while German artists like Wilhelm Schulz were atmospheric and painterly in their rendering.

While picture stories in the first half of the nineteenth century included text, their visual/verbal blend was restricted to combining narrative captions with illustrated panels. In *The Origins of Comics*, Thierry Smolderen points out that graphic narratives at this time did not include text for diegetic sound: panels did not include sound effects and the sporadic word balloons were used for identification and labeling purposes, not to indicate direct speech.[42] The step to omitting the narrative captions from picture stories, a transition that started in the 1860s and quickly became common, had a two-fold effect: it meant removing the reading instructions for the viewers and it changed the page structure.

With the removal of textual guidelines, readers of these picture stories instead had to pay closer attention to the images. One minor form of signposting for readers that was sometimes retained was the numbering of panels.[43] The imagery did not change significantly from captioned strips to wordless strips, as can be seen in studying works by Wilhelm Busch and Caran D'Ache, two artists who produced both silent and captioned comics. On the whole, the amount of visual information offered to the reader remained similar, and it was left up to the reader to decipher it. One result of wordlessness on narrative that Smolderen points out is that storylines often became more causality-driven. Especially in the silent strips in *Fliegende Blätter*, "the drawings presented a perfectly self-sufficient explanation of the chain of actions, and the fact that they didn't need (or entice) any paraphrase or commentary was probably their most salient feature: these purely visual 'sentences' were clearly the self-propelled products of the modern industrial age."[44] While these mechanical gags, often revolving around technology going haywire, were one result of the wordless trend, another result was the dreamlike comic without a reasoned narrative in which *Chat Noir* specialised.[45]

The blocks of captions in picture narratives from Hogarth onward had encouraged a structured page layout to accommodate under-panel caption texts, and the result of removing captions was a page structure that could be freer and more fluid. Steinlen and Willette's *Chat Noir* strips of the 1880s made full use of the flexibility an unstructured page design offered. Meanwhile, the illustrations in Smolderen's *Origins of Comics* show that eventually, captioned comics began to emulate this more fluid page structure as well, reducing the length of captions and inserting them in less obtrusive ways so that there too the visuals of the page became more important.[46]

One piece of text that wordless comics did retain was the title. In some cases the title was only generic, for example the commonly used 'histoire sans parole.' At other times, the title was purely descriptive, such as Hans Schliessmann's *Ein Bubenstreich*, or 'a scoundrel's trick', showing an errand boy playing a trick on an older man.[47] In some cases, the title provides extra meaning or irony to the silent comic, as with the examples discussed above, or it may even provide a key to understanding the strip. Caran D'Ache's famous strip *Une vache qui regarde passer le train*, ('a cow watching a train go by') does not actually show a train, only the cow. Just about the only thing moving in this eight-panel strip is the cow's eyes, which slowly move from left to right, and it is this phlegmatic reaction to a train that is only implied which makes the gag.[48]

Whatever differences existed between national schools and traditions, short silent picture stories were esteemed and sought-after in the late nineteenth century in Continental Europe, as evidenced by their inclusion in high circulation newspapers such as *Le Figaro*, as well as critically admired periodicals such as *Chat Noir* and *Jugend* from the 1880s onwards. These wordless comics were popular, even mainstream at the time, in a way that they have not been since then, until this very decade.[49]

Notes

1. Kunzle, D. (2001) "The Voices of Silence: Willette, Steinlen and the Introduction of the Silent Strip in the *Chat Noir*, with a German Coda." in Varnum, R. And Gibbons, C. *The Language of Comics: Word and Image*. Jackson: University Press of Mississippi, pages 190 – 191.
2. Research for this chapter was made possible in part by the generous support from the Modern Literature and Culture Research Centre at Ryerson University and a SSHRC postdoctoral fellowship, which allowed me to go to the archive of the Cité internationale de la bande dessinée et de l'image (CIBDI) in Angoulême to study the *Chat Noir* magazine.
3. Smolderen, T. (2014) *The Origin of Comics*. University Press of of Mississippi, page 75.
4. Groensteen, T. (1997) "Histoire de la bande dessinée muette. Première partie." in *9e Art (Neuvième art)* 2, page 64.
5. Hayward, J. (1997) *Consuming Pleasures: Active Audiences and Serial Fictions from Dickens to Soap Opera*. Lexington: University Press of Kentucky, page 90.
6. Ibid., page 93.
7. Kunzle, D. (2001) "The Voices of Silence: Willette, Steinlen and the Introduction of the Silent Strip in the *Chat Noir*, with a German Coda." in Varnum, R. And Gibbons, C. *The Language of Comics: Word and Image*. Jackson: University Press of Mississippi, page 5.
8. Gordon, I. (1998) *Comic Strips and Consumer Culture: 1890-1945*. Washington: Smithsonian Institution Press, page 24.
9. Kunzle, D. (2001) "The Voices of Silence: Willette, Steinlen and the Introduction of the Silent Strip in the *Chat Noir*, with a German Coda." in Varnum, R. And Gibbons, C. *The Language of Comics: Word and Image*. Jackson: University Press of Mississippi, page 12.
10. In a chapter called *The Piano in the American Home*, Foy and Marlin's edited collection includes an example of a wordless Howarth strip that shows a boy playing his parents off against one another to get out of having to practice playing the piano, which was published in *Puck* in 1895.

11 Gordon, I. (1998) *Comic Strips and Consumer Culture: 1890-1945*. Washington: Smithsonian Institution Press, pages 34 – 36.
12 Ibid, page 6. And Kunzle 1990:377 – 378.
13 Gardner, J. (2012) *Projections: Comics and the History of Twenty-First-Century Storytelling*. Stanford: Stanford Uuniversity Press, page 4.
14 Jonathan Crary discusses these devices at length in *Techniques of the Observer: On Vision and Modernity in the Nineteenth Century*. Cambridge: MIT Press, 1990, pp. 107-110. See also Gardner, J. (2012) *Projections: Comics and the History of Twenty-First-Century Storytelling*. Stanford: Stanford University Press, page 4.
15 Smolderen, T. (2014) *The Origin of Comics*. University Press of Mississippi, page 3.
16 Ibid., page 11.
17 Hogarth's scenes include major and minor characters and meaningful objects in the fore- and backgrounds, blending his satiric caricature with traditions of fine art painting, especially historical painting.
18 Kunzle, D. (1990). *The History of the Comic Strip. Vol. 2: The Nineteenth Century*. Berkeley: University of California Press, 1990, page 10.
19 Jennifer Hayward discussed the heyday of serialised newspaper comics narrative in the 1930s in *Consuming Pleasures*, with Milton Caniff's *Terry and the Pirates* as her case study. Harward, J. (1997) *Consuming Pleasures: Active Audiences and Serial Fictions from Dickens to Soap Opera*. Lexington: University Press of Kentucky, pages 84 – 134.
20 Sabin, R. (2009) "Ally Sloper: The First Comics Superstar?" in Heer, J. and Worcester, K. Ed. *A Comics Studies Reader*. Jackson: University Press of Mississippi, page 177.
21 By the 1890s, there were several recurring characters in the French popular press, mostly developed by Christophe (pseudonym of Georges Colombe). His series included *La Famille Fenouillard* and *Le Sapeur Camember*.
22 Kunzle, D. (1990). *The History of the Comic Strip. Vol. 2: The Nineteenth Century*. Berkeley: University of California Press, 1990, page 244.
23 Groensteen, T. (1997) "Histoire de la bande dessinée muette. Première partie." in *9e Art (Neuvième art)* 2, page 60.
24 Kunzle, D. (1990). *The History of the Comic Strip. Vol. 2: The Nineteenth Century*. Berkeley: University of California Press, 1990, page 178; Groensteen 1997, 62).
25 Groensteen, T. (2002) "Caran d'Ache : le retour du *Maestro*." in *9e Art (neuvième art)* 7, page 10).
26 The *Histoires sans paroles du Chat Noir* published by the Musée de la bande dessinée, Angoulême, in 1998 is a collection of *Chat Noir* strips, including episodes about artists on pages 11, 16, 41, 52, and 62, for example.
27 Kunzle, D. (1990). *The History of the Comic Strip. Vol. 2: The Nineteenth Century*. Berkeley: University of California Press, 1990, page 192.
28 Many twentieth-century instances of this rivalry are discussed in Bart Beaty's *Comics versus Art*. See, for example, pages 53 and 54.
29 Information about the contributors to the *Simplicissimus* magazine can be found on the website collecting all the scanned issues. Schulz' information is here: http://www.simplicissimus.info
30 The *Histoires sans paroles du Chat Noir* (see note 26) includes episodes that deal with prostitution in some way on pages 34, 56, 57, and 59. I found many more instances in the issues of the *Chat Noir* in the archives of the CIBDI.

31 Complete runs of both *Simplicissimus* and *Jugend* have been digitised and can be found online at http://www.simplicissimus.info/ and http://www.jugend-wochenschrift.de/ respectively.
32 Smolderen argues convincingly that comics did not start using balloons to "synchronise" sound until the turn of the twentieth century, at which point the comics finally "created an audiovisual stage on paper". See Smolderen, T. (2014) *The Origin of Comics*. University Press of Mississippi, pages 146 and 147.
33 Kunzle, D. (2001) "The Voices of Silence: Willette, Steinlen and the Introduction of the Silent Strip in the *Chat Noir*, with a German Coda." in Varnum, R. And Gibbons, C. *The Language of Comics: Word and Image*. Jackson: University Press of Mississippi, pages 5 and 9.
34 Ibid., pages 6 and 10.
35 Kunzle, D. (1990). *The History of the Comic Strip. Vol. 2: The Nineteenth Century*. Berkeley: University of California Press, 1990, page 5 and 308.
36 Ibid, page 5.
37 Ibid., page 5 and 314.
38 Ibid., page 375.
39 Kunzle, D. (2001) "The Voices of Silence: Willette, Steinlen and the Introduction of the Silent Strip in the *Chat Noir*, with a German Coda." in Varnum, R. And Gibbons, C. *The Language of Comics: Word and Image*. Jackson: University Press of Mississippi, page 4.
40 Kunzle, D. (1990). *The History of the Comic Strip. Vol. 2: The Nineteenth Century*. Berkeley: University of California Press, 1990, page 178.
41 Ibid.
42 Ibid.
43 I discuss the current popularity of wordless comics, as well as some possible reasons for this popularity, in my chapter "Silent Comics" in the *Routledge Companion to Comics and Graphic Novels*, forthcoming in 2015.
44 Smolderen, T. (2014) *The Origin of Comics*. University Press of Mississippi, page 85.
45 Ibid., page 113.
46 Kunzle. D. (2001) "The Voices of Silence: Willette, Steinlen and the Introduction of the Silent Strip in the *Chat Noir*, with a German Coda." in Varnum, R. And Gibbons, C. *The Language of Comics: Word and Image*. Jackson: University Press of Mississippi, page 6.
47 Smolderen, T. (2014) *The Origin of Comics*. University Press of Mississippi, pages 77 and 88.
48 Ibid., page 114.
49 Groensteen, T. (1997) "Histoire de la bande dessinée muette. Première partie." *9e Art* (*Neuvième art*) 2, pages 62 – 63 and Smolderen, T. (2014) *The Origin of Comics*. University Press of Mississippi, page 129.

References

d'Ache, C. (1999) *Maestro*. Angoulême: Musée de la bande dessinée.
d'Ache, C. (1886) "L'Humidité." In *Chat Noir* 29 May, page 711.
Beaty, B. (2012) *Comics versus Art*. Toronto: University of Toronto Press.
Beronä, D. A. (2008) *Wordless Books: The Original Graphic Novels*. New York: Abrams.
Cham (1871) *Les Folies de la Commune*. Paris: L'Eclipse.
Crary, J. (1990) *Techniques of the Observer: On Vision and Modernity in the Nineteenth Century*. Cambridge: MIT Press.

Engl, J. B. (1896) "Der Triumph des Realismus." in *Jugend* 20 June, page 403.

Engl, J. B. (1896) "Inspiration." in *Simplicissimus* 23 May, page 5.

Foy, J. H. and Marling, K. A. Ed. (1994) *The Arts and the American Home, 1890-1930*. Knoxville: University of Tennessee Press.

Gardner, J. (2012) *Projections: Comics and the History of Twenty-First-Century Storytelling*. Stanford: Stanford Uuniversity Press.

Gordon, I. (1998) *Comic Strips and Consumer Culture: 1890-1945*. Washington: Smithsonian Institution Press.

Groensteen, T. (2002) "Caran d'Ache : le retour du *Maestro*." In *9e Art (neuvième art)* 7, pages 10 – 15.

Groensteen, T. (1998) "Histoire de la bande dessinée muette. Deuxième partie." *9e Art (Neuvième art)* 3, pages 92 – 105.

Groensteen, T. (1997) "Histoire de la bande dessinée muette. Première partie." *9e Art (Neuvième art)* 2, pages 60 – 75.

Hayward, J. (1997) *Consuming Pleasures: Active Audiences and Serial Fictions from Dickens to Soap Opera*. Lexington: University Press of Kentucky.

Kunzle, D. (2009) "Rodolphe Töpffer's Aesthetic Revolution." in Heer, J. and Worcester, K. Ed. *A Comics Studies Reader*. Jackson: University Press of Mississippi, pages 17-24.

Kunzle, D. (2001) "The Voices of Silence: Willette, Steinlen and the Introduction of the Silent Strip in the *Chat Noir*, with a German Coda." in Varnum, R. And Gibbons, C. *The Language of Comics: Word and Image*. Jackson: University Press of Mississippi.

Kunzle, D. (1990). *The History of the Comic Strip. Vol. 2: The Nineteenth Century*. Berkeley: University of California Press.

Kunzle, D. (1972). *The History of the Comic Strip. Vol. 1: The Early Comic Strip, c. 1450-1825*. Berkeley: University of California Press.

Poitevin, F. "Cruelle Énigme." *Chat Noir* 19 Dec. 1885: 615.

Sabin, R. (2009) "Ally Sloper: The First Comics Superstar?" in Heer, J. and Worcester, K. Ed. *A Comics Studies Reader*. Jackson: University Press of Mississippi, pages 177 – 189.

Schulz, W. (1896) "Umsonst." in *Simplicissimus* 7 Nov.

Smolderen, T. (2014) *The Origin of Comics*. University Press of Mississippi.

Unnamed authors. (1998) *Histoires sans paroles du Chat Noir*. Angoulême: Musée de la bande dessinée.

Part 3

Using the Victorians: appropriation, adaptation and historiography

Marie-Luise Kohlke

"Abominable pictures": neo-Victorianism and the tyranny of the sexual taboo

Constituting a self-conscious re-engagement with the nineteenth century and its aesthetic, socio-political, and ideological legacies, the cultural phenomenon of neo-Victorianism is fundamentally intertwined with notions of transgression and subversion, both of the norms of the period and our assumptions about it.[1] Neo-Victorian works simultaneously acknowledge our predecessors' continuing influence over our own postmodern culture and revolt against it, attempting to assert our essential difference from our historical Others. In the neo-Victorian novel, this is nowhere more apparent than in the insistent exposure of the supposedly repressed Victorians' secret sex lives and illicit carnal practices and pursuits, often combined with poking fun at the excessive value which the nineteenth century placed on modesty and decorum in all matters of the human body, especially its sensual and reproductive capabilities.[2] J. G. Farrell's 1973 *The Siege of Krishnapur*, set at the time of the Indian Mutiny – or, to respect postcolonial sensitivities, India's First War of Independence – provides a resonant example in point. Early on in the novel, the tourist George Fleury, recently arrived at an outlying cantonment, visits the local Maharaja's palace as a guest of Hari, the ruler's son and heir, a voluble admirer of all things British from fashion to science and technology. During a tour of the royal residence, as the young men look in on the sleeping Maharaja, Hari promises to show Fleury "many wonderful things", swiftly adding the enquiry: "First and foremost, you would like perhaps to see abominable pictures?"[3] An affirmative is clearly assumed to be a foregone conclusion. The tantalising invitation to sensationalised spectatorship self-consciously, even metafictionally, focalises one of the main attractions of neo-Victorianism as a cultural phenomenon: to indulge in "abominable" re-imaginings of the nineteenth century so as to attack, deconstruct, and violate the period's one-time taboos – as well as some of our own.

Lighted rags having been brought to illuminate the shadowy bedroom wall, "a large and disgusting oil painting sprang out of the gloom", depicting "such an intricate mass of limbs that [Fleury] was quite unable to fathom what it was all about (though it was clearly very lewd indeed)".[4] The scene is self-evidently comedic, even more so for today's readers than Farrell's immediately post Sexual Revolution audience, for the two-dimensional static figures we are asked to envisage could hardly compete in lewdness with the real-life moving images of simulated and actual copulation omnipresent on today's cinema, television, and computer screens, on internet sites and in hardcore pornography. The picture precipitates a self-reflexive break in the fictional illusion, akin to that in *I Need Light*, the first episode of the BBC's 2012-2013 *Ripper Street*, Series One, in which Detective Inspector Edmund Reid (Matthew Macfadyen) of H Division in London's East End and his co-investigators, Detective Sergeant Bennett Drake (Jerome Flynn) and the forensic specialist Homer Jackson (Adam Rothenberg), realise that a murder, staged to look like another Jack the Ripper killing, is actually linked to a burgeoning industry in experimental sex and snuff movies. At one point Jackson describes the "more ... evolved" graphic stills of "the act itself" as "the future of smut" – namely the Victorians' future we now inhabit.[5] Later, after discovering a segment of film in the darkroom of the photographer Cecil Creighton (Julian Bleach), Reid wonders "Now what, what if you could make these images move? And make them be real?", causing Drake to anticipate that "Then they'd make more" – and ever more thereafter in an exponential propagation, as the audience knows all too well.[6] We cannot help but draw a parallel with our own historical moment and the further proliferation of sexual, obscene, and illegal images through postmodernity's comparable technological innovations: the internet with its radical impact on society since the 1990s and, more lately, mobile phone technology. Unsurprisingly, *The Siege of Krishnapur* likewise foresees this pornographically liberated future in a subsequent scene, in which the 'fallen woman' Lucy Hughes is covered by swarms of flying black cockchafers and tears off her clothes in panic, only to have the insects envelop her white flesh over and over again as soon as she brushes them away or they fall off from their own combined weight. The "flickering image of Lucy's delightful nakedness", alternately exposed and obscured, produces a quasi-cinematic effect of a tantalising striptease caught on early black-and-white film, inspiring Fleury to conceive of the possibility of "a series of daguerreotypes which would give the impression of movement."[7]

In the earlier scene, however, Fleury declines Hari's offer to show him "more disgraceful pictures", claiming that he is "not very well up in this sort of thing", an attitude applauded by Hari, who misreads it to mean that "[f]or a gentleman 'well up' in science and progress" lewd imagery "is not in the least rather interesting."[8] Yet as obvious to the reader, and as confirmed by Fleury's first ever sight of a (living) naked female body in the later cockchafer scene, the English protagonist's dismissive attitude stems not from superior scientific interests but disconcerted ignorance: although in his twenties, Fleury is a male version of the sexual ingénue, a repressed Victorian virgin. Hari's abashed response to having Fleury witness the subsequent intrusion of a sacred cow into the Maharaja's bed chamber – "This is most backward" – resonates ironically with Fleury's inhibited attitude towards the tabooed pleasures of the flesh, as well as our own progressive age's increasing, rather than lessening, obsession with all things sexual.[9] The humour arises from the contrast between Fleury's sexual nescience and Farrell's readers' sexual sophistication: Fleury's flustered embarrassment at something no longer objectionable strikes us as ludicrous, not to say pathetic, for a grown man. Metaphorically, Farrell is slaughtering the Victorian's sacred cow of self-disciplining restraint on the subject of sex. Like the Indians who will shortly rise up against their colonial overlords, the neo-Victorian novel stages a would-be War of Independence against sexual repression, which the Victorians and their mainstream literature continue to embody in the cultural imaginary regardless of contradictory evidence about the period.[10]

We live in a world where the taboo as that which is unthinkable and unspeakable has become largely redundant.[11] At least in most of Western secularised culture, and especially with regards to sexuality, the very idea of the taboo has been relegated to categories of the repressively antiquated and "backward". Not least, as Sue Harper and Justin Smith remark, the popular "slogan 'the personal is political'" ensured that post-1960s "the concepts of privacy and decorum would never be the same again."[12] Admittedly there are a handful of exceptions, namely what might be termed the 'ultimate' taboos, but most one-time unmentionables in nineteenth-century polite society, such as homosexuality, interracial relationships, blasphemy, profanity, bodily display and pornography, are now accepted as commonplace and, if not necessarily endorsed or tolerated by all, are officially recognised and increasingly protected by the law, including in areas such as free speech and expression, anti-discrimination legislation, and marriage and adoption rights for gay and lesbian couples.[13] Postmodernity's 'no-go' areas are no longer primarily delimited by proscribed objects, persons, acts and practices, but rather by politically incorrect attitudes – sexism, racism, homophobia, ableism, etc. – towards other individuals, by any attempts at perceived illegitimate intervention in, or regulation of, those subjects' morality, lifestyle choices, and self-expression, and by inappropriate language that is felt to violate others' rights. As Kate Burridge puts it:

> the new taboos are legally recognised sanctions against what might be dubbed -IST *language* (sexist, racist, ageist, religionist, etc. language). The basic human right of respect is understood to mean that people can no longer speak of or to others in terms that are considered insulting and demeaning and there is a new apprehensiveness and shunning of anything that may be interpreted as discriminatory or pejorative.[14]

Yet with the reliance on incontestable authorities and master narratives having been rendered questionable, if not defunct, by post-structuralism's relativism, the whole notion of taboo is also cast into doubt. For who or what is left to arbitrate on political correctness, determining what is and is not "insulting" and "discriminatory"?[15] Indeed, since the taboo, though always historically and culturally contingent, relies on prohibitions collectively assumed to be sacrosanct and self-evident, 'Taboo' – like 'Empire' or 'Progress' – can be understood as a master narrative, becoming ethically suspect. In the pluralist age of freedom for all, interdiction itself risks being proscribed as a form of prejudicial invasion of privacy and/or individual rights – not least the right to desire. Put differently, the one-time taboo is transformed into a category not of abhorrence but desire (though paradoxically also a desire for abhorrence, as will be shown).

There is an unexpected problem, however, with attempting any straightforward reading of Farrell's "abominable pictures" scene as an iconoclastic jettisoning of outworn taboos. To reduce the passage to a self-congratulatory pillorying of the benighted Victorians as part of a celebration of our own sexual liberation misses the point of the irony. Farrell, after all, is mocking Fleury, the representative of Western enlightenment, "science and progress", as much as and more than the "backward" indigene. In a sense, Fleury functions as the herald of his society's future and hence as the stand-in for the modern reader. Even as we are invited to view the Victorians as our pitiable Others (akin to how Farrell's British protagonists regard the 'primitive' Indians), as historical curiosities and oddities, embodiments of outmoded values, attitudes, and ideologies long superseded, we are also implicitly aligned/identified with those same disparaged Victorians as the target of the text's irony.

Michel Foucault's "repressive hypothesis" famously postulated that the Victorians' often alleged and derided repression on the subject of sex actually facilitated, in direct proportion, an increased craving for and "steady proliferation of discourses concerning sex" via new channels developed or adapted for the purpose, resulting in "an institutional incitement to speak about it, and to do so more and more."[16] Among others, these channels included medicine (the study of hysteria, gynaecology, sexology, etc.), sensationalist journalism (such as W.T. Stead's 1885 *The Maiden Tribute of Modern Babylon* and the 1895 coverage of Oscar Wilde's trial), legal campaigns (for example, against the Contagious Diseases Acts and to raise the age of consent), advertising (not least, for corsetry and other undergarments), and debates on sanitation and housing reform (partly justified on the basis of combating incest among the urban poor). Analogously, one might argue that today's no-holds-barred free-for-all concerning sex, its explicit representation and ubiquitous saturation of all levels of culture generates a corresponding yearning for and writing about its opposite, namely repression – or at least for a re-imagined new/old repressive framework or context that whets jaded appetites by rendering sexuality once more subversively 'transgressive' and thus more potently exiting. Shani Rousso's concept of "nostalgia for the limitations of taboo" suggests something similar:

from the position of relative liberalism of the late twentieth/early twenty-first century, historical frameworks might be employed in order to recreate a sense of heightened sexual desire for the unobtainable and forbidden object, and to reconstruct the sexual charge of transgressing social boundaries.[17]

Rousso specifically identifies the turn to the repressive Victorian past as the correlative to the current comparative lack of sexual restraint.[18] Similarly, Christian Gutleben contends that the re-imagined nineteenth-century setting acts as a guarantor for the recovery of a lost subversive edge to sexuality: any "intrusion of sex" into the fictional world "constitutes *ipso facto* an offence against the rules of modesty. One could say that, in the context of a Victorian fabula, the phallus is necessarily shamelessly subversive."[19] Repression becomes not just desirable, but *essential* for subversion to take place, since without repression it would no longer *be* subversion and lose all its audacious potential to shock, infringe, defile, profane, and scandalise.[20] Neo-Victorianism thus exemplifies what might be termed the 'anti-repressive hypothesis'.

The resulting sexual irony, one which rebounds upon the reader as in *The Siege of Krishnapur*, occurs in other prominent neo-Victorian novels. In John Fowles' iconic 1969 *The French Lieutenant's Woman*, the interminable build-up to the consummation scene between Charles Smithson and Sarah Woodruff, the titular, presumed fallen woman (though actually a virgin), functions as a veritable narrative 'tease'. When it finally happens, however, the sex-act for which Fowles' readers, like Charles, have waited for so long is begun and concluded in a mere one-and-a-half minutes:

He began to ejaculate at once.
  'Oh, my dearest. My dearest. My sweetest angel … Sarah, Sarah … oh, Sarah.'
  A few moments later he lay still. Precisely ninety seconds had passed since he had left her to look into the bedroom.[21]

Likewise the consummation itself takes no longer (actually rather less) than "ninety seconds" to read, so that it comes across more akin to *coitus interruptus* than the anticipated 'money shot'.[22] The payoff for the readers' investment in the narrative proves comically disappointing, forcing us to question whether we have not over-invested in a new master narrative of Sexual Liberation. The violation of Victorian taboos thus enables writers to play unsettling games with reader expectations.

Similarly, A.S. Byatt's 1990 *Possession: A Romance*, which chronicles two parallel romantic relationships in the Victorian and the late twentieth century, turns exceedingly coy when it comes to the sex scenes themselves, re-enacting the constraint exercised in mainstream nineteenth-century literature. In "The White Bed of Desire" in A.S. Byatt's *Possession*, Jennifer M. Jeffers fittingly notes the novel's curious "achromatic" politics, its extensive employment of white rather than, as one might expect, the colour red as the "trope of desire."[23] I would suggest that this can also be read as a strategic blanking or renewed obscuration of sexuality; as the modern-day protagonist Roland Michell pointedly remarks of 'écriture féminine' criticism, in Byatt's novel too, "[s]exuality [is] like thick smoked glass", afforded and affording limited visibility.[24] When the (fictional) Victorian poets Randolph Henry Ash and Christabel LaMotte finally come together, LaMotte's body is wholly covered in "a high-necked white lawn nightdress", and the consummation itself is rendered as a lacuna, disappearing into the white space of a line break on the page:

> When he took her in his arms, it was she who said, harshly, 'Are you afraid?'
> 'Not in the least, now,' he said. 'My selkie, my white lady, Christabel.'
>
> That was the first of those long strange nights. She met him with passion, fierce as his own, [...] she exacted her pleasure from him, opened herself to it, clutched for it, with short animal cries.[25]

This is a curiously cool, insubstantial recreation of the sex act; the lovers' couch hardly proves a bed of white-hot desire. While pretending to be open and explicit about sex – "pleasure", "passion", "clutched", "animal cries" – the passage depicts hardly anything at all, leaving the physical encounter to the reader's imagination. It comes nowhere near to what Byatt's self-conscious narrator elsewhere describes as postmodernity's exposure-driven, "proliferated sexual language" so well-known to the novel's twentieth-century protagonists and literary critics, Roland Michell and Maud Bailey: "they knew about phallocracy and penisneid, punctuation, puncturing and penetration, about polymorphous and polysemous perversity, orality, good and bad breasts, clitoral tumescence, vesicle persecution, the fluids, the solids, the metaphors for these."[26] In the Victorian sex scene, there is neither a single glimpse of breasts, genitals, or buttocks, nor a single drop of sweat, vaginal or seminal fluid in sight.[27] So too in the case of Michell and Bailey's consummation towards the close of *Possession*, where Byatt once more resorts to oblique and euphemistic 'Victorian' language, as signalled with metafictional emphasis:

> Roland finally, *to use an outdated phrase*, entered and took possession of all her white coolness that grew warm against him, so that there seemed to be no boundaries, and he heard towards dawn, from a long way off, her clear voice crying out, uninhibited, unashamed, in pleasure and triumph.[28]

Meanwhile the long-term lesbian relationship implied to exist between LaMotte and the painter Blanche Glover, who live together, goes wholly unrepresented.[29] Put differently, while sexual desire drives the novel's narrative action, sex itself is excised, as though (once more) too taboo to be pictured outright.[30]

In spite of "there seem[ing] to be no boundaries" to what can be spoken or shown, boundaries are reinstated through the conscious artifice of resorting to a new/old spurious prudery which, crucially, takes itself quite seriously rather than being intended as parodic. As Gutleben puts it, "[i]n the light of retro-Victorian fiction's art of unrestrained exhibition, it is easy to find new values to Victorian euphemisms and understatements, to the unsaid and unshown, to the latent and implicit, to potentiality and imagination."[31] Byatt's narrative stratagem demonstrates the anti-repressive hypothesis at work, playfully reactivating the taboo to rekindle the mystery of sexuality as an almost arcane power, now implicitly lost, to make it intrigue and fascinate anew in an age of hypersexual desensitisation and exhaustion. Drawing on Roland Barthes' 1973 *The Pleasure of the Text*, Jeffers explains that "desire is 'in' the game, in the ruses, in the spaces, between the said, the not said" of Byatt's text, where "the game [...] of perpetuation through lack" is continued indefinitely to tantalise and prolong readerly desire.[32] As Jeffers concludes – this time extemporising on Foucault's improvisation on Steven Marcus' work[33] – "taboo is the very ruse that arouses and titillates those Other Victorians – as well as We 'Other Victorians'."[34] The transgression of Victorian taboos conversely ends in the embrace of the anti-repressive hypothesis, to the point that Michell and Bailey at times seem envious of their Victorian counterparts and what they deem Ash and Lamotte's more vital connection with the instinctual life of the senses and emotions, as opposed to their own isolated cerebral lives.

The emerging picture, then, is arguably more complicated than Jonathan Loesberg suggests, in attributing a shared theme to *The French Lieutenant's Woman* and *Possession*: the attempted "declaration of some form of freedom" from the Victorians and 'their' repression, ironically based on the same quest pursued by the Victorians, namely "to find a truth about sexuality" taken to define the self.[35] While Loesberg rightly asserts that both texts fundamentally rely on an assumed "prior contrast between Victorian reticence and modern openness" about sexuality, it seems to me that the writers' deployments of this distinction, regardless of the negative or positive connotations they imbue it with, primarily serve another purpose than facilitating oppositional identity-formation for characters and readers.[36] Not least, the texts repeatedly conflate 'us' with the Victorians, while illustrating a sort of 'repression-envy' rather than disavowing repression altogether. As Michell and Bailey discover, the postmodern disavowal of the taboo does not necessarily make for happier (sex) lives, leading to a reflexive repression-envy for the very thing we so eagerly cast off as outdated. In much the same way, obliquely evoking Christianity's primal taboo and transgression, namely the forbidden Tree of Knowledge and the apple theft in Genesis, the narrator of *The French Lieutenant's Woman* ironically remarks that

> desire is conditioned by the frequency it is evoked: our world spends a vast amount of its time inviting us to copulate, while our reality is as busy in frustrating us. We are not so frustrated as the Victorians? Perhaps. But if you can only enjoy one apple

a day, there's a great deal to be said against living in an orchard of the wretched things; you might even find apples sweeter if you were allowed only one a week. So it seems very far from sure that the Victorians did not experience a much keener, because less frequent, sexual pleasure than we do; and that they were not dimly aware of this, and so chose a convention of suppression, repression and silence to maintain the keenness of the pleasure.[37]

By reinstating what Virginia Woolf called the past's "barriers of reticence and reserve",[38] *The French Lieutenant's Woman* and *Possession* seek to recapture what Fowles' narrator terms "the keenness of the pleasure", rendering the sex-act not a revealed or revelatory truth, but once again *a construct of fantasy and desire* left to the reader's tantalised imagination to concretise.

Admittedly, other neo-Victorian texts resist this renewed turn to reticence, most obviously when engaging with nineteenth-century sexual subcultures, the Victorian pornography business and sex industry, or any combination of these. Thus Sarah Waters' 1998 *Tipping the Velvet* re-imagines well-to-do Sapphist and working-class lesbian circles and clubs, where sex is explicitly discussed just as it is graphically represented on the novel's pages (definitely with bodily fluids, unlike in *Possession*) – perhaps most famously in scenes involving the rich hedonist Diana Lethaby's dildo, notoriously lingered over in Andrew Davies' screenplay for the 2002 BBC adaptation. A Victorian euphemism for cunnilingus, Waters' choice of title, of course, blatantly highlights sexuality's central role in her lesbian *Bildungsroman*, and one of the stages of her protagonist Nancy Astley's sexual education involves prostituting herself as a cross-dressing rent 'boy'. The novel's carnality insistently re-materialises what Terry Castle famously termed the "apparitional lesbian" within cultural consciousness, clothing the historically occluded spectre of non-heteronormative sex with wanton flesh.[39] So too in Waters' 2002 *Fingersmith* which depicts the hapless Maud Lilly groomed to service the mania of her bibliophile uncle, forced to help him compile "his *Universal Bibliography of Priapus and Venus*" at his country mansion of Briar, as well as giving salacious readings from his collection for visiting London suppliers and fellow aficionados.[40] Following Mr Lilly's death, Maud not only becomes a writer of pornography to support herself, but implicitly initiates her lover Susan Trinder into the trade.[41] Michel Faber's 2002 *The Crimson Petal and the White* casts a prostitute, Sugar, as its main protagonist, following her trajectory from brothel inmate to kept mistress of William Rackham, a rich industrialist, to 'governess' in Rackham's family home and his eventual cast-off. As well as depicting Sugar writing a violent pornographic revenge novel, the text sees Rackhams' dissolute cronies, Philip Bodley and Edward Ashwell, publishing a guide to London prostitutes for "*Men About Town*", and includes detailed depictions of brothel visits and back alley sex with streetwalkers.[42] Belinda Starling's 2007 *The Journal of Dora Damage* chronicles the corrupting encounter of the titular protagonist with the pseudoscientific *Les Sauvages Nobles* society (based on the historical Cannibal Club), whose 'anthropological' pornographic works she binds and beautifies to ensure the survival of her family and the failing bindery business. A good amount of the action of *Ripper Street* is set in the brothel run by Jackson's partner and secret wife, Madam 'Long' Susan Hart (MyAnna Buring), with various episodes involving actual or former prostitutes as victims of crime and sometimes as the investigators' helpers. Besides the girls' sex work, the series also features more reprehensible aspects of the trade, such as white slavery, sexual trafficking and pornographic snuff movies. Similarly, the 2010 French television series *Maison Close*, set in an 1871 up-market Paris brothel, focuses on sexual exploitation, including forced induction into prostitution and women being auctioned off to the highest bidder.

Such more explicit texts might seem to contradict, at least in part, the anti-repressive hypothesis, by using the nineteenth-century context merely for gratuitous sexploitation: that is, for the extra shock effect, sensationalism, and titillation derived from displaying sex in historical fancy dress. Indeed the already mentioned *Ripper Street* episode *I Need Light* self-consciously signals awareness of this potential criticism via the costume drama in which the slumming Sir Arthur Donaldson (Mark Dexter), who likes to star in the films he finances, sexually abuses one of Madam Hart's girls, Rose Erskine (Charlene McKenna). In a 'mise-en-abyme', *Ripper Street*'s audience witnesses Donaldson, wearing a Romanesque toga, being filmed raping and asphyxiating the drugged and battered Erskine, dressed as a slave-girl, against the same painted backdrop of Ancient Egypt featured in another snuff movie he earlier forced her to watch. The historical stage set is clearly intended to add frisson to the proceedings and heighten nineteenth-century viewers' enjoyment by providing a re-imagined context in which 'uncivilised' offences (slavery, rape, indiscriminate killing for pleasure) could realistically have taken/take place. The neo-Victorian employs an analogous temporal displacement to indulge in and 'justify' transgression, what I have elsewhere called "sexsation" – the eroticised re-imagining of the nineteenth century as "a sensationalised realm of desire and novelty, where any and every sexual fantasy may be gratified", a libidinal free zone of excess.[43] In spite of the episode's metafictionality, the primary aim of its sexsation appears to be the gratuitous breaking of Victorian taboos for the sake of it, an aggressive demonstration not so much of present-day sexual liberation as of anarchic sexual 'laissez-faire'. At most, the simulated past could be said to reflect today's so-called 'rape culture'.[44]

This sexsational trend also becomes obvious in instances of film adaptations of nineteenth-century and/or neo-Victorian classics that add sexually suggestive or explicit material not actually found in the source texts. Mira Nair's 2004 *Vanity Fair*, for instance, incorporates a belly/slave dance scene starring Reese Witherspoon as Becky Sharp in harem girl costume, with the harem, of course, constituting a favourite motif of Victorian pornography.[45] Meanwhile, Oliver Parker's 2006 *Dorian Gray* features drug-induced orgies, and the attic that contains the horrid portrait of the protagonist (Ben Barnes) also functions as the traumatic site of his grandfather's intimate abuse, possibly sexual, of Dorian as a child. Similarly, the *Tipping the Velvet* adaptation introduces a new street scene where Nancy, who restricts her rent boy services to oral sex, is subjected to attempted anal rape by a punter.

Yet as Eckart Voigts-Virchow remarks, inadvertently even representations of subversive "Victorian subcultures may reinforce the auto-stereotype" of the nineteenth-century "mainstream" as the fulcrum of "pre-liberation Western culture", by inviting readers to imagine themselves as "sexually liberated, open-minded" historical subjects having "to live furtively under the regime of Victorian repression."[46] Hence it should come as no surprise that even sexsational texts may end up reaffirming some taboos in the very process of violating Victorian restraint. The ultimate taboo of paedophilia proves an illustrative case in point. *The Crimson Petal and the White*, for instance, specifically identifies Sugar as a former child-prostitute, sold by her own madam mother at a tender age. Yet the offence's actual representation is severely circumscribed, limited to a single flashback in which the adult Sugar recalls examining her "inflamed genitals" in a mirror the morning after her violation, together with the grotesque euphemistic words of her first abuser, strongly reminiscent of the language of Victorian pornographic texts: "*I have a clever middle finger, yes I have!* was what he'd told her, as he poked and prodded between her legs. *A most frolicsome little fellow! He loves to play with little girls, and make them happier than they've ever been!*"[47] Faber deliberately 'blanks out' Sugar's abused childhood – in effect, figuring it as an unrepresentable trauma – and opts to focus his narrative on the adult protagonist, insulating himself and his readers against potential accusations of producing or enjoying literary paedophiliac porn.

Such blanking can assume various textual forms. In structural terms, as in Faber's novel, the offence can be relegated to the un-narrated past, taking place before the action commences. In psychological terms, it can be repressed, only resurfacing indirectly through characters' traumatic symptoms: such as flashback, as in the case of Sugar and Dorian Gray; sleepwalking, as in Byatt's 2009 *The Children's Book*, in the case of Pamona Fludd, abused by her father; or at the level of dreams, as in the case of Grace Marks in Margaret Atwood's 1996 *Alias Grace*, another instance of (implied) paternal incest. In the latter example, the dream's manifest content is left to be deciphered by the reader, who has to elicit the 'hidden' offence; the text thus invites the taboo's imaginative transgression and infilling by the audience, while itself respecting the taboo on representing child sex abuse outright. Finally, the tabooed act can be displaced into alternative contexts or sublimated into art. In *The Journal of Dora Damage*, for instance, the child's sexual violation is ghosted by another form of physical – namely medical – violation: Dora's powerful patrons threaten to perform a forced clitoridectomy on her epileptic daughter Lucinda unless the bookbinder agrees to continue to work for them. In *The Children's Book*, meanwhile, incestuous paedophilia is also encoded via ekphrasis in the descriptions of the potter Benedict Fludd's obscene ceramics depicting his nude daughters in explicit sexual poses. Following the patriarch's apparent suicide, these pots are buried by Pamona, relegated to a sort of symbolic re-repression.

In contrast to *The Crimson Petal and the White*, Waters' *Fingersmith* dwells at length on Maud's traumatic childhood and her 'grooming' by Mr Lilly, who exposes her to sexually explicit materials before she can even understand their contents. Yet the novel never transgresses so far as to imagine actual incest by the abuser or his pimping of Maud to others – bar the symbolic prostitution of having her read aloud for the titillation of his guests – even though this would constitute a logical development in line with criminological understandings of patterns of habitual abuse as well as prevalent storylines of Victorian pornographic texts.[48] Moreover, though specifically set within the contexts of the pornography trade, *Fingersmith* proves curiously reticent about that industry's publications, only incorporating the briefest of snippets of actual (and/or fictional) nineteenth-century sources, none of which contain explicit child sex abuse, in spite of paedophilia certainly featuring within such writings.[49] *Fingersmith*, in other words, self-consciously performs itself as a *non*-paedophiliac text in spite of its controversial subject matter.

Interestingly, even the novel's oblique hints at child sex abuse are almost completely excised from Aisling Walsh's 2005 adaptation for the BBC. The childhood 'flagellation' scene of Mr Lilly striking Maud's hands with "a line of metal beads, bound tight with silk, for keeping down springing pages", which "sting like a whip", is drastically foreshortened: the implement used is not clearly depicted, the impact on her flesh is never shown (the camera focusing instead on the girl's wincing face), and Maud's intense weeping thereafter is cut from the scene.[50] All references to the young Maud's frequent beatings and other "punishments", including physical restraint, and to Lilly ordering the servants to "whip her [...] if she prove troublesome" disappear entirely from the adaptation.[51] Upon Susan's arrival at Briar, she is scandalised by the adult Maud's indecorously short skirts, reminiscent of a child's dress, "show[ing] her ankles" and exposing "her calves" when she leans over; Maud's improper attire adds to the sexual frisson afforded by her readings, emphasising her enforced simulated childlikeness.[52] On screen, however, these childish clothes are replaced by full length Victorian gowns. Just as crucially, the orchestrated rape of Maud's maid, the fifteen-year-old Agnes, in which Maud conspires with the conman Richard 'Gentleman' Rivers, is transformed into a romantic tryst interrupted by the housekeeper, with Agnes portrayed as a consenting adult. This constitutes a further striking sanitisation of Waters' treatment of taboo subjects, which itself already evinces a degree of self-policing. In the novel, for instance, Agnes' rape is never witnessed outright; instead Maud listens to the girl's violation from her bedroom next door, imaginatively fleshing out the scene:

> Her voice [...] lifts high, in surprise, in indignation and then—I suppose—a kind of panic; but then it drops, is stifled or soothed, gives way in a moment to whispers, to

the rub of linen or limbs ... Then the rub becomes silence. And the silence is worst of all: not an absence of sound, but teeming [...] with kicks and squirming movements. I imagine her shuddering, weeping, her clothes put back—but her freckled arms closing despite herself, about his plunging back, her white mouth seeking out his – [53]

The "abominable pictures" are constituted only within Maud's and the readers' minds, presented as mental but never literal images in the text. As Mr Lilly notes of the more subtle stimulations afforded by written as compared to photographic erotic images, "words [...] seduce us in darkness, and the mind clothes and fleshes them to fashions of its own."[54] The narrative's visual elision conscripts the reader into thinking the unthinkable – vicariously violating the taboos of both rape and paedophilia – as the text performs the neo-Victorian's simultaneous fascination and consternation with their transgression.

Akin to *Fingersmith*'s adaptation, *Ripper Street* employs sanitising elision. The first series is ghosted by the spectre of child sex abuse encoded in the gradually unfolding backstory of Reid's lost daughter Mathilda, who disappeared on a boating accident during an excursion the detective employed as cover for his investigation of one Victor Trumper aka Silver (David Oakes). In the final episode, *What Use Our Work*, in which the criminal resurfaces, Silver and his siblings hold a number of female captives whom they intend to traffic to South America, among them a young girl Reid futilely hopes might turn out to be Mathilda. Although never expressly stated, Reid evidently fears that Mathilda, if still alive, has been or will be forced into the sex trade. The abductions are initially referenced in the Duty Sergeant's report of "Two missing persons, both teenage girls."[55] Later, however, the girls are specifically identified as being aged nineteen and seventeen, hence both over sixteen, the UK legal age of consent both in 1889 and today, which (for females) had been raised from twelve to thirteen in 1875, and then to sixteen in 1885, following social purity campaigns assisted by Stead's crusade against child prostitution. Similarly, the filmmakers take pains to ensure that all the prostitutes featured are depicted as older than sixteen.[56] While some historians question how widespread Victorian child prostitution actually was, they nonetheless agree on its definite existence. Hence *Ripper Street*'s deliberate suppression of the subject not only comes across as unrealistic, but also as overly careful (paranoid?) not to offend viewer sensibilities – a slightly odd, if perhaps understandable concern in light of the UK news having been dominated by child sex abuse scandals in the run-up to the series' first UK airing on 30 December 2012, involving the Rochdale sex trafficking gang (convicted in May 2012) and the deceased celebrity TV presenter Jimmy Savile (from September 2012 onwards). Only right at the end of *What Use Our Work* do the filmmakers gesture towards these current anxieties in an oblique evocation of Stead's purchase of a child virgin in *The Maiden Tribute*. Silver's accessory in crime, his sister Clarissa or 'Clara' (Ruta Gedmintas), claims she and her brothers "nurture" the young girl, adding that "when she has grown just a few more years, well, *imagine* the price we shall fetch for her."[57] The offence of paedophilia is projected into the future, with viewers, like Reid and the readers of *Fingersmith*, drawn into the defiling collusion of imagining the unrepresented violation.

Neo-Victorian texts, then, may be described as "boundary-walkers", to adapt Harper and Smith's cinematic concept: they "hedge their bets in adopting ambivalent attitudes" to sexuality, "walk the boundaries between the sacred and profane", and "display an awareness of the power of taboo and the dangerous exaltations which ensue from its destruction", whether real or imagined.[58] By constituting the forbidden through its circumscription, the boundary (between representation/non-representation) itself becomes eroticised, enabling as it does the experience of transgression. As Carl B. Holmberg explains:

> taboos are borders. An edge, however, suggests a place individuals [...] can teeter before going over the edge and transgressing that border, if indeed they ever go over the edge. Individuals 'on edge' may be characterised as consciously or unconsciously intensified in their awareness of themselves, others, and the situations in which they find themselves. 'On edge' begins to describe the appeal [Georges] Bataille calls the fascination of the transgression.[59]

Assuming a surprisingly normative position of (albeit always teetering) moral centrism, these neo-Victorian texts construct 'the child' as a twenty-first-century new/old taboo – in the term's alternative sense of something *'sacred'* and *'revered'*, which must be protected at all costs from defilement (that is, outright sexualised representation) and risks contaminating others in turn. Bringing about what Franz Steiner termed "a kind of socialisation of danger", "the principle of contagion" thus serves "two separate social functions" covered by the same term of 'taboo': "social participation in danger" and purification therefrom.[60] At once registering and disavowing the taboo, neo-Victorian texts self-consciously play on the fears of reciprocal pollution of the taboo (the sacred made 'dirty') and of its transgressors (self-contaminating readers/viewers tempted to engage in 'filthy' imaginings of child victims). As I have argued elsewhere, neo-Victorianism invites "*reading for defilement*", both the defilement of our historical Others and ourselves; by "pander[ing] to a seemingly insatiable desire for imagined perversity", it allows us to "extract politically incorrect pleasure from what has become inadmissible or ethically *unimaginable* as a focus of desire in our own time."[61] This facilitates a concurrent temporary purging or disowning of those same desires at individual and/or cultural levels at the very moment that paedophilia, assisted by new technologies, becomes an omnipresent feature of postmodernity. Such an ambiguous conflation of self-violating danger and attraction constitutes the very nature of the taboo, according to E. F. O'Doherty: "desire and aversion arise together in respect of the same object", leading to "a deep-seated conflict."[62] As much is seen in neo-Victorian texts' schizophrenic approach to paedophiliac images as both rigorously repressed and employed for illicit enticement. Neo-Victorianism resorts to self-policing measures of "verbal hygiene", a linguistic concept which Deborah Cameron links not just to political correctness, but more generally to "language-using" as "paradigmatically a social, public act", so that "talking (and writing and signing) must be carried on with reference to norms", even when such norms are being contested or pushed to their limits.[63] Image-making constitutes part of language-using, and in neo-Victorian texts verbal hygiene works hand-in-hand with an unacknowledged new orthodoxy or consensus of 'image hygiene' on page and screen.

Of course figurative circumvention of sexual violence, or representation through non-representation, can also be read as self-conscious ethical reserve, particularly evident in neo-Victorian figurations of non-white subalterns as victims of sex abuse. In Toni Morrison's 1987 *Beloved*, for instance, the ex-slaves Sethe and Paul D struggle to hold memories of sexual trauma at bay. The novel provides an apt illustration of what Martin Swales identifies as a typical "stylistic mode" of rendering taboo experiences: "thematic repression is both replicated by and deconstructed by narratological repression."[64] Thus Sethe's implied rape at the hands of the overseer Schoolteacher's nephews is euphemised by the victim as "those boys [...] took my milk."[65] Paul D's flashback to his first day on the chain-gang and the oral sex black prisoners were forced to perform on the white guards is likewise figured with deliberate obliquity: re-titled "breakfast" offered to the hungry "nigger" and shrouded in morning "mist"; this act too is not described or witnessed outright, as Paul D studies his hands while kneeling beside the violated man, "smelling the guard, listening to his soft grunts".[66] The reader as secondary witness 'sees' but does not 'see'. The scene actively resists visualisation through its depersonalisation and apperception's diversion from vision to other senses: to hearing (as in the case of Agnes' rape in *Fingersmith*) and smell. While in Waters' novel such deflection stimulates complicit yearning for the missing image (modelled by the seemingly aroused Maud's visualisation), Morrison's novel merely invites alienated disgust. There is no emotional 'hook' offered to its readers, on which to hang their desire for transgressive envisaging.

In Barbara Chase-Riboud's 2003 *Hottentot Venus: A Novel*, a biofiction of the historical Sarah Baartman, the protagonist's rape by her Boer master's brother and later 'manager', Hendrick Caesar, is handled similarly to the Ash and Lamotte consummation in *Possession*. It disappears into a textual gap, here signalled by ellipses:

> – The Hottentot apron – I thought it was a legend, a myth like mermaids, he whispered. But you're real …
> When he finished, he straightened up, contrite, and untied my hands.[67]

This self-chosen silencing is particularly striking, since the scene, like the bulk of Chase-Riboud's novel, is narrated from Baartman's posthumous perspective: even a spectre, it seems, remains bound by at least some taboos. Equally disconcerting, however, is the way the passage cannot exclude the insidious appeal to the reader's transgressive imagination altogether, as underlined by Caesar's fascination with fantasy made "real". Richard Flanagan's 2008 *Wanting* also employs non-representation for the quasi-incestuous, paedophiliac rape of the Aboriginal Mathinna by Sir John Franklin, her adoptive father and governor of Tasmania, at a costume ball in which he appears dressed as a black swan:

> Looking down on Mathinna, her diminutive body, her exposed black ankles, her dirty little feet, the suggestive valley of her red dress between her thin legs, Sir John felt thrilled. And after, was thrilled no more.[68]

Tammy Ho Lai-Ming argues that elision here "forces the readers to imagine the event's details, thus making them complicit in the problematic desires the narrative implies and arouses."[69] Yet simultaneously, the grotesque scene of Franklin's re-enactment of Zeus' mythical rape of Leda short-circuits desire which, as for Franklin, tips over into its opposite: disgusted turn-off. The sex act in *Wanting* is further de-materialised by Flanagan's typical postcolonial use of the rape trope "as a metaphor for British colonialism."[70] As Mathinna becomes a nineteenth-century Leda, emblematic of both her land and people, their plundering and despoliation, her individual sexual suffering is depersonalised and abstracted. Chase-Riboud resorts to the same trope in the latter part of *Hottentot Venus*, during Baron Georges Léopold Cuvier's public dissection of Baartman's corpse. Employing animalistic, Ripperesque, and cannibalistic imagery, the scene is figured as the culmination of the scientist's rape fantasy of Baartman as "the Dark Continent, dissected, violated, probed, raped by dead white men since Roman times", compensating for the failure of Cuvier's prior attempt at Baartman's literal rape while she was still living.[71] Triumphantly, he excises her 'Hottentot apron' or enlarged labia that, like a murderer's trophy, is passed round the "braying [...] mob" of attending anatomists in a "bell jar" for their delectation.[72] Neither the inanimate cadaver nor its monstrous violator, nor even Baartman's narrating spectre, provide viable points of reader identification in this deliberately 'kinky' scene, implicitly aligning us with Cuvier's avid audience lapping up the Gothic spectacle. Her corpse's violation places the genitalia Baartman deemed most private and inviolable – and resolutely kept hidden from view (hence, taboo) – on public display. Once again, readers are implicated in transgression of the taboo, not just rape, racism, cannibalism, and mutilation, but also a kind of necrophilia – almost as though the novel were hammering home that this is the logical endpoint of deeming anything and everything permissible to be spoken, written, and shown, unfettering representation completely.

Fittingly, at various earlier points in Baartman's narration, the novel self-consciously reflects on the instrumentalisation of her stigmatised bodily image: constructed as a primitive to be lampooned for sport in cartoons peddling racist ideologies of white

Western supremacy; as a sex-object/celebrity to sell newspapers and advertise consumer goods; as a prodigy or freak of nature to draw in crowds to her exhibits; as the contested ground on which to build scientific reputations. Put differently, Chase-Riboud's text constitutes an on-going metafictional meditation on *what we do with* (and what profit and pleasure we derive from) the images that we create, circulate, and consume. For not to address taboo subjects altogether would risk turning the "word-taboo" – and/or image-taboo – into "a taboo on thinking itself."[73] Neo-Victorianism self-reflexively employs the taboo to think through (and make readers think through) its own politics (and readers' expectations) of representation.

Hence a more positive interpretation for non-representation offers itself. In the aforementioned examples from *Beloved*, *Hottentot Venus*, and *Wanting*, self-imposed reticence also serves an ethical imperative, even if not always convincingly accomplished: to protect subalterns from further extreme objectification and sexual exploitation, which would re-enact in textual form the historical violations to which they and other real-life subjects like them were subjected in the past (and/or continue to be subjected in the present). Though powerfully written and forcing readers into awareness of their own voyeuristic transgression against Baartman, Chase-Riboud's sexsational dissection scene is perhaps less successful than it might have been, because horror finally overrides ethical concerns. Yet perhaps more than any of the other examples, the scene also makes clear the fundamental ambivalence of neo-Victorianism's managing of reader responses through strategic exposure and/or concealment.

Admittedly, the flourishing field of Neo-Victorian Studies is varied and rich enough to accommodate contradictory examples and support alternative readings to those offered here.[74] My intention, then, is not to construct a monolithic reading of neo-Victorian representations of sexuality, but rather to highlight a particularly prominent trend and to demonstrate that neo-Victorianism's relation to the taboo is significantly more complicated, conflicted, and equivocal than it initially appears. Neo-Victorianism's hate/love affair with sexual prohibition pursues an ongoing confrontation with the taboo rather than its exorcism, and this is achieved in two distinct ways. First, neo-Victorianism reinstates a historical context of proscription, once again imbuing the now commonplace subject of sexuality with the controversial charge of (lost) risqué impropriety, frisson, and offensiveness, illustrating what I have called 'the anti-repressive hypothesis' and 'repression-envy'. Second, it enables transgression (of today's demanded political correctness) via the re-presentation – and invited vicarious identification with – now unacceptable nineteenth-century attitudes of sexism and sexual exploitation under the guise of their deconstructive critique and contestation. Consequently, neo-Victorian texts raise uncomfortable questions with regards to their intended reader response. To what extent are we meant to indulge and revel in a new illicitness or, conversely, experience guilty shame and revulsion at the offensive attitudes and behaviours portrayed? As evident from the examples of paedophilia and sexually abused subalterns of colour, the two impulses can never be wholly distinguished: dubious pleasures may be derived from either or both responses. Put differently, neo-Victorian works want to have their cake and eat it too: sexsation and mystery; sexploitation and sexual/textual ethics. Opportunistically, neo-Victorianism reworks nineteenth-century sexuality into a fetishistic 'cult' object, which simultaneously breaches and reinstates the tyranny of the taboo. While recreating the past's 'old' taboos and inscribing 'new' taboos of the present, the neo-Victorian cannot resist the lure of their outright or imagined violation. Deliberately blurring the lines between desirable and undesirable images – and interrogating the limits (and limitlessness) of image producers' and image consumers' desiring – this essential hybridity of the taboo, its functions and effects resides at the heart of neo-Victorianism's "abominable pictures" of the nineteenth century.

Notes

1. Neo-Victorian media include literature, film, graphic novels, videogames, steampunk fashion, visual and aesthetic arts, pornography, theme parks, and architectural adaptive reuse, among others. Admittedly, there is still much debate about the appropriateness and parameters of the term 'neo-Victorian', carrying as it does connotations of Britishness and hence implicated in a potential cultural neo-imperialism when applied to other geographical, especially non-Anglophone contexts and other nations' historical fictions set in the nineteenth century. In spite of these complications, 'neo-Victorianism' has emerged as the favoured term, accompanied by a new academic field of 'Neo-Victorian Studies' and a dedicated e-journal of the same title, launched in 2008 (http://www.neovictorianstudies.com).
2. The term 'neo-Victorian novel' encompasses a wide range of works, including texts that pastiche or parody nineteenth-century aesthetic conventions; intertextual works that borrow from nineteenth-century texts and their characters; biofictions of actual historical personages of the period; examples of historiographic metafiction, magic realism, and postcolonial fiction set in the nineteenth century, often incorporating historically marginalised viewpoints; and dual/multiple time-frame as well as fantasy time-travel novels. Neo-Victorian novels also cover all literary genres, though arguably Gothic, sensation fiction, detective fiction, and trauma narratives predominate.
3. Farrell, J. G. (1999) *The Siege of Krishnapur*. London: Orion Books, page 77.
4. Ibid.
5. Shankland, T. Dir. (2012) *I Need Light. Ripper Street*, Series One, Episode 1. Screenplay by Richard Warlow. BBC, 30 December, 29.28-29.30, original pause.
6. Ibid., 42.31-42.37, 42.55-42.56.
7. Farrell, op. cit., page 231.
8. Ibid., page 77.
9. Ibid.
10. Thus Matthew Sweet's popular 2001 *Inventing the Victorians* aims at dispelling spurious myths regarding nineteenth-century prudery and supposedly sex-negative culture, while historians

of sexuality have long been involved in a radical revision of our understanding of Victorian repression; see, for example Zisowitz Stearns, C. and Stearns, P. N. (1985) "Victorian Sexuality: Can Historians Do It Better?" in *Journal of Social History,* Volume 18, Number 4, Summer, pages 625 – 34.

11   Strictly speaking, in anthropological terms, 'taboo' also refers to what is prohibited on account of its sacredness rather than its offensiveness, that is, what is approached with excessive reverence rather than extreme revulsion (see Steiner, F. (1956) *Taboo*. London: Coehn & West, page 34). In this chapter, however, I employ the term mainly in its latter relation to abhorrence, arguably the more prevalent usage in Western culture today.

12   Harper, S. and Smith, J. (2012) "Boundaries and Taboos." in Harper, S. and Smith, J. Ed. *British Film Culture in the 1970s: The Boundaries of Pleasure*. Edinburgh: Edinburgh University Press, page 140.

13   Ultimate taboos include cannibalism and sexual violence, in particular paedophilia and/or incest, where the social injunction coincides with a legally specified, criminal and prosecutable offence. Yet even these taboos feature regularly in neo-Victorian fiction. Perhaps not coincidentally perpetrated against a child victim, literal cannibalism, for instance, occurs in Robert Edric's 2000 *The Book of the Heathen*; so too in Carol Birch's 2011 *Jamrach's Menagerie*, albeit given a more elegiac treatment as a last resort for survival. Paedophilia tends to be implied or alluded to, as in the brothel scene in John Fowles 1969 *The French Lieutenant's Woman* or Sarah Waters' 2002 *Fingersmith*. Yet apart from the odd exception, such as Sheri Holman's 1999 *The Dress Lodger*, it is rarely depicted outright even when at the heart of a text's mystery and denouement, as in Isabel Colegate's 1991 *The Summer of the Royal Visit*, or Anthony Horowitz's 2011 *The House of Silk*, two texts respectively involving ritual and institutionalised child sex abuse. The same applies to the incest theme, which may be found in works including Matthew Kneale's 1992 *Sweet Thames,* Margaret Atwood's 1996 *Alias Grace*, Jem Poster's 2006 *Rifling Paradise* and A. S. Byatt's 2009 *The Children's Book*, as well as her earlier 1992 novella *Morpho Eugenia*.

14   Burridge, K. (2010) "Linguistic cleanliness is next to godliness: taboo and purism." in *English Today,* Volume 26, Issue 2, June, page 4, original emphasis.

15   Appropriately, Christian Gutleben notes how, from being a progressive "right-minded movement" concerned with securing and protecting minority rights, political correctness became first a "consensual" and then "an obliged attitude" (Gutleben, C. (2001) *Nostalgic Postmodernism: The Victorian Tradition and the Contemporary British Novel*. Amsterdam and New York: Rodopi, page 167), or perhaps more accurately, an obligatory and hence itself restrictive attitude. Although, strictly speaking, neo-Victorianism predates the 1970s emergence of 'political correctness' in its common usage today, namely as the insisted upon respectfulness towards all forms of cultural and personal difference (including sexual orientation and lifestyle), the neo-Victorian phenomenon only came fully into its own in the final decades of the twentieth century. Gutleben thus finds something potentially suspect in the neo-Victorian (or as he also terms it, 'retro-Victorian') novel's drive towards equality and liberation, implicitly also freedom from the taboo: "What seems undecidable is whether the spreading of the politically correct made the birth of the retro-Victorian novel possible or whether the retro-Victorian novel developed out of a resolution to exploit an ideological trend which had reached a consensus. Because most neo-Victorian novels were actually written in the 1990s, that is to say after political correctness had become widespread, one cannot help harbouring the suspicion of an opportunistic drive." (Ibid., page 168).

16   Foucault, M. (1990) *History of Sexuality: An Introduction*. Translated by Robert Hurley. London: Penguin, page 18.

17   Rousso, S. (2008) "Beyond Liminality towards Similarity: The Representation of Desire in

Literature." in Kohlke, M-L. and Orza, L. Eds. *Probing the Problematics: Sex and Sexuality*. Oxford: Inter-Disciplinary Press, page 306 (ebook).
18   Rousso is discussing the role of lesbian desire in Sarah Waters' neo-Victorian writing, but her reflections are equally relevant to neo-Victorianism more generally.
19   Gutleben, C. (2005) "Phallus in Fabula: The Shameless Abuse of Victorian Intertextuality in Contemporary British Fiction" in *Symbolism: An International Annual of Critical Aesthetics*, Volume 5, page 155.
20   Gutleben further emphasises the crucial function of the repressive context by comparing sexual explicitness in neo-Victorian novels and those with contemporary settings where no repression operates: "In the frame of a late twentieth-century reading pact (in Western civilisation), wanton speculations, adultery, and homosexuality have no scandalous propriety – on the contrary, they correspond to the choice themes of today's reading habits and expectations" (ibid., page 160).
21   Fowles, J. (1981) *The French Lieutenant's Woman*. Bungay, Suffolk: Triad/Granada, page 304, original ellipses.
22   The term refers to the cinematic shot of a male performer's actual ejaculation in pornographic films, although Fowles' novel, of course, can hardly be described as pornographic. At the end of Chapter 40, in Charles' earlier encounter with a London prostitute after a dissolute night on the town, Fowles likewise frustrates readers' expectations of a graphic sex scene: upon hearing that the girl's name is also Sarah, Charles, already nauseous from too much drink, succumbs to a vomiting fit and is left unable to perform.
23   Jeffers, J. M. (2002) "The White Bed of Desire in A.S. Byatt's *Possession*." in *Critique: Studies in Contemporary Fiction,* Volume 43, Issue 2, Winter, page 135.
24   Byatt, A. S. (1990) *Possession: A Romance*. London: Vintage, page 246.
25   Ibid., page 283.
26   Ibid., page 423.
27   Only retroactively, the morning after their love-making, does Ash discover "traces of blood on his thighs" (Ibid., page 284).
28   Ibid., page 507, added emphasis.
29   The following day, Ash reflects with curiosity on the discrepancy between LaMotte's virginity and the "informed desire" or sexual experience she demonstrated in their lovemaking, implicitly deducing the "to him slightly repugnant" possibility of lesbianism (Ibid., page 285). Jonathan Loesberg argues that this passage contains "the distinct traces of the pornographic narrative in which earlier female lesbian dalliance, presented for male pleasure, is construed as preparatory to the more serious heterosexual experience that follows" (Loesberg, J. (2007) "The Afterlife of Victorian Sexuality: Foucault and Neo-Victorian Historical Fiction." in *Clio,* Volume 36, Issue 3, Summer, page 387). Yet the novel's restrained language and lack of physical explicitness could not be further removed from pornographic discourse.
30   The rather lack-lustre and radically simplified 2002 film adaptation of Byatt's novel likewise proves ambiguously 'Victorian' in its mere pretence of a more explicit representation of sexuality. In the consummation scene between Ash (Jeremy Northam) and LaMotte (Jennifer Ehle), Ash is depicted helping his lover partially unlace her corset and then kissing and biting her shoulders, before the lovers kiss passionately and his hand caresses LaMotte's buttocks through her petticoats. The camera then shifts to the sex act itself, which shows Ash kneeling on the bed and holding the entwined LaMotte – still in her virginal white shift – on his lap. Apart from the merest side-on hint of his buttock outline, his own nakedness remains decorously concealed by LaMotte's form, of which merely exposed

shoulders and legs are on view, before the camera goes into soft focus fade-out. Thereafter the lovers are shown sleeping in each other's embrace, with LaMotte still wearing her shift. After a brief switch to the twentieth-century protagonists, LaMotte wakes to find Ash sitting up in bed, and the lovers talk and then resume their love-making, but the whole scene is shot 'above the waist' and the viewer is allowed no glimpse 'beneath the covers' as it were. A later flashback to their lovemaking, close to the end of the film, likewise depicts no more than Ash's torso, while LaMotte remains clothed. Just as ironically, Michell and Bailey's consummation is never depicted at all.

31 Gutleben, "Phallus in Fabula", op. cit., page 166.
32 Jeffers, op. cit., pages 138 and 145.
33 Part One of Foucault's 1978 *The History of Sexuality: An Introduction*, is entitled We 'Other Victorians', in homage to Steven Marcus' 1966 *The Other Victorians: A Study of Sexuality and Pornography in Mid-Nineteenth-Century England*.
34 Jeffers, op. cit., page 146.
35 Loesberg, op. cit., page 363.
36 Ibid., page 388.
37 Fowels, op. cit., pages 233 – 234.
38 Woolf, V. (1978) *Moments of Being: Unpublished Autobiographical Writings*. Frogmore, St Albans: Triad/Panther Books, page 200. Woolf employs the expression in her much cited recounting of the moment in 1908 when Lytton Strachey first used the word 'semen' in mixed company, which for her spelled the proper end of the Victorian age: "there was now nothing that one could not say" (Ibid., pages 200 – 201). Loesberg opens his article with a discussion of this passage from Woolf's posthumously published essays.
39 Castle, T. (1993) *The Apparitional Lesbian: Female Homosexuality and Modern Culture*. New York: Columbia Press.
40 Waters, S. (2002) *Fingersmith*. London: Virago, page, 201. Waters based Lilly and his work on the historical Henry Spencer Ashbee and his 1877 *Index Librorum Prohibitorum* as well as later catalogues, published pseudonymously under 'Pisanus Fraxi'.
41 The confines of this chapter do not permit an in-depth analysis of depictions of non-heteronormative sexuality, a theme which, though prominent in neo-Victorian criticism, remains comparatively scarce in terms of its fictional representation. Apart from Waters' neo-Victorian trio, which also includes her 1999 *Affinity*, and more recently, Emma Donoghue's 2008 *The Sealed Letter*, other neo-Victorian lesbian texts, such as Isabel Miller's 1969 *Patience and Sarah* (originally published as *A Place for Us*), Nevada Barr's 1984 *Bittersweet*, Elana Dykewoman's 1997 *Beyond the Pale* and Patricia Duncker's 1999 *James Miranda Barry*, have received no sustained critical attention as yet. Male homosexuality too is still under-represented, but features, for example, in Chris Hunt's 1986 *Street Lavender*, an acknowledged source of inspiration for *Tipping the Velvet*, and biofictions involving Oscar Wilde, such as Gyles Brandreth's 2007 *Oscar Wilde and the Candlelight Murders* and further volumes in his *Oscar Wilde Murder Mysteries* series.
42 Faber, M. (2003) *The Crimson Petal and the White*. Edinburgh: Canongate Books, page 584.
43 Kohlke, M-L. (2008) "Sexsation and the Neo-Victorian Novel: Orientalising the Nineteenth Century in Contemporary Fiction." in Kohlke, M-L. and Orza, L. Eds. *Negotiating Sexual Idioms: Image, Text, Performance*. Amsterdam and New York: Rodopi, page 53.
44 See, for instance, widespread newspaper and internet coverage of the prevalence of rape jokes at the 2013 Edinburgh Fringe Festival and of notorious rape scandals, such as the 2012 Steubenville High School case in the US.

45 On the prevalence of the harem trope in Victorian pornographic texts, see Sigel, L. Z. (2002) *Governing Pleasures: Pornography and Social Change in England, 1815-1914*. New Brunswick, New Jersey and London: Rutgers University Press, pages 41 – 45.
46 Voigts-Virchow, E. (2009) "In-yer-Victorian-face: A Subcultural Hermeneutics of Neo-Victorianism." in *Literature Interpretation Theory*, Volume 20, Issues 1-2, page 113.
47 Faber, op. cit. p. 538, original italics.
48 In the anonymously published the 1891 *The Yellow Room*, for example, another uncle initiates his orphaned, eighteen-year-old niece into the dubious pleasures of incestuous sadomasochism.
49 See, for example, *The Romance of Lust*; or *Early Experiences*, appearing between 1873 and 1876 (discussed in Sigel, op. cit., pages 93 – 95), or *Lady Pokingham* or *They All Do It*, serialised in *The Pearl* between 1879 and 1880 (reprinted in 1995 in *The Pearl: Three Erotic Tales*. Wordsworth, Ware, Hertfordshire: Wordsworth Classic Erotica, pages 7-107).
50 Waters, op. cit., page 187.
51 Ibid., pages 192 and 194.
52 Ibid., pages 66 and 70.
53 Ibid., pages 238 – 239, un-bracketed ellipses in the original.
54 Ibid., page 216.
55 Wilson, A. Dir. (2013) *What Use Our Work. Ripper Street*, Series One, Episode 8. Screenplay by Richard Warlow. BBC, 24 February, 17.05-17.06.
56 Explicit mention of child prostitution only occurs in a single instance, as far as I am aware. In Episode 5, *The Weight of One Man's Heart*, Rose briefly recalls knowing "a girl, Peggy, worked on her back from ten years of age" (McCarthy, C. Dir. (2013) *The Weight of One Man's Heart. Ripper Street*, Series One, Episode 5. Screenplay by Toby Finlay. BBC, 27 January, 3.11-3.13). *Threads of Silk and Gold*, Episode 5 from *Ripper Street*, Series Two, focuses on male prostitution, but once again the 'boys' involved are depicted as young adults rather than children.
57 Wilson, op. cit., 51.55-52.03, added emphasis.
58 Harper and Smith, op. cit., pages 141 and 147.
59 Holmberg, C. B. (1998) *Sexualities and Popular Culture*. Thousand Oaks, California, London and New Delhi: Sage Publications, page 93.
60 Steiner, F. (1956) *Taboo*. London: Coehn & West, pages 114 – 115.
61 Kohlke, op. cit., page 55, original emphasis.
62 O'Doherty, E. F. (1960) "Taboo, Ritual and Religion." in *Studies: An Irish Quarterly Review*, Volume 49, Number 194, Summer, page 132.
63 Cameron, D. (1995) *Verbal Hygiene*. London and New York: Routledge, pages 116 – 165 and 2.
64 Swales, M. (1996) "Text and Sub-Text: Reflections on the Literary Exploration of Taboo Experience." in Jackson, D. Ed. *Taboos in German Literature*. Providence, Rhode Island and Oxford: Berghahn Books, page 24.
65 Morrison, T. (2005) *Beloved*. London: Vintage, page 19.
66 Ibid., page 127.
67 Chase-Riboud, B. (2003) *Hottentot Venus: A Novel*. New York: Doubleday, page 53, original ellipses.
68 Flanagan, R. (2010) *Wanting*. London: Atlantic Books, page 152.
69 Ho Lai-Ming, T. (2012) "Cannibalised Girlhood in Richard Flanagan's *Wanting*." in *Neo-Victorian Studies*, Volume 5, Issue 1, page 20.
70 Ibid., page 21.
71 Chase-Riboud, op. cit., page 281.

72 Ibid., pages 281 and 283.
73 Hardin, G. (1978) *Stalking the Wild Taboo*. California: William Kaufmann, Inc, page viii.
74 For instance, it remains to be determined whether other 1960s/70s examples (besides those by Fowles and Farrell) or still earlier neo-Victorian works may engage in other ways with questions of the taboo and position themselves differently vis-à-vis the anti-repressive hypothesis than do their later counterparts, particularly those from the twentieth century's own 'naughty nineties' and the following 'noughties', which constitute my primary focus. Such an investigation, however, is beyond the scope of the present chapter.

References

Anonymous. (1995) "The Yellow Room." in *The New Epicurean & The Yellow Room*. Ware, Hertfordshire: Wordsworth, pages 69 – 127.

Anonymous. (1995) "Lady Pokingham or They All Do It." in *The Pearl: Three Erotic Tales*, Ware, Hertfordshire: Wordsworth, pages 7 – 107.

Atwood, M. (1996) *Alias Grace*. London: QPD in association with Bloomsbury.

Barr, N. (2001) *Bittersweet*. New York: Perennial/Harper Collins.

Barthes, R. (1973) *The Pleasure of the Text*. Translated by Richard Miller, With a Note on the Text by Richard Howard. Hill and Wang: New York.

Birch, C. (2011) *Jamrach's Menagerie*. Edinburgh: Canongate.

Brandreth, G. (2007) *Oscar Wilde and the Candlelight Murders*. London: John Murray.

Burridge, K. (2010) "Linguistic cleanliness is next to godliness: taboo and purism." in *English Today*, Volume 26, Issue 2, June, pages 3 – 13.

Byatt, A. S. (1990) *Possession: A Romance*. London: Vintage.

Byatt, A. S. (1992) "Morpho Eugenia". In *Angels and Insects*. London: Chatto & Windus, pages 1 – 160.

Byatt, A. S. (2009) *The Children's Book*. London: Chatto & Windus.

Cameron, D. (1995) *Verbal Hygiene*. London and New York: Routledge.

Castle, T. (1993) *The Apparitional Lesbian: Female Homosexuality and Modern Culture*. New York: Columbia Press.

Chase-Riboud, B. (2003) *Hottentot Venus: A Novel*. New York: Doubleday.

Colegate, I. (1991) *The Summer of the Royal Visit*. London: Hamish Hamilton.

Donoghue, E. (2008) *The Sealed Letter*. New York: Harcourt.

Duncker, P. (1999) *James Miranda Barry*. London: Serpent's Tail.

Dykewomon, E. (1997) *Beyond the Pale*. Vancouver: Press Gang Publishers.

Edric, R. (2000) *The Book of the Heathen*. London: Anchor/Transworld Publishers.

Faber, M. (2003) *The Crimson Petal and the White*. Edinburgh: Canongate Books.

Farrell, J. G. (1999) *The Siege of Krishnapur*. London: Orion Books.

Flanagan, R. (2010) *Wanting*. London: Atlantic Books.

Foucault, M. (1990) *History of Sexuality: An Introduction*. Translated by Robert Hurley. London: Penguin.

Fowles, J. (1981) *The French Lieutenant's Woman*. Bungay, Suffolk: Triad/Granada.

Gutleben, C. (2001) *Nostalgic Postmodernism: The Victorian Tradition and the Contemporary British Novel*. Amsterdam and New York: Rodopi.

Gutleben, C. (2005) "Phallus in Fabula: The Shameless Abuse of Victorian Intertextuality in Contemporary British Fiction." in *Symbolism: An International Annual of Critical Aesthetics*, Volume 5, pages 151 – 167.

Hardin, G. (1978) *Stalking the Wild Taboo*. California: William Kaufmann, Inc.

Harper, S. and Smith, J. (2012) "Boundaries and Taboos." in Harper, S. and Smith, J. Eds. *British Film Culture in the 1970s: The Boundaries of Pleasure*. Edinburgh: Edinburgh University Press, pages 138 – 154.

Ho Lai-Ming, T. (2012) "Cannibalised Girlhood in Richard Flanagan's *Wanting*." in *Neo-Victorian Studies* Volume 5, Issue 1, pages 14 – 37.

Holman, S. (2000) *The Dress Lodger*. London: Hodder and Stoughton.

Holmberg, C. B. (1998) *Sexualities and Popular Culture*. Thousand Oaks, California, London and New Delhi: Sage Publications.

Horowitz, A. (2001) *The House of Silk*. London: Orion Books.

Hunt, C. (1998) *Street Lavender*. London: GPM Publishers.

Jackson, D. Ed. (1996) "Introduction." in *Taboos in German Literature*. Providence, Rhode Island and Oxford: Berghahn Books, pages 1 – 15.

Jeffers, J. M. (2002) "The White Bed of Desire in A.S. Byatt's *Possession*." in *Critique: Studies in Contemporary Fiction,* Volume 43, Issue 2, Winter, pages 135 – 147.

Kohlke, M-L. (2008) "Sexsation and the Neo-Victorian Novel: Orientalising the Nineteenth Century in Contemporary Fiction." in Kohlke, M-L. and Orza, L. Eds. *Negotiating Sexual Idioms: Image, Text, Performance*. Amsterdam and New York: Rodopi, pages 53-77.

Kneale, M. (2001) *Sweet Thames*. London: Penguin Books.

Loesberg, J. (2007) "The Afterlife of Victorian Sexuality: Foucault and Neo-Victorian Historical Fiction." in *Clio*, Volume 36, Issue 3, Summer, pages 361 – 89.

Marcus, S. (1996) *The Other Victorians: A Study of Sexuality and Pornography in Mid-Nineteenth-Century England*. London: Weidenfeld and Nicolson.

Miller, I. (2005) *Patience and Sarah*. Vancouver: Arsenal Pulp Press.

Morrison, T. (2005) *Beloved*. London: Vintage.

O'Doherty, E. F. (1960) "Taboo, Ritual and Religion." in *Studies: An Irish Quarterly Review,* Volume 49, Number 194, Summer, pages 131 – 43.

Poster, J. (2006) *Rifling Paradise*. St Ives: Sceptre.

Rousso, S. (2008) "Beyond Liminality towards Similarity: The Representation of Desire in Literature." in Kohlke, M-L. and Orza, L. Eds. *Probing the Problematics: Sex and Sexuality*. Oxford: Inter-Disciplinary Press, pages 303-9 (ebook).

Sigel, L. Z. (2002) *Governing Pleasures: Pornography and Social Change in England, 1815-1914*. New Brunswick, New Jersey and London: Rutgers University Press.

Starling, B. (2007) *The Journal of Dora Damage*. London: Bloomsbury.

Steiner, F. (1956) *Taboo* (with a preface by E.E. Evans-Pritchard). London: Coehn & West.

Swales, M. (1996) "Text and Sub-Text: Reflections on the Literary Exploration of Taboo Experience." in Jackson, D. Ed. *Taboos in German Literature*. Providence, Rhode Island and Oxford: Berghahn Books, pages 17 – 26.

Sweet, M. (2001) *Inventing the Victorians*. London: Faber and Faber.

Voigts-Virchow, E. (2009) "In-yer-Victorian-face: A Subcultural Hermeneutics of Neo-Victorianism." in *Literature Interpretation Theory,* Volume 20, Issues 1-2, pages 108 – 25.

Waters, S. (1999) *Affinity*. London: Virago.

Waters, S.(2002) *Fingersmith*. London: Virago.

Waters, S.(2002) *Tipping the Velvet*. London: Virago.

Woolf, V. (1978) *Moments of Being: Unpublished Autobiographical Writings*. Frogmore, St Albans: Triad/Panther Books.

Zisowitz Stearns, C. and Stearns, P. N. (1985) "Victorian Sexuality: Can Historians Do It Better?" in *Journal of Social History*, Volume 18, Number 4, Summer, pages 625 – 34.

Filmography

Hawkes, K. Dir. (2013) *Threads of Silk and Gold*. *Ripper Street*, Series Two, Episode 5. Screenplay by Thomas Martin and Toby Finlay. BBC, 25 November.

LaBute, N. Dir. (2002) *Possession*. Screenplay by David Henry Hwang, Laura Jones, and Neil LaBute. Focus Features/Warner Bros. Pictures.

McCarthy, C. Dir. (2013) *The Weight of One Man's Heart*. *Ripper Street*, Series One, Episode 5. Screenplay by Toby Finlay. BBC, 27 January.

Nair, M. Dir. (2004) *Vanity Fair*. Screenplay by Matthew Faulk, Julian Fellowes, and Mark Skeet. Focus Features.

Ouaniche, J. Creator. (2010-present) *Maison Close*. Noé Productions.

Parker, O. Dir. (2009) *Dorian Gray*. Screenplay by Toby Finlay. Momentum Pictures.

Sax, G. Dir. (2002) *Tipping the Velvet*. Screenplay by Andrew Davies. BBC.

Shankland, T. Dir. (2012) *I Need Light*. *Ripper Street*, Series One, Episode 1. Screenplay by Richard Warlow. BBC, 30 December.

Walsh, A. Dir. (2005) *Fingersmith*. Screenplay by Peter Ransley. BBC.

Wilson, A. Dir. (2013) *What Use Our Work*. *Ripper Street*, Series One, Episode 8. Screenplay by Richard Warlow. BBC, 24 February.

Ian Hague

Drawing "the apprenticeship of a man of letters": adapting *Remembrance of Things Past* for 'bande dessinée'[1]

Marcel Proust's *Remembrance of Things Past* is one of the signal achievements not only of twentieth-century French modernism, but of literature as a whole.[2] Comprising well over one million words and usually published in multiple volumes, the work arguably exceeds the limits of what could reasonably be called a novel and becomes something else entirely.[3] As Walter Benjamin has written:

> It has rightly been said that all great works of literature establish a genre or dissolve one — that they are, in other words, special cases. Among these cases, [*Remembrance of Things Past*] is one of the most unfathomable. From its structure, which is at once fiction, autobiography, and commentary, to the syntax of boundless sentences (the Nile of language, which here overflows and fructifies the plains of truth), everything transcends the norm.[4]

While it is impossible to summarise the work adequately in the space available here (in fact it could be argued that Proust's work cannot be summarised: it must simply be read) it is perhaps helpful to outline a few of the key moments in the plot to orient the reader who is unfamiliar with the text in the discussion that follows.[5]

Remembrance of Things Past recounts the life of the book's narrator from his early years holidaying in the fictional town of Combray to the point at which he has resolved to withdraw from Parisian society in order to write a major work. Between these two points, the reader learns of the narrator's youth and early love for Gilberte Swann, daughter of Charles Swann (whose own relationship with Odette de Crécy, the woman who will be Gilberte's mother, is related at length in an extensive flashback that comprises most of *Swann's Way*, the first volume of *Remembrance*). The narrator holidays in the seaside town of Balbec, where his youthful (and unrequited) love for Gilberte is replaced with an infatuation with a group of girls who are also holidaying there. Among them is Albertine Simonet, who will later become a key figure in the narrator's life. The reader is told of the narrator's entry into Parisian society; over time he comes to dine regularly with members of the aristocracy, whose heritage, habits and infidelities he describes in scrupulous detail, with particular attention paid to cultures of homosexuality. Eventually he reconnects with Albertine and they begin a romance, but this is derailed by the narrator's paranoia and/or Albertine's possible infidelity and lesbianism. Albertine dies. The narrator suffers immense grief but does eventually come to terms with the event. He renews his friendship with Gilberte, now married to his friend Robert de Saint-Loup. The work's final volume, *Time Regained*, deals with the culture of Paris during WWI, and concludes at a party where the narrator realises how he might express in literature the history and nature of his life and memories.

Major subjects discussed in the book include the properties of time, and the ways in which society works and is structured. The book also integrates lengthy discussions of various social, cultural and philosophical ideas, an extensive account of the concepts that underpin the work, and descriptions of how it is possible to write such a text. Key among *Remembrance*'s themes is memory (particularly involuntary memories of the type prompted by encounters with specific sensory stimuli): in one famous moment the narrator sips a cup of tea with a few crumbs of madeleine cake in it, and their smell and taste unfold memories of his time in Combray. Yet although the theme of involuntary memory is perhaps the most well-known aspect of Proust's writing it is not, Giles Deleuze has suggested, "[w]hat constitutes the unity of [*Remembrance of Things Past*]".[6] "What is involved is not an exposition of involuntary memory," he writes, "but the narrative of an apprenticeship: more precisely, the apprenticeship of a man of letters".[7] Throughout the book, the narrator is in the process of becoming a writer; from early attempts while at Combray through to initial publications in the newspaper *Figaro* following the death of Albertine, and finally a resolution that the only way to write a book of the scope and significance that he has in mind is to withdraw from society and isolate himself in order to establish the conditions necessary to complete his proposed work. *Remembrance of Things Past*, then, is fundamentally bound up with the act of writing, what it means to write, and the process by which one becomes a writer. Similarly, the novel concerns itself with the nature and expression of ideas in *written* language or text. We have already encountered Walter Benjamin's description of the book as 'the Nile of language', and in a similar vein director Mary Zimmerman, writing on her process in adapting Proust's work for the theatre, has asserted:

I cannot think of another text that is so textual, so bound to its print form. Its sentences are unspeakably long, its ideas so intricate the reader must often retrace his steps. The plot is glacial in pace but not in weight, and although there is some dialogue it is neither frequent nor particularly persuasive. Most challenging of all, its almost exclusive concern is the unspoken, invisible, interior life of a person. Its method is to record the smallest of human interactions – a glance, an interrupted phrase, a movement of the hand – and then to dwell on these moments for pages; seeing the thing first one way and then another, taking it through thought after thought, metaphor after metaphor, and finally deducing from it a general rule of human behavior. All of this conspires against an evening in the theatre.[8]

Yet Zimmerman did adapt Proust's life and work for the theatre on two occasions: in a one-person show entitled *M. Proust* that drew on the memoir of Proust's housekeeper Celeste Albaret, and in a site-specific work called *Eleven Rooms of Proust* that dramatised selected scenes and ideas from *Swann's Way*. While neither endeavoured to be a straightforward presentation of the novel's plot upon the stage, both employed Proust's language and in so doing suggested that the novel's sentences were not (or at least not entirely) unspeakable.

There have also been numerous adaptations of *Remembrance* on film. 1984's *Swann in Love* (directed by Volker Schlöndorff) was a fairly straightforward presentation of the plot of the book's first volume, *Swann's Way*, with Jeremy Irons in the title role. 2000's *The Captive* (directed by Chantal Akerman) took its inspiration from the novel's fifth volume in depicting the charged and paranoid relationship between Simon (Stanislas Merhar) and Ariane (Sylvie Testud) – thinly veiled reimaginings of the narrator and Albertine – but transplanted the plot to a modern setting. 1999's *Time Regained* (directed by Raul Ruiz) ostensibly adapted only the final volume of Proust's novel, but used points of remembering to return the protagonist to moments drawn from previous books in the sequence as well. It is perhaps this last adaptation that is the most successful of the three mentioned here, since it expresses not only Proust's plot but also some of the structural features of his novel as well.

Film is not the only medium in which adaptors have sought to work with Proust. In 1998, Delcourt published the first part of Stéphane Heuet et al.'s adaptation of *Remembrance of Things Past* in the 'bande dessinée' format. Yet producing this most textual and 'writerly' of works in a form that, even in its very name, emphasises the act of drawing ('bande dessinée' translates literally as 'drawn strip'), presents some significant opportunities and challenges for the adaptation of Proust's work. Over the remainder of this chapter I will consider these challenges, and look at the ways in which the adaptation of *Remembrance of Things Past* for 'bande dessinée' deals with the expression of information and the communication of ideas in the original novel.

Traditionalist grumblings about the complexity of Proust's language and ideas aside, there are some good reasons to think that 'bande dessinée' represents a superb opportunity for the adaptation of *Remembrance of Things Past*, and offers significant scope for the reworking of Proust's ideas in meaningful ways. In aspects as disparate as publishing systems, visual content and structural mechanisms, 'bande dessinée' suggests means by which *Remembrance* might be open to reinterpretation and adaptation.

Format and organisation: although the serialised mode of publication has now generally fallen out of fashion in the realm of prose fiction, it is still alive and well in the fields of comics and 'bande dessinée'. Whether in long-running but now completed series such as *The Adventures of Tintin*, or in ongoing serials such as the *Asterix* albums, which have lasted even beyond the death of one of their original authors, serialisation is a key aspect of publication in 'bande dessinée'. And while each of these examples may be picked at for the relatively limited interconnection of the albums, there are some examples of complete works that have been published over extensive periods of time.[9] By this I mean works in which the various sections comprise not sequels to an original self-contained narrative, but parts of a single whole that would be rendered incomplete were they to be removed. Dave Sim and Gerhard's *Cerebus*, which appeared between 1977 and after 2004, which was serialised across three hundred individual comic book issues and then collected into sixteen lengthy paperback volumes is one such work. In this regard, comics and 'bande dessinée' offer an interesting platform for the re-presentation of *Remembrance*, given that they are able to echo both the fragmented format that editions of the work generally take, and the serialised nature of its original publication from 1913-1927.[10] At the time of this writing in July 2014, six volumes of Heuet's adaptation have been published in French. The first four of these have been translated into English. Where each of the seven volumes of the original runs to hundreds of pages each, however, the 'bande dessinée' versions are shorter, with the first volume, entitled *Combray*, being just seventy-two pages, and the subsequent instalments shorter still.[11] As Jan Baetens notes, the primary methods Heuet uses to reduce Proust's 2,500-plus page novel to the more limited page count of the 'bande dessinée' format (usually between 48 and 64 pages per album, though some variation is possible) are the "contraction and removal" of content, each of which offer certain possibilities to the author in presenting the information in a manner that goes beyond illustration and prompts the images and text to enter into meaningful relationships with each other.[12] Heuet's version does not, however, simply present Proust's narrative in a compressed form, it also reorganises the material of the plot in a manner that significantly alters the reader's position relative to it. Specifically, the prose version's first volume (*Swann's Way*) begins with two chapters, entitled *Overture* and *Combray* respectively, which introduce the narrator and the notion of involuntary memory through the episode with the madeleine, then outline his time in Combray. The third chapter, *Swann in Love*, then segues into a flashback detailing the relationship between Swann and Odette that takes up most of the rest of the volume. By contrast, Heuet's work covers the content of the *Overture* and *Combray* in its first volume (also entitled *Combray*) but then skips to the content of the prose book's second volume

(*Within a Budding Grove*) for its second and third books (which are entitled *Within a Budding Grove Volume 1* and *Volume 2*). It then takes up the story of Swann and Odette in volumes four and five (entitled *Swann in Love Volume 1* and *Volume 2* – this title of course being taken from the third chapter of the prose book's first volume), before returning to the final chapter of *Swann's Way* in volume 6.

While this switch may seem a relatively minor modification, it does represent a substantial reorganisation of the original's plot in the new version. This can be understood in purely quantitative terms with reference to the original work: were we to enact this change upon the prose novel it would mean moving 174 pages of material back by some 448 pages in the edition I am consulting, a fairly major reworking. It also means a refocusing of the text upon the narrator as a character, and a shift away from the early focus on Swann that characterises the prose novel. This is significant since in the original Swann serves as a sort of precursor to the narrator: like the narrator he experiences moments of involuntary memory that sweep him back into the past (in Swann's case it is a "little phrase" in a piece of music by the composer Vinteuil that pulls him into reverie), and his paranoia over and obsession with Odette's infidelities prefigure the narrator's own love for Albertine.[13] In addition to being a thematic forebear, Swann is a historical precursor to the narrator, his story providing a context for the narrator's since Swann is a socialite in the period prior to the narrator's trips to Combray, and he is a married man with a child (Gilberte) at the time of the holidays that the narrator describes. Indeed Swann, whose house is close to the narrator's aunt's (where the narrator and his family stay while in Combray) often visits the family in the evenings. The reorganisation in Heuet's version therefore represents a postponement of this historical context and a reduction of the novel's social backstory in favour of an increased focus upon the individual story of the narrator. In this way, Heuet arguably brings the novel more into line with the 'bande dessinée' trope of the young male protagonist as seen in examples such as Tintin or Spirou. Swann, then, takes the position of older supporting character, and should we wish to take the Tintin comparison further, we might also note that the lengthy flashback to Swann and Odette's romance that plays out in volumes four and five of Heuet's adaptation bears some resemblance to the tale Captain Haddock relates about his famous ancestor in *The Secret of the Unicorn* in that both employ significant events from the past in telling stories that influence the lives of the characters in the present.[14]

Yet this modification is not wholly unproblematic, and the amendment does bring about a critical change: in the novel, the final chapter of *Swann's Way* (which comes after *Swann in Love*) and the first chapter of *Within a Budding Grove* detail the narrator's friendship and early infatuation with Gilberte Swann (who is the product of the relationship described in *Swann in Love*). In the 'bande dessinée', however, these chapters are missing – the plot skips straight from the end of the chapter *Combray* to the second chapter of *Within a Budding Grove*, only coming back to the Gilberte storyline in the sixth volume, much later than it appears in the novel. Here it becomes difficult to agree with Jan Baetens' assertion that Heuet's "reduction isn't an amputation," since the adaptation involves the reorganisation of a substantial portion of one of the novel's most important relationships and in the first instance this does involve a reduction that removes at least a few digits, if not a whole limb.[15] Where Proust has the narrator's love for Gilberte arising first from a brief and wordless encounter during a walk in Combray, and then from a substantial friendship that is described in some detail across two chapters of the novel, Heuet at first retains only the initial meeting in Combray. This plays out across just three pages, and Gilberte only actually appears on two of them, which makes the opening of *Within a Budding Grove* somewhat bizarre as the narrator declares "I'd come to a state of almost complete indifference concerning Gilberte, when, two years later, I left [Paris] for Balbec with my grandmother".[16] In Proust's version this makes sense, since the narrator has by this point described his friendship and infatuation with Gilberte as something that takes place over a period of time; in the 'bande dessinée' it makes the narrator appear truly obsessive by implying that the momentary encounter in Combray led to him devloping a two-year crush on her. Nor are the effects of this limited to this encounter only, since just as Swann prefigured the narrator Gilberte prefigures Albertine, and the implication of an obsessive narrator at this point colours the reader's impression of him going forwards but does not offer the more nuanced and sympathetic portrayal that Proust is able to present. Heuet does, however, present the narrator/Gilberte relationship in the sixth volume of the adaptation (not published in English at the time of this writing), much later than its appearance in the prose, suggesting a 'renewal' (or multiple remembrances) of the affections the narrator has for Gilberte rather than positioning those affections clearly at a particular point in the narrator's life as the novel does. It remains to be seen how this will play out in the later volumes; at the time of this writing the adaptation of *The Captive* has not been published. Nevertheless we can say that in its initial volumes at least Heuet's work presents a simpler and more obsessive narrator than Proust's original. He is less self-aware, and less able to account for his thoughts and actions. He is perhaps a different character.

As David Carrier has observed, 'bande dessinée' is rich in possibilities for the adaptation of *Remembrance* because Proust's novel engages frequently with visual and partially-visual arts such as painting, theatre, photography and magic lantern projections.[17] I will not repeat Carrier's discussion, which considers the implications of visually depicting the scenes, people and objects that Proust describes, here. Instead, I will look at two specific structural aspects of 'bande dessinée' and consider how they function to express particular qualities of Proust's novel in Heuet's adaptations. The first of these aspects is the inset, which I will discuss in relation to Proust's frequent use of parentheses; the second is braiding, which I will look at relative to the idea of involuntary memory that Proust presents in the book.

Parentheses and the inset: one of the qualities for which *Remembrance of Things Past* is best known is its use of long, detailed sentences that involve numerous digressions and meditations on things outside what could strictly be termed the 'plot'. Although many things do happen in the book it would be difficult to argue that it is action-packed: its language is dense and rich (though not without rhythm), and moves forwards slowly and carefully. While this has been viewed favourably by some (see the quotation from Mary Zimmerman, above, for example – although she argues this type of language is difficult to adapt for the theatre she is largely positive about it as an aspect of a work of literature), it has been derided by others. Germaine Greer, for example, is vitriolic in her assessment:

> If Proust did not make such a snobbish to-do about diction, it might be easier to forgive him for his battering of the sentence to rubble and his apparent contempt for the paragraph. He relies on commas and semi-colons to do what should be done by full stops, of which there are far too few, many of them in the wrong place. Sentences run to thousands of words and scores of subordinate clauses, until the reader has no recollection of the main clause or indeed whether there ever was one.[18]

Although this claim does not apply to the whole work, and Proust does vary his style to some degree across the seven volumes of *Remembrance*, it is true to say that as a general rule the book does employ long sentences with complex structures, and contains within these sentences more than is common in literature. In contrast with Greer, I would argue that Proust's paragraphs do not indicate any "contempt" for the device as such; rather they represent the limits of what a paragraph can be, and push them further than literature generally does. Each tends to relate to a single idea, but develops that idea so fully and in so much detail that it can often be as rich as a whole chapter might be in another work. Proust's chapters, made up of these often very long paragraphs (themselves comprised of very long sentences) might very well be volumes in and of themselves (many are over 100 pages in length). Yet what is most notable in all these structures is the rigour with which Proust approaches his subjects, and the way in which the narrator is positioned. Often, sentences employ lengthy parentheses (whether these are contained within brackets or, more often, commas) that serve to figuratively 'bracket off' the narrator from the situation in which he is engaged at the same time as retaining a position within the space of the plot. The narrator is both within the situation and outside it (i.e. in a position to analyse it) at the same time, and the reader is required to hold these two positions in their head at the same time (hence the challenge of "recollection" outlined by Greer).

In Heuet's adaptations, this 'dual position' is generally represented visually through the use of narration boxes that contain only text in a typeset font (albeit one which looks like a formal style of handwriting). These narration boxes are not impenetrable; on occasion they also play host to images in silhouette, but they do generally serve to bracket off the narrator's comments about the situation from the situation itself, which proceeds both in images and dialogue (dialogue employs a less formal typography).

Part 3: Using the Victorians

Fig. 12. Heuet, S. and Dorey, V. (2001) *Remembrance of Things Past: Combray*. New York: NBM, page 8.

The narration boxes are also presented in a consistent yellow colour, while speech and thought bubbles are white. Thus, Heuet's adaptation makes clear the distinction between what is happening and what the narrator is narrating about what is happening. In one instance though, Heuet also takes an interesting approach to page layout that suggests an additional means by which Proust's parentheses might be represented, employing a variant of what Thierry Groensteen has described as an "inset" panel. Groensteen describes the inset as a configuration of panels "that find[s] a frame welcomed within one or several other frame(s)."[19] Generally this takes the form of a small panel whose borders are physically within a larger one, and there are two common purposes for insets:

> the inset serves the purpose of the picture when it magnifies the background panel, whereas it more clearly serves the story when its purpose is the contextualisation of the inset panel. In the first case, it allows itself to be reduced to a simple *superimposition*; in the second, it puts in place a dialogic *interaction* between the concerned panels.[20]

In the first volume of Heuet's adaptation, we can see a slightly varied form of the inset early in the story when the narrator is listening to his relatives speaking about Swann (see Fig. 12.).

In the fifth panel, we see a broad view of the situation, with the narrator sitting on a stool between his aunts and his grandfather, who are sat on a couch and a chair respectively. His great aunt is seen in the foreground. At the bottom of the page, however, the framing is much tighter: first it focuses upon the narrator's great aunt who comments upon Swann, then upon the narrator's aunts who continue the discussion. The final panel returns to the great aunt, but between this last panel and the one with the two aunts we see the narrator tightly enclosed in a small panel filled with a substantial pair of thought balloons. Although this panel does not strictly fall into Groensteen's description of the inset since a gutter does separate it from the panels that surround it, I would argue that it is nonetheless an example of an inset since it does effectively cut into the shapes of the panels around it (note that these are the only panels on the page that are not rectangular). Those larger panels, despite not being absolutely contiguous with the smaller one, do physically enclose it and serve visually to bracket off the narrator with his own thoughts. In this sense the page layout echoes the structure of the book's sentences, since the narrator is both enclosed within the situation by the surrounding panels and held outside it by the gutters and panel borders. This goes beyond "the [magnification of] the background panel", since it offers a different perspective upon a sequence whose context is elaborated in the broader panel above it, but it does not go as far as "[putting] in place a dialogic 'interaction' between the concerned panels" since the inset does not actually affect the sequence with the aunts and the great aunt (in fact, it is precisely the narrator's inability to affect this sequence that is the point of the inset). It therefore sits somewhere in between Groensteen's two purposes for insets, and indicates just how complex Proust's

Part 3: Using the Victorians

language and narration are. In this way the structure of parentheses that Proust used to express the tension between the narrator's position 'inside' and 'outside' situations in language is successfully substituted for a structural function of comics.

Involuntary memory and braiding: the specific qualities of the medium of comics also come into play in Heuet's representation of one of Proust's most famous subjects: involuntary memory. As outlined above, involuntary memory is a prevalent theme throughout the novel, being experienced by both Swann (whose remembrances are prompted by hearing Vinteuil's "little phrase") and by the narrator (most famously in relation to the madeleine, but in other sequences as well, particularly in *Time Regained*). Importantly, in speaking of involuntary memory, the text is not simply referring to our recollection of experiencing particular sensations, but to our re-experiencing of the sensations themselves, something that Proust suggests enables them to exist outside time. Among the most helpful expressions of this idea in the book is the following passage:

> let a sound, a scent already heard and breathed in the past be heard and breathed anew, simultaneously in the present and in the past, real without being actual, ideal without being abstract, then instantly the permanent and characteristic essence hidden in things is freed and our true being which has for long seemed dead but was not so in other ways awakes and revives, thanks to this celestial nourishment. An instant liberated from the order of time has recreated in us man liberated from the same order, so that he should be conscious of it. And indeed we understand his faith in his happiness even if the mere taste of a madeleine does not logically seem to justify it; we understand that the name of death is meaningless to him for, placed beyond time, how can he fear the future?[21]

The ability of comics to express the perspective of a character that stands outside time is something I have already discussed at some length elsewhere, but I would like to expand on that discussion in a slightly different direction here by drawing upon another term described by Thierry Groensteen: 'braiding' ('tressage').[22] Groensteen describes braiding thus:

> within the paged multiframe that constitutes a complete comic, every panel exists, potentially if not actually, in relation with each of the others. This totality, where the physical form is generally, according to French editorial norms, that of an album, responds to a model of organisation that is not that of the strip nor that of the chain, but that of the network.

Jan Baetens and Pascal Lefèvre have justly noted that "far from presenting itself as a chain of panels, the comic demands a reading capable of searching, beyond linear

184

relations, to the aspects or fragments of panels susceptible to being networked with certain aspects or fragments of other panels." Braiding is precisely the operation that, from the point of creation, programs and carries out this sort of bridging. It consists of an additional and remarkable structuration that, taking account of the breakdown and the page layout, defines a *series* within the sequential framework.[23]

A series then, is a set of panels (which may be more or less expansive depending on the example) whose connection and relationships derive from visual similarity but not necessarily physical contiguity. One of the most well-known examples cited by Groensteen in *The System of Comics* comes from the repeated use of the smiley face icon in *Watchmen*: a recurring visual motif that threads throughout the graphic novel in a complex and polysemic way. In his adaptation of *Remembrance of Things Past*, Stéphane Heuet regularly employs braiding to create just such series.

The most frequently (re)used image in Heuet's adaptation is probably that of the eyes of the narrator superimposed onto a scene or (more commonly) a montage within a panel, that indicates a summation of the events and moments that have preceded it. The image appears on the endpapers of the first two volumes of the adaptation, and is used within the narrative from the first page of the first volume (see Fig.13.). It recurs across the books at moments that emphasise the act of remembering. In the examples seen in Fig. 13, the narrator speaks of how his "memory was set in motion" and a later appearance of the motif towards the end of the volume picks up on sensory experiences that also prompt the re-experiencing of moments across time that is indicated in the extract from Proust that is quoted above, a narration box asserting: "That scent of hawthorn collecting along the hedge, an echo-less sound of steps on the gravel of an alley, a bubble formed by the river water beside a water-plant and which immediately bursts …"[24] Yet despite its repetition across this first volume, the image of the eyes is not visually contextualised until the final page of the first volume, its position in the panel sequence echoing that of the first page, as the narrator's adult face comes into view in a wordless panel. This panel then, serves to identify the eyes, and to indicate the one who is remembering. In later volumes the eyes appear less frequently than in the volume *Combray*, only featuring on the endpapers of *Within a Budding Grove Volume 1* (though the end papers are hardly an unprivileged location in 'bande dessinée', as readers of *Tintin* who are familiar with the sets of portraits that contextualise Hergé's stories will know). They return within the narrative (but lose their position on the endpapers) in *Within a Budding Grove Volume 2*, where they underpin the narrator's discussion of diners in a restaurant who "hadn't taken a wider view of things which sheds for them their customary appearance and allows us to perceive analogies."[25] Here again, they serve to identify a point of detachment from the moment and emphasise reflection upon a situation. In *Swann in Love Volume 1* the eyes again appear only once, but in an important location: the first panel. Here they remind the reader of the presence of the narrator as a character who appears within the plot (rather than an omniscient being

Part 3: Using the Victorians

PART ONE

COMBRAY

Fig. 13. Heuet, S. and Dorey, V. (2001) *Remembrance of Things Past: Combray*. New York: NBM, page 3.

who stands outside it) before introducing a story in which the narrator does not appear. The narration box above the panel (which also integrates a silhouetted image of the narrator in bed) reads:

> thus did I often remain through the morning, thinking about times in Combray, ...and by association of memories, about what I'd learned, many years after having left that small town, concerning a love affair that Swann had had before my birth...[26]

Note that this passage does not strictly make sense following Heuet's reorganisation of the text as detailed in section II of this chapter, since the narrator has by this point in the adaptation moved on from talking about Combray and discussed his time at Balbec at length across the two volumes of *Within a Budding Grove*. The text makes more sense if it is read directly after the chapter *Combray*, which reflects the position of the chapter *Swann in Love* in the original novel. Here though, I would suggest, we find further evidence for the notion that Heuet's reorganisation of the text is intended to reinforce the reader's connection to the narrator and emphasise his role as character within the books. By shifting the Balbec sequence forwards, the reader has more visual exposure to the narrator and is able to identify him within the narrative either by his full visual appearance or by the motif of the eyes. By the time we reach *Swann in Love* then, we are sufficiently familiar with the character that a single panel showing the eyes is enough to situate the story told to us in that book as 'a story that is told by our narrator'; we are not tempted to view it as an independent tale related by an omniscient narrator. In this way, Heuet visually indicates the relationships between the stories, and emphasises that *Swann in Love* does relate to the rest of *Remembrance* in a specific and direct fashion. As I will discuss later in this chapter, this positioning of the narrator as a character is not itself unproblematic, but for the moment it is enough to note that braiding is a very effective means of expressing the unity of the work.

Heuet also uses braiding to communicate another important theme in Proust's text: recognition, something that is closely related to involuntary memory since as the extract from Proust above emphasises, the remembrance of things past could also be a recognition of sensations that recur. Yet as Proust's work also makes clear, recognition is sometimes partial or incomplete – we cannot always call to mind exactly *why* we recognise someone or something, or what it reminds us of. This occurs, and is expressed visually, in Heuet's adaptations extremely effectively. In the volume *Combray*, for example, while on a carriage ride the young narrator sees the church steeples at Martinville and they inspire him to produce his first sustained piece of writing.[27] Later, in *Within a Budding Grove Volume 1*, the narrator has a similar encounter:

> Suddenly I was filled with that profound happiness that I'd not often felt since Combray, a happiness analogous to that which, among other things, the steeples in Martinville had caused me. / But this time, it remained incomplete. / I'd just spied

three trees that probably served as an entry point for a shaded road / and formed a sketch that I wasn't seeing for the first time. / I was unable to recall this place from which it was almost like they were detached, but I sensed that it was familiar to me in the past. / Where had I seen them before? There was no place around Combray where a roadway opened up like that. / Soon, at a crossroads, the carriage left them behind. It was carrying me far from what I believed was alone real, from that which would have made me truly happy, it resembled my life. / I saw the trees drawing away, waving their desperate arms, seeming to say to me: 'What you don't learn from us today, you'll never know. If you let us sink into the depths of this road from which we'd sought to raise ourselves to you, a whole part of yourself that we were bringing to you will forever fall into nothingness.'[28]

In his depiction of this sequence, Heuet enables the reader to undergo similar experiences to the narrator, and expresses clearly the notion of a recognition that remains just out of reach. In the latter sequence, the shapes and positions of the trees, both within the panels and in the page layout more broadly, are similar to those of the steeples of Martinville's church as they are depicted in the previous volume. They are not absolutely identical, however, so while the reader may have a sense of recognition it is not possible to link the two instances absolutely directly, and braiding here serves as much to confound as to connect. A similar technique is used later in *Within a Budding Grove Volume 1* to connect the character of the Baron de Charlus to Gilberte Swann through a similarity of posture, reflecting an impression made upon the narrator that the two may be related.[29] The reader thus experiences the sense of ambiguous recognition (or misrecognition) that the narrator expresses verbally, though unlike the narrator the reader does have the advantage of being able to flip back to the previous volume and compare the two images should (s)he wish to do so.

Although the adaptation of *Remembrance of Things Past* is in many ways extremely effective in working with the form of 'bande dessinée' to express visually what Proust conveys through language, there are certain areas where issues do arise. One of the most striking of these is the representation of point of view, which brings with it issues of identity. To put the matter simply: Proust's novel is narrated throughout by a single individual whose point of view is (in principle) limited. Although he does know more than we might reasonably expect a real person to know about the thoughts and feelings of people exterior to himself (most obviously Swann, but others too) and situations in which he was not involved, there is a sense throughout that the narrator came to know about these things from a specific source (even if this source is not actually identified within the novel). The narrator, then, is not omniscient. Importantly though, the narrator's identity is not absolutely clear within the novel as my use of the term 'narrator', rather than a character name, to identify him indicates. In fact while his descriptions are generally very precise and detailed, the narrator remains coy when it comes to revealing his own name within the work. Generally speaking, the narrator is known as 'Marcel' when the work is discussed, but this name comes only from a few short sequences in the book's fifth volume (*The Captive*). The first of these remains vague, not committing to the name for the character:

> The uncertainty of awakening revealed by her silence was not at all revealed in her eyes. As soon as she was able to speak she said: 'My –' or 'My dearest –' followed by my Christian name, which, if we give the narrator the same name as the author of this book, would be 'My Marcel', or 'My dearest Marcel'.[30]

This hardly represents a straightforward statement that the narrator's name is indeed Marcel, and ambiguity around this aspect is again emphasised later in this volume:

> I embraced her, told her that I was going to take a turn outside, she half opened her eyes, said to me with an air of astonishment – indeed the hour was late: 'But where are you off to, my darling –' calling me by my Christian name, and at once fell asleep again.[31]

The book does subsequently use Marcel as the narrator's name more confidently in a note sent by Albertine to the narrator:

> 'My darling, dear Marcel, I return less quickly than this cyclist, whose machine I would like to borrow in order to be with you sooner. How could you imagine that I might be angry or that I could enjoy anything better than to be with your? It will be nice to go out, just the two of us together; it would be nicer still if we never went out except together. The ideas you get into your head! What a Marcel! What a Marcel! Always and ever your Albertine.'[32]

Yet this more direct naming of the narrator as Marcel does not hold. In the final volume (*Time Regained*), we read:

> I noticed that the servants had recognised me and whispered my name, and a lady said she had heard them remark in their vernacular: 'There goes old – ' (This was followed by my name).[33]

While it may seem excessive to pick out each occasion on which the narrator's name appears (or explicitly does not appear) it is worth noting that these few instances represent (as far as I am aware) all the occasions in the entire work of around one and a quarter million words in which the narrator's name is indicated. At no point can the reader be certain of even the most basic facts about the narrator who guides them through this massive text

Part 3: Using the Victorians

– a character with whom they are likely to spend a significant amount of time if they read the book in its entirety. Not that this has stopped scholars and critics from identifying the narrator concretely as Marcel and from drawing (or attempting to draw) direct comparisons between Marcel as the narrator/character and Marcel Proust as the author.[34]

These comparisons, and the ambiguity that surrounds the narrator, complicate the process of adapting *Remembrance of Things Past* for visual media, where much is shown rather than (or in addition to) being told. Much of the complexity here arises from the issue of focalisation, since the novel's fairly restricted internal focalisation (that is, internal to the narrator, even if he speaks of characters that are external to him) does not lend itself well to visual arts such as comics and film, where a) consistent internal focalisation is rare and b) multimodality makes consistent focalisation difficult. There are some examples of comics and films that *do* employ very limited focalisation in conveying their narratives, such as Peter Bagge's *My Pad and Welcome to It!* (in *Hate* #1), which is a 16 page comic that is visually and verbally addressed to the reader, who is given a tour of Buddy Bradley's new house by Bradley himself.[35] Throughout the sequence the images are shown from a (loosely) fixed point of view: that of a person that Bradley is talking to, and this is employed consistently except during a few short flashbacks that take the reader outside the physical space of the house and show the stories that Bradley narrates. John Byrne et al's *The House That Reed Built* (from *Fantastic Four* v.1 #265), Baru's *Sur la route encore* and films such as *The Blair Witch Project*, of 1999, directed by Daniel Myrick and Eduardo Sánchez, *Cloverfield*, of 2008, directed by Matt Reeves and Neil Blomkamp's 2009 *District 9*, have made similar use of limited focalisation in visual narratives, more or less consistently.[36] But in each of these cases the comic or film was the initial instance of the plot, it was not an adaptation of an existing narrative. In the case of *Remembrance of Things Past*, by contrast, there is a question around how much flexibility is possible or desirable when it comes to representing point of view, since we already know that the novel is narrated entirely from one point of view: that internal to the narrator. Were that point of view to shift, questions would arise around how much liberty could be taken with the text – should the narrator be shown? If so, what should he look like? Should he bear a resemblance to Marcel Proust?

In most adaptations in which the narrator features, he is shown, and Stéphane Heuet's graphic adaptation is no exception. The narrator appears in various stages of development: as a young boy at Combray, an adolescent at Balbec, and as an adult in various scenes that relate to the older narrator as he remembers (for example in the incident with the madeleine). In some cases, Heuet has clearly taken inspiration from images of Proust himself; a panel depicting the narrator in bed at the end of *Combray* seeming to have been taken directly from a specific (and anonymous) photograph of the author looking directly into the camera with his fingers resting against his chin and cheek. Heuet has removed the hand from the photograph, but the provenance of the image is obvious. Yet it would be unwise to suggest that this is necessarily an attempt on Heuet's part to connect Proust to the narrator in a literal fashion. The various descriptions of the narrator that are to be found in the novel do indicate visual similarities between him and Proust, so it is unsurprising that Heuet depicts them in this way, yet there is enough ambiguity in the drawn image to believe that the narrator is not necessarily intended to be Proust himself, and he is thus able to remain a fictional character.[37]

A more substantial issue exists around the broader question of focalisation. In depicting the narrator from an external position, Heuet (and indeed any adaptation of *Remembrance*) ruptures the internal focalisation found in the novel. In the case of Heuet's adaptation this rupture is multiplied since in addition to the sequences of images that show the narrator, there are also various levels of textual content that are ontologically split along lines that do not arise in the novel, where everything that is said or thought is filtered through the internal point of view of the narrator. In Heuet's version we find distinctions made between the narration (contained within narration boxes), speech (in speech bubbles) and thoughts (in thought bubbles), along with the use of typographic features such as exclamation marks and question marks within images, used to indicate things that are neither visible nor directly convertible into language 'per se', such as alarm or puzzlement. In Heuet's version then, we are witness to a narrative that jumps around between focal and narrative points quite extensively, first speaking from the narrator's internal point of view, then moving outside the narrator and showing him speaking and being responded to by other characters. In some cases panels do show us scenes or objects from what appears to be the narrator's ocular viewpoint, but these panels are occasional, not the norm. As Ann Miller and Kai Mikkonen have pointed out, heterodiegetic narration is common in comics, and it is unusual to find a comic that does employ a limited focalisation as consistently as *My Pad and Welcome to It!*[38] This is not problematic in itself, but when it comes to an adaptation it is worth paying attention to, since it can have a substantial effect upon the way in which the text is perceived. Of particular note in this instance is how the multiplication of narrative points of view affects the intimacy between the narrator and the reader of Proust's novel. As Laurence Grove has observed:

> In general, [the words] of the characters are expressed by the 'bulles' [speech bubbles], and those of the narrator by the 'récitatif' [narration boxes], although any divergence from these norms (e.g., having the character as a narrator) can unsettle the reader or, alternatively, create an effect of shared confidence.[39]

In the case of Heuet's adaptations, I would suggest that the effect of the multifocal narration depends very much upon the reader. If the reader is not familiar with Proust's original work, then the narration boxes that offer insights into the narrator's thoughts will create precisely the sense of "shared confidence" that Grove describes, and offer a means by which the narrator as character might explain what lies beneath the actions that are depicted in the images without speaking directly to the reader within those depictions and in effect 'breaking the spell' of the story.[40] But for the reader who is familiar with the novel before reading the adaptation, the exterior focalisation to be found in the panels, which serves to position the reader outside the narrator (looking at him rather than 'through' him) will undermine the notion of a shared confidence and have the effect of "[unsettling] the reader" mentioned by Grove. The relatively concise and heavily edited nature of the narration in the adaptation, along with the reorganisation of material discussed above and the use of braiding also combine with the heterogeneity of the narration to further strengthen the idea of the narrator as a character. The reader occupies a shared space with the narrator, but there remains an unresolved distance between them; the gap does not close and allow the reader to encounter situations from the position of the narrator as (arguably) occurs in the novel.

Remembrance of Things Past confounds many of the conventional questions we commonly ask when thinking about adaptations. The old question of fidelity and whether an adaptation should seek to be faithful to the original or to inject its own character into the plot and ideas of the original work, for example, is essentially meaningless in this context.[41] It is unclear what an adaptation would be faithful to: the plot, the ideas and concepts, the characters, the style, the structure or something else. The sheer scope of Proust's work makes it difficult to see how any adaptation could express everything within it, and in this regard the novel is, I would suggest, immune to adaptation in the conventional sense. This does not mean, however, that it cannot be expressed in other media, or that adaptations are inherently lesser works because they do not convey the whole of Proust's vast project. While it is true that Heuet's graphic novels omit much, reshuffle the narrative, and position the narrator differently to Proust's originals, they are also inventive and intelligent in their employment of 'bande dessinée's' structural capabilities to express the style and ideas of the novels. David Carrier has asserted that:

> Compared to Proust's novel, Heuet's *Remembrance of Things Past* is only a slight work of art. And yet, I would not scorn the comic, both because Heuet's book does raise extremely interesting philosophical questions about the nature of visual and verbal narratives and, also, because it's fun rereading the novel alongside the comic. When you do that [...] you will find that Heuet's little books can teach us something about Proust's great novel.[42]

More than this, I would suggest that Heuet's work offers both an introduction to the plot and ideas of Proust's, and a taste of that work's style and nature. For the reader who has not yet read Proust's novel this taste will likely be blunt and unsophisticated: sour or sweet – it will either put them off Proust for life since despite certain connections to the field the comic's slow, meandering narrative is arguably dull when compared to the pacier high adventure narratives of *Tintin* or many of its other peers in the realm of 'bande dessinée', or it will entice them to read more and engage more fully with the 'whole text' of which Heuet's adaptation is only a part. For the reader who has read Proust though, it is likely to be generally unsatisfying and to fall into the realm of the "slight work of art" as David Carrier has suggested. It is only a light apéritif by comparison with the vast banquet represented by Proust's original. And yet… in that apéritif the reader might well discover, in select moments, particular images and turns of phrase, a resonance with the novel that returns to the present the experiences that it offers. The 'bande dessinée' may only offer a taste of *Remembrance of Things Past*, but let us not forget the power that Proust ascribed to taste:

> when from a long-distant past nothing subsists, after the people are dead, after the things are broken and scattered, still, alone, more fragile, but with more vitality, more unsubstantial, more persistent, more faithful, the smell and taste of things remain poised a long time, like souls, ready to remind us, waiting and hoping for their moment, amid the ruins of all the rest; and bear unfalteringly, in the tiny and almost impalpable drop of their essence, the vast structure of recollection.[43]

Notes

1. I would like to thank Jan Baetens for providing me with a copy of his article *Marcel Proust en 48CC*, and Hayleigh Nash for generously taking the time to translate it for me for the purposes of this chapter.
2. Although the title of Proust's novel is now more commonly translated as *In Search of Lost Time*, I will be referring to the English language translation of the text by C.K. Scott Moncrieff, and the English translation of the 'bande dessinée' published by NBM, both of which use the older translated title *Remembrance of Things Past*, so I have employed that version consistently here, and amended any quotations that use *In Search of Lost Time* to *Remembrance of Things Past* in order to avoid confusion. The translation of Proust's work is a tricky area, and there are numerous versions in print. Throughout this article I refer to literature in translation (both Proust's and Heuet's). I do not see this as inherently problematic since my focus here is on the mechanics of adaptation and the broad ideas of the work rather than the specifics of Proust's language, but I am aware that there are some who would chastise me for engaging with the text in translation.
3. The number of volumes the book has depends upon the edition. Throughout this chapter I refer to Wordsworth Classics' two volume edition, which collects three books in the first volume (*Swann's Way*, *Within a Budding Grove* and *The Guermantes Way*) and four books in the second volume (*Cities of the Plain*, *The Captive*, *The Sweet Cheat Gone* and *Time Regained*). Different editions sometimes translate these titles (and the titles of chapters) differently but I have remained consistent with the edition I have used here.
4. Benjamin, W. (2005) "On the Image of Proust." in *Walter Benjamin: Selected Writings. Vol. 2, Part 1, 1927 – 1930*. Cambridge, MA: The Belknap Press of Harvard University Press, page 237.

Part 3: Using the Victorians

5 For a humorous indication of the difficulties of explaining Proust's plot, see Monty Python's *All England Summarise Proust Competition* sketch.
6 Deleuze, G.(2008) *Proust and Signs*. London & New York: Continuum, page 3.
7 Ibid.
8 Zimmerman, M. (2009) "Adapting Proust: A Moment in the Red Room," in *Triquarterly*, Volume 134, page 58.
9 Certain characters, tropes and storylines persist, but neither *Tintin* nor *Asterix* could convincingly be argued to have a very clear 'beginning' and 'end' point outside the boundaries of each individual album – characters do not generally age and the impact of one album upon subsequent instalments is usually (but not always) slight.
10 Proust died in 1922.
11 Verdaguer, P. (2005) "Fictionalising Proust." in *Contemporary French and Francophone Studies* Volume 9 Number 2, page 165.
12 Baetens, J. (2012) "Marcel Proust en 48 CC." in *Cahiers Marcel Proust 9*. Amsterdam & New York: Editions Rodophi B. V, pages 173 – 84. For more on the album format, see: Dejasse, E. and Capart, P. (2014) "In Search of the Lost Serial." in Miller, A. and Beaty, B. Eds. *The French Comics Theory Reader*. Leuven: Leuven University Press, pages 313 – 20.
13 Proust, M. (2006) *Remembrance of Things Past: Volume One* [*Swann's Way*, *Within a Budding Grove*, *The Guermantes Way*]. Ware: Wordsworth Editions. See particularly pages 208 – 13.
14 It is not wholly unfair to compare Heuet's protagonist to Tintin since Heuet's art style does fall into the 'ligne claire' (clear line) style made famous by Hergé, though as Jan Baetens has observed, "Only a distracted or hurried reader will mistake Heuet for a belated or lesser Hergé," and there are some important differences between them, particularly in terms of depth of field (Baetens, J. (2012) "Marcel Proust en 48 CC." in *Cahiers Marcel Proust 9*. Amsterdam & New York: Editions Rodophi B. V). Yet we might also find similarities between Proust's relatively anonymous narrator and Tintin as characters as well, particularly if we compare the argument that: "The reader does not read to learn facts about the author, the reader reads to discover him or her self" from Ingrid Wassenaar's introduction to *Remembrance of Things Past: Volume One*, page 10, with the oft-repeated argument that Tintin is a blank slate, whose appeal comes from his "complete lack of any personality, making it possible for every reader to identify with him" (see Aishwarya Subramanian, A. (2013) "Fanboy Lichtenstein and the 'blank slate' that is Tintin." *The Sunday Guardian* 11/05/2013, accessed 02/08/2014, http://www.sunday-guardian.com/bookbeat/fanboy-lichtenstein-and-the-blank-slate-that-is-tintin).
15 See Baetens, note 14, above). For a similar claim that Heuet's amendments are essentially undamaging to the novel's plot, see Ferslt, P. (2010) "Novel-Based Comics." in Berninger, M., Ecke, J. and Haberkorn, G. Eds. *Comics as a Nexus of Cultures: Essays on the Interplay of Media, Disciplines and International Perspectives*. Jefferson & London: McFarland & Company, page 64.
16 Heuet, S. and Brézet, S. (2002) *Remembrance of Things Past: Within a Budding Grove 1*. New York: NBM, page 3.
17 Carrier, D. (2012) "Proust's *In Search of Lost Time*: The Comics Version." in Meskin, A. and Cook, R. T. Eds. *The Art of Comics: A Philosophical Approach*. Chichester: Wiley-Blackwell, pages 188 – 202.
18 Greer, G. (2009) "Why do people gush over Proust? I'd rather visit a demented relative." *The Guardian* 08/11/2009, accessed 02/08/2014, http://www.theguardian.com/culture/2009/nov/08/germaine-greer-proust
19 Groensteen, T. (2007) *The System of Comics*. Jackson: University Press of Mississippi 2007, page 86.

20 Ibid. Italics in original. For more on the inset, see particularly: ibid. pages 85 – 91.
21 Proust, M. (2006) *Remembrance of Things Past: Volume Two* [*Cities of the Plain*, *The Captive*, *The Sweet Cheat Gone*, *Time Regained*]. Ware: Wordsworth Editions 2006, page 1151.
22 Hague, I. (2012) "Adapting *Watchmen*." in Allen, S. and Hubner, L. Eds. *Framing Film: Cinema and the Visual Arts*. Bristol: Intellect, pages 37 – 55.
23 As note 19, page 146. Italics in original. For more on braiding see pages 145 – 147 and 156 – 158. For more on Groensteen's concept of the series, and the distinction between this and the sequence, see pages 146 – 147 and Groensteen, T. (2012) "Narration as Supplement: An Archaeology of the Infra-Narrative Foundations of Comics." in Miller, A. and Beaty, B. Eds. *The French Comics Theory Reader*. Leuven: Leuven University Press, pages 163 – 181, especially page 176.
24 Heuet, S. and Dorey, V. (2001) *Remembrance of Things Past: Combray*. New York: NBM, page 71.
25 Heuet, S. and Brézet, S. (2003) *Remembrance of Things Past: Within a Budding Grove 2*. New York: NBM, page 7.
26 Heuet, S. (2007) *Remembrance of Things Past: Swann in Love 1*. New York: NBM, page 3.
27 Heuet, S. and Dorey, V. (2001) *Remembrance of Things Past: Combray*. New York: NBM, pages 69 – 70.
28 Heuet, S. and Brézet, S. (2003) *Remembrance of Things Past: Within a Budding Grove 2*. New York: NBM, page 26.
29 As note 27, page 54 and as note 28, page 38.
30 Proust, M. (2006) *Remembrance of Things Past: Volume Two* [*Cities of the Plain*, *The Captive*, *The Sweet Cheat Gone*, *Time Regained*]. Ware: Wordsworth Editions 2006, page 507.
31 Ibid., page 541.
32 Ibid., page 575.
33 Ibid., page 1195.
34 Carrier, D. (2012) "Proust's *In Search of Lost Time*: The Comics Version." in Meskin, A. and Cook, R. T. Eds. *The Art of Comics: A Philosophical Approach*. Chichester: Wiley-Blackwell, page 193.
35 Bagge, P. (2007) *Hate #1*. Seattle: Fantagraphics.
36 For more on *Sur la route encore* see: Miller, A. (2007) *Reading Bande Dessinée: Critical Approaches to French-language Comic Strip*. Bristol & Chicago: Intellect, pages 109 – 110.
37 This question is addressed differently in other media. In Raoul Ruiz's film *Time Regained*, for example, Patrice Chereau provides the voice of Marcel Proust, but the character of the novel's narrator (here called Marcel) is played primarily by Marcello Mazzarella (other actors occasionally appear as Marcel at different stages of his life).
38 As note 36, pages 105 – 108 and Mikkonen, K. (2012) "Focalisation in Comics. From the Specificities of the Medium to Conceptual Reformulation." in *The Scandinavian Journal of Comic Art* Volume 1, Number 1, pages 69 – 95. See also: Groensteen, T. (2013) *Comics and Narration*. Jackson: University Press of Mississippi. Particularly pages 79 – 131. Also Schneider, C. W. (2013) "The cognitive grammar of 'I': Viewing arrangements in graphic autobiographies." in *Studies in Comics* Volume 4, Number 2, pages 307 – 332.
39 Grove, L. (2010) *Comics in French: The European Bande Dessinée in Context*. New York & Oxford: Berghahn Books, page 33.
40 For a useful discussion of intimacy and narrative perspective in the prose novel see: Forster, E. M. (2005) *Aspects of the Novel*. London: Penguin, particularly pages 81 – 84. Forster also considers the implications of the author taking the reader "into his confidence about his characters" (page 84).
41 For more on fidelity in relation to 'bande dessinée' adaptations of novels, see Blin-Rolland, A.

(2013) "Fidelity versus Appropriation in Comics Adaptation: Jacques Carelman's and Clément Oubrerie's *Zazie dans le métro*." in *European Comic Art* Volume 6, Number 1, pages 88 – 109 (the entirety of this issue of *ECA*. is devoted to the subject of comics adaptations of literary works, and is a useful resource on this topic). See also note 22 above, pages 40 – 43.

42 Carrier, D. (2012) "Proust's *In Search of Lost Time*: The Comics Version." in Meskin, A. and Cook, R. T. Eds. *The Art of Comics: A Philosophical Approach*. Chichester: Wiley-Blackwell, pages 201.

43 See note 13, page 63. I have discussed this idea (and indeed this specific quotation) in relation to comics at more length in: Hague, I. (2014) *Comics and the Senses: A Multisensory Approach to Comics and Graphic Novels*. New York & London: Routledge, pages 126 –127.

References

Baetens, J. (2012) "Marcel Proust en 48 CC." In *Cahiers Marcel Proust 9*. Amsterdam & New York: Editions Rodophi B. V, pages 173 – 84.

Bagge, P. (1990) *Hate #1*. Seattle: Fantagraphics.

Benjamin, W. (2005) "On the Image of Proust." In *Walter Benjamin: Selected Writings. Vol. 2, Part 1, 1927 – 1930*. Cambridge, MA: The Belknap Press, pages 237 – 47.

Blin-Rolland, A. (2013) "Fidelity versus Appropriation in Comics Adaptation: Jacques Carelman's and Clément Oubrerie's *Zazie dans le métro*." *European Comic Art* Volume 6, Number 1, pages 88 – 109.

Carrier, D. (2012) "Proust's *In Search of Lost Time*: The Comics Version." in Meskin, A. And Cook, R. T. *The Art of Comics: A Philosophical Approach*. Chichester: Wiley-Blackwell, 188 – 202.

Dejasse, E. and Capart, P. (2014) "In Search of the Lost Serial." in Miller, A. And Beaty, B. Eds. *The French Comics Theory Reader*. Leuven: Leuven University Press, pages 313 – 20.

Deleuze, G. (2008) *Proust and Signs*. London & New York: Continuum.

Ferslt, P. (2010) "Novel-Based Comics." in Berninger, M., Ecke, J. And Haberkorn, G. Eds. *Comics as a Nexus of Cultures: Essays on the Interplay of Media, Disciplines and International Perspectives*. Jefferson & London: McFarland, pages 60 – 69.

Forster, E. M. (2005) *Aspects of the Novel*. London: Penguin.

Greer, G. (2009) "Why do people gush over Proust? I'd rather visit a demented relative." *The Guardian* 8 November 2009, accessed 2 September 2014, http://www.theguardian.com/culture/2009/nov/08/germaine-greer-proust.

Groensteen, T. (2013) *Comics and Narration*. Jackson: University Press of Mississippi.

Groensteen, T. (2014) "Narration as Supplement: An Archaeology of the Infra-Narrative Foundations of Comics" in Miller, A. And Beaty, B. Eds. *The French Comics Theory Reader*. Leuven: Leuven University Press, pages 163-81.

Groensteen, T. (2007) *The System of Comics*. Jackson: University Press of Mississippi.

Grove, Laurence. (2010) *Comics in French: The European Bande Dessinée in Context*. New York & Oxford: Berghahn Books.

Hague, I. (2012) "Adapting *Watchmen*." In Allen, S. And Hubner, L. Eds. *Framing Film: Cinema and the Visual Arts*. Bristol: Intellect, pages 37 – 55.

Hague, I. (2014) *Comics and the Senses: A Multisensory Approach to Comics and Graphic Novels*. New York & London: Routledge.

Heuet, S. (2007) *Remembrance of Things Past: Swann in Love 1*. Johnson. New York: NBM.

Heuet, S. and Brézet, S. (2003) *Remembrance of Things Past: Within a Budding Grove 2*. New York: NBM.

Ibid. (2002) *Remembrance of Things Past: Within a Budding Grove 1*. New York: NBM.

Heuet, S. and Dorey, V. (2001) *Remembrance of Things Past: Combray*. New York: NBM 2001.

Mikkonen, K. (2012) "Focalisation in Comics. From the Specificities of the Medium to Conceptual Reformulation." *The Scandinavian Journal of Comic Art* Volume 1, Number 1, pages 69 – 95.

Miller, A. (2007) *Reading Bande Dessinée: Critical Approaches to French-language Comic Strip*. Bristol & Chicago: Intellect.

Proust, M. (2006) *Remembrance of Things Past: Volume One* [*Swann's Way*, *Within a Budding Grove*, *The Guermantes Way*]. Ware: Wordsworth Editions.

Proust, M. (2006) *Remembrance of Things Past: Volume Two* [*Cities of the Plain*, *The Captive*, *The Sweet Cheat Gone*, *Time Regained*]. Ware: Wordsworth Editions.

Schneider, C. W. (2013) "The cognitive grammar of 'I': Viewing arrangements in graphic autobiographies." *Studies in Comics* Volume 4, Number 2, pages 307– 32.

Subramanian, A. (2013) "Fanboy Lichtenstein and the 'blank slate' that is Tintin." *The Sunday Guardian* 11 May 2013, accessed 2 August 2014, http://www.sunday-guardian.com/bookbeat/fanboy-lichtenstein-and-the-blank-slate-that-is-tintin.

Verdaguer, P. (2005) "Fictionalizing Proust," *Contemporary French and Francophone Studies* Volume 9, Number 2, pages 165 – 73.

Zimmerman, M. (2009) "Adapting Proust: A Moment in the Red Room," *Triquarterly* Number 134, pages 57 – 65.

Aarnoud Rommens

Allegories of graphiation: Alberto Breccia's counter-censorial versions of E. A. Poe's *Valdemar*[1]

First, an apparent puzzle. In 1992, a year before his death, Argentine comics artist Alberto Breccia (1919-1993) completed his retelling of Edgar Allan Poe's *The Facts in the Case of Mr. Valdemar*. Or rather, Breccia 'revisited' the story of Valdemar as this was already his second version of the same tale: together with scenario writer Carlos Trillo he had finished a first adaptation of Poe's tale in 1980.[2] A question arises: given that Breccia rarely if ever repeated earlier work, why did he feel the need for a remake? And why reprise this particular story? However, instead of framing the question as if it were a traditional detective story wherein establishing intentionality clears up the mystery, it would seem more worthwhile to allow time to do its work. In other words, perhaps the time-lag does not so much point to a riddle as it is an invitation to read both versions in the 'key' of 'après-coup.'[3] This delinearisation of texts and images allows for the superposition of before and after, 'original' and derivative, source and adaptation. From this perspective I will read both versions as after-images of one another, with each comic recoding the other while simultaneously re-figuring Poe's *Valdemar*. Not only are they adaptations of Poe's text, they equally transfigure Breccia's work, making for a complex constellation.

Furthermore, against the backdrop of a contemporary Argentina still working through the 1976-83 'Process of National Reorganisation,' Breccia's comic adaptations appear as 'blurry' memory images: their equivocalness is a correlative for the uncertainty about how to fix and mourn a past that refuses to settle.[4] More precisely, Breccia's bequest – his twin Valdemar – is an analogue to the instability, the historical plasticity, of the ambiguous figure of the 'desaparecidos,' those 'disappeared' by the military regime. The 'disappeared' foreground the ambiguity between presence and absence, positive and negative space, figure and ground. I will argue that in his adaptations of Poe's *Valdemar*, Breccia makes this vacillation palpable by presenting readers with an allegory of 'graphiation', to use Philippe Marion's neologism of 1993, intimating how to leave one's mark in the face of censorship.[5] This intertwining of poetics and politics is the focus of my investigation.

In 1976 the military took power in Argentina, and for more than seven years they engaged in what they called the 'Process of National Reorganisation' (1976 – 1983) – simply referred to as the 'Proceso' – a mission to rid the country of subversion and restore 'healthy' values. During this 'Dirty War', the media were subject to state censorship, complete with bans, book burnings, and the abduction and murder of critical voices. Approximately 30,000 so-called 'subversive elements' were kidnapped, tortured, and executed, never to be seen again: they were 'disappeared' by the state apparatus. Around 1981 repression was somewhat relaxed, and after the disastrous Malvinas/Falklands War the military lost all support. After the first democratic election after the junta stepped down, Raúl Alfonsín was sworn in as President in 1983.[6] However, pressured by the strong military class and fearing for reprisals, Alfonsín passed amnesty laws releasing lower level officers while restricting the scope of legal investigations into the crimes committed by the junta. This reign of amnesia would find its climax during the ten-year rule of Carlos Menem from 1989 to 1999. His radical neo-liberal reform was accompanied by the extension of amnesty laws to the higher ranking officers who had ordered most of the atrocities.[7] Today, the amnesty laws have all been revoked, and new trials are still bringing those responsible to court. There is also a heated debate about what form the official memorialisation of this painful period in Argentina's history should take, and what the precise role of the government should be in facilitating remembrance. Overall, you could say that it is only now that mourning and memory work are taking place.[8] It is against this backdrop that counter-censorship should be understood.

Research in the field of literature and theatre produced during military dictatorships in South America has come up with the concept of counter-censorship ('contracensura') as a way to overcome the binary between censorship and self-censorship. As opposed to the latter concepts, counter-censorship supposedly allows for agency in terms of covert resistance. In literature and theatre, counter-censorship refers to rhetorical figures and practises such as allegory, metaphor, the orphaned quote, parody and other means of distantiation that "disarticulate the repressive discursive system." What emerges is a covert "discourse [that would be] censored by that very system" had the artworks not been inoculated against erasure through techniques of indirection.[9] Counter-censorship is thus essentially ironic: the work is made to say something it disavows, like the detours of the 'negative dialectics' of the work of art.[10] Moreover, counter-censorship is precarious: it is historically situated, idiosyncratic and affective, always skirting the possibility, perhaps even the necessity, of over-interpretation. It always depends on the active engagement from its audience, and actualises itself with each reading, staging endless interpretative performances.

With respect to the visual, it could be argued that counter-censorship manifests itself in what Dario Gamboni defines as a 'potential image.' In his conception, potential images are "the instrument and the result of [the] type of aesthetic communication which aims at and depends upon an active collaboration between artist, artwork, and 'onlooker'."[11] Ambiguity is a central feature of such potential images. Gamboni invokes Odilon Redon's understanding of 'mystery' as the perpetuation of "continuous ambiguity, (...) with forms that are about to come into being or will take their being from the onlooker's state of mind"[12] However, unlike Gamboni who still insists on the intentionality of ambiguity, I believe this to be irrelevant from a counter-censorial point of view. This, I think is vital: as opposed to most studies on censorship and counter-censorship alike, the agency ascribed to counter-censorship is an agency exerted by the artwork in dialogue with the reader or viewer. This entails that the precise meaning of what is encrypted is, and must, remain unclear: there cannot be one 'correct' deciphering, otherwise the censor would intervene. The challenge of reading is to allow meanings to proliferate in an intimate encounter with a work that demands that the reader/viewer de-censor it.

I contend that the adaptation of a literary text into a comic can be read as a counter-censorial tactic. As I will argue, Breccia's work harbours an implicit politics of adaptation.[13] This means that both adaptations are not only legible as graphic narratives, which they certainly are. They are also disarticulations of narration that create spaces for memory and critical thinking. Moreover, by virtue of being counter-censorial they test the limits of the language of comics insofar as the latter is a narrative medium. They in fact indicate more poetic, expressive and performative possibilities of comics.

First published in 1845, Edgar Allan Poe's *The Facts of the Case of M. Valdemar* is a parable of modern death: a death without redemption, where flesh becomes (written) word only to dissolve–to 'liquefy'–into its own materiality.[14] The tale is presented in the form of a transcription of a gruesome mesmeric experiment. Using one of his characteristically unreliable narrators, Poe frames the story through the eyes and words of a certain Mister P. who provides us with a retrospective account of this baffling event. The narrator aims to rectify the misunderstandings, speculation and exaggerations that followed when the case became public knowledge. The report's intent is to demystify what happened, to clear up "misrepresentations" and "disbelief" and establish, once and for all, the truth of the matter.[15] The exposition should dispel any doubt by invoking the aura of science by associating it with the language of the medical case study.[16] Of course, the narrator ends up doing the exact opposite: his writing further perpetuates the enigma and the absurdity of the experiment.

The supposedly irrefutable 'facts' concern the hypnosis of Ernest Valdemar, the narrator's terminally ill friend. Since no one had ever thought of mesmerising a man at the point of death, Mister P. takes it upon himself to do just that. At his deathbed, Valdemar is mesmerised: under hypnosis he first reports that he is sleeping. After persistent questioning by Mr. P. asking whether he is still asleep, the patient finally intones, to the horror of all present that "Yes; – no; – I have been sleeping – and now – now – I am dead."[17] Once calm has returned to the bedchamber, the physicians check for vital signs only to conclude that indeed, physically speaking, Valdemar is dead. The hypnotised remains in this trance for seven months, after which the narrator decides to awaken his patient from his living death. While completing the procedure for reawakening, Valdemar opens his eyes, repeatedly crying out that he is dead, "ejaculations of 'dead! dead!' absolutely bursting from the tongue and not from the lips of the sufferer." The mesmerist manages to end the trance, after which Valdemar's body rots in a few seconds' time, leaving behind nothing but a "nearly liquid mass of loathsome–of detestable putridity."[18]

Unlike Poe's story *Mesmeric Revelation* in which the dying patient reveals that the "substance" of God is "unparticled matter", *Valdemar* does not offer a vista of transcendence but insists on the finality of the dissolution of flesh and word.[19] Death brings no ultimate revelation except for the certainty of life's unravelling. As such, *Valdemar* enacts the literalisation of denouement: what is unknotted is language ("the tongue"), bringing it back to its a-semiotic, material condition, with a liquefied pool of black ink on white sheets ready to rise up and reassemble itself into meaningful lines.

In fact, it is thanks to Breccia's adaptations that this interpretive possibility in Poe's text can be fully registered, because the comics foreground their own material conditions of possibility, thereby interrogating the limits of meaningfulness and narration. There are moments in the graphic narratives that give form to those negative spaces – the blanks – that enable narration but which should have remained unseen to ensure diegetic flow.[20] The 'invasion' of plastic, negative space within some of Breccia's frames heightens the opacity and loosens "iconic solidarity", making such images move into the direction of abstraction rather than figurative transparency, ultimately calling into question narrative cohesion.[21]

A brief comparison with other graphic retellings of Poe's *Valdemar* sheds light on Breccia's poetics of visual indeterminacy and allows a glimpse of his politics of adaptation. By comparing the apotheosis of the story that discloses the full horror of the putrefying body with other re-imaginings, Breccia's strategy of literary adaptation will stand out.

Although not a comic but a literary book illustration, Harry Clarke's rendition for the 1919 edition of Poe's *Tales of Mystery and Imagination* sets the tone for subsequent visualizations. The hideousness of Valdemar's liquefying body is rendered in expressionist black and white: the veins of the dripping lines of ink give form to the trickling of the flesh which has changed into liquid. Ink, blood, flesh, line-work and putrefaction engage in a complex shadow play of transmutation.

If Clarke's image still has some self-reflexive nuance, then the following adaptations try to outdo themselves in graphic horror, leaving little room for ambiguity. This small selection from the vast corpus of comic adaptations of Poe's texts highlights the singularity of Breccia's approach. For instance, Carlos Giménez's *El Extraño caso del señor Valdemar*, of 1975, heightens the effect of terror through cutting up the sequence of awakening, while enlarging the words "I am dead" so that the final image – a skull with putrid flesh – can take on its full force. As in the other comics, black and white is the visual language of choice for adapting Poe. In the 1985 *El caso del señor Valdemar*, Joan Boix shifts registers and appropriates Valdemar for the genre of gore comics, making a spectacle of the rotting corpse – its liquid flesh dripping from the bones, one rotting hand reaching out to the viewer. The reader must experience the full emotional force of disgust. Gore had already reached a crescendo in an earlier publication however, such as Isidro Mones's 1975 *Facts in the Case of M. Valdemar*. This hyperbole should come as no surprise since it was published in *Creepy* magazine, whose readership had built up a certain tolerance to gore: it is 'too graphic,' which is of course the whole point of the genre.[22] It is not that these versions merely submit to what Groensteen calls the "tyranny of the plot".[23] These comics stick to Poe's story in order to further exceed Poe's "unity of effect", which is simultaneously the unity of affect.[24] In this case it is the reader who must fully submit to the "tyranny" of repulsion, which is also to submit to the (guilty?) pleasure of gore. Gore produces a kind of 'useless' excess that traditional narratology cannot account for: it is just too much.

By contrast, Breccia's adaptations seem almost tame: against the explicitness of gore his versions appear cerebral (See Fig. 14. and Fig. 15.). This restraint is counteracted by the use of colour, which seems counterintuitive. Especially in the second version, the vibrant palette of the first pages contrasts with the black and white of other Poe adaptations, which, with their precise lines and contours draw our attention to every single anatomical detail of bodily decomposition. By contrast, Breccia's versions seem rather 'festive' at first glance: thick, coloured contours delineate discrete zones of vivid tints; speech balloons are embossed, encircled by dense, contoured bands in colour instead of the usual thin black line. The frames resemble figurative stained glass windows. This graphic distinctiveness also signals that Breccia's renditions seek a different affective engagement than gore. As both versions end in equivocation (coupled to a process of 'whitening'), it is precisely this ambiguity that his comics seek to replicate viscerally. More precisely, I read these opaque adaptations as allegories that examine the limits of narration. On the condition that the reader is attentive to these moments of abstraction, he or she will have to engage with the irresolution communicated by the images.

Breccia's first version of *Valdemar*, with a scenario by Carlos Trillo, ends with a strong, enigmatic image (Fig. 14.). In the comic, Edgar Allan Poe appears as a character: he is the mesmerist responsible for arresting death. Poe's text is cut down, which, incidentally, is

Part 3: Using the Victorians

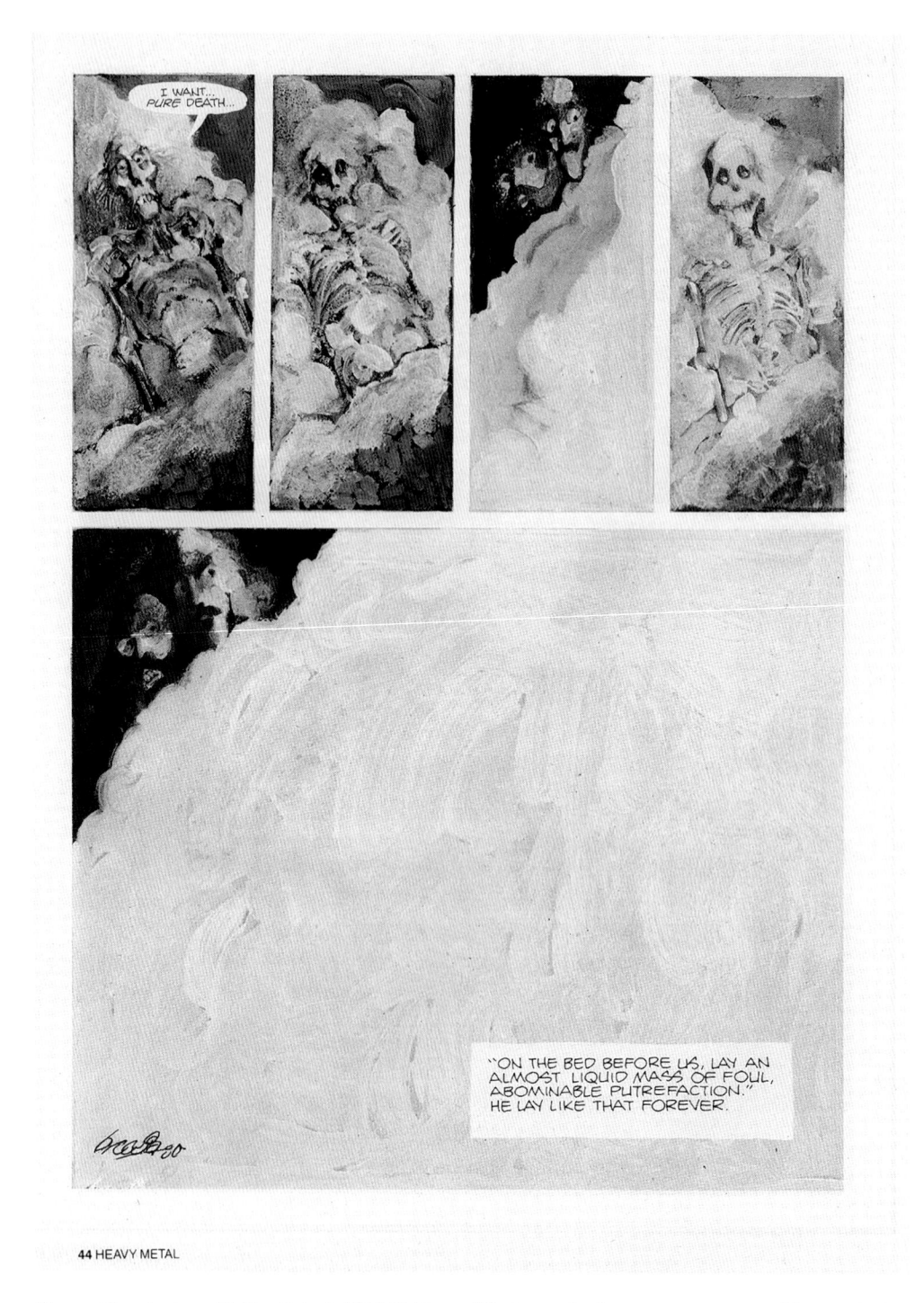

Fig. 14. Breccia, A. and Trillo, C. (1982) "Mr Valdemar." in *Heavy Metal* 6, no. 7, page 44. Used by permission of the heirs of Alberto Breccia.

also the case in the later version. In fact, both versions of Breccia's *Valdemar* are textually austere, erasing the loquaciousness of Poe's narrator. Plastic vibrancy counteracts the aniconic discipline of literature that must evoke the visual through the word. The pathological mania for detail which makes Poe's text such a self-reflexive meandering, textual labyrinth is cut short. Against the automatism of elaboration and the endless nuance of Poe's *Valdemar*, Breccia's *Valdemar* exploits the indeterminacy of the image.

The climax of the story shows an enigmatic image and a caption with the final (somewhat rephrased) words of Poe's text: "On the bed before us lay an almost liquid mass of foul, abominable putrefaction." One line that is not in Poe's original text has been added, as a kind of coda: "He lay like that forever" (Fig. 14.). The image is inundated by shades of white crossing into the panel. The acrylic paint with its modulations of white and grey, the darker lines revealing the strokes of the brush – this frenzied eruption of brushstrokes billows outward and threatens to engulf the two characters, their speech, the space of the panel, and, by extension, narrative space as a whole. Like an ink-spill, the formless blob unravels the 'iconic solidarity' that the comic was so careful to construct: the plastic whitespace confronts us in its illegibility, making palpable the fading of meaning. This moment of abstraction refuses to help in the deciphering of the text: "putrefaction" is figured as if it were a matter of returning the page to pristine white, of white-washing the horror of a death beyond redemption. It is an image of iconoclasm that mobilizes the aniconism of white. The billowing cloud is the whiteout that foregrounds the raw material out of which the story emerged: paint and paper.

When compared to the other adaptations of *Valdemar*, Breccia's final image becomes visible as a hermetic plastic sign: its abstract silence keeps it from figurative decoding and attendant narrative integration. Its opacity provokes a double-take. What emerges is an allegory of the limit of reading: the whitespace makes manifest the negative space – the gutters – on which the comic relies, as a narrative medium. The space of indetermination, which is supposed to remain hidden, takes over the diegetic surface, upsetting it with its painted strokes. It is as if a narrative device had incarnated itself through graphiation: the device suddenly becomes all too visible, as if it were both the tool and the artefact produced by it. What is counter-censorial about the image is that it denies any possible intervention by the censor, by staging the act of censorship. The image makes palpable the effect of censorship, the gesture of repression, which had to be disavowed in ordinary discourse. Through mimicry it denies the pleasure of interdiction and the exercise of authority: by speaking the truth through abstraction – the whitespace being a synecdoche for an institutional apparatus of covering up – it outmanoeuvres authority However, the "active collaboration" required from the reader to create the 'potential image' acquires a sinister ring.[25] It makes the reader complicit in the oscillation between figuration and de-figuration. The support becomes plastic, material, and the reader is faced with the task of literally making and unmaking the image: bringing the image into being as an image of effacement also brings about that very effacement.

Part 3: Using the Victorians

Fig. 15. Breccia, A (1995) "Monsieur Valdemar." in *Le cœur révélateur et autres histoires extraordinaires d'Edgar Poe*. Genève: Les Humanoïdes Associés. Plate 9. Used by permission of the heirs of Alberto Breccia.

The agency that is meant to be, specific to counter-censorship is made problematic: this is a dark allegory foregrounding the reader's complicity, the self-censorship he or she must adopt, just to get by in daily life. Breccia's *Valdemar* inverts the pleasure of gothic transgression into an uncomfortable commentary on clandestine, everyday horror. In this climate of fear, the only stories worth writing and reading are those that stage what they know only to conceal it. In 1980, to expose and denounce the repressive apparatus directly would have resulted in detention, torture, and disappearance. Yet, these horrifying practises were anything but unknown: they were 'open secrets' requiring that everyone submit to the duplicitous transparency of official versions of events. Thus, counter-censorship is double: to read is to recreate the gesture of censorshi, through the graphiation of crossing out, redaction, whiteout, etc., while making it legible as a simulacrum of censorship is also to circumvent that gesture.

The abstract interruption of the final frame is an analogue to amnesia: the denouement of the narrative is not the dissolution of Mr Valdemar but the evacuation of the story from our field of vision. The 'whitespace' is a memory screen upon which 'disappeared' meanings can be projected. A space for trauma is cleared: the wiping of the blackboard makes room for the inscription of memory traces and allusions to the repressed reality of the 'desaparecidos', those spectral figures haunting everyday Argentina. Breccia's *Valdemar* is a paradoxical mnemonic encounter: it is paradoxical because nothing is left behind. There is nothing attesting to a life, since even Valdemar's corpse is wiped out. This is precisely what it means to be 'disappeared.' Since there are no material remains, no corpses pointing to a lived past, with the regime thus effectively circumventing the principle of 'habeas corpus' – only negative space can attest to the former presence of the 'desaparecidos': their absence is the only trace they leave behind.

Breccia's second version captures the uncanny temporality of censorship and counter-censorship. In the light of this new version, the previous adaptation can be read as a prolepsis of the version to come. On the other hand, the second version is the working through, the remembering of Breccia's initial version. Yet, as I will try to show it also branches out into the future as it poses the problem – the impossibility, even – of a univocal representation of the 'desaparecidos.'

The work's graphiation bears the traces of its context. During the 1990s, a regime of forgetting was established which, in a sense, was the continuation of the dictatorship. Decrees were passed that pardoned most of the officers in charge during the 'Dirty War' in the name of 'national re-unification.' Amnesty was awarded to those who had previously been sentenced, while former concentration camps were to be demolished. It went even so far that President Menem threatened "those critical of his government with arrest, suggesting that they toe the self-censoring line." Albeit on a smaller scale, even the practice of disappearance continued, while "journalists continue[d] to be threatened, and some [...] even murdered. A militaristic presence continued to make itself felt even under democratic government."[26]

Like the first adaptation, the final image of this reworking ends not so much in a denouement as the foreclosure of an ending: the story is what unravels (Fig. 15). Negative space becomes all the more evident as the colour pattern moves from bright to white, creating a chromatic rhythm. It is the inverse of the colouring book: colour is evacuated as the experience of reading continues. The bright colours at the beginning of the comic literally fade to white. What is peculiar is that the figure in the closing frame seems to contradict the notion of instant 'liquefaction', of flesh dissolving upon waking. Throughout the comic, the main focus is Valdemar's face, which seems to have petrified within the cracked surface of the pillow after a slow process of becoming mineral. Instead of instantaneity, the image conjures up the protracted temporality of "ruin time" or even the inhuman vastness of geological time, the time of fossilisation.[27]

Like a timeworn, ancient fresco, it looks as if paint has been steadily flaking, once again revealing the surface underneath. The main figure dissolves, destined to disappear into the white of the 'wall', the blank page. It even seems as if time is running in reverse, suggesting a slow rewind during which the composition will eventually return to its unpainted state. Perhaps this is an over-exposure, with particles of light corroding the integrity of the image, as in ancient cave paintings disintegrating through contact with oxygen and flashlights. No matter how one imagines the receding of the image (a chipping away, a dissolve, time looping back), the slow dissolve contrasts sharply with Poe's story, and evokes the twelve-year lapse between the first and second adaptation. As in the previous version, there is a movement towards de-figuration and whitening, with abstraction functioning as a visual equivalent to the unutterable.

At the same time however, the image can also be read inversely: instead of vanishing, the figure emerges out of its ground, slowly revealing itself. If so, then instead of erosion, a lengthy metamorphosis is taking place, with a monstrous figure tentatively rising up out of the liquid that is now Valdemar. This double dynamic between focus and blur makes this image a 'crypto-image.' To quote Jean-Didier Urbain a crypto-image is "a sign that oscillates between the desire to be disclosed (to be an image) and the temptation of the void satisfied by utter effacement (being a non-image)."[28] This oscillation is preceded by an uncanny sequence of frames. It is a moment in the graphic narrative that foreshadows the opacity of the final image and heightens the allegorical register of Breccia's adaptation.

I have in mind plate six in particular (See Fig. 16.). In the second row of panels we see the hand of the mesmerist making his gestures in order to wake Valdemar from his trance. Something in the image seems off however. Is the head not too small, is the hand not drawn too large considering the scale? Is there not a basic mistake in perspective and shading, omitting the suggestion of the distance between hand and head, thus making things appear disproportionate? Significantly, this anomaly corresponds with the scene in Poe's text where Valdemar's skin undergoes a sudden transformation. As Poe writes: "The eyes rolled themselves slowly open, the pupils disappearing upwardly; the skin generally assumed a cadaverous hue, resembling not so much parchment as white paper."[29] The large hand of the mesmerist moves over Valdemar's miniature head surrounded by white space, and in the following images there is a radical, but almost imperceptible reversal of monstration. The last frame of the strip of images contains a perplexing reverse shot sucking us into the space of the image: through shreds of white paper we make out the faces of the two physicians who look on as perplexed as we are. It is as if the two are dumbfounded at the incredible feat of the graphiator who just performed a radical reversal from "zero" to "internal ocularisation."[30]

Through a trick of the medium the reader becomes the mesmerist's 'medium' as he or she not only inhabits the field of vision of Valdemar but also – at least by metaphoric extension – the twilight zone between life and death. The gutter is the margin through which we 'cross over' to the 'other side' – the inside of the story, the position of the viewing eye as well as that of the speaking and writing 'I', the I of "I am dead." As readers of a comic, we cannot but follow the captivating rhythm of the 'mise en page' to reach the end of the story. Along the way, we must undergo the uncanny shift in monstration: we are 'mesmerised' by the steady sequencing of panels that at the same time induces a reflection on the medium of comics as such. Indeed, the graphiator has put us under his spell. Not only does the alternating rhythm between panels and gutter make possible the 'suturing' of individual panels into narrative cohesion, it also – in conjunction with the shift in occularisation of the individual panel – effects our entry into the story and the opening up of the allegorical register. Moreover, owing to the opacity of the closing image and its resistance to (clear) meaning, the ultimate dissolution of coherence has the final word. Transfixed, our eyes follow the narrative route laid out by the mesmerist-graphiator, which at the same time occasions a reflection on the making (and unmaking) of the comic itself and the limits of narration.

Breccia has made graphiation manifest: we see the hand of the mesmerist, the hand that makes the plot move forward. Simultaneously, this hand is also the hand of the graphiator; it is the hand that refers back to the gesture of drawing. The graphiating mesmerist wakes us up to the graphic act we co-construct during the reading process forcing "our eyes [to roll] themselves slowly open" to face the visual opacity that will reach its peak in the 'potential image' of the final frame. We are being read and examined by the narrative itself, with the two empirical researchers looking in amazement as we wander into the frame, leaving our mark. The hand of the mesmerist, who in Poe's text is said to "make use of the customary passes" that puts patients in a trance or awakens them, is the hand of the graphiator.[31] creating our reading path through the 'customary gesture' of drawing and painting by hand.[32] Like a musical conductor tracing lines in the air following a 'score' we perform, the graphiator draws us in, quite literally. *Valdemar* has become a ghost story wherein we move through the space in-between presence and absence, never completely in or out of the graphic narrative, as if it is the viewer who haunts its pages. This is what makes

Part 3: Using the Victorians

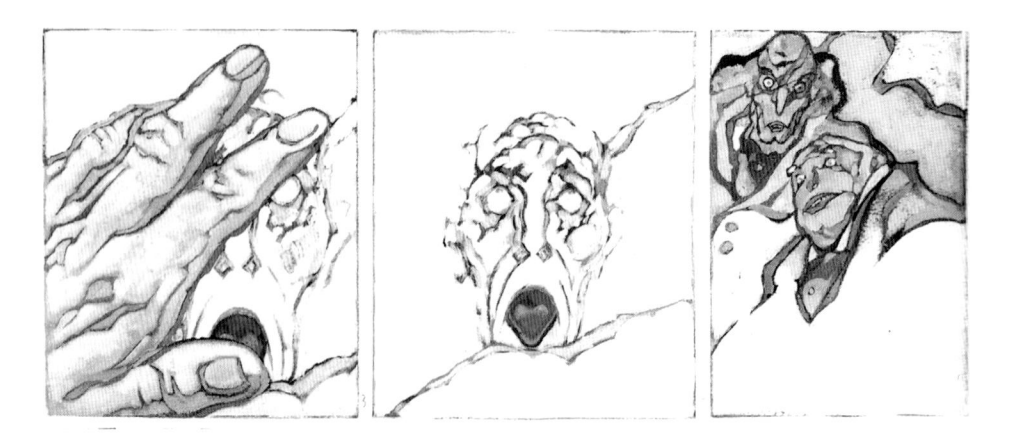

Fig 16. Breccia, A (1995) "Monsieur Valdemar." in *Le cœur révélateur et autres histoires extraordinaires d'Edgar Poe*. Genève: Les Humanoïdes Associés, Plate 6, row 2. Used by permission of the heirs of Alberto Breccia.

it an allegory of graphiation: we must reckon with the irreducible materiality of line-making, lettering, colouring (the whole repertoire of graphiating acts) to which we owe our reading. In fact, self-conscious graphiation insinuates itself in the final image Valdemar sees before his dissolution – the third frame of the page (See Fig. 15.) – and is signalled by a modification of colour tonality accompanying the uncanny internal ocularisation. The contours of the two witnesses are in the same shade as that of the decomposing head. The last thing Valdemar sees are the contours of decay mirroring his own, in a frame that looks like a solarised photograph. The dead sees a memento of his own death, thus adding a further impossibility absent in Poe's original text by virtue of a modulation in graphiation.

Breccia uses the power of comics and their propensity for endless visual association to charge Poe's text with unexpected nuance, as can be gleaned from the last frame (See Fig. 15.). I believe that there is a possible association with the artistic intervention of the 'siluetazo' ('silhouetting'), which would indicate that Breccia's *Valdemar* reactivates the trace of the disappeared. The politico-aesthetic tactic of 'siluetazo' emerged in 1983, just before the weakened military stepped down.[33] The event hinged on the participation of the viewer, who was invited to outline his or her body on paper (or any other support), and then paste the silhouette all over the city. Together, these silhouettes were reminders of the disappeared, indicating the massive scale of the regime of terror. Silhouetting plays on the tension between memory and embodiment, self and other: the contours of your own body identify with erased figures. For a while, Buenos Aires was filled with these ghostly figures, demanding attention from passers-by, forcing a disavowed reality to take on shape in memory.[34]

Breccia's silhouette in the final frame (See Fig. 15.) mobilises a similar politics of memory, presenting a poignant image, especially considering the progressive institutionalisation of forgetting at the time of the story's publication. Breccia's silhouette is a mnemonic interpellation of the viewer by graphiating the 'siluetazo' into the comic. The image explores the same ambiguity between appearance and disappearance as the 'siluetazo', and the precariousness of creating memory images: while the contours are slowly emerging out of the white to form a silhouette, at the same time the emerging figure seems not even to be safe from the work of time and memory. Wavering between a sign and a non-sign within the architecture of the comic, this crypto-image as trace opens the floodgates of visual association and endless reinterpretation. A crypto-image is then not so much a distinct image, but a process, a dynamic that is well suited to the medium of comics.

In fact, the constitutive ambiguity of crypto-images can be considered as a visual correlative to the ambiguity inherent in Gothic literature that Breccia refashions into a counter-censorial tactic of adaptation. In Gothic fiction "[a]mbivalence and uncertainty obscure single meaning" and it is this principled uncertainty that Breccia transposes to his graphiation.[35] As "Gothic figures have continued to shadow the progress of modernity with counter-narratives displaying the underside of enlightenment and humanist values", so does Breccia counter the deceptive transparency of the discourse of 'National Reorganisation' through a visual opacity that indirectly mimics the (silenced) terror of the everyday and the disappeared haunting Argentina.[36] In fact, Breccia's practice of adapting Gothic tales spans more than two defining (and violent) decades in the history of Argentina between 1973 and 1993. During this period he interpreted the grim tales of H. P. Lovecraft, Edward Plunkett, Horacio Quiroga and others as a means to intimate the censored reality of mass murder. Adaptation was a 'stealth manoeuvre' evoking a dark socio-political context that countered the junta's doublespeak with the opacity of the crypto-image.

Breccia started working on his Poe cycle as early as 1973, and by the time of his death had adapted a considerable selection of the American writer's short stories. The author's work proved an ideal vehicle for counter-censorial allusiveness, as his tales are pervaded by "inscrutability," meaning that "the true horror of Poe's writings […] is less the fear of the unknown, which at least suggests the possibility of knowing and hence of dispelling the fear, than the terror of unknowability" – a terror Breccia transfers to his graphic narratives.[37] Unknowability is at the heart of Breccia's opaquing procedure: what, indeed, does the final image 'mean'? What does the discrepancy between the textual ("putridity") and the image (the billowing white or the figure in ruin time) signify? In the final analysis, what Breccia's adaptations perform are their own illegibility, imprinting the inscrutability of everyday terror by graphiating an encounter with the terror of indeterminacy.

In closing, a reading experiment. Let us take the two final frames of Breccia's *Valdemar* and superimpose the one over the other. The image with the billowing cloud of white (See Fig. 14.) will serve as our 'ground'; the final image with the enigmatic creature in the second version (See Fig. 15.) serves as our 'figure'. Imagine making the latter more transparent so that it seems as if the cloud of white of the first version envelops the monstrous silhouette in the second version. Through the mist, the two characters of the original version of *Valdemar* express their horror upon discerning the strange shape of the 'future' adaptation. The virtue of this admittedly unorthodox reading strategy is that a dynamic, transversal reading of comics becomes possible approximating the dynamic of the crypto-image. Furthermore, I believe that the braiding (through superimposition) of comics across space and time lights up political subtleties that might be overlooked during a first reading.

Out of the cloud of indeterminacy in the 1980 version a silhouette from the future, post-1992, appears, functioning as a comment on the emptying of the frame in the first version, as if reproaching the final image of the earlier version for 'disappearing' its silhouette. In this reading, *Valdemar* (version 2) testifies to the enduring need for counter-censorship even (or especially) in societies that deem themselves democratic, as Argentina did under Menem's rule. Following the logic of the crypto-image, the silhouette comes into being only to vanish, and the text Carlos Trillo added to Poe's text in the first adaptation now assumes an unanticipated resonance. Reading the two final panels as if they were in sequence, a never-ending loop between materialisation and blanketing is created, indicated by the word forever: "'On the bed before us, lay an almost liquid mass of foul, abominable putrefaction.' He lay like that forever." As a 'potential image', the silhouette journeys back and forth between past and present, appearing in the cloud of the 'previous' version as the uncanny after-image of the later version. Valdemar is caught in the limbo of appearing and disappearing, echoing the plight of the disappeared. If there is a moral to this parable, it is the suggestion that there is no stable, permanent memory-image of the 'desaparecido.' In fact, the figure's formlessness might indicate that there should never be an institutionally sanctioned visual identity of the disappeared.

Notes

1. I would like to thank Pablo Turnes and Matthieu Mevel for their help in tracking down the first version of Breccia's *Valdemar* as well as their insightful comments on this essay.
2. Alberto Breccia finished his retelling of Poe's *The Facts in the Case of Mr. Valdemar* in 1992, with a French version published in 1995. The first version, with a scenario by Carlos Trillo was finished in 1980 and was published two years later in Europe in the Italian magazine *Alter Alter* and in the US in *Heavy Metal*.
3. No work is "fully significant and historically effective in the first instance" (see Foster, H. [1996] *The Return of the Real: The Avant-Garde at the End of the Century*. Cambridge, MA: MIT Press). Adaptations testify to this 'Nachträglichkeit' that is characteristic of cultural production.
4. The fact that there is still no political consensus about how to 'properly' represent the 'disappeared' in museums for instance serves as an indication of their 'blurriness'; there are multiple and overlapping strategies of remembrance, none of which have (yet) attained hegemonic status. For an example, see Jens Andermann's discussion of the disagreements on how to integrate the former concentration camp housed at the ESMA (Navy School of Mechanics) in Buenos Aires into an overarching discourse of remembrance (see Andermann, J. [2012] "Returning to the Site

of Horror: On the Reclaiming of Clandestine Concentration Camps in Argentina." in *Theory, Culture & Society Volume* 29, Number 1, pages 76 – 98).

5   As Phillipe Marion developed the concept in *Traces en Cases*, graphiation refers to "the graphic and narrative enunciation of comics" (see Baetens, J. [2001] "Revealing Traces: A New Theory of Graphic Enunciation." in Varnum, R. and Gibbons, C. Eds. *The Language of Comics: Word and Image*. Jackson: University Press of Mississippi, page 147) and includes the drawing, colouring, lettering, form of captions, balloons and panels, and so on – in short, all traces that refer back to the act of graphic enunciation. For the purposes of this essay, the distinction between monstration and graphiation is vital. In film theory, monstration refers to what is given to view within a shot, as the basic unit with narrative potential. As Marion points out, this concept is insufficient for the analysis of comics, since, contrary to cinematic monstration, "monstration in comics by no means has the same figurative transparency, the same transitivity as in film where the process of monstration hides itself behind the powerful analogical simulacrum it usually produces. By contrast, in comics the graphic material always resists, and is always opaque, thereby preventing monstration from being fully transitive" (see Marion, P. (1993) *Traces en cases. Travail graphique, figuration narrative et participation du lecteur*. Louvain-la-Neuve: Academia, page 36; my translation). I will demonstrate that Breccia's work effects an opaquing procedure, in the end interrogating the narrative import of monstration and transitivity, bordering on the hermetic.

6   Marchak, M. P., and Marchak, W. (1999) *God's Assassins: State Terrorism in Argentina in the 1970s*. Montreal: McGill University Press, pages 146 – 68.

7   Feitlowitz, M. (2011) *A Lexicon of Terror*. Oxford: Oxford University Press. Foster, H. (1996) *The Return of the Real: The Avant-Garde at the End of the Century*. Cambridge, MA: MIT Press, pages 301 – 36).

8   Andermann, J. (2012) "Returning to the Site of Horror: On the Reclaiming of Clandestine Concentration Camps in Argentina." in *Theory, Culture & Society Volume* 29, Number 1, pages 76 – 98.

9   See Graham-Jones, J. (2000). *Exorcising History: Argentine Theater under Dictatorship*. Lewisburg: Bucknell University Press and Cánovas, R. (1981) "Lectura de Purgatorio. Por donde comenzar." in *Hueso húmero* Number 10, page 171.

10 An investigation of counter-censorship in relation to Theodor Adorno's 1997 *Aesthetic Theory* is work for the future. Let me just note that art's inalienable 'enigmaticalness' ensures that it has a certain power that cannot be exhausted by hermeneutics, or any discourse that (however implicitly) claims mastery such as art history (or any theory of art), or practices informed by historically determinate socio-political contexts (most evident in censorship). From this perspective, in order to deserve the honorific 'art,' a work must exhibit (at some point in time) a counter-censorial kernel: "All artworks– and art altogether–are enigmas; since antiquity this has been an irritation to the theory of art. That artworks say something and in the same breath conceal it expresses this enigmaticalness from the perspective of language" (see Adorno, T. [1997] W. *Aesthetic Theory*. London: Athlone Press, page 120).

11 Gamboni, D. (2002) "Visual Ambiguity and Interpretation." in *RES: Anthropology and Aesthetics* Number 41, page 8.

12 Ibid.

13 In terms of output alone, it is quite striking that during the reign of the military regime Breccia primarily turned to adaptations. He not only started adapting H.P. Lovecraft, E. A. Poe and other writers of the macabre, but also contemporary Latin American authors. The only notable

exception was *Buscavidas*, which he started working on with Carlos Trillo in 1981 – 82 when the junta was losing its grip. For an account of *Buscavidas*, see Rommens, A. (2008) "*Buscavidas* and the 'Terror of the Uncertain Sign'." in *Art & Fact* Number 27, pages 70 – 75.

14 I am indebted to Kennedy, J. G. (1987) *Poe, Death, and the Life of Writing*. New Haven, CT: Yale University Press.

15 Poe, E. A. (2006) "The Facts in the Case of M. Valdemar." in *The Portable Edgar Allan Poe*. London: Penguin Books, page 71.

16 The irony of course was that the hoax was taken as factual at the time of publication. Antoine Faivre ascribes the propensity of Poe's tales to command belief to the still uncertain status of science at the time, and the discovery of the wonders of electric magnetism in particular. The precise meaning of what we call science today was not yet secure, hovering somewhere between inductive rigour and (black) magic (see Faivre, A. [2007] "Borrowings and Misreading: Edgar Allan Poe's 'Mesmeric' Tales and the Strange Case of their Reception." in *Aries* Number 7, pages 21 – 62).

17 Ibid., page 78.

18 Ibid., page 79.

19 Poe, E. A. (1987) "Mesmeric Revelation." in *The Science Fiction of Edgar Allan Poe*. Harmondsworth: Penguin, page 127.

20 I am of course referring to Wolfgang Iser's notion of 'Leerstellen,' those indeterminate gaps that the reader fills, revises and dynamically reinterprets through the interminable process of interpretation (see Iser, W. [1978] *The Act of Reading: A Theory of Aesthetic Response*. Baltimore: Johns Hopkins University Press).

21 Groensteen, T. (207) *The System of Comics*. Jackson: University Press of Mississippi.

22 Joan Boix's version appeared in the Spanish edition of *Creepy* published by Toutain, based in Barcelona. See Boix, J. (1985) "El caso del señor Valdemar." in *Creepy: El comic del terror y lo fantastico* Number 70, pages 19 – 27.

23 Groensteen, T. (2013) *Comics and Narration*. Jackson: University Press of Mississippi, page 34.

24 Poe, E. A. (2006a) "On Unity of Effect." in *The Portable Edgar Allan Poe*. London: Penguin Books, page 529.

25 Gamboni, D. (2002) "Visual Ambiguity and Interpretation." in *RES: Anthropology and Aesthetics* Number 41, pages 5 – 15.

26 Graham-Jones, J. (2000). *Exorcising History: Argentine Theater under Dictatorship*. Lewisburg: Bucknell University Press, page 604.

27 "Time creates the ruin by making it something other than what it was, something with a new significance and signification, with a future that is to be compared with its past. Time writes the future of a ruin. Ruin time creates the future of a ruin, even the return of the man-made part to the earth (…). Ruin time unites. It is beyond historical time. It includes the biological time of birds and moss." In Hetzler, F. M. (1998) "Causality: Ruin Time and Ruins." in *Leonardo* Volume 21, Number 1, page 55. In the final instance, it also involves "cosmological time," "the sidereal time of the stars, sun and clouds that shine upon it, shadow it and are part of it" (ibid., page 51).

28 Urbain, J-D. (1991) "La crypto-image ou le palimpseste iconique." in *Eidos* Number 5, page 2.

29 Poe, E. A. (2006) "The Facts in the Case of M. Valdemar." in *The Portable Edgar Allan Poe*. London: Penguin Books, page 76.

30 Film theorist François Jost employs the term 'ocularisation' to designate "the imaginary axis of the camera-eye" (Jost, F. [2004] "The Look: From Film to Novel. An Essay in Comparative Narratology." in Stam, R. and Raengo, A. Eds. *A Companion to Literature and Film*. Oxford: Blackwell, page 74), a useful concept in comics studies as long we keep in mind that graphiation will always modulate

monstration. Jost distinguishes two basic positionings: either "a shot is anchored in the regard of an instance internal to the diegesis," in which case we speak of "internal ocularisation," or such anchoring is absent, in which case we speak of "zero ocularisation" (ibid.). My argument is that the shift in this comic's ocularisation is allied to an increasing display of the work of graphiation, a process precipitating the allegorical register. Moreover, as the final frame approximates plastic abstraction and thereby insists on graphiation's visual opacity, it makes the conceptual apparatus of ocularisation, monstration, narration and so on appear as a catachresis of visuality.

31 Poe, E. A. (2006) "The Facts in the Case of M. Valdemar." in *The Portable Edgar Allan Poe*. London: Penguin Books, page 79.

32 For this particular sequence, one could say that the interplay between the individual panel's monstration and the structural sequencing of the lay-out works towards a transmedial approximation of Poe's poetics of the short story which "aimed to induce a kind of mesmeric submission in [the] reader". In Breccia's *Valdemar*, the graphiator is the narrating instance ensuring, in Poe's words, that "during the hour of perusal the soul of the reader is at the writer's control" (Elmer, J. [1995] "Terminate or Liquidate? Poe, Sensationalism, and the Sentimental Tradition." in Rosenheim, S and Rachman, S. Eds. *The American Face of Edgar Allen Poe*. Baltimore: Johns Hopkins University, pages1 11 and 112.

33 Conceived by artists Rodolfo Aguerreberry, Julio Flores and Guillermo Kexel, the original 'siluetazo' project was a collective intervention that took place on the plaza de Mayo on September 21, 1983. The event inspired many similar ones that played on the same visual language. For photographs of 'siluetazo' actions, see for instance the website of the Human Rights Archive of the Museo Nacional Centro de Arte Reina Sofia (http://www.museoreinasofia.es/biblioteca-centro-documentacion/archivo-de-archivos/archivo-derechos-humanos).

34 Druliolle, V. (2009) "Silhouettes of the Disappeared: Memory, Justice and Human Rights in Post-Authoritarian Argentina." in *Human Rights & Human Welfare* Number 9, pages 77 – 89.

35 Botting, F. (1996) *Gothic*. London: Routledge, pages 1 and 2).

36 One of the major aims of the military junta was to restore "family values" against "subversion" and thereby realign Argentina with "Western, Christian Civilization" as General Videla characterised his mission (quoted in Troncoso, O. (1984) *El Proceso de Reorganización Nacional*. Buenos Aires: Centro Editor de América Latina, page 26.

37 Tally, R. T. Jr. (2014) *Poe and the Subversion of American Literature: Satire, Fantasy, Critique*. New York: Bloomsbury Academic, page 70.

References

Andermann, J. (2012) "Returning to the Site of Horror: On the Reclaiming of Clandestine Concentration Camps in Argentina." in *Theory, Culture & Society* Volume 29, Number 1, pages 76 – 98.

Adorno, T. (1997) W. *Aesthetic Theory*. London: Athlone Press.

Baetens, J. (2001) "Revealing Traces: A New Theory of Graphic Enunciation." in Varnum, R. and Gibbons, C. Eds. *The Language of Comics: Word and Image*. Jackson: University Press of Mississippi, pages 145 – 155.

Boix, J. (1985) "El caso del señor Valdemar." in *Creepy: El comic del terror y lo fantastico* Number 70, pages 19 – 27.

Botting, F. (1996) *Gothic*. London: Routledge.

Breccia, A. and Trillo, C. (1982) "Mister Valdemar." in *Heavy Metal* Volume 6, Number 7, pages 38 – 44.

Breccia, A. and Trillo, C. (1982) "Mister Valdemar." in *Alter Alter* Volume 9, Number 4, pages 60 – 66.

Breccia, A. (1995) "Monsieur Valdemar." in Reichert, F. and Imparato, L. Eds. *Le cœur révélateur et autres histoires extraordinaires d'Edgar Poe*. Genève: Les Humanoïdes Associés, no page.

Cánovas, R. (1981) "Lectura de Purgatorio. Por donde comenzar." in *Hueso húmero* Number 10, pages 170 – 177.

Druliolle, V. (2009) "Silhouettes of the Disappeared: Memory, Justice and Human Rights in Post-Authoritarian Argentina." in *Human Rights & Human Welfare* Number 9, pages 77 – 89.

Elmer, J. (1995) "Terminate or Liquidate? Poe, Sensationalism, and the Sentimental Tradition." in Rosenheim, S and Rachman, S. Eds. *The American Face of Edgar Allen Poe*. Baltimore: Johns Hopkins University, pages 91 – 120.

Faivre, A. (2007) "Borrowings and Misreading: Edgar Allan Poe's 'Mesmeric' Tales and the Strange Case of their Reception." in *Aries* Number 7, pages 21 – 62.

Feitlowitz, M. (2011) *A Lexicon of Terror*. Oxford: Oxford University Press.

Foster, H. (1996) *The Return of the Real: The Avant-Garde at the End of the Century*. Cambridge, MA: MIT Press.

Gamboni, D. (2002) "Visual Ambiguity and Interpretation." in *RES: Anthropology and Aesthetics* Number 41, pages 5 – 15.

Giménez, C. (1975) "El Extraño caso del señor Valdemar." in *Club de Amigos de la Historieta: Suplemento de Boletines* Number 4, no page.

Graham-Jones, J. (2000). *Exorcising History: Argentine Theater under Dictatorship*. Lewisburg: Bucknell University Press.

Graham-Jones, J. (2001) "Broken Pencils and Crouching Dictators: Issues of Censorship in Contemporary Argentine Theatre." in *Theatre Journal* Volume 53, Number 4, pages 595 – 606.

Groensteen, T. (2013) *Comics and Narration*. Jackson: University Press of Mississippi.

Hetzler, F. M. (1998) "Causality: Ruin Time and Ruins." in *Leonardo* Volume 21, Number 1, pages 51 – 55.

Iser, W. (1978) *The Act of Reading: A Theory of Aesthetic Response*. Baltimore: Johns Hopkins University Press.

Jost, F. (2004) "The Look: From Film to Novel. An Essay in Comparative Narratology." in Stam, R. and Raengo, A. Eds. *A Companion to Literature and Film*. Oxford: Blackwell, pages 71 – 80.

Kennedy, J. G. (1987) *Poe, Death, and the Life of Writing*. New Haven, CT: Yale University Press.

Marchak, M. P., and Marchak, W. (1999) *God's Assassins: State Terrorism in Argentina in the 1970s*. Montreal: McGill University Press.

Marion, P. (1993) *Traces en cases. Travail graphique, figuration narrative et participation du lecteur*. Louvain-la-Neuve: Academia.

Mones, I. (1975) "The Facts in the Case of M. Valdemar." in *Creepy* Number 69, pages 53 – 60.

Poe, E. A. (2006) "The Facts in the Case of M. Valdemar." in *The Portable Edgar Allan Poe*. London: Penguin Books, pages 71 – 79.

Poe, E. A. (2006a) "On Unity of Effect." in *The Portable Edgar Allan Poe*. London: Penguin Books, page 529.

Poe, E. A. (1987) "Mesmeric Revelation." in *The Science Fiction of Edgar Allan Poe*. Harmondsworth: Penguin, pages 124 – 134.

Rommens, A. (2008) "*Buscavidas* and the 'Terror of the Uncertain Sign'." in *Art & Fact* Number 27, pages 70 – 75.

Tally, R. T. Jr. (2014) *Poe and the Subversion of American Literature: Satire, Fantasy, Critique*. New York: Bloomsbury Academic.

Troncoso, O. (1984) *El Proceso de Reorganización Nacional*. Buenos Aires: Centro Editor de América Latina.

Urbain, J-D. (1991) "La crypto-image ou le palimpseste iconique." in *Eidos* Number 5, pages 1 – 16.

Peter Wilkins

An incomplete project: graphic adaptations of *Moby-Dick* and the ethics of response

In using the term 'ethics of response' in my title regarding the graphic adaptations of Herman Melville's *Moby-Dick*, I mean the way an adaptation feels obliged to produce a certain kind of work by making particular choices about and actions upon the source material. Adaptations, illustrations, and even allusive works of art establish a continuity that establishes an ethical responsibility in that they invite the audience to trace their obligation to the prior work: when we listen to Led Zeppelin's instrumental *Moby-Dick*, we immediately seek a rationale for the name, an analogue between John Bonham's extensive drum solo and the white whale or book. The same happens when we look at abstract paintings that refer directly to *Moby-Dick* in their titles, such as those by Jackson Pollock, Sam Francis, and Frank Stella.

While any adaptation or re-mediation of a work of art invokes this responsibility, *Moby-Dick*'s status as what Umberto Eco calls 'an open work' makes it especially pressing. Eco describes the open work as one that challenges the reader to help create it as he or she performs it.[1] The 'open' work asserts an obligation on the part of the performer/audience to construct it. Eco uses the musical compositions of Berio and Stockhausen as examples: "In primitive terms we can say that they are quite literally 'unfinished': the author seems to hand them on to the performer more or less like the components of a construction kit"[2] Melville's novel is just such a work, one that re-imagines the novel's form by combining multiple discourses and genres, of which the 'story' of Ahab's quest for the whale is but one strand in the weave of the text. The reader's chief task is in to connect that story to all the other pieces. Any adaptor or illustrator might be expected to engage with this aspect of the text as well, and in doing so must decide how to deal with *Moby-Dick's* incompleteness.

Long as it is, *Moby-Dick* is indeed a novel of unfinished business: the novel ends, but Ahab's quest for absolute knowledge fails. Ishmael's discourse on whales and whaling that surrounds the quest, meanwhile, is a deconstruction of encyclopedism; it mimics the would-be comprehensive work that says all there is to say about whales and whaling, but undermines the idea at the same time. That is, as much as Ishmael narrates on the subject, something is always missing:

> But now I leave my cetological System standing thus unfinished, even as the great Cathedral of Cologne was left, with the crane still standing upon the top of the uncompleted tower. For small erections may be finished by their first architects; grand ones, true ones ever leave the copestone to posterity.[3]

On nearly every topic related to whales, Ishmael uses a language of incompletion or of the failure of representation. On the subject of visually representing the whale, for instance, he says:

> the great Leviathan is that one creature in the world which must remain unpainted to the last. True, one portrait may hit the mark much nearer than another, but none can hit it with any very considerable degree of exactness. So there is no earthly way of finding out precisely what the whale really looks like.[4]

Any graphic adaptation of *Moby-Dick* must grapple with its rhetoric of incompleteness and impossibility, or else run the risk of representing it as antithesis. Needless to say, many visual adaptations bearing the name *Moby-Dick* are actually anti-*Moby-Dicks*.

A better term to describe these adaptations is mono-*Moby-Dicks*. They identify entirely with Ahab and his monomaniacal, tyrannical ethic at the expense of Ishmael's discursive, democratic one. Ahab's ethic demands revelation, that nothing be hidden behind impediments to the perception of the truth about the world. In short, the very language of incompletion and impossibility that governs Ishmael's rhetoric is the enemy of Ahab's demand for the absolute. The uncertainties and ambiguities of the world that inspire Ishmael are anathema to Ahab. The fact that Ishmael lives, Ahab dies, and the absolute truth remains veiled suggests that Ishmael's ethic triumphs, and that the person who can engage with uncertainty and ambiguity triumphs over the person who would eradicate them. In other words, the novel celebrates the democrat over the 'absolute monarch'.

The democratic dimension of *Moby-Dick* is part and parcel of its 'openness' in Eco's sense. Ishmael himself represents a common man willing to think about weighty subjects like ontology, existence, perception, and politics, and his implication of the reader in his discourse suggests that we should show a similar willingness to engage with him. 'Here is my thinking on the subject,' Ishmael appears to say, 'what is yours?' Insofar as *Moby-Dick* is the great American novel it is because it espouses this democratic ideal of freedom of thought and expression. Anyone, regardless of rank and status, can and should think deeply about the most meaningful subjects and have others respect and engage with that thinking; one does not have to be a philosopher who has "broken his digester."[5] The novel's ethical demand upon the artist who would adapt it is that the art should engage with this type of thinking rather than be faithful to its plot. Fidelity to the idea of engaged thinking trumps fidelity to plot, style, or period trappings.

My hunch is that *Moby-Dick's* democratic mode of engagement is the reason that so many artists have responded to it with works of their own. As Elizabeth Shultz argues in *Unpainted to the Last*, visual artists must have adapted, illustrated, re-mediated, and interpreted *Moby-Dick* more than just about any other novel of the nineteenth century.[6] It is fairly easy to see how visual artists, in particular, would be drawn to the novel. The multiple references in the text to mark-making and to non-alphabetic visual communication such as scrimshaw, tattoos and hieroglyphs invite the visual imagination. While we might imagine that Ishmael's assertion of the sublimity of his subject matter would put visual artists off – why try to depict something that the text has said is impossible to depict? – in fact it does the opposite. Democratic sublimity is an invitation to represent. When Ishmael argues that the whale is unpaintable, he also says 'one portrait may hit the mark nearer than another,' which suggests that fact that the whale remains 'unpainted' is no check on attempts to paint it. After all, the impossibility of representing the whale in language does not prevent Ishmael from providing hundreds of pages of words on the subject.

The Kantian version of the sublime explains this phenomenon. Kant's *Third Critique* focuses on the relationship between the beautiful and the sublime. The beautiful is representation without a concept and the sublime is a concept without a representation: "if something arouses in us... a feeling of the sublime, then it may indeed appear, in its form, contrapurposive for our power of judgment, incommensurate with our power of exhibition, and as it were violent to our imagination, and yet we judge it all the more sublime for that."[7] It is impossible to say what idea a beautiful object represents. But that impossibility does not stop us from discussing the matter. We keep testing ideas against the object even though none fits. In the case of the sublime, the positions are reversed; we have an idea, like infinity or the absolute, but no way of adequately representing it. Again, we do not necessarily stop our efforts to represent the sublime idea. This notion of sublimity accords with the democratic imperative of the novel: that there is no adequate form that would represent what Ishmael is trying express means there is no ideal form either. Other artists are thus freed to produce their own versions. Just as the whale is unpaintable, so is Melville's novel: all the more reason to give it a go. Democracy, like the whale, is a sublime

Part 3: Using the Victorians

idea. We can never get it right, so we have to keep working at it. The irony here is that the very difficulty of *Moby-Dick* is the basis of its openness to responsive adaptation.

The way visual or graphic adaptors respond to the heterogeneity of discourses, rhetorics, and genres in *Moby-Dick* is key to the ethics of their response.[8] Melville's novel is multimodal before illustrators and comics artists get their hands on it, making the challenge of adaptation more complex. This multimodality and heterogeneity are themselves part of Melville's interrogation of the democratic project in *Moby-Dick*. A democracy needs many languages, modes, and types of people, whereas a tyranny needs only one voice. Those adaptations that close down heterogeneity and close off Ishmael's ethic of sublime incompletion unwittingly support Ahab's univocal tyranny and, when they depict the failure of his mad project, do so in a way that renders it meaningless. Those adaptations that engage with Ishmael's ethic sustain the novel's openness by transforming it.

Comics adaptations that present themselves as 'easy' versions to give younger readers an introduction to a novel they otherwise might not read, such as the 1976 Marvel and the 1956 Classics Illustrated adaptations, tend not to rise to the challenge of Ishmael's ethic.[9] In fact, most of them erase the sublimity of Melville's text so that everything is comprehensible and representable; even though they depict Ahab's failure, they subscribe to his ethic of the explicable world. Ishmael generally, though not always, remains the narrator, but his role is to frame the plot rather than provide a reflexive, metafictional counterpoint to it. If we are lucky, we get a few of Ishmael's aphorisms, like "Better sleep with a sober cannibal than a drunken Christian", but usually none of his meditations.[10] Instead, these adaptations use sequential art to represent the plot of Ahab's obsessive revenge against Moby Dick. These versions cut to the chase, even though it is only one dimension of a multi-dimensional narrative.

While it is tempting to accuse the writers and artists of these adaptations of doing Melville's novel an injustice because they fail to engage with Ishmael's ethic, such works demonstrate a contest of responsibilities between those to Melville's novel and those to the intended audience of the adaptation: children and adults who wouldn't otherwise engage with the novel. In making the choices that they do, these adaptations show that they believe that the sections demonstrating Ishmael's ethic are either too complex or too dull to engage with their intended audience. Perhaps the adaptors feel that Ishmael does too much telling and not enough showing.

In their attempts to excise the Ishmaelean sublime, the classics comics characterise Queequeg and Ahab, who play key roles in the novel's opposition of ambiguity to absolute clarity, in ways that do not make sense. Both characters bear marks upon their bodies that symbolise their relationship to the world: Ahab has a single scar, purportedly running the entire length of his body, and Queequeg's body is covered in tattoos. Ahab's scar matches his linear monomania:

The path to my fixed purpose is laid with iron rails, whereon my soul is grooved to run. Over unsounded gorges, through the rifled hearts of mountains, under torrents' beds, unerringly I rush! Naught's an obstacle, naught's an angle to the iron way![11]

Queequeg's tattoos, meanwhile, represent intentional but indeterminate, uninterpretable marks:

And this tattooing had been the work of a departed prophet and seer of his island, who, by those hieroglyphic marks, had written out on his body a complete theory of the heavens and the earth, and a mystical treatise on the art of attaining truth; so that Queequeg in his own proper person was a riddle to unfold; a wondrous work in one volume; but whose mysteries not even himself could read, though his own live heart beat against them; and these mysteries were therefore destined in the end to moulder away with the living parchment whereon they were inscribed, and so be unsolved to the last.[12]

We should note that each of these kinds of 'marks' cry out for graphic representation; we would expect comics adaptations of *Moby-Dick* to pick up on them as significant opportunities to produce meaningful images. But because most adaptations have their own 'fixed purpose', those expectations are largely disappointed.

The novel associates Ishmael's ethic with Queequeg because of the way that ethic must respect Otherness, including but not limited to race, in order to be properly democratic. Ishmael sees Otherness of various kinds everywhere he looks, the hieroglyphic being the primary conceptual example. Queequeg is the hieroglyph personified, or at least embodied. Ishmael's 'marriage' to Queequeg, and his later use of the image of himself and Queequeg tied together by the monkey rope, a safety rope that prevents a sailor working over the side of the ship from falling into the ocean, demonstrates the dependence of Ishmael's model of thinking on a collective of different people: "I saw that this situation of mine was the precise situation of every mortal that breathes; only, in most cases, he, one way or other, has this Siamese connexion with a plurality of other mortals."[13] But each classics comics adaptation has a distinct uneasiness in depicting Queequeg, treating him more as a freak than an exemplary figure of humanity.

The 1976 Marvel adaptation by Shapiro and Niño expresses this uneasiness in its refusal of Melville's language; it refers to Queequeg as 'a wild man' rather than a cannibal presumably because Irwin Shapiro and Alex Niño have concluded either that the child reader cannot handle the horror of cannibalism, that the term is offensive, or that the word itself is too difficult for the audience easily to comprehend. The fact that Father Mapple's sermon is re-named 'special talk' suggests the latter. Nevertheless, cannibalism is an essential theme to the novel – the Pequod is 'a cannibal craft', the whale's teeth on the bulwarks make it appear like a machine for eating whales, and reading about the whale through a magnifying lens composed of its own skin is equated with cannibalism. "Who is not a cannibal?" asks Ishmael, with a rhetorical question that matches his famous "who ain't a slave?"[14] The socially levelling nature of Ishmael's language, though problematic, suggests a need to view Queequeg as an equal.[15] Translating the question into "Who is not a wild man?" does not make the same kind of sense, as it privileges individual, temporary behaviour over cultural or religious and general behaviour. If we consider the Marvel adaptation's child reader, we must ask what a child is to make of the term 'wild man' exactly? Such a substitution seems to exchange one problem – how to simplify the text for children – for another – how to represent Queequeg's cultural and philosophical significance to the narrative.

While the 'wild man' problem is one of language, the image of Queequeg in the Marvel edition is equally loaded. In fact, Shapiro and Niño's Queequeg looks more like a mid-twentieth-century Western film's image of the 'red Indian' than a Pacific Islander. His tattoos are limited to indistinct dots on his face, a poor place-holder for an unreadable 'theory of the heavens and earth'.

The 1956 Classics Illustrated adaptation presents Queequeg visually as pure caricature of 'Otherness', as if the artist could not figure out what stereotype to rely on.[16] As Elizabeth Schultz remarks: "The anonymous illustrator…makes Queequeg a bizarre composite of several cultures: he wears a Sufi's conical hat and medieval tunic, while his hatchet-peace pipe swings bizarrely from his neck."[17]

While this adaptation has no reservations about calling Queequeg a cannibal, it takes pains to make him look as unthreatening as possible, almost childlike. His position is analogous to that of Tintin's friend Chang in Herge's *The Blue Lotus*, a non-threatening ethnic sidekick whose presence validates the white, European character as a decent fellow. This depiction identifies Queequeg as 'Other' but also as 'nothing in particular.' A 'cannibal' ends up being a fantastic multi-ethnic being who offers the child reader no specific locus for cannibalism except the generalised Other. In evading its responsibility, the Classics Illustrated 1956 adaptation escapes being particularly racist by being generally racist.

Like the Marvel adaptation, the Classics Illustrated adaptation identifies Queequeg's Otherness but fails to engage with its significance. This failure is symptomatic of both adaptations' unwillingness to engage in anything at all reflexive in the source text, as if *Moby-Dick* presents a series of rabbit holes that the adaptors fear falling into and never emerging from. This fear leads them to quick and dirty depictions of Queequeg that, rather than help their intended audience to understand the ideas he intersects with in the novel, simply make him an absurd element.

These adaptations' representations of Ahab also verge on absurdity. In Melville's novel, Ahab is a complex character in spite of the strict linearity of his thinking. On the one hand, his usurpation of the ship to accomplish his personal goal of revenge against the white whale, coupled with his requirement of fealty from his crew, makes him seem anti-democratic, tyrannical even. And yet, his demand for absolute freedom speaks to an American individualism that acts as a counterweight to equality. For him, Moby Dick is a symbol of his inability to act unfettered in the world. To put it simply, though, Ahab is a bad example in the novel: his actions, aimed at destroying the barriers to his absolute freedom, end in his death by entanglement in the means he uses to pursue that freedom: the technology of whaling. A harpoon line wraps around his neck and Moby Dick drags him down to a watery grave. Not only that, his folly kills everyone on board the Pequod save Ishmael, the advocate of human interdependence. Ahab's demand for transparency pits his project against the incompletion and unrepresentability of Ishmael's ethic. Rather than embrace the obscurity of the world, Ahab would eradicate it.

Both the Marvel and Classics Illustrated adaptations use the same material from the source text to represent Ahab's frustration at the limitations on his ability to perceive the world and its truth, using visual cues to convey Ahab's state of mind. The Marvel version shows Ahab as a scruffy-looking lunatic, almost humorous in appearance, whose motivation and power over his crew are difficult to fathom. The Classics Illustrated version, meanwhile, makes Ahab look like a harried middle-aged man, an office worker. Again, the visual depiction doesn't carry much force: Ahab doesn't look powerful or persuasive enough to convince his crew to take up his challenge. Each of these adaptations depicts Ahab as a ridiculous figure as it strips the novel down to its plot, on the assumption that it is its 'essence'. In fact, Ahab's story is neither compelling nor comprehensible without the interplay between what he represents and what Ishmael (and Queequeg) represents. The purpose of these adaptations appears to be to show how a rollicking adventure story underlies the discursive, reflective elements of the novel that we must strip away to get to that story. But what they deem ephemeral is crucial; without it, we get nothing but an angry, crazy man chasing a whale.

This obliviousness to anything but plot prevents the 1976 Marvel and 1956 Classics Illustrated adaptations from exploiting the full range of comics 'discourses' available to them. For instance, with all of its historical and technological information about whaling, *Moby-Dick* would be well suited to the strategies of the information comic, like those used in *Look and Learn* and *World of Wonder*.[18] Just about the only distinguishing feature of the 2009 Campfire adaptation by Lance Stahlberg and Lalit Kumar Singh is its use of information comic strategies to illustrate features of the sperm whale and the whaling ship to conclude the volume.[19] Curiously, these pages are based on general research of the kind one could look up in an encyclopedia rather than on Melville's text itself.

So many comics adaptations tread the same stripped down, plot-oriented ground that it would seem in their interest to set themselves apart from other adaptations. Instead, they are like English grammar and style books, which, in spite of there being hundreds of versions, all present more or less the same thing. These versions may be more obliged to the codes of adapting classic literature in general and of their particular series than to this particular text. The important thing for them is to have 'a' *Moby-Dick* in their series, not necessarily to have a great adaptation of the novel.

However, Bill Sienkiewicz and Dan Chichester's 1990 update of the Classics Illustrated *Moby-Dick* presents a radical revision of the line's *modus operandi* for adaptation.[20] No longer does the audience appear to be school children but rather what Bart Beaty calls the 'comics art world.'[21] This adaptation shows much less desire to simplify the source text, as we can see from the way Sienkiewicz challenges conventional comics page structure in his adaptation. Panels are irregular, with many different ways of marking their boundaries, including insets and free hand drawn frames. Sienkiewicz incorporates symbolic visual elements, such as rows of whales' teeth around panels or pages to signify the cannibalism theme. The text boxes float over the images on the page rather than being compartmentalised at the tops and bottoms of panels, giving the effect of being in front of the images and causing the reader to look behind them. Furthermore, the images operate in counterpoint to the text rather than as mere support of it. The effect is a powerful one that shows the adaptors interpreting a way of looking that challenges easy consumption through simplification. In fact, Sienkiewicz and Chichester are willing to be unclear in order to promote 'looking' at the pages in a way that corresponds with Ishmael's examination of ideas: 'this is not easy,' they appear to be saying.

For instance, many of the pages have a dense, obscure, veiled look, as if Sienkiewicz were interfering with our direct apprehension of what he is depicting. In these cases, we see an adaptation engaging with ideas beyond that of revenge; Sienkiewicz and Chichester are responsible not only to ideas in the source text but also to their own aesthetic ideas. This dual responsibility exemplifies the kind of adaptation that I argue *Moby-Dick* encourages. This is not to say that the other 'classics' I have discussed in this section of the paper do not have their own 'style', just that those styles are detached from the perspectives and concepts of the novel.

Although Sienkiewicz and Chichester's adaptation is more or less as plot-oriented as the other classics comics, they employ multiple 'discourses' in their visual adaptation of the rhetoric of the text. Or, to put it another way, we see an effort to adapt style in visual terms, not just characters and events. Thus, Sienkiewicz and Chichester perform the kind of adaptation that Simon Grennan achieves with Anthony Trollope's *John Caldigate*, actively seeking visual analogues for prose style.[22] For example, in Sienkiewicz's *Moby-Dick* Father Mapple's sermon appears as a pastiche of a Turner painting that tilts at a sublime feeling, as Turner paintings do. This allusion also has its analogue in the novel. Several critics have noted that Turner's paintings influenced Melville's prose. Here, Sienkiewicz transfers that influence back into images. Finally, Sienkiewicz and Chichester's visual experimentalism frees them to include different kinds of content from the novel. It includes several of the 'gams', the meetings at sea between the Pequod and other whalers, and some informational pages whose style indicates a shift in discourse.

While the Sienkiewicz and Chichester Classics Illustrated adaptation is no more 'true' to the novel in terms of giving a comprehensive picture of *Moby-Dick* than the other two texts we have examined, it is more receptive to Ishmael's invitation to respond to rather than simply capture his language: Sienkiewicz and Chichester take up the challenge that the novel puts forward to interpret its interpretation of the enigmatic world in a way that stretches its own medium.

Comics co-optations do not 'adapt' *Moby-Dick* exactly. Rather, they allude to and incorporate elements from Melville's novel in their own narratives. In the *Leviathan* story arc of *The Unwritten*, by Mike Carey, Peter Gross, Vince Locke, and Al Davison, characters from the comics series enter the novel as if it were an alternate reality.[23] *Dylan Dog #15 Sulla rotta di Moby-Dick* (*On the Route of Moby-Dick*) by Tiziano Sclavi, Angelo Stano, Bruno Brindisi, and Tito Faraci presents a sequel/revision of the plot in a contemporary setting.[24] Both of these texts are less interesting for any visual analogue to Melville's language or rhetoric than for how they play with narrative ideas. But while plot is once more king, these co-optations have a reflexive register that engages with Ishmael's ethic of sublime incompletion.

The Unwritten plays with multiple styles and discourses to show the different levels of its own story as it moves Tom Taylor, the central character, in and out of different diegetic worlds from classic literature. Tom is engaged in an Oedipal power struggle with his author father, Wilson Taylor, who has 'used' him as the main character of a Harry Potter-like adventure series. *The Unwritten* is savvy in its relationship to the texts it invokes. Its intertexts generally concern the relationship between the author/creator and his text/creation: Frankenstein's monster and Pinocchio are key figures. Tom tries to discover the source of his father's power, which requires a picaresque journey through several well-known literary works. Diegesis becomes a metafictional science fiction concept.

Further, by linking Harold Bloom's concept of the anxiety of influence to Tom's Oedipal struggle with his father/creator, the comic says something about its own relationship to the literature with which it engages. This relationship engages medium – the relationship between culturally debased comics and esteemed literature – and content – the relationship between this story and canonic narratives. *The Unwritten* critiques the conventional classics comics' occlusion of these relationships to create a 'complete' story in a tidy package. The classics comics adaptations are thus classic Oedipal texts: paradoxically obedient and murderous. *Moby-Dick* meanwhile is distinctly 'anti-Oedipal'; in spite of its status as a 'great work,' the novel invites transformative engagement of the sort that *Unwritten* performs. In place of the 'don't touch me' aura of the 'masterpiece,' *Moby-Dick* says 'play with me'.

In *The Unwritten's* brief pass through *Moby-Dick*, Tom's tyrannical father is Ahab, and Tom is Bulkington, a character who appears as if he is going to play a prominent role in Melville's text and then disappears from it. Both character transcriptions display a keen understanding of the novel. Authorial power is exactly what Ahab demands, and the curious uncertainty of Bulkington's status in the text fits Tom's unstable position in

The Unwritten: he might disappear at any time. Tom quickly moves on to other literary works with whales in them, including *One Thousand and One Nights* and Thomas Hobbes' *Leviathan*. *The Unwritten* stays true to the novel's intertextual web by weaving itself into the network of whale literature into which Melville wove *Moby-Dick*.

Dylan Dog is an Italian horror comics series featuring a paranormal investigator of the same name who lives in London. He is a mashup of different literary detectives, not the least of whom is Sherlock Holmes. His sidekick is Groucho Marx. The series was initiated by Tiziano Sclavi, but, as with many comics, other writers and artists have taken up the writing and drawing duties. As Giorgio Mariani writes, *Sulla rotta di Moby-Dick* sets itself up as a sequel/prequel to Melville's novel, suggesting a cycle in which Ahab and Moby Dick will forever be re-fighting their battle. In the way it relates to Melville's novel, Mariani suggests, "our Dylan Dog graphic novel not only opts for a contemporary setting but is also conceived as a sequel. Rather than a retelling of *Moby-Dick*, it is its own invention."[25] It is an invention that cleverly co-opts Melville's novel as a component of its own tale: the sequel frames and begets the 'original.'

Like *The Unwritten*, *Dylan Dog* represents travel through time and worlds. But *Dylan Dog* is diegetically the reverse of *Unwritten*: Ahab (and Queequeg, as his sidekick Tamura) come into the present from the past and to 'reality' from the world of fiction to chase Moby Dick, who has also moved through the 'time vortex', once more. The comic thus takes up *Moby-Dick*'s presentation of itself as an open-ended parable: it is a stone tossed towards the future for others to take up, interpret, and pass on. The way in which the comic ends by sending both Ahab and Moby Dick back into 1850 to start their battle over again in Melville's novel suggests an infinite cycle, an ouroboros.

It is fitting then that *Dylan Dog* takes up of the theme of technological cannibalism in the novel where Ahab's whale bone prosthetic leg participates in the same logic as the whale's teeth around the Pequod's bulwarks that transform it into a giant mouth for eating whales. Ahab's leg signifies the 'becoming-whale' of the world in a kind of autophagic loop: dead whales pursue live ones to consume them in another kind of ouroboros. In *Dylan Dog*, the present Moby Dick is a military experiment gone awry and Ahab has a high-tech prosthetic leg rather than one carved out of whale bone – he has been fully technologised to suggest that technology is now consuming us. In linking the temporal ouroboros to the technological one *Dylan Dog* recycles *Moby-Dick* in a way that reads it forward so that it updates the novel's nineteenth-century themes for the twentieth century.

In terms of conceptual play, both *Unwritten: Leviathan* and *Dylan Dog: Sulla rotti di Moby-Dick* exemplify the ethics of response that *Moby-Dick* invokes. These engagements with the text qualify at least in part as adaptations (they include about as much of the original as the more 'strict' adaptations do proportionally), but they are interpretive and transformative, questioning the source text as much as 'reproducing' it. Georgio Mariani puts this point very well in his analysis of *Dylan Dog*:

In postmodern fashion, our graphic novel indicates that the meaning or content of a literary masterpiece like *Moby-Dick* resides not so much in our trying to reconstruct its author's original intentions as in questioning what open-ended future can be read into the traumatic trace registered in Melville's novel.[26]

At risk of sounding theoretically naive and old-fashioned, I would suggest that this questioning is exactly what Melville intended, or at least that this result follows logically from the rhetorics of sublimity and incompletion in *Moby-Dick*.

So far in this discussion, the adaptations and co-optations of *Moby-Dick* that follow the Ishmael ethic of response, with the exception of the Sienkiewicz adaptation, have been notable more for their concepts and narrative play than their images. Only Sienkiewicz has manipulated the visual resources of comics to create visual analogues to feelings, tones, and ideas in Melville's novel. That is, the art in the other texts is figurative, 'realistic', and sequential. Formally conventional is the best way to express their approaches and effects. Visual experimentation with *Moby-Dick* has generally been the purview of fine artists like Frank Stella and Sam Francis, who give abstract artworks allusive names from the novel that challenge the viewer to find connections between what they are looking at and the text. Matt Kish's 2011 *Moby-Dick in Pictures, One Drawing for Every Page* lies somewhere between the fine art world and the comics art world. The project sets constraints for itself that oblige it to approach the novel in a different way from other adaptations.[27]

For one thing, *Moby-Dick in Pictures* is as much a response to Zak Smith's similar work with *Gravity's Rainbow* as it is to Melville's novel, so it really has two source texts.[28] But even the inspiration from Smith fits the ethos of 'every man thinking', or in this case 'every man drawing and painting', that *Moby-Dick's* Ishmael ethic encourages. Kish's sense that "I could do that… in my own way with a different text" is right in line with that ethic. If anything, Kish's obligation to Smith enhances his response to *Moby-Dick*.

Second, the project is as much about Kish and the constraints and challenges he places upon himself as it is about *Moby-Dick*. Unlike the classics comics adaptors, Kish is upfront about his strategy for deciding what material to include in his book, as the title indicates: he selects a passage to draw from each page of the Signet Classic edition of *Moby-Dick*. This constraint ensures proportional representation of the totality of the novel and a direct link between Melville's language and Kish's drawing: Kish includes the specific text that inspires each drawing, suggesting a multi-modal poeisis, a springing forth of the image from the language of the text. This strategy also avoids the huge cuts that the comics adaptations make, while testifying to Ishmael's rhetoric of impossibility. Kish can only make a drawing for every page, not every sentence or word.

Finally, in addition to making a drawing for every page, Kish challenged himself to complete a drawing every day until he was finished, a commitment analogous to going to sea; he could not return to normal life until the project was done. The constraints that Kish imposes on his project lend it an Ishmaelean obsessiveness for exploring ambiguity that contrasts with Ahab's monomaniacal desire to rip the veil off of truth. Kish's obsessiveness as an artist matches that of the text in its efforts to say everything possible about whales and whaling. In fact, Kish credits the novel with inspiring this sort of obsessive behaviour. He describes his obsession as that of a 'reader' of the book who performs it in pictures: "I have been obsessed with *Moby-Dick* for most of my life."[29] A certain level of subjective, readerly obsession is a requirement for getting through *Moby-Dick*. Kish himself says that when he first read the novel in its entirety, he was struck by how dull some of it was. And yet, this aesthetic of boredom is a necessary component of any physical or intellectual quest: like a journey up a mountain, or discovering the Antarctic, reading *Moby-Dick* demands both slogging and strategy. This is how the reader participates in the bookish analogy for whaling that Ishmael sets up in the 'Cetology' chapter and elsewhere.

Like any obsessive, Kish is reflexive and self-aware, qualities that are also missing from most of the comics adaptations apart from the Sienkiewicz and Chichester version. For instance, in the Marvel version, Shapiro and Nino depict Ahab's obsession in an objective manner, but not the obsessiveness of the text itself, particularly Ishmael's part of it, nor that of the reader who takes on the book. Indeed, we could say that the aim of these adaptations is to control, reduce, and objectify obsessiveness rather than participate in it.

At first glance, it would be difficult to assert that *Moby-Dick in Pictures* is a comic. While the drawings are sequential in that they follow the physical sequence of the book, there are no obvious grid or gutters to invoke closure in the sense that Scott McCloud presents it in *Understanding Comics*, and we don't read it as if it were a comic; rather, we tend to browse through it, dipping in and out of it. Nevertheless, it is possible to understand *Moby-Dick in Pictures* as a kind of 'uncomic,' as a radical undercutting of the classics comics adaptations of the novel. Kish's book exposes the impossibility of reducing and capturing *Moby-Dick* with neatly sequential art by drawing our attention to what the classics comics texts occlude in their gutters. The fact that Kish is able to draw, or be inspired to draw by, only a couple of sentences from each page of the Signet edition means that the other sentences remain "unshored, harbourless immensities" as Ishmael would say.[30] Instead of trying to put *Moby-Dick* together, Kish is trying to explode it in a way that shows its parts, like an exploded diagram of a machine or flat pack furniture.

The diagrammatic dimension of *Moby-Dick in Pictures* is significant both for the way it engages with the novel and for its relationship to comics. Kish draws on found paper, which frequently has been inscribed with technical drawings for television sets and other electronics. The superimposition of Kish's drawings over these found images invokes the most significant passage of the novel regarding the semiotics of interpreting marks:

> In life, the visible surface of the Sperm whale is not the least among the many marvels he presents. Almost invariably it is all over obliquely crossed and re-

crossed with numberless straight marks in this array, something like those in the finest Italian line engravings. But these marks do not seem to be impressed upon the isinglass substance above mentioned, but seem to be seen through it, as if they were engraved upon the body itself. Nor is this all. In some instances, to the quick, observant eye, those linear marks, as in a veritable engraving but afford the ground for far other delineations. These are hieroglyphical; that is, if you call those mysterious cyphers on the walls of pyramids hieroglyphics, then that is the proper word to use in this connection.... Besides all the other phenomena which the exterior of the Sperm Whale presents, he not seldom displays the back, and more especially his flanks, effaced in great part of the regular linear appearance, by reason of numerous rude scratches, altogether of an irregular, random aspect.[31]

The sperm whale's skin is marked up like Queequeg's, with similar obscurity. The 'engraving' simile suggests an intentionality supported by the hieroglyphical 'other delineations'. These finer lines contrast with the 'accidental' 'rude scratches' that are 'irregular' and 'random'. Kish's drawings superimposed on pre-existing diagrams combine the 'intentional' and ' the accidental' in the same way. We find ourselves peering through the drawings to the diagrams. Kish explains his use of palimpsest in his introduction:

I had experimented with painting robots on the more abstract television repair diagrams, and I was fascinated with the way certain elements of the diagrams showed through the paint, almost at random. To me, this hinted at a greater complexity and a hidden structure.... Melville's book is so densely, deeply, and at times confusingly layered with narrative and symbolism that I wanted to mirror that structure in the art I was making. With each image, I wanted there to be bits of text or strange lines and pictures showing through the paint or peeking around a sailor or a harpooner to hint to the viewer that there is much more to all this than he or she might see at first.[32]

The visual presentation of 'complexity' and 'hidden structure' symbolizes something that defies representation and thus engages with the sublime in Ishmael's rhetoric. What Kish sees in *Moby-Dick*, Ishmael sees in Queequeg's tattoos, the marks on the whale's skin, and the world at large--a tension between what is intentional and what is accidental. When he identifies this dichotomy and presents it in his drawings, Kish shows his understanding of *Moby-Dick*'s openness and his willingness to engage with it.

The structure of technology and its relationship to cannibalism is the most dangerous example of this tension in *Moby-Dick* because it industrial, machine-based capitalism consuming the organic forms of consumption that preceded it. The rigid, mechanical schematic diagrams under Kish's impressionistic, frequently 'loose' drawings do the same sort of thing: the newer world frames and consumes the older one.

Part 3: Using the Victorians

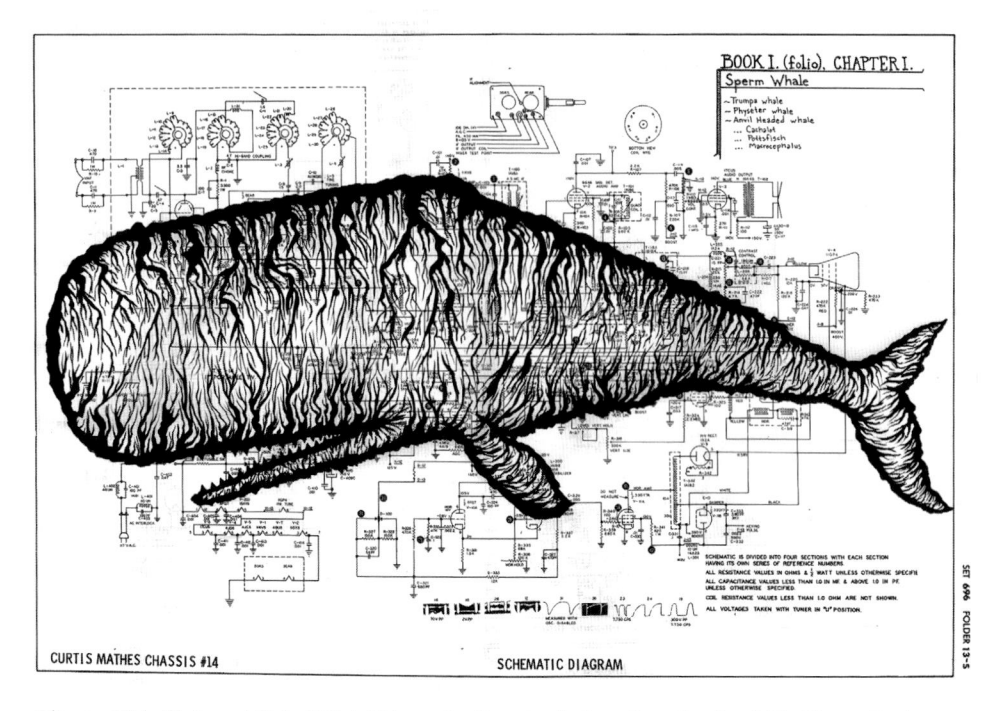

Fig. 17. Kish, M. (2011) *Moby-Dick in Pictures, One Drawing for Every Page*. Portland: Tin House Books, no page.

The classics comics versions of *Moby-Dick* treat it from a 'museum culture' perspective; the object is to fix the essence of the novel in a visual adaptation that will not make us ask questions but allow us to fit it into the collection or library and appreciate it from a distance. In this way, Scott McCloud's definition of closure in comics becomes aligned with the kind of closure that reconstructs rather than deconstructs *Moby-Dick*. This closure consequently works against the idea that Melville's novel is an 'open work'. The adaptations and co-optations that reflexively highlight their interpretation, distortion, and transformation of the 'original' respond to the text in the way that it invites us to do. The Ishmaelean ethic is more interested in participating in an open-ended network of conversations than in being 'preserved'.

Through the Ishmaelean ethic of sublime incompletion *Moby-Dick* issues an imperative to those who would respond to it, whether in works of language or visual art, which is to take up where it leaves off to produce something new in response. In this sense, *Moby-Dick* resists adaptation in favour of response. While we might imagine the phenomenon of fan fiction, aided by the immediacy of the internet and social media, as a twenty-first-century phenomenon, great works of literature have always been 'fan fiction'; they have continued a conversation started by a work somewhere else in the network.

The Unwritten's notion that literary works have special bridges that connect their diegetic worlds is not far off the truth. *The Aeneid* is, in its way, an adaptation of *The Odyssey*, which transfers the epic structure from Greece to Rome. The difference between this instance of 'adaptation' and what *Moby-Dick* encourages is that Melville is less interested in one 'great' work answering another than in a democratic, often combative, explosion of voices, ideas, and images unfiltered by taste police deciding what is good or not, something like the fan fiction we see on the internet today. Matt Kish's *Moby-Dick in Pictures* emerges from this world of fan fiction, having begun as a blog that was ultimately collected and published in print. Clearly, Ishmael's invitation has had as significant an impact on artists who want to draw and re-draw as it has on writers.

In Melville's model of the literary and visual arts network, being 'true' to a prior text means to play with its ideas, not to preserve them. *Moby-Dick* is a parable: an enigmatic story whose lesson requires continual rethinking, and whose relationship to the future is also parabolic, like a stone tossed forward into the future to be picked up, considered, and tossed forward again. The most ethical responses to *Moby-Dick* are those that revise, rethink, and recast it forward. A great unfinished book is sustained by those who continue to contribute to it, making it less and less finished over time.

Notes

1. Eco, U. (1984) *The Role of the Reader: Explorations in the Semiotics of Texts*. Bloomington: Indiana University Press, page 47.
2. Ibid., page 49.
3. Melville, H. and Feidelson, C. (1985) *Moby-Dick, Or, The Whale*. Indianapolis: Macmillan, page 195.
4. Ibid., page 352.
5. Ibid., page 83.
6. Schultz, E. A. (1995) *Unpainted to the Last: Moby-Dick and Twentieth-Century American Art*. Lawrence: University Press of Kansas.
7. Kant, I. (1987) *Critique of Judgment*. Indianapolis: Hackett, page 99.
8. See also Thomas Leitch's discussion of Roland Barthes' distinction between the 'readerly' and 'writerly' text and Mikhail Bakhtin's distinction between 'authoritative discourse' and 'internally persuasive discourse' in Leitch, T. (2009) *Film Adaptation and Its Discontents: From Gone with the Wind to The Passion of the Christ*. Baltimore: Johns Hopkins University Press, page 12.
9. Melville, H., Shapiro, I. and Niño, A. (1976) *Moby-Dick*. New York: Marvel Comics Group.
10. Melville, H. and Feidelson, C. (1985) *Moby-Dick, Or, The Whale*. Indianapolis: Macmillan, page 151.
11. Ibid., page 227.
12. Ibid., page 612.
13. Ibid., page 416).
14. Ibid., pages 393 and 28.
15. Asking 'who ain't a slave?' rhetorically elides the particular African-American experience and suffering of slavery.

16. The Classics Illustrated adaptation has been worked over at least 3 times. While I refer to the 1956 version, with art attributed to Norman Nodel, it appears to be a transformation of the 1951 edition.
17. Schultz, E. A. (2001) "Visualising Race: Images of Moby-Dick." in *Leviathan: A Journal of Melville Studies* Volume 3, Number 1, page 44.
18. Published serially by Fleetway 1962-1982 and 1970-1975 respectively.
19. Stahlberg, L., Kumar Singh, L. and Melville, H. (2010) *Moby Dick*. New Dehli, India: Campfire, Kindle edition.
20. Sienkiewicz, B., Chichester, D., Schubert, W. and Melville, H. (1990) *Moby Dick*. New York: Berkley.
21. Beaty, B. (2012) *Comics versus Art*. Toronto: University of Toronto Press, Chapter 2.
22. Grennan, S. (2015) *Dispossession*. London: Jonathan Cape.
23. Carey, M., Gross, P., Locke, V. and Davison, A. (2011) *The Unwritten: Leviathan*. New York: Vertigo/DC Comics.
24. Sclavi, T., Stano, A., Brindisi, B. and Faraci, T. (2005) *Dylan Dog: Sulla Rotta Di Moby Dick*. Milano: Mondadori.
25. Mariani, G. (2013) "Pulp(y) Fiction: A Dylan Dog Adaptation of Moby-Dick." in *Leviathan: A Journal of Melville Studies* Volume 15, number 3, page 91.
26. Ibid., page 98.
27. Kish, M. (2011) *Moby-Dick in Pictures: One Drawing for Every Page*. Portland: Tin House Books.
28. *Moby-Dick* and *Gravity's Rainbow* have a certain kinship besides both being large novels. Each is a novel of American apocalypse that plays with themes of encyclopedism and absolutism.
29. Kish, M. (2011) *Moby-Dick in Pictures: One Drawing for Every Page*. Portland: Tin House Books, page v.
30. Melville, H. and Feidelson, C. (1985) *Moby-Dick, Or, The Whale*. Indianapolis: Macmillan, page 179.
31. Ibid., page 400.
32. (Kish, M. (2011) *Moby-Dick in Pictures: One Drawing for Every Page*. Portland: Tin House Books, page ix.

References

Anonymous (2013) *Classics Illustrated …5: Moby-Dick Herman Melville*. N.P: Trajectory, Kindle Edition.

Beaty, B. (2012) *Comics versus Art*. Toronto: University of Toronto Press.

Bloom, H. (1973) *The Anxiety of Influence; a Theory of Poetry*. New York: Oxford University Press.

Carey, M., Gross, P., Locke, V. and Davison, A. (2011) *The Unwritten: Leviathan*. New York: Vertigo/DC Comics.

Eco, U. (1984) *The Role of the Reader: Explorations in the Semiotics of Texts*. Bloomington: Indiana University Press.

Groensteen, T. (2007) *The System of Comics*. Jackson: University Press of Mississippi.

Kant, I. (1987) *Critique of Judgment*. Indianapolis: Hackett.

Kish, M. (2011) *Moby-Dick in Pictures: One Drawing for Every Page*. Portland: Tin House Books.

Leitch, T. (2009) *Film Adaptation and Its Discontents: From Gone with the Wind to The Passion of the Christ*. Baltimore: Johns Hopkins University Press.

Mariani, G. (2013) "Pulp(y) Fiction: A Dylan Dog Adaptation of Moby-Dick." in *Leviathan: A Journal of Melville Studies* Volume 15, number 3, pages 90 – 103.

McCloud, S. (1994) *Understanding Comics: The Invisible Art*. New York: Harper Perennial.

Melville, H., Shapiro, I. and Niño, A. (1976) *Moby-Dick*. New York: Marvel Comics Group.

Melville, H. and Feidelson, C. (1985) *Moby-Dick, Or, The Whale*. Indianapolis: Macmillan.

Schultz, E. A. (1995) *Unpainted to the Last: Moby-Dick and Twentieth-Century American Art*. Lawrence: University Press of Kansas.

Schultz, E. A. (2001) "Visualising Race: Images of Moby-Dick." in *Leviathan: A Journal of Melville Studies* Volume 3, Number 1, pages 31–60.

Sclavi, T., Stano, A., Brindisi, B. and Faraci, T. (2005) *Dylan Dog: Sulla Rotta Di Moby Dick*. Milano: Mondadori.

Sienkiewicz, B., Chichester, D., Schubert, W. and Melville, H. (1990) *Moby Dick*. New York: Berkley.

Smith, Z. (2006) *Gravity's Rainbow Illustrated: One Picture for Every Page*. Portland: Tin House Books.

Stahlberg, L., Kumar Singh, L. and Melville, H. (2010) *Moby Dick*. New Dehli, India: Campfire, Kindle edition.

Index

About Faces 83, 86
A Confidential Agent 99, 100, 106, 253
action space 44
Adams, Neal 44
adaptation 5, 9, 13, 15, 16, 17, 18, 19, 20, 21, 23, 26, 27, 30, 34, 41, 47, 55, 62, 65, 89, 149, 158, 160, 161, 162, 169, 177, 178, 179, 180, 183, 185, 187, 188, 190, 191, 192, 193, 199, 201, 202, 207, 208, 211, 212, 217, 218, 220, 221, 222, 223, 224, 225, 227, 230, 232
Adaptation and Appropriation 30, 32
Adaptations 30, 32
Adorno, Theodor 213, 215
Aesthetic Theory 213, 215
Aguerreberry, Rodolfo 215
A Haunt of Fears 127, 128
Ainsworth, Harrison 90, 105
Airy Alf and Bouncing Billy 112, 117
Akerman, Chantal 177
Albaret, Celeste 177
Alfonsín, Raúl Ricardo 200
Alias Grace 160, 172
Alice in Wonderland 93
allegory 71, 76, 77, 83, 200, 205, 207, 210
All the Year Round 115, 116
Ally Sloper 108, 109, 111, 112, 113, 114, 115, 116, 117, 119, 120, 121, 122, 124, 125, 126, 127, 128, 133, 135, 145, 147, 253
Ally Sloper's Half-Holiday 108, 109, 112, 113, 115, 116, 117, 119, 120, 121, 122, 125, 126, 127, 128, 135, 253
Alter Alter 212, 216
A Meet of Sir Clifford Constable's Stag Hounds at Burton Constable 106
anaphoras 37, 41, 42, 46, 47
An Old Man's Love 74, 78, 79, 85, 86
apparatus 44, 45, 46, 49, 200, 205, 207, 215

appropriation 5, 149
Arcades Project 71, 83, 84, 86
Ardizzone, Edward 49
Arnold, Mathew 84, 87, 110, 124, 125
Ars poetica 31
A Short History of America 22
As You Like It 101
Atwood, Margaret 160, 172
Austen, Jane 101
Australia 55, 60, 62, 63, 64, 77, 78, 82
Australian 7
Babette 31, 32
Baetens, Jan 5, 8, 10, 15, 31, 32, 65, 66, 67, 178, 180, 184, 193, 194, 196, 213, 215
Bagge, Peter 190, 195, 196
Bailey, Maud 156
Baker, Kyle 67
Bakhtin, Mikhail 231
bande dessinée 5, 137, 144, 145, 146, 147, 175, 177, 178, 179, 180, 185, 188, 193, 195, 197
Banville, Scott 113, 126, 127, 128
Barchester Towers 80, 81, 85, 86
Barthes, Roland 17, 30, 32, 50, 52, 76, 84, 85, 157, 172, 231
Bathers 62
Battaglia, Dino 5, 8, 10, 22, 23, 26, 27, 28, 29, 30, 32, 248
Baudelaire, Charles 72
Baudry, Jean Louis 44, 46, 49, 51, 52
BBC television 62
beat 22, 23, 25, 221
Beaty, Bart 145, 146, 194, 195, 196, 224, 232
Beloved 164, 166, 171, 173
Benjamin, Walter 56, 71, 72, 76, 77, 78, 83, 84, 85, 86, 87, 175, 176, 193, 196
Berio, Luciano 217
Besant, Walter 119
Biers, Katherine 18, 19, 30, 32
Big Budget 108, 112, 117, 121
Big Numbers 60, 66

Index

Bildungsroman 158
Blackwoods Magazine 30
Bleak House 51, 52, 73
Blomkamp, Neil 190
Bloom, Harold 225, 232
body schemas 45
Boix, Joan 203, 214, 215
Bone 47, 52, 53
Bonham, John 217
Boughton, Rutland 128
Boule de Suif 5, 15
Bourdieu, Pierre 111, 126, 128, 129
Boys Will Be Boys 126
braiding 180, 184, 185, 187, 188, 192, 195, 212
Breccia, Alberto 6, 12, 16, 30, 32, 199, 200, 201, 202, 203, 204, 205, 206, 207, 208, 209, 210, 211, 212, 213, 215, 216, 259, 260, 261
Brighton Society 113
Brindisi, Bruno 225
Bring on the Books for Everybody 30, 32
British Quarterly Review 126
British Socialists and the Politics of Popular Culture, 1884-1914 125, 129
Brooks, Peter 19, 30, 32
Browne, Hablot Knight 92
Brown, Ford Maddox 62, 84, 86
Browning, Elizabeth Barrett 95
Burns, Charles 58, 59, 66, 68
Burridge, Kate 153, 168, 172
Buscavidas 214, 216
Busch, Wilhelm 11, 135, 143
Busiek, Kurt 47, 51, 52
Byatt, A. S. 155, 156, 157, 160, 169, 172, 173
Byrne, John 190
Caillebotte, Gustave 10, 42, 48
Camden Town Murder 98, 105
camera 35, 81, 161, 169, 190, 214
Cameron, Deborah 164
Caniff, Milton 21, 22, 31, 145

Can You Forgive Her? 73, 86
Caran d'Ache 11, 137, 139, 141, 142, 143
Carey, Mike 225
Carrier, David 180, 192, 193, 194, 195, 196
Castle, Terry 158
catachresis 45, 215
censorship 127, 200, 201, 205, 207, 212, 213
Cerebus 178
Cezanne, Paul 43
Cham 9, 49, 132, 146
Chaplin, Charlie 56
Chase-Riboud, Barbara 164, 165, 166, 172
Chat Noir 131, 135, 136, 137, 139, 140, 141, 143, 144, 145, 146, 147, 255
Chavs 127, 129
Chichester, Dan 224
Chomsky, Noam 109, 125, 128
cinematograph 135
Clarke, Harry 202
Classics Illustrated 56, 107, 220, 222, 223, 224, 225, 232
Cloverfield 190
Clowes, Daniel 58, 66, 68
Collins, Wilkie 16, 30, 32, 76, 84, 86, 100, 172
colore 49
colorito 49
Combe, William 91
Combray 175, 176, 178, 179, 182, 185, 186, 187, 190, 195, 197, 257, 258
Comic Cuts 108, 109, 112, 116, 121, 126
Comics and Language 31, 32
Comics and Narration 31, 32, 195, 196, 214, 216
Comics: Ideology, Power and the Critics 127
Coming Home from Church 92
Commedia dell'Arte 44
Contagious Diseases Acts 154
Contes et nouvelles de guerre 5, 10, 28, 32, 248
contracensura 200
Copper Calhoun 21, 22, 31

Cornhill Magazine 90, 103, 105
Courir deux lièvres 89, 104
Cousin Henry 75, 76, 79
Creepy 203, 214, 215, 216
critics 57, 95, 108, 109, 112, 113, 114, 115, 118, 119, 120, 121, 122, 123, 124, 127, 156, 190, 224
Cruelle Énigme 140, 147
Cruikshank, George 11, 40, 50, 53, 89, 90, 91, 115, 121, 134, 142
Crumb, Robert 22
Cultural Studies 124, 125, 129
Culture and Anarchy 125
Culture and Anomie 85, 86
Cunningham, Michael 16
Cuvier, Georges Léopold 165
Daily Graphic 8
Danaë 56, 64, 67
Dark Knight Returns 37, 39, 46
Daumier, Honoré 10, 18, 25, 49, 62
Davies, Andrew 158, 174
Davison, Al 225
depiction 34, 37, 39, 42, 43, 45, 46, 47, 49, 56, 62, 64, 72, 188, 222, 223
depictive regime 40, 43, 48, 50
Derby Day 43
Der Triumph des Realismus 140, 147
Dickens, Charles 8, 11, 51, 52, 72, 73, 75, 76, 79, 83, 84, 86, 89, 90, 91, 92, 105, 106, 112, 132, 135, 144, 145, 147
Dictionary of Nineteenth-Century Journalism 125, 128
Didi-Huberman, Georges 64, 67, 68
diegesis 34, 39, 40, 41, 47, 50, 81, 215
Dirks, Rudolph 133
disegno 49
Dispossession 5, 7, 9, 10, 12, 13, 16, 17, 21, 24, 25, 26, 27, 30, 32, 33, 34, 35, 36, 37, 38, 39, 40, 41, 43, 44, 47, 49, 50, 52, 55, 56, 57, 58, 59, 60, 61, 62, 63, 64, 65, 67, 68, 89, 101, 104, 107, 232, 247, 249, 250

distance 22, 23, 25, 26, 29, 34, 35, 41, 48, 76, 121, 192, 209, 230
Distinction 126, 128
District 9 190
divisions of action 35
Doctor Thorne 77
Dombey and Son 92, 105
Dorian Gray 159, 160, 174
drawing 17, 18, 23, 26, 33, 37, 40, 41, 43, 44, 45, 46, 47, 48, 49, 56, 58, 60, 64, 99, 135, 137, 140, 177, 184, 188, 190, 209, 213, 226, 227, 228
Drawing Words & Writing Pictures 46
Dr Jekyll and Mr Hyde 65
Dr Wortle's School 75
duration 17, 20, 21, 23, 25, 30, 31, 91, 92
Duval, Marie 39, 40, 133
Dylan Dog #15 Sulla rotta di Moby-Dick 225
Eco, Umberto 217, 218, 231, 232
Egan, Pierce 89
Ein Bubenstreich 144
Eisner, Will 41, 45, 51, 52
Eleven Rooms of Proust 177
El Extraño caso del señor Valdemar 203, 216
Eliot, George 93, 95
emic 48
Engl, Joseph Benedict 140, 147
equivocation 9, 18, 26, 34, 39, 41, 47, 49, 97, 166, 203
Ericksen, Donald H. 42, 51, 52
esoterica 58
etic 48
evenness 17, 19, 20, 23, 25, 26, 27
Faber, Michel 84, 86, 158, 160, 170, 172, 173
facies hippocratica 77
facture 41, 44, 48, 49
Faivre, Antoine 214, 216
Fantastic Four 190
Faraci, Tito 225, 232, 233
Farrell, J. G. 151, 152, 153, 154, 167, 172
Ferrand, Nathalie 90, 105, 106

237

Index

fidelity 15, 16, 17, 192, 195, 219
Fingersmith 161, 162, 164, 168, 170, 174
Flanagan, Richard 165, 172, 173
flâneur 72
Fliegende Blätter 137, 143
Floc'h, Jean-Claude 59, 66, 68
Flores, Julio 215
focalisation 71, 80, 81, 82, 190, 191, 192
folk culture 118, 122
Forceville, Charles 45, 46, 51, 52
form 15, 17, 22, 23, 27, 29, 39, 42, 45, 49, 55, 56, 58, 60, 62, 65, 66, 67, 71, 76, 77, 79, 80, 81, 83, 89, 92, 97, 103, 104, 107, 108, 109, 112, 114, 115, 119, 124, 125, 131, 132, 133, 135, 137, 141, 142, 143, 154, 157, 160, 166, 170, 177, 178, 183, 184, 188, 200, 201, 202, 211, 213, 217, 219
Foucault, Michel 154, 157, 169, 173
Fowles, John 155, 158, 168, 169, 173
Framley Parsonage 11, 93, 95, 99, 106
Francis, Sam 217, 227
Franco-Prussian war 27
Freeman's Journal and Daily Commercial Advertiser 126
Frey, Hugo 5, 8, 10, 55, 57, 59, 61, 63, 65, 66, 67, 68
Friedman, Norman 80, 81, 85, 86
Frith, William Powell 43
From the Penny Dreadful to the Ha'Penny Dreadfuller 125, 129
Funny Cuts 112
Funny Wonder 108, 121
Gamboni, Dario 201, 213, 214, 216
Garageland 128
Gardner, Jared 133
Genette, Gérard 19, 20, 31, 32, 80, 81, 85, 86
genre 21, 47, 57, 65, 72, 137, 142, 175, 203
Gerhard 178
Germinal 128
Gibbons, Dave 10, 23, 31, 32, 50, 53, 66, 68, 144, 146, 147, 215

Gillray, James 91, 115, 121, 142
Giménez, Carlos 203, 216
Gladstone, William 118
Glasgow Herald 121, 126
Golden Age 91, 132
Gordon, Ian 78, 106, 133, 134, 144, 145, 147
Grandmother's Money 94, 95, 251
graphiation 6, 12, 199, 200, 205, 207, 209, 211, 213, 215
Graphic Women 66, 68
Gravity's Rainbow 227, 232
Greer, Germain 181, 194, 196
Grennan, Simon 5, 7, 8, 9, 10, 12, 13, 16, 18, 20, 21, 23, 24, 25, 26, 27, 29, 30, 32, 33, 35, 36, 37, 38, 39, 41, 43, 45, 47, 49, 50, 51, 52, 53, 55, 56, 57, 58, 59, 61, 62, 63, 64, 65, 66, 67, 68, 89, 101, 104, 107, 224, 232, 247, 249, 250
grid 23, 25, 27, 43, 55, 57, 61, 62, 228
gridding 33
Groensteen, Thierry 22, 23, 31, 32, 33, 50, 52, 83, 86, 132, 137, 144, 145, 146, 147, 183, 184, 185, 194, 195, 196, 203, 214, 216, 232
Gross, Peter 225
Grove, Laurence 5, 7, 191, 192, 193, 194, 195, 196, 197
Gutleben, Christian 155, 157, 168, 169, 173
Hague, Ian 5, 7, 12, 175, 195, 196, 199
Happy Hooligan 133
Harper, Sue 50, 51, 53, 153, 163, 168, 172, 173, 232
Harry Potter 16, 225
Hate #1 190, 195, 196
Haussmann, Georges-Eugène 72
Hayward, Jennifer 132, 144, 145, 147
Heath, William 8
Heavy Metal 204, 212, 216, 259
Hergé 10, 58, 59, 185, 194
Heuet, Stéphane 12, 177, 178, 179, 180, 181, 182, 183, 184, 185, 186, 187, 188, 190, 191, 192, 193, 194, 195, 196, 197, 257, 258

238

Index

Histoire de Monsieur Cryptogame 132
Histoire de M. Vieux Bois 132
historiography 5, 149
Hitch, Bryan 44, 47, 51, 53
Hitchcock, Alfred 59
Hobbes, Thomas 226
Hoffmann, Ernst Theodor Amadeus 81
Hogarth, William 11, 91, 92, 115, 121, 128, 134, 142, 143, 145
Ho Lai-Ming, Tammy 165, 172, 173
Holloway, Stanley 74, 105
Holman Hunt, William 10, 42, 43
Holmberg, Carl B. 163, 171, 173
Hopkins, Arthur 99, 214, 215, 216, 231, 232
Horace 31
horror comics 110, 111, 124, 226
Horse Frightened by a Lion 43
Hottentot Venus 164, 165, 166, 172
Howarth, Franklin Morris 133
How to do Things With Books in Victorian Britain 127, 129
Hugo, Victor 8
icon 37, 39, 185
iconic solidarity 202, 205
Ill Effects 127, 128
illusion 5, 10, 37, 55, 56, 57, 58, 59, 60, 61, 62, 63, 65, 66, 67, 92, 104, 152
Illustrated Books and Newspapers 114
Illustrated Chips 108, 109, 112, 121
illustration 17, 29, 42, 64, 89, 90, 91, 92, 94, 95, 97, 100, 101, 103, 104, 105, 164, 178, 202, 251
imagery 49, 67, 71, 77, 114, 143, 152, 165
impact flashes 47
Impressionism 141
I Need Light 152
inset 180, 183, 195
internal ocularisation 209, 210, 215
Introduction to the Structuralist Analysis of Narratives 84, 85
Iser, Wolfgang 214, 216

Is He Popenjoy 74, 84, 87
isochronic tics 20, 22
isochrony 19
It's All the Fault of the Naughty Birds 100
Jack Shepperd 90
James, Henry 18, 19, 30, 32, 72, 81, 84, 85, 86, 170, 172
Jeffers, Jenifer M. 155, 157, 169, 173
JLA/Avengers ...2 47
John Caldigate 5, 13, 15, 17, 18, 21, 23, 34, 35, 42, 48, 49, 55, 67, 68, 73, 75, 76, 77, 78, 81, 82, 84, 85, 87, 89, 97, 224
Jost, François 214, 215, 216
Judy 8, 107, 109, 116, 121, 135
Jugend 140, 141, 144, 146, 147
Jugendstil 140, 141
Kant, Emmanuel 219, 231, 232
Kept in the Dark 75
Kexel, Guillermo 215
kinetoscope 135
Kish, Matt 227, 228, 229, 230, 231, 232, 261
Kohlke, Marie-Luise 5, 9, 11, 151, 169, 173
Kumar Singh, Lalit 223, 232, 233
Kunzle, David 131, 132, 133, 134, 137, 139, 141, 142, 143, 144, 145, 146, 147
Lakoff, George 48, 51, 52
Laokoon 8
La Place de l'Europe, temps de pluie 42
Larks! 108, 112
Last Day in the Old Home 62
Laurel, Stan and Hardy, Oliver 56
Le Brun, Charles 83
Le Charivari 8
Le Chat Noir 8, 11
Le Cœur révélateur et autres histoires extraordinaires 30, 32
Le cœur révélateur et autres histoires extraordinaires d'Edgar Poe 206, 260
Led Zeppelin 217
Lefèvre, Pascal 184
Le Figaro 137, 139, 144

239

Index

Leighton, Frederick 95
Leitch, Thomas 231
Le Monde Illustré 8
Les Folies de la Commune 132, 146
Lessing, Gotthold Ephraim 8, 19, 42, 43, 51, 53
Leuven University 16
Leviathan 218, 225, 226, 232, 233
L'Humidité 136, 137, 140, 146, 255
Life 8, 66, 68, 106, 129, 133, 214, 216
ligne claire 55
L'Illustration 9, 132
Lire Tintin 66, 68
literary voice 17, 34, 39
Livres vus, livres lus 90, 105, 106
Lloyd, Harold 56
Locke, Vince 225, 232
Loesberg, Jonathan 157, 169, 170, 173
Look and Learn 223
Look at her, Matt 99, 100, 253
Lord Glamis and his Staghounds 105
Lovecraft, H. P. 211, 213
Macmillan's Magazine 95
Maëstro 137
magic 56, 58, 60, 65, 167, 180, 214
Magritte, René 60, 67, 68
Maison Close 159, 174
Mannerism 44
Manufacturing Consent 125, 128
Marcus Clarke's Bohemia. Literature and Modernity in Colonial Melbourne 83, 86
Marcus, Steven 83, 86, 157, 170, 173
Mariani, Giorgio 226, 232
Marion Fay 71, 74, 82, 83, 85, 86
Marion, Philippe 71, 74, 75, 82, 83, 85, 86, 200, 213, 216
Martin Chuzzlewit 105
Martineau, Robert Braithwaite 62
Marvel 43, 46, 47, 51, 53, 220, 221, 222, 223, 228, 231, 232
Marx, Groucho 226

Maupassant, Guy de 5, 10, 15, 16, 26, 27, 29, 30, 31, 32, 248
Maus 57, 58, 60, 61, 66, 68
Max und Moritz 135
Mayhew, Henry 123
Maynard, Patrick 33, 50, 53
McChesney, Robert 109, 125, 129
McCloud, Scott 37, 228
McDougall, Walt 123, 128
McLuhan, Marshall 21
melodrama 19, 25, 26, 35, 45, 46, 48, 73
Melodrama, and the Mode of Excess 30, 32
Melville 7
Melville, Herman 12, 217, 219, 220, 221, 222, 223, 224, 225, 226, 227, 229, 230, 231, 232, 233
memory 62, 176, 178, 179, 180, 184, 185, 187, 199, 200, 201, 207, 210, 211, 212
Menem, Carlos 200, 207, 212
Meskin, Aaron 31, 32, 109, 125, 129, 194, 195, 196
Mesmeric Revelation 202, 214, 216
Meta-Maus 58, 66
Metz, Christian 44, 51, 53
Mevel, Matthieu 212
Meyerhold, Vsevolod 35, 50, 53
Michell, Roland 156, 157, 170
Miers, John 5, 8, 9, 10, 33, 35, 37, 39, 41, 43, 45, 47, 49, 51, 53
Mikkonen, Kai 191, 195, 197
Millais, John Everett 8, 11, 91, 93, 95, 96, 97, 98, 99, 100, 101, 102, 103, 104, 105, 106, 252, 253, 254
Miller, Ann 191
Miller, Frank 31, 32, 37, 85, 86, 170, 173, 194, 195, 196, 197
Millidge, Gary Spencer 55, 58, 66, 68
Milne, Alan Alexander 112
mimesis 81
mise en abime 64
Moby-Dick 6, 12, 217, 218, 219, 220, 221,

222, 223, 224, 225, 226, 227, 228, 229, 230, 231, 232, 233
Moby-Dick in Pictures, One Drawing for Every Page 227, 230, 261
Modan, Rotu 44, 49, 53
Mones, Isidro 203
Monkton Grange 101, 102, 105, 254
Monsieur Lajaunisse 132
Moore, Alan 10, 23, 31, 32, 35, 50, 53, 55, 58, 60, 66, 68
Morel-Retz, Louis 9
Morrison, Toni 164
Morris, William 118
movie 16, 37, 39, 40, 41, 42, 44, 45, 46, 47, 59, 159
Mr Scarborough's Family 74, 75
M. Töpffer invente la bande dessinée 83, 86
music hall 57, 108, 114, 116, 118, 122
Music Hall and Modernity 125, 129
Muybridge, Eadweard 35
My Pad and Welcome to It! 190
Myrick, Daniel 190
mystery 17, 57, 58, 75, 76, 140, 142, 157, 167, 168, 199, 201
Nair, Mira 159
narrative 17, 19, 20, 21, 22, 23, 25, 27, 29, 31, 33, 37, 40, 41, 42, 43, 45, 47, 55, 57, 58, 59, 60, 62, 63, 65, 66, 80, 82, 84, 89, 90, 91, 92, 97, 99, 100, 101, 104, 131, 132, 133, 135, 137, 139, 141, 142, 143, 145, 154, 155, 156, 157, 160, 162, 165, 169, 176, 178, 185, 187, 190, 191, 192, 195, 201, 202, 205, 207, 208, 209, 213, 216, 220, 222, 225, 227, 229
Narrative 31, 32, 51, 52, 53, 66, 68, 85, 86, 133, 195, 196
Narrative Discourse. An Essay In Method 31, 32
narrator 26, 27, 29, 39, 71, 75, 79, 80, 81, 82, 91, 98, 115, 156, 157, 158, 175, 176, 177, 178, 179, 181, 183, 184, 185, 187,

188, 189, 190, 191, 192, 194, 195, 201, 202, 205, 220
national traditions in comics 131, 142
Nat Turner 67
neo-Victorian 9, 57, 67, 151, 153, 155, 158, 159, 162, 163, 164, 166, 167, 168, 169, 170
neo-Victorianism 5, 151, 163, 166, 167, 168, 169
Newcastle Weekly Courant 122
New Journalism 108, 125
New South Wales 7, 41
Nisbet, Hume 120, 121
Nobbler and Jerry 112
Noé, Amédée de 9
Novel Violence 31, 32
Oberländer, Adolf 137
O'Doherty, E. F. 163, 171, 173
Ohmart, Carol 31
Oliver escapes being bound apprentice to the sweep 91
Oliver Surprised 89
Oliver Twist 89, 91, 112
One Thousand and One Nights 226
Opper, Frederick Burr 133
Orley Farm 11, 95, 96, 98, 99, 101, 102, 105, 106, 252, 254
Other Victorians 157, 170, 173
Overture 178
pace 20, 21, 23, 135, 177
painting 30, 42, 43, 46, 48, 56, 98, 105, 141, 142, 145, 152, 180, 210, 224, 227, 229
Pall Mall Gazette 127
Pan 95
paragone 16, 30, 31, 49
parentheses 180
Parker, Oliver 159
pauses of mutual agitation 46
Payn, James 99, 100, 106, 253
Pennell, Elizabeth 122, 123, 128
penny dreadful 65, 110, 116, 117, 124, 127
Perez, George 47, 51, 52

Index

Peuples exposés, peuples figurants 67, 68
phenakistiscope 134
Phineas Finn 75, 99
Phineas Redux 75, 76
photo-collage 44
photography 30, 42, 43, 44, 49, 56, 114, 135, 180
phrenology 79
physiognomy 26, 71, 72, 73, 74, 79, 83
pillar box 7
Piper, John 49
plotlessness 41
Plunkett, Horatio 211
Poe, Edgar Allan 6, 7, 12, 16, 72, 199, 200, 201, 202, 203, 205, 208, 209, 210, 211, 212, 213, 214, 215, 216
Poitevin, F. 140, 147
Pollock, Jackson 217
Popular Culture and Performance in the Victorian City 125, 128
Popular Reading and Publishing in Britain 1914-1950 125, 127, 129
Possession 11, 155, 156, 157, 158, 164, 169, 172, 173, 174
Postema, Barbara 5, 9, 11
Post-Impressionism 141
Post Office 7, 76
postures 41, 45, 46, 48
'practice-based' research 30
Pratt, Hugo 58, 66, 68
Pre-Raphaelite Brotherhood 95
Pride and Prejudice 101
Process of National Reorganisation 199, 200
Promethea 60, 66, 68
Proust, Marcel 7, 12, 175, 176, 177, 178, 180, 181, 183, 184, 185, 187, 188, 190, 191, 192, 193, 194, 195, 196, 197
Puck 8, 133, 145
Pulling the Devil's Kingdom Down 126, 129
Pulp Fiction 59
Punch 8, 93, 107, 109, 112, 115, 121, 123, 142

Purcell, Edmund Sheridan 82
Quiroga, Horacio 211
Rachel Ray 99
Raeburn, Henry 56
Rawson, Phillip 43, 51, 53
Reader's Digest 21
realism 17, 18, 19, 20, 23, 26, 27, 35, 43, 59, 60, 73, 76, 80, 81, 92, 141, 167
Redon, Odilon 201
Reeves, Matt 190
Remembrance of Things Past 5, 12, 175, 176, 177, 178, 180, 182, 185, 186, 188, 190, 192, 193, 194, 195, 196, 197, 257, 258
Renaissance 10
Rendez-vous de Sevenoaks 59
repression-envy 12, 157, 166
Reynolds Newspaper 127
rhythm 19, 20, 21, 22, 23, 25, 29, 33, 35, 48, 181, 208, 209
ribbon paths 47
Rich Media, Poor Democracy 125, 129
Ripper Street 11, 152, 159, 162, 171, 174
Rivière, François 59, 66, 68
Robert Walter Skating on Duddingston Loch 56
Robinson, Frerick William 94, 251
Rommens, Aarnoud 6, 7, 12, 214, 216
Romola 95
Rose, Jonathan 119, 127, 129, 171
Ross, Charles 133
Rousso, Shani 154, 155, 169, 173
Rowlandson, George 11
Rowlandson, Thomas 89, 91, 134, 142
Ruiz, Raul 177, 195
Sabin, Roger 5, 9, 11, 107, 135, 145, 147
Sala, Augusta 113, 115, 127
Salis, Rodolphe 139
Sánchez, Eduardo 190
Sanders, Joe Sutliffe 30, 32, 40, 50, 53
Savile, Jimmy 162
scale 44, 58, 208, 210
Schliessmann, Hans 144

Schlöndorff, Victor 177
Schulz, Wilhelm 139, 143
Sclavi, Tiziano 225, 226, 232, 233
Scott McCloud 230
Scott, Walter 103, 106, 193
Seduction of the Innocent 126, 129
Self-Help 113
sequence 43, 45, 47, 56, 57, 58, 60, 63, 64, 90, 91, 134, 177, 183, 185, 187, 188, 190, 195, 203, 208, 212, 215, 228
Seven Dials 89
Shakespeare, William 90, 101, 114, 115, 119
Shapiro, Irwin 221
Shepherd, Simon 46, 48, 51, 53
Shultz, Elizabeth 219
Sienkiewicz, Bill 224, 225, 227, 228, 232, 233
Signet Classic 227
siluetazo 210, 211, 215
Sim, Dave 178
Simon Grennan, Simon 7
Simplicissimus 134, 138, 139, 140, 141, 145, 146, 147, 256
Sketches by Boz 72, 89
Skilton, David 5, 8, 11, 80, 85, 86, 89, 105, 106
slippage 57
Small House at Allington 95, 100, 105, 106
Smiles, Samuel 113, 114, 126
Smith, George 95
Smith, Jeff 37, 41, 46, 47, 48, 50, 52, 53
Smith, Justin 153
Smith, W. H. 112
Smith, Zac 227, 233
Smolderen, Thierry 125, 129, 134, 143, 144, 145, 146, 147
Soirées de Médan 30
sous-exposé 64
Spiegelman, Art 57, 58, 60, 61, 66, 68
Stahlberg, Lance 223, 232, 233
Stanislavski, Constantin 35, 50, 53

Stano, Angelo 225, 232, 233
Starling, Belinda 158
Stead, W. T. 154
Steinlen, Théophile Alexandre 135, 141, 142, 143, 144, 146, 147
Stella, Frank 217, 227
Steve Canyon 21
Stevenson, Robert Louis 65
Stockhausen, Karlheinz 217
Stop 9
storyboard 33, 34, 35, 37, 39
Strangehaven 55, 59, 66, 68
Stubbs, George 10, 43, 103
style 17, 19, 21, 29, 30, 34, 35, 39, 42, 48, 60, 61, 90, 91, 95, 103, 109, 119, 124, 132, 135, 137, 139, 140, 141, 143, 181, 192, 194, 219, 223, 224
Sugar Skull 59, 66, 68
superhero 21, 43, 46, 47
sur-exposé 64
Sur la route encore 190, 195
suturing 209
Swales, Martin 164, 171, 173
Swann in Love 177, 178, 179, 185, 187, 195, 196
Swann's Way 176, 177, 178, 179, 193, 194, 197
synecdoche 205
tableaux 19, 25, 35, 42
taboo 5, 11, 151, 153, 154, 156, 157, 160, 161, 163, 164, 165, 166, 168, 172
tabularity 23, 31
Take Your Son Sir! 62
Talbot, Bryan 67, 68
Tales of Mystery and Imagination 202
Talmy, Leonard 47, 51, 53
Tenniel, John 11, 93, 94, 95, 142, 251
Tennyson, Alfred 91
Thackeray, William Makepeace 90, 91, 105, 106
The Adventures of Luther Arkwright 67, 68

243

Index

The Adventures of Philip 90, 105, 106
The Adventures of Tintin 178
The Aeneid 231
The Ambassadors 18
The American Senator 75, 77, 84, 85, 87
The Art of the Novel 30, 32
The Awkward Age 81
The Blair Witch Project 190
The Blue Lotus 222
The Bourgeois Interior 84, 86
The Boys Brigade Gazette 127
The Calculus Affair 59
The Captive 177, 180, 189, 193, 195, 197
The Castafiore Emerald 59
The Children's Book 160, 172
The Children's Holiday 42
The Contemporary Review 118, 122, 128
The Crimson Petal and the White 158, 160, 161, 170, 172
The English Constitution 77, 85
The Ethiopians 58
The Eustace Diamonds 73, 75, 76, 84, 86
The Facts in the Case of Mr. Valdemar 199, 212
The Fixed Period 81
The Forbes Collection of Victorian Pictures and Works of Art 105
The French Lieutenant's Woman 11, 155, 157, 158, 168, 169, 173
The Gentleman's Magazine 128
The Glasgow Looking Glass 8
The Golden Bowl 18
The Graphic Novel 66, 67
The Great Cow Race 47
The Hive 59, 66, 68
The Hours 16
The House That Reed Built 190
The Intellectual Life of the British Working Classes 127
The Journal of Dora Damage 158, 160, 173
The Katzenjammer Kids 133
The Landleaguers 75, 77, 81

The Law and the Lady 100
The Leeds Mercury 127
The London Illustrated News 8
The Maiden Tribute 154, 162
The Maiden Tribute of Modern Babylon 154
The Melodramatic Imagination 30, 32
The Modern Comic Newspaper 122
The Name on the Beam 90
The Necklace 31, 32
The Odyssey 231
The Old Curiosity Shop 72, 84, 86
The Origin of German Tragic Drama 84, 85, 86
The Origins of Comics 125, 143
The Pallisers 62
The Piece of String 31, 32
The Prime Minister 73, 80
The Progress of Mr. Lambkin 40
The Property 44, 49, 53
The Routledge Companion to Comics 31, 32
The Secret of the Unicorn 179
The Siege of Krishnapur 151, 152, 155, 167, 172
The Siege of Krishnapur, 11
The Small House of Allington 99
The Spectator and the City in Nineteenth-Century American Literature 83, 86
The Suspicions of Mr. Whicher 84, 86
The Three Lodgers 112
The Time Machine 65
The Unwritten 225, 226, 231, 232
The Victorian Country House 106
The Victorian Eye 83, 84, 86
The Violent Effigy 86
The Walking Dead 67, 68
The Warden 52, 73
The Way We Live Now 78, 80, 85, 86
The Work of Art in the Age of Mechanical Reproduction 56
time 5, 17, 19, 20, 21, 22, 23, 25, 26, 27, 29, 30, 31, 33, 34, 35, 37, 39, 41, 42, 43, 44, 45, 47, 48, 49, 50, 58, 59, 64, 65, 76, 80, 90, 95, 101, 104, 109, 112, 114, 115, 116,

244

123, 124, 126, 134, 137, 142, 143, 144, 151, 153, 157, 167, 176, 178, 180, 181, 184, 185, 187, 190, 193, 208, 209, 211, 212, 213, 214, 218, 226
Time Regained 176, 177, 184, 189, 193, 195, 197
Tipping the Velvet 11, 158, 160, 170, 174
Tit-Bits 114, 115
Töpffer, Rodolphe 9, 83, 86, 132, 134, 135, 142, 147
transmediality 16
Trillo, Carlos 199, 203, 204, 212, 214, 216, 259
Trollope
   An Autobiography 84, 87, 98, 105, 106
Trollope, Anthony 5, 7, 8, 9, 10, 11, 12, 13, 15, 16, 17, 18, 19, 20, 21, 23, 25, 26, 27, 30, 34, 35, 39, 41, 48, 49, 52, 55, 57, 61, 62, 63, 64, 65, 66, 67, 68, 71, 72, 73, 74, 75, 76, 77, 78, 79, 80, 81, 82, 83, 84, 85, 86, 87, 89, 91, 95, 96, 97, 98, 99, 101, 102, 103, 104, 105, 106, 107, 112, 114, 135, 224, 252, 254
Trust Me 98
Truth 8
Turner, Joseph Mallord William 52, 126, 129, 224
Turnes, Pablo 212
typography 181
Ultimates 47, 51, 53
Umsonst 138, 139, 147, 256
uncanny 59, 60, 61, 207, 208, 209, 210, 212
Understanding Comics 46, 50, 51, 53, 228, 232
Une vache qui regarde passer le train 144
Unpainted to the Last 219, 231, 233
Urbain, Jean-Didier 208, 214, 216
ut pictura poesis 31
Van Dam, Frederik 5, 8, 11, 84, 87
Vanity Fair 159, 174
verisimilitude 18, 44, 60
Victorian Interpretation 85
Virtual Modernism 30, 32

visual style 34
Voigts-Virchow, Eckart 160, 171, 174
volk 118, 123, 124
Walker, Joseph Francis 105, 126, 129
Walsh, Aisling 161
Wanting 165, 166, 172, 173
Ware, Chris 10, 21, 40, 55, 172, 194, 195, 197
Washington Square 18
Was it not a lie? 95
Watchmen 23, 31, 32, 35, 50, 53, 55, 66, 68, 185, 195, 196
Waters, Sarah 158, 169
Weary Willie and Tired Tim 112, 117, 123
Weekly News and Courier 128
Wells, Herbert George 65
Wertham, Frederic 111, 126, 129
What Use Our Work 162, 174
Wilkins, Peter 6, 7, 12, 217
Willette, Adolphe 135, 141, 142, 143, 144, 146, 147
Winnie-the-Pooh 112
Wiradjuri 7, 41, 56, 60, 63, 64
Within a Budding Grove 179, 185, 187, 188
Wolstenholme Snr, Dean 105
Women and Achievement in Nineteenth-Century Europe 127, 129
Woolf, Virginia 34, 50, 53, 158, 170, 174
Wordsworth, William 114, 172, 193, 194, 195, 197
World of Wonder 223
writing style 34
X'ed Out 59
Yahav, Amit 20, 31, 32
Your son, Lucius, did say – shopping 95, 96, 252
Youth, Popular Culture and Moral Panics 126, 129
Zimmerman, Mary 176, 177, 181, 194, 197
Zizek, Slavoj 128
zoetrope 134
Zola, Emile 128

Gallery with colour figures

Fig. 1. Grennan, S. (2015) *Dispossession*. London: Jonathan Cape, page 23.

Fig. 2. Battaglia D. (2002) *Contes et nouvelles de guerre*. St-Égrève: Mosquito, page 72.

Fig. 3. Grennan, S. (2015) *Dispossession*. London: Jonathan Cape, page 2.

Fig. 4. Grennan, S. (2015) *Dispossession*. London: Jonathan Cape, page 21.

Fig. 5. Tenniel, J. (1862) Untitled illustration in Robinson, F. W. (1862) *Grandmother's Money*. London: Hurst and Blackett, frontispiece.

"Your son Lucius did say—shopping."

Fig. 6. Millais, J. E. (1862) "Your son, Lucius, did say – shopping." in Trollope, A. (1862) *Orley Farm*. London, Chapman and Hall, page 97.

Fig. 7. Millais, J. E. (1880) "Look at her, Matt." in Payn, J. (1880) *A Confidential Agent*. London: Chatton & Windus, frontispiece.

Fig. 9. Anonymous (1886) Illustration in *Ally Sloper's Half-Holiday*. London: Gilbert Dalziel, October 30, no page.

255

"Monkton Grange."

Fig. 8. Millais, J. E. (1862) "Monkton Grange." in Trollope, A. *Orley Farm*. London, Chapman and Hall, page 215.

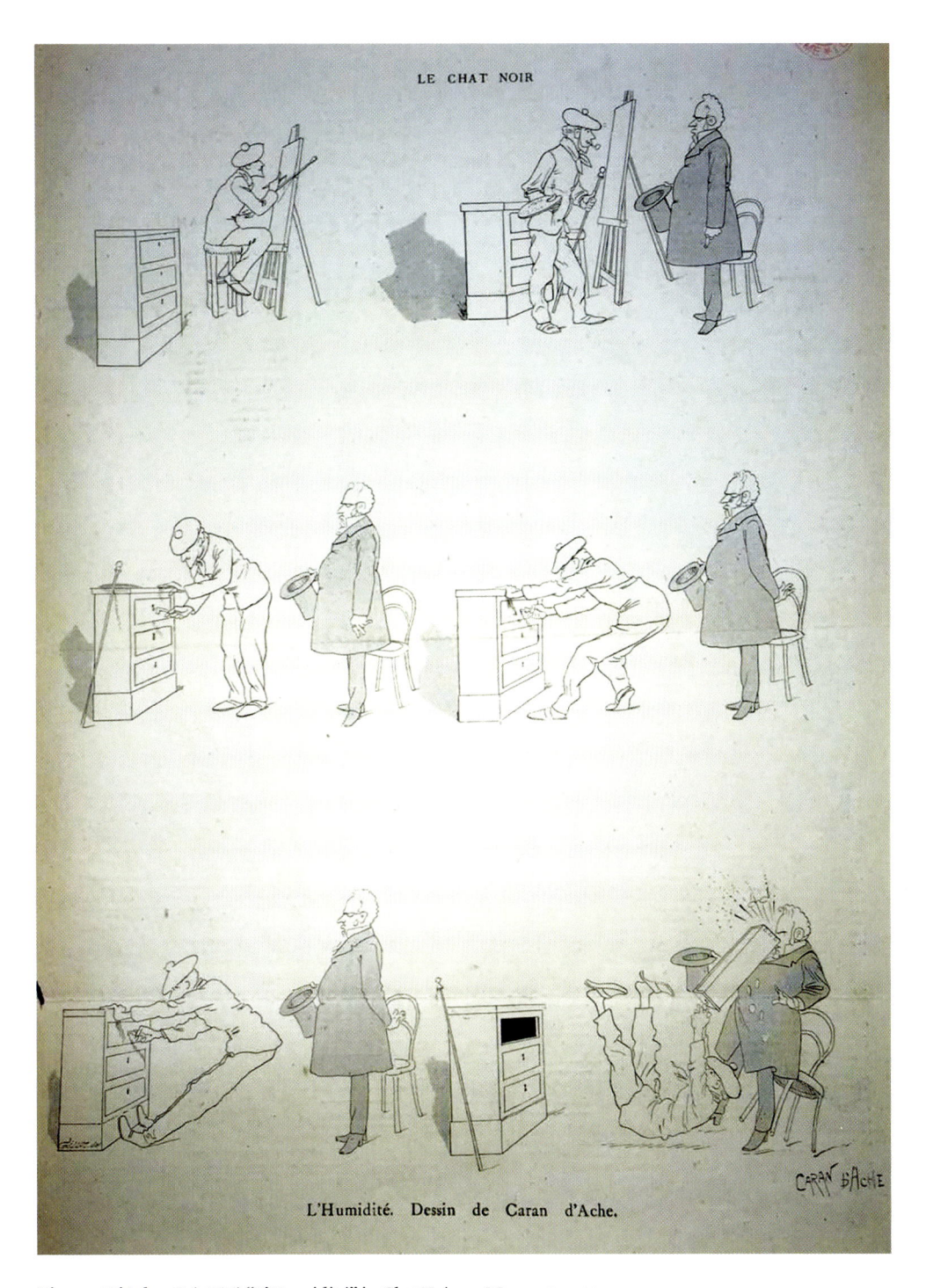

Fig. 10. D'Ache, C. (1886) "L'Humidité" in *Chat Noir*, 29 May, page 711.

Fig. 11. Schulz, W. (1896) "Umsonst" in *Simplicissimus*, 7 November, page 8.

Fig. 12. Heuet, S. and Dorey, V. (2001) *Remembrance of Things Past: Combray*. New York: NBM, page 8.

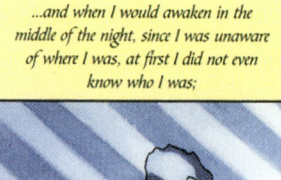

Fig. 13. Heuet, S. and Dorey, V. (2001) *Remembrance of Things Past: Combray*. New York: NBM, page 3.

Fig. 14. Breccia, A. and Trillo, C. (1982) "Mr Valdemar." in *Heavy Metal* 6, no. 7, page 44. Used by permission of the heirs of Alberto Breccia.

Fig. 15. Breccia, A (1995) "Monsieur Valdemar." in *Le cœur révélateur et autres histoires extraordinaires d'Edgar Poe*. Genève: Les Humanoïdes Associés. Plate 9. Used by permission of the heirs of Alberto Breccia.

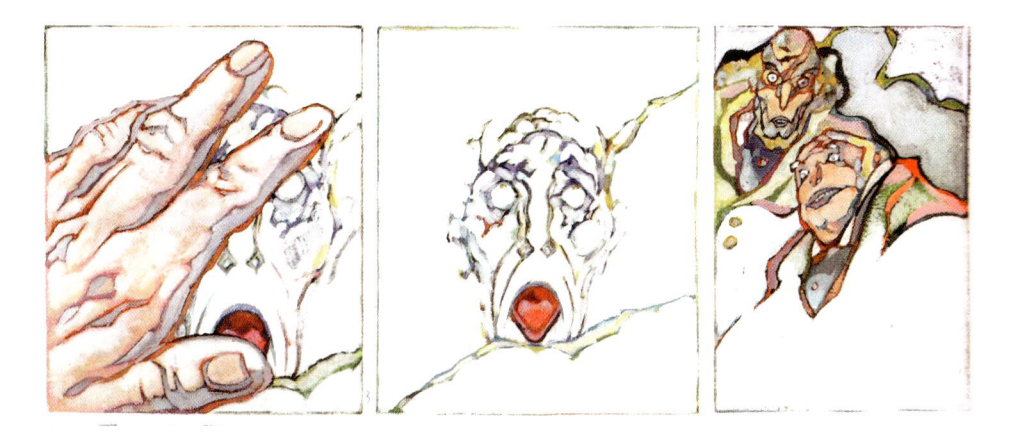

Fig 16. Breccia, A (1995) "Monsieur Valdemar." in *Le cœur révélateur et autres histoires extraordinaires d'Edgar Poe*. Genève: Les Humanoïdes Associés, Plate 6, row 2. Used by permission of the heirs of Alberto Breccia.

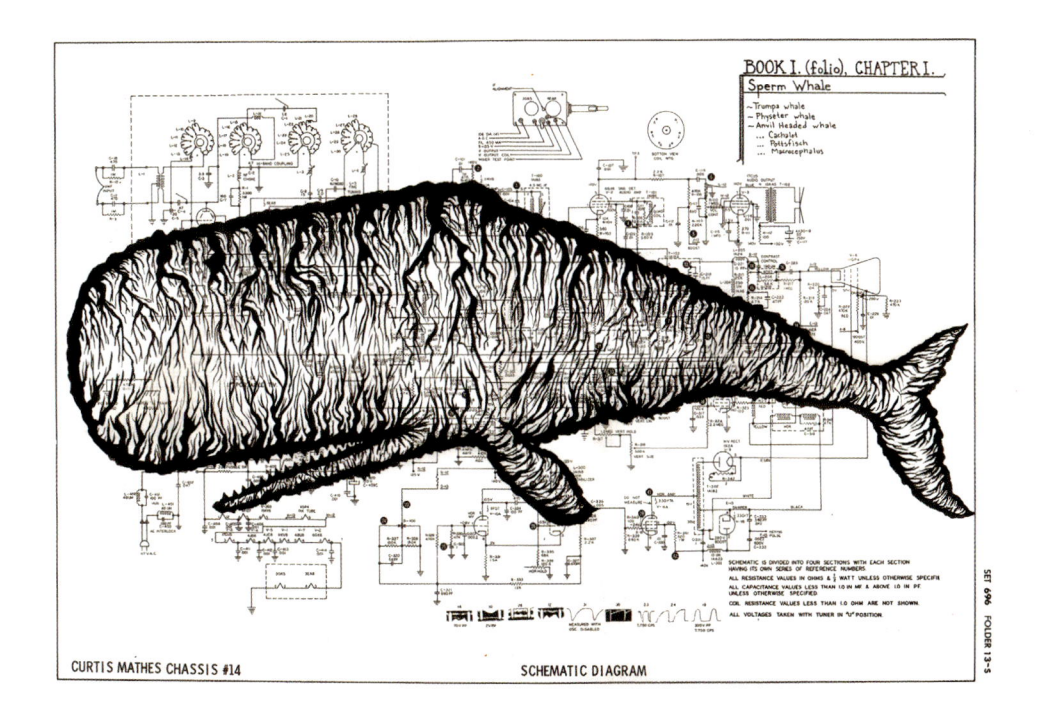

Fig. 17. Kish, M. (2011) *Moby-Dick in Pictures, One Drawing for Every Page*. Portland: Tin House Books, no page.